Footprints 1

Teacher's Book

- **Syllabus** — page 2
- **Introduction to *Footprints***
  - Who *Footprints* is for — page 14
  - Components of *Footprints 1* — page 14
  - Description of the course materials — page 15
  - Key features of *Footprints 1* — page 18
  - Classroom language — page 20
  - Twenty ways to use the finger puppets — page 21
- **Teaching notes**
  - Introduction — page 24
  - 1 My birthday — page 31
  - 2 My classroom — page 55
  - 3 My body — page 79
  - 4 My clothes — page 103
  - 5 Food I like — page 127
  - 6 My toys — page 151
  - 7 My family — page 175
  - 8 My pets — page 199
  - 9 Treasure! — page 223
  - Christmas — page 247
  - Easter — page 251
  - Father's Day — page 254
  - Mother's Day — page 257
- **Photocopiable pages**
  - Christmas cut-out — page 261
  - Easter cut-out — page 262
  - Father's Day cut-out — page 263
  - Mother's Day cut-out — page 264
  - Achievement Certificate — page 265

Carol Read

Footprints 1 syllabus

Title	Structures and grammar	Vocabulary	Main receptive language
Introduction	• What's your name? • I'm ... • Who's this? • It's ... Recycled: • How are you? • I'm fine.	• Core: *desk, chair, window, book, door, board, clock, floor* • Other: *friends, rainbow, tell, come, look* • Recycled: *Hello / Hi / Goodbye, please,* colours, numbers 1–5	• *follow, footprints, find, treasure, clue*
Unit 1 My birthday	• How old are you? / I'm ... • Are you ...? • Yes, I am. / No, I'm not. • Here's a ... (for you)! • The ... is a ... • This is a ... Recycled: • What's your name? • I'm ...	• Core: *cake, candle, present, balloon, hat, card, biscuit, sandwich, plate, cup* • Other: *birthday, mat, party, late boy, girl* • Content / culture: *circle, rectangle, triangle, square, happy, dear* • Recycled: *Thank you, desk, chair, window, door, book, board, clock,* numbers 1–10, colours	• *shape, different, object* • *recognise* • *How many ...?*
Unit 2 My classroom	• What's this? • It's a ... • Can I have the ..., please? • Here you are. • This / My ... is ... • Me, too. Recycled: • It's ... • Here ... • The / A ...	• Core: *school bag, file, notebook, pen, pencil, crayon, rubber, pencil sharpener, pencil case, ruler* • Other: *wolf, hungry, Mum, Dad, school* • Content / culture: *plastic, wood, natural, trees, hard, soft, paper, stone, scissors, hurry, late, close* • Recycled: *yes, no, thank you, chair, door, come,* numbers, colours	• classroom objects • *difference between ...* • *made of ...*

BASIC COMPETENCIES KEY			
C1: Competency in linguistic communication.	C3: Competency in knowledge of and interaction with the physical world.	C6: Competency in social awareness and citizenship.	
C2: Competency in mathematics.	C4: Competency in use of new technologies.	C7: Competency in learning to learn.	
	C5: Competency in the use of new technologies.	C8: Competency in learning autonomous personal initiative.	

Communicative competence

Understanding	Speaking	Writing
Listening • Can understand greetings (C1, C5) • Can understand when someone asks your name (C1, C5) • Can identify key items in the classroom • Can recognise numbers 1–5 (C1, C2) • Can recognise colours (C1) **Reading** • Can recognise words for items in the classroom (C1, C3) • Can recognise colours (C1) • Can recognise two questions to find out names (C1, C5)	**Spoken interaction** • Can exchange greetings (C1, C5) • Can ask and say your name (C1, C5) • Can ask about and identify others (C1, C3) **Spoken production** • Can name key items in the classroom (C1, C3) • Can sing the *Hello song* (C1, C6) • Can sing the song *What's your name?* (C1, C6) • Can name colours (C1) • Can say numbers 1–5 (C1, C2) • Can sing the *Goodbye song* (C1, C6)	• Can copy and write words for items in the classroom (C1, C3, C7, C8) • Can copy and write colour words (C1, C7)
Listening • Can recognise words related to birthdays and birthday parties (C1) • Can understand when someone asks your age (C1, C5) • Can understand the episode of the story (C1, C6, C8) • Can recognise numbers to ten (C1, C2) • Can follow instructions in a game (C1, C5, C7) **Reading** • Can recognise words related to birthdays and birthday parties (C1, C3) • Can recognise words for numbers to ten (C1, C2) • Can read questions and answers related to age (C1, C2) • Can read sentences about the shape of objects (C1, C2, C3, C4)	**Spoken interaction** • Can ask and say your age (C1, C5) • Can ask and respond to questions to check age (C1, C5) • Can offer things and say *thank you* (C1, C5) **Spoken production** • Can sing the *Hello song* (C1, C6) • Can name objects related to birthdays and birthday parties (C1) • Can count to ten (C1, C2) • Can say your age (C1, C2) • Can say the shapes of objects (C1, C2) • Can sing the song *A card, a balloon* (C1, C6) • Can say the rap *One, two, three* (C1, C6) • Can sing *Happy birthday* (C1, C6) • Can produce the sounds /æ/ and /eɪ/ (C1) • Can sing the *Goodbye song* (C1, C6)	• Can copy and write words related to birthdays and birthday parties (C1, C3, C7, C8) • Can copy and write words for numbers to ten (C1, C2, C7) • Can copy and write words for shapes (C1, C2, C3, C7) • Can complete short sentences (C1)
Listening • Can recognise words for classroom objects (C1) • Can understand the episode of the story (C1, C6, C8) • Can understand questions and answers to identify things (C1, C5) • Can understand requests and responses (C1, C5) • Can understand simple statements about classroom objects (C1, C3) **Reading** • Can recognise words for classroom objects (C1, C3) • Can read short exchanges about classroom objects (C1) • Can read requests and responses (C1, C5) • Can read sentences about plastic and wood (C1, C3, C4)	**Spoken interaction** • Can ask and respond to questions about classroom objects (C1, C3, C5) • Can make and respond to requests (C1, C5) • Can use *please* and *thank you* appropriately (C1, C5) **Spoken production** • Can sing the *Hello song* (C1, C6) • Can name classroom objects (C1, C3) • Can say whether objects are plastic or wood (C1, C3) • Can sing the song *A pencil! A pencil!* (C1, C6) • Can sing the song *Can I have the rubber, please?* (C1, C6) • Can say the rhyme *One, two, three, four* (C1, C6, C7) • Can say a tongue-twister with /p/ (C1) • Can sing the *Goodbye song* (C1, C6)	• Can copy and write words for classroom objects (C1, C3, C7, C8) • Can copy and complete sentences about what classroom objects are made of (C1, C3)

Title	Structures and grammar	Vocabulary	Main receptive language
Unit 3 **My body**	• *This is my ...* • *These are my ...* • *eye / eyes* • *I brush / wash / have ...* • *We ...* • *Our ...* Recycled: • *I'm ...* • *Are you ...?* • *Yes, I am. / No, I'm not.* • *my / your*	• Core: *head, ears, eyes, nose, mouth, chin, arms, legs, fingers, toes* • Other: *happy, sad, tired, scared* • Content / culture: *germs, hands, teeth, hair, shower, every day / week, before / after meals* • Recycled: *please, hungry,* numbers 1–10	• *noise, lie, tiny, everywhere, ill, strong, body, fight germs*
Unit 4 **My clothes**	• *I've got (a) ..., (too).* • *Is this your ...?* • *Yes, it is. / No, it isn't.* • *Are these your ...?* • *Yes, they are. / No, they aren't.* Recycled: • *This ... / These ...* • *It's ...* • *Can I ...?* • *Your / My ...*	• Core: *coat, gloves, trousers, shirt, t-shirt, dress, skirt, shoes, jumper, socks* • Other: *shorts, everybody, put on, giant, beanstalk, castle, new* • Content / culture: *jeans, tracksuit, wool, cotton, warm, cool, bed, cross, river, crocodile* • Recycled: *hat,* colours, numbers	• *material, clothes, pocket* • *natural, new* • *plant, sheep* • *take care*
Unit 5 **Food I like**	• *I like ... / I don't like ...* • *Do you like ...?* • *Yes, I do. / No, I don't.* • *Is / Are ... good for you?* Recycled: • *What's this?* • *It's ...* • *Yes, it is / No, it isn't.* • *Yes, they are. / No, they aren't.* • *I'm ...* • *Me, too!*	• Core: *hamburger, chicken, chips, salad, pizza, ice cream, chocolate, yogurt, apple, banana* • Other: *delicious, horrible, house, food, witch, key, table* • Content / culture: *good for you, water, sweet, coffee, tea, apple pie, roast beef, cheese, soup* • Recycled: *hungry, boy, girl, biscuit, sandwich, cake,* colours	• *body, need, food, drink, snack, lunch, train, pot, important* • *my friend*

BASIC COMPETENCIES KEY			
C1: Competency in linguistic communication.	C3: Competency in knowledge of and interaction with the physical world.	C6: Competency in social awareness and citizenship.	
C2: Competency in mathematics.	C4: Competency in use of new technologies.	C7: Competency in learning to learn.	
	C5: Competency in the use of new technologies.	C8: Competency in learning autonomous personal initiative.	

Communicative competence

Understanding	Speaking	Writing
Listening • Can recognise words for parts of the body (C1, C3) • Can understand words for feelings (C1, C5) • Can understand the episode of the story (C1, C6, C8) • Can understand statements about parts of the body (C1, C3) • Can understand some personal daily routines (C1, C5) • Can recognise singular and (regular) plural words (C1) Reading • Can recognise words for parts of the body (C1) • Can read statements about feelings and parts of the body (C1, C5) • Can recognise singular and plural words (C1) • Can read sentences about germs and personal daily routines (C1, C3, C4, C5)	Spoken interaction • Can ask about and respond to questions about feelings (C1, C5) • Can respond to a question about personal daily routines (C1, C3, C5) Spoken production • Can sing the *Hello song* (C1, C6) • Can name parts of the body (C1, C3) • Can say the rap *One head* (C1, C6) • Can say sentences to describe parts of the body (C1, C3) • Can sing the song *These are my eyes* (C1, C6) • Can sing the song *This is the way* (C1, C6) • Can say sentences to describe some personal daily routines (C1, C3, C5) • Can say singular and (regular) plural words (C1) • Can sing the *Goodbye song* (C1, C6)	• Can copy and write words for parts of the body (C1, C3, C7, C8) • Can complete short sentences with singular or plural words (C1)
Listening • Can recognise clothes words (C1, C3) • Can recognise words for two materials used to make clothes (C1, C3) • Can understand the episode of the story (C1, C6, C8) • Can understand statements about clothes (C1, C3) • Can understand questions and answers about clothes (C1, C3, C5) • Can discriminate between the sounds /s/ and /ʃ/ at the start of words (C1) Reading • Can recognise clothes words (C1) • Can read statements about clothes (C1) • Can read questions and answers about clothes (C1) • Can read sentences about wool and cotton (C1, C3, C4)	Spoken interaction • Can ask about and respond to questions about clothes (C1, C5) • Can ask for permission in a game (C1, C5, C8) Spoken production • Can sing the song *I'm ready for English* (C1, C6) • Can name clothes (C1) • Can say the chant *Everybody put on your coat* (C1, C6) • Can say sentences about clothes (C1, C5) • Can say the chant *Is this your hat?* (C1, C3) • Can say the rhyme *Diddle, diddle, dumpling* (C1, C6) • Can say words which start with /s/ and /ʃ/ (C1) • Can sing the song *Shake your head* (C1, C6)	• Can copy and write words for clothes (C1, C3, C8) • Can complete questions and sentences with words for clothes (C1)
Listening • Can recognise food words (C1, C3) • Can understand the episode of the story (C1, C6, C8) • Can understand when people say they like or don't like food (C1, C3, C5) • Can understand questions about food you like (C1, C3) • Can understand questions and answers about whether food is good for you (C1, C3) Reading • Can recognise food words (C1) • Can read statements about food people say they like and don't like (C1, C3) • Can read questions and answers about food you like (C1) • Can understand questions and answers about whether food is good for you (C1, C3, C4)	Spoken interaction • Can ask about and respond to questions about food you like (C1, C5) • Can ask and answer questions about whether food is good for you (C1, C3, C5) Spoken production • Can sing the song *I'm ready for English* (C1, C6) • Can name food (C1) • Can sing the song *Delicious for me, delicious for you!* (C1, C6) • Can say sentences about food you like and don't like (C1, C3) • Can say the chant *Do you like yogurt?* (C1, C6) • Can say the chant *The lunch train* (C1, C6) • Can say a skipping game rhyme (C1, C5, C7) • Can say a tongue-twister with /tʃ/ (C1) • Can sing the song *Shake your head* (C1, C7)	• Can copy and write words for food (C1, C3, C7, C8) • Can complete questions and sentences about food you like and don't like (C1)

Title	Structures and grammar	Vocabulary	Main receptive language
Unit 6 **My toys**	• Where's the ...? • It's in / on / under ... • Where are the ...? • They're ... • How many ...? Recycled: • I've got ... • What's this? • It's ... • Can I have a ...? • Here you are.	• Core: *doll, bike, ball, car, train, marbles, skates, plane, robot, computer game*, numbers 11–20 • Other: *cave, genie, magic, lamp, box, jar, shelf, big, small* • Content / culture: *wheel, skateboard, bus, scooter, teddy bear, driver, chatter, hoot, hot, cold* • Recycled: *table, chair, children, thank you*, numbers 1–10	• *shape, things, move,* • *have got ...* • *dark*
Unit 7 **My family**	• Who's he / she? • He's / She's my ... • His / Her name is ... • He's / She's got ... Recycled: • Who ...? • I've got ... • This is ... / These are ... • my / your • ..., too	• Core: *mother, father, brother, sister, baby, grandmother, grandfather, aunt, uncle, cousin* • Other: *love, fair, house, soup, name, goat* • Content / culture: *colour, glasses, lap, nap, clap, fold* • Recycled: *boy, girl, friend, eyes, hair, brown, blue, red, green, black, hat, hands, arms, fantastic, delicious*, numbers 1–20	• *similar to* • *members, family* • *also, special* • *Let's ...*
Unit 8 **My pets**	• It's got ... • What's its name? • Its name is ... • What a ...! • It's the ... • I ... my ... Recycled: • It's ... • I like ... • I've got ... • I brush my ... • This is ... • my / your • Here's the ... • Hurry! • Can I ...?	• Core: *cat, dog, pony, mouse, rabbit, hamster, bird, fish, guinea pig, turtle* • Other: *goat, troll, cross, bridge, medium, pet, tail, fur, whiskers, long, short* • Content / culture: *feed, clean, give water, take for walks, little, fly, shiny, curly* • Recycled: *brush, play, eyes, ears, nose, legs, big, small, colours*	• *live, home, keep,* • *important, kind* • *care for*

BASIC COMPETENCIES KEY			
C1: Competency in linguistic communication.	C3: Competency in knowledge of and interaction with the physical world.	C6: Competency in social awareness and citizenship.	
C2: Competency in mathematics.	C4: Competency in use of new technologies.	C7: Competency in learning to learn.	
	C5: Competency in the use of new technologies.	C8: Competency in learning autonomous personal initiative.	

Communicative competence

Understanding	Speaking	Writing
Listening • Can recognise names of toys (C1, C3) • Can understand the episode of the story (C1, C6, C8) • Can understand when people ask and say where things are (C1, C3) • Can understand the question *How many ...?* (C1) • Can recognise numbers to 20 (C1, C2) • Can recognise word stress (in two-syllable words) (C1) **Reading** • Can recognise the names of toys (C1) • Can recognise numbers to 20 (C1, C2) • Can read questions and answers about where things are (C1, C3) • Can read sentences about the wheel (C1, C3, C4)	**Spoken interaction** • Can ask about and respond to questions about where things are (C1, C5) • Can ask and answer questions about how many (C1, C2, C5) **Spoken production** • Can sing the song *I'm ready for English* (C1, C6) • Can name toys (C1) • Can sing the song *I've got a car and a ball* (C1, C6) • Can say where things are (C1, C3) • Can say the chant *How many marbles are in the jar?* (C1, C2, C6) • Can say familiar two-syllable words with the correct stress (C1) • Can count to 20 (C1, C2) • Can sing the song *The wheels on the bus* (C1, C6, C7) • Can sing the song *Shake your head* (C1, C6)	• Can copy and write words for toys (C1, C3, C7, C8) • Can copy and write words for numbers to twenty (C1, C2, C7, C8) • Can complete questions and sentences about where things are (C1)
Listening • Can recognise words for members of the family (C1, C3) • Can understand the episode of the story (C1, C, C8) • Can understand questions which ask and say who people are (C1, C3) • Can understand statements about people's hair and eye colour (C1, C3) • Can recognise the difference between /ð/ and /θ/ (C1) **Reading** • Can recognise words for members of the family (C1, C3) • Can read sentences that describe the colour of eyes and hair (C1, C3) • Can read questions and answers about who people are (C1, C3) • Can read about ways we are similar to other members of our family (C1, C3, C4)	**Spoken interaction** • Can sing the song *I like English* (C1, C6) • Can ask and respond to questions about who people are (C1, C3, C5) **Spoken production** • Can name members of the family (C1, C3) • Can sing the song *My mother and father* (C1, C6) • Can say who people are (C1, C3) • Can sing the song *She's my friend* (C1, C6) • Can say words with /ð/ and /θ/ correctly (C1) • Can describe people's hair and eye colour (C1, C3) • Can say the rhyme *These are grandmother's glasses* (C1, C6, C7) • Can sing the song *Are you ready to finish?* (C1, C6)	• Can copy and write words for members of the family (C1, C3, C7, C8) • Can copy and write words for the colour of hair and eyes (C1, C3, C7, C8) • Can complete questions and sentences about who people are (C1)
Listening • Can recognise words for pets (C1, C3) • Can understand the episode of the story (C1, C6, C8) • Can understand statements describing pets • Can understand statements about ways to care for pets (C1, C3) **Reading** • Can recognise words for pets (C1, C3) • Can recognise words to describe pets (C1, C3) • Can read simple statements about pets (C1, C3) • Can read about ways to care for pets (C1, C3, C4)	**Spoken interaction** • Can ask and say the names of pets (C1, C3, C5) **Spoken production** • Can sing the song *I like English* (C1, C6) • Can identify pets (C1, C3) • Can sing the song *I like pets!* (C1, C6) • Can describe and say the names of pets (C1, C3) • Can say the chant *This is my dog* (C1, C6) • Can say a tongue twister with /h/ (C1) • Can say what you do to care for pets (C1, C3) • Can sing the song *Little Peter Rabbit* (C1, C6, C7) • Can sing the song *Are you ready to finish?* (C1, C6)	• Can copy and write words for pets (C1, C3, C7, C8) • Can copy and write words to describe pets (C1, C3, C7, C8) • Can complete sentences about pets (C1)

Title	Structures and grammar	Vocabulary	Main receptive language
Unit 9 Treasure!	• *Where are you?* • *Let's ... to the ...!* • *Good idea!* • *Put it in ...!* Recycled: • *What's this?* • *It's ...* • *Are you ...?* • *Yes, I am. / No, I'm not.* • *Where ...?* • *I'm ...* • *in / on / under* • *We ...*	• Core: *tree, flower, grass, rock, river, hill, bush, path, fence, gate* • Other: *jump, hop, run, walk, skip* • Content / culture: *paper, glass, tin cans, bin, know, show, three times* • Recycled: *put, plastic, clean, blue, yellow, green, red, happy, clap hands,* numbers 1–20	• *countryside, rubbish, recycle, throw away*
Christmas	• *... has got ...* • *I like ... / don't like ...* • *What ...!* • *We love you!* • *Please help me!* Recycled: • *... is happy / sad*	• Core: *Christmas, short, antlers, yellow, Santa, reindeer, sleigh.* • Recycled: *yellow, happy, sad, present*	• *Christmas Eve, guide, children*
Easter	• *go ...* • *finds ...* Recycled: *It's ...*	• Core: *Easter, rabbit, egg, little, hunt, eat, run away* • Recycled: *big, play,* colours, numbers 1–5	
Father's Day	• *I love ...* • *How about you?* • *He loves me, too* Recycled: *... is ...*	• Core: *Father, day, Dad, love* • Recycled: *fantastic, great, brilliant, happy*	• *shirt, tie* • *play, read*
Mother's Day	• *Make a ...* • *Give a ...* Recycled: • *I love ...*	• Core: *Mother, day, hug, surprise* • Recycled: *Mum, present, card, flowers*	• *special, things*

BASIC COMPETENCIES KEY
C1: Competency in linguistic communication.
C2: Competency in mathematics.
C3: Competency in knowledge of and interaction with the physical world.
C4: Competency in use of new technologies.
C5: Competency in the use of new technologies.
C6: Competency in social awareness and citizenship.
C7: Competency in learning to learn.
C8: Competency in learning autonomous personal initiative.

Communicative competence

Understanding	Speaking	Writing
Listening • Can recognise words for things in the countryside (C1, C3) • Can understand the episode of the story (C1, C6, C8) • Can understand questions and answers about where you are (C1, C3) • Can understand suggestions (C1, C5) • Can understand what people recycle (C1, C3, C4, C5) • Can identify words which rhyme (C1) Reading • Can recognise words for things in the countryside (C1, C3) • Can recognise words to describe where people are (C1, C3) • Can recognise action words (C1, C3) • Can read statements about recycling (C1, C3, C4, C5)	Spoken interaction • Can ask and say where you are (C1, C3) • Can make and respond to suggestions (C1, C5) Spoken production • Can sing the song *I like English* (C1, C6) • Can identify things in the countryside (C1, C3) • Can sing the song *Where's the treasure?* (C1, C6) • Can say where you are (C1, C3) • Can say the rhyme *Follow me* (C1, C6) • Can say what you and your family recycle (C1, C3, C5) • Can sing the song *If you're happy* (C1, C6, C7) • Can say rhyming words (C1) • Can sing the song *Are you ready to finish?* (C1, C6)	• Can copy and write words for things in nature (C1, C3, C7, C8) • Can complete sentences about where people are (C1, C3, C7, C8) • Can complete suggestions (C1)
Listening • Can understand a Christmas story (C1, C6, C8) Reading • Can read key sentences in the story (C1, C6, C8)	Spoken interaction • Can answer questions about the story (C1, C5, C6) Spoken production • Can act out the story (C1, C5, C6) • Can sing the song *Jingle bells* (C1, C6, C7) • Can sing the *Goodbye song* (C1, C6)	
Listening • Can understand an Easter song (C1, C6, C7) • Can identify numbers and colours (C1, C2, C3) Reading • Can read numbers and colour words (C1, C2, C3)	Spoken interaction • Can answer questions about the colour of Easter eggs (C1, C3, C7) Spoken production • Can sing the song *Five little rabbits go out to play* (C1, C6, C7) • Can sing the song *Shake your head* (C1, C6)	
Listening • Can understand a Father's Day song (C1, C6, C7) Reading • Can read a message in a Father's Day card (C1, C7)	Spoken interaction • Can answer questions about what you do with your father (C1, C5, C7) Spoken production • Can sing the Father's Day song *I love Dad* (C1, C6, C7) • Can sing the song *Are you ready to finish? / Shake your head* (C1, C6)	• Can complete a Father's Day card (C1, C6, C8)
Listening • Can understand things to do for Mother's Day (C1, C7) Reading • Can read things to do for Mother's Day (C1, C7)	Spoken interaction • Can answer a question about what you'd like to do for Mother's Day (C1, C5, C7) Spoken production • Can say things you'd like to do for Mother's Day (C1, C5, C7) • Can sing the song *Shake your head / Are you ready to finish?* (C1, C6)	• Can complete a Mother's Day card (C1, C6, C8)

Footprints 1 syllabus guide

Title	Content links	Learning strategies and thinking skills
Introduction		• Following a model (C1, C7) • Imitating and repeating (C1, C7) • Associating pictures and characters (C1, C3, C7) • Associating music with greetings (C1, C6, C7) • Associating rhythm and actions with vocabulary (C1, C6, C7) • Taking turns (C5, C7) • Activating previous knowledge (C8)
Unit 1 **My birthday**	• *Maths:* recognition of shapes	• Recognising learning objectives (C7) • Following simple instructions (C1, C5, C7) • Using mime and gesture (C1, C6, C7) • Associating rhythm with a language pattern (C1, C6, C7) • Making logical deductions (C1, C2, C3, C7) • Observing shapes in pictures and in the classroom (C1, C2, C7) • Classifying objects according to their shape (C1, C2, C7) • Reflecting on learning (C7, C8)
Unit 2 **My classroom**	• *Science:* differences between plastic and wood	• Recognising learning objectives (C7) • Using music and rhythm to memorise language (C1, C6, C7) • Sequencing (C1, C2, C7) • Making use of prior knowledge (C3, C7, C8) • Using visual and other clues to make predictions and guesses (C3, C7) • Associating shape and touch with vocabulary (C2, C3, C7) • Classifying classroom objects according to whether they are plastic or wood (C1, C3, C7) • Reflecting on learning (C7, C8)
Unit 3 **My body**	• *Social sciences:* germs and personal hygiene	• Recognising learning objectives (C7) • Following simple instructions (C1, C5, C7) • Associating vocabulary with touch (C1, C3, C7) • Relating parts to the whole (C3, C7) • Associating sounds with meaning (C1, C6, C7) • Using mime and gesture (C1, C6, C7) • Reflecting on learning (C7, C8)
Unit 4 **My clothes**	• *Science:* wool and cotton	• Recognising learning objectives (C7) • Following simple instructions (C1, C5, C7) • Associating colours and materials with clothes (C1, C3, C7) • Associating vocabulary with touch (C1, C3, C7) • Classifying (C1, C3, C7) • Making logical deductions (C1, C2, C3, C7) • Using mime and gesture (C1, C6, C7) • Reflecting on learning (C7, C8)
Unit 5 **Food I like**	• *Social sciences:* food that is good for you	• Recognising learning objectives (C7) • Associating vocabulary with personal preferences (C1, C7) • Completing a chart (C2, C3, C7) • Cooperating with others (C5, C7) • Classifying (C1, C3, C7) • Using rhythm to memorise vocabulary and language patterns (C1, C6, • Reflecting on learning (C7, C8)

BASIC COMPETENCIES KEY
C1: Competency in linguistic communication.
C2: Competency in mathematics.
C3: Competency in knowledge of and interaction with the physical world.
C4: Competency in use of new technologies.
C5: Competency in the use of new technologies.
C6: Competency in social awareness and citizenship.
C7: Competency in learning to learn.
C8: Competency in learning autonomous personal initiative.

Children's culture	Values and attitudes
• Identifying fairytale characters (C1, C3, C7)	• Interest in learning English (C1, C8) • Pleasure in exchanging greetings and asking and saying your name in English (C1, C5, C8) • Enjoyment in meeting the course characters (C1, C3) • Awareness that fairytale characters exist in English (C1, C3, C6)
• Singing a traditional birthday song: *Happy birthday* (C1, C3, C5, C6, C7) • Playing a version of a traditional birthday party game: *Pass the present* (C1, C5, C6, C7)	• Pleasure in celebrating a birthday in English (C1, C5, C6, C7) • Interest in recognising and identifying shapes (C1, C3) • Awareness that it's polite to say *thank you* when people give you a present (C1, C5, C8)
• Saying a traditional rhyme: *One, two, three, four* (C1, C6, C7) • Playing a traditional children's game: *Paper, stone, scissors!* (C1, C5, C6, C7)	• Interest in being able to talk about classroom objects in English (C1, C3, C5) • Recognition that classroom objects are made of different materials (C1, C3) • Awareness that it's polite to say *sorry* if you're late (C1, C5, C8)
• Singing a song: *This is the way …* (C1, C6, C7) • Playing a dice game: *Body dice!* (C1, C5, C6, C7)	• Interest in being able to name parts of the body in English (C1, C3) • Awareness of the importance of personal hygiene (C1, C3, C5) • Awareness of the importance of washing your hands (C1, C3, C5)
• Saying a version of a traditional rhyme: *Diddle, diddle, dumpling* (C1, C6, C7) • Playing a version of a traditional game: *Mr Crocodile!* (C1, C5, C6, C7)	• Enjoyment in being able to talk about your clothes in English (C1, C3, C5) • Interest in materials used to make clothes (C1, C3) • Awareness of the importance of taking care of your clothes (C1, C3, C5, C8)
• Saying a chant: *The lunch train* (C1, C6, C7) • Playing a traditional skipping game: *Coffee and tea!* (C1, C5, C6, C7)	• Pleasure in expressing personal likes and dislikes (C1, C5) • Interest and respect for other people's opinions (C1, C5, C8) • Awareness that it is important to eat food that is good for you (C1, C3) • Awareness of the importance of eating a good lunch (C1, C3, C8)

Title	Content links	Learning strategies and thinking skills
Unit 6 **My toys**	• *Science:* things with wheels	• Recognising learning objectives (C7) • Associating vocabulary with personal possessions (C1, C3, C7) • Classifying (C1, C3, C7) • Using rhythm to memorise vocabulary and language patterns (C1, C6, C • Observing objects and pictures in close detail (C3, C7) • Associating language with spatial positions (C1, C2, C7, C7) • Reflecting on learning (C1, C7, C8)
Unit 7 **My family**	• *Science* ways in which we are similar to other members of our family	• Recognising learning objectives (C7) • Associating vocabulary with people you know (C1, C3, C7) • Using pictures to memorise vocabulary and language patterns (C1, C3, • Observing people in close detail (C1, C3, C7) • Guessing who people are (C1, C3, C7) • Deducing (C1, C3, C7) • Reflecting on learning (C7, C8)
Unit 8 **My pets**	• *Social sciences:* ways to care for pets	• Recognising learning objectives (C7) • Associating vocabulary and pictures (C1, C3, C7) • Using mime to memorise language patterns (C1, C6, C7) • Identifying features of pets (C1, C3, C7) • Deducing from a description (C1, C3, C7) • Expressing personal preferences (C1, C3, C5, C7) • Reflecting on learning (C7, C8)
Unit 9 **Treasure!**	• *Science:* recycling	• Recognising learning objectives (C7) • Associating vocabulary with pictures (C1, C3, C7) • Using actions to memorise language patterns (C1, C3, C7) • Deducing (C1, C3, C7) • Sorting and counting (C1, C2, C7) • Associating colours and materials (C1, C3, C7) • Reflecting on learning (C7, C8) • Recognising own progress (C7, C8)
Christmas	• *Art and craft:* cut-out story book	• Predicting and hypothesising what happens in a story (C3, C6, C7, C8) • Associating pictures and language patterns (C1, C3, C7) • Using actions to memorise a song (C1, C6, C7)
Easter	• *Art and craft:* counting cut-out	• Identifying key words in a rhyme (C1, C6, C7) • Using rhythm and repetition to memorise language patterns in a rhyme (C1, C6, C7, C8) • Associating counting with manipulating a cut-out (C1, C2, C6, C7)
Father's Day	• *Art and craft:* Father's Day card	• Using rhythm and repetition to memorise language patterns in a song (C1, C6, C7) • Associating pictures and personal experience (C1, C3, C7) • Personalising a card (C1, C5, C6, C7)
Mothers's Day	• *Art and craft:* Mother's Day card	• Listening and reading in order to make personal choices (C1, C5, C7) • Expressing personal preferences (C1, C5, C7) • Personalising a card (C1, C5, C6, C7)

BASIC COMPETENCIES KEY
C1: Competency in linguistic communication.
C2: Competency in mathematics.
C3: Competency in knowledge of and interaction with the physical world.
C4: Competency in use of new technologies.
C5: Competency in the use of new technologies.
C6: Competency in social awareness and citizenship.
C7: Competency in learning to learn.
C8: Competency in learning autonomous personal initiative.

Children's culture	Values and attitudes
• Singing a traditional song: *The wheels on the bus* (C1, C6, C7) • Playing a version of a traditional game: *Where's the …?* (C1, C5, C6, C7)	• Enjoyment in talking about toys in English (C1, C5) • Awareness that many things have got wheels (C1, C2, C3) • Awareness of noise level when you chat with friends (C1, C5, C8)
• Saying a rhyme: *These are grandmother's glasses* (C1, C6, C7) • Playing a version of a traditional game: *Grandmother's footsteps!* (C1, C5, C6, C7)	• Pleasure in talking about your family in English (C1, C5) • Recognition that we are similar to other members of our family (C1, C3, C5) • Awareness that your family is special (C1, C5)
• Singing a song: *Little Peter Rabbit* (C1, C6, C7) • Playing a version of a traditional game: *Cat and mouse!* (C1, C5, C6, C7)	• Pleasure in talking about pets in English (C1, C5) • Awareness of the responsibility of having a pet (C1, C3, C5) • Recognition that it is important to be kind to pets (C1, C5)
• Singing a song: *If you're happy* (C1, C6, C7) • Playing a traditional game: *Follow my leader!* (C1, C5, C6, C7)	• Recognition of the value of recycling (C1, C3, C5, C8) • Sense of achievement in completing *Footprints 1* (C1, C5, C8) • Pleasure in how much English you know (C1, C5)
• Listening to a story about a Christmas reindeer (C1, C6, C7) • Singing a version of a well-known Christmas song: *Jingle bells* (C1, C6, C7)	• Pleasure in celebrating Christmas (C1, C3, C5) • Enjoyment in a Christmas story and song (C1, C3, C6, C8) • Awareness that it's wrong to mock or laugh at others (C1, C5, C7)
• Singing an Easter song: *Five little rabbits go out to play* (C1, C6, C7) • Identifying coloured eggs in an Easter egg hunt (C1, C5, C6, C7)	• Pleasure in celebrating Easter (C1, C3, C5) • Enjoyment in a well-known Easter tradition (C1, C3, C7, C8) • Awareness that it's important to share things with others (C1, C5, C7)
• Singing a Father's Day song (C1, C6, C7) • Making a Father's Day card (C1, C6, C7, C8)	• Pleasure in celebrating Father's Day (C1, C3, C5) • Recognition of the importance of family (C1, C3, C5) • Enjoyment in making a card to give to your father (C1, C7, C8)
• Reading about ways to celebrate Mother's Day (C1, C5) • Making a Mother's Day card (C1, C6, C7, C8)	• Pleasure in identifying things to do for Mother's Day (C1, C3, C5) • Recognition of the importance of family (C1, C3, C5) • Enjoyment in making a card to give to your mother (C1, C6, C7, C8)

Introduction to *Footprints*

1 Who *Footprints* is for

Footprints is a six-level course for children who have started learning English at pre-school or for children who have no previous knowledge of English and are being taught at a faster pace. *Footprints* is designed to develop children's communicative competence to A2 level within the Council of Europe's Common European Framework for Modern Languages (CEF) and to maximise successful learning outcomes at every age and stage on the way to attaining this.

The main aims of *Footprints*

- To enable children to communicate confidently and competently in English.
- To develop all language skills in a balanced, systematic and integrated way.
- To learn content from other areas of the curriculum through English.
- To develop intercultural learning and citizenship skills.
- To provide motivating, challenging and enjoyable materials.
- To support teachers and children in preparing for external exams and tests.
- To help children become responsible, reflective, independent learners.

2 Components of *Footprints 1*

Pupil's Book: 80 full-colour pages comprising a list of contents, a summary of the syllabus, a two-page Introduction, nine units and material for four festivals (Christmas, Easter, Father's Day and Mother's Day). Each unit comprises eight pages, one per lesson. These include *Vocabulary presentation* (Lesson 1), *Language input and story* (Lesson 2), *Communication and grammar* (Lesson 3), *Communication, grammar and pronunciation* (Lesson 4), *Content input* (Lesson 5), *Content and personalisation* (Lesson 6), *Children's culture* (Lesson 7) and *Unit review* (Lesson 8). There is also a pull-out double page of colour stickers inserted in the centre of the book.

Activity Book: This comprises 96 black and white pages, with a range of engaging activities for children to practise language skills. Each unit comprises eight pages, one per lesson. This corresponds to the organisation of units and lessons in the Pupil's Book and makes the materials very convenient to use. In addition, the Activity Book contains a two-page Picture Dictionary which provides a useful reference and a record of the key vocabulary that children learn. It also includes nine cut-outs, one for each unit. The cut-outs include finger puppets of the course characters (Unit 1), vocabulary picture / word cards (Units 2, 4, 6 and 8) and 'little books' (Units 3, 5, 7 and 9).

All About Me **Portfolio Booklet:** This is a 24-page booklet in A5 format which allows children to build up a personalised record of learning. At the start of the booklet, children complete their portrait and passport, including information about the language(s) they speak and learn at school. For each unit, children draw and write personalised information relating to the topic and language of the unit. They also carry out a self-assessment in the form of 'can do' statements relating to what they have learnt in the unit. If children are using language portfolios, the *All About Me* booklet is designed to form part of these. If not, the booklet provides a motivating format for additional, enjoyable, personalised language practice and self-assessment.

Finger puppets: A pack of two attractive, multi-coloured finger puppets made out of soft material is also included as part of the course materials. These represent the two magical, mischievous, miniature course characters, Pip and Squeak, who accompany Alex and Katie (the children) and Frodo (the frog) on the *Footprints* adventure in the book of fairy tales. The finger puppets are easy to manipulate (you can pick things up and even write on the board while wearing them) and their size reflects the pixie- / fairy-like course characters they represent. The finger puppets are strongly differentiated in colour and shape, and children can easily identify them flying about on your fingers even in big classrooms. There are many advantages in having two puppets – for example, when demonstrating activities or playing whole-class games. A section in the Teacher's Book, *Twenty ways to use the finger puppets* (see page 21), provides more ideas for using the finger puppets, in addition to those included in the teaching notes for each unit.

Audio CDs: The three audio CDs contain recordings of all the *Follow the footprints* vocabulary activities, episodes of the story, songs, rhymes, chants, raps, musical games and other listening activities that are included in *Footprints 1*. All the songs and chants are followed by 'karaoke' versions, with music or percussion only, which can be used when children are familiar with the words.

Flashcards / Word cards: A pack of 96 full-colour flashcards illustrating key vocabulary and corresponding word cards is included to support children's learning in *Footprints 1*. These are used for presenting and practising key vocabulary as well as for showing understanding of songs, rhymes and chants, revision activities and games. Detailed instructions for using the flashcards and word cards are given in the teaching notes for each unit.

Teacher's Book: This includes facsimile pages from the Pupil's Book and the Activity Book, making it very convenient and easy to use in class. The Teacher's Book aims to provide clear guidelines and support for teachers using *Footprints 1* and includes:

- *Footprints 1* **syllabus**
- **Introduction to** *Footprints 1*
- *Twenty ways to use the finger puppets:* Included in the introduction is a section of twenty additional ideas for ways to use the finger puppets to provide varied extra language practice and to help you manage your classes effectively.
- **Detailed teaching notes:** These contain the syllabus objectives of the unit followed by detailed stage-by-stage guidelines for teaching all the lessons, including

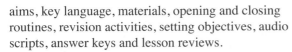

aims, key language, materials, opening and closing routines, revision activities, setting objectives, audio scripts, answer keys and lesson reviews.

- **Photocopiable cut-outs:** These include cut-outs to be used optionally as part of the festival materials for Christmas, Easter, Father's Day and Mother's Day. There is also a photocopiable Achievement Certificate to be given to children at the end of *Footprints 1*.

Additional resources

For children:

Stories and Songs CD: A CD containing every episode of the *Footprints 1* story as well as the songs, rhymes, raps and chants in each unit is included with the Pupil's Book for each child. This allows for enjoyable additional listening practice and reinforcement of learning in the children's own time at home.

CD-ROM: A CD-ROM of interactive activities and games which relate to each unit is also included with the Pupil's Book for each child. The CD-ROM motivates children to practise and extend their learning. It provides reinforcement activities in a medium which children enjoy. The CD-ROM can be used independently either in class or at home.

For teachers:

Tests and Photocopiable Resources CD-ROM Pack: This is a CD-ROM with all the evaluation and assessment material for *Footprints 1*, plus 54 supplementary worksheets which allow children to consolidate their knowledge. The tests, exams and classroom practice worksheets are in PDF format ready to download and print out and photocopy whenever you need them. The exams practice worksheets contain activities which can be used with children preparing to take the Trinity and Cambridge Young Learners exams. The CD-ROM includes answer keys for all the activities. The CD-ROM comprises the following:

- **Tests (plus teacher's notes and answer keys)**
  - Diagnostic test (three pages)
  - End-of-unit tests (27 pages)
  - Three term tests (after Units 3, 6 and 9) (nine pages)
  - End-of-year test (four pages)
- **Exams practice worksheets (plus teacher's notes and answer keys)**
  - Listening, reading, writing and speaking practice exam materials for Units 1–9 (18 pages)
- **Child assessment sheets:**
  - Observation of speaking activity (one page)
  - Child assessment sheets (two pages)
  - Class assessment sheets (four pages)
  - Learning-to-learn reflection sheet (one page)
- **Classroom practice worksheets (plus teacher's notes and answer keys)**
  - Mixed ability worksheets (two worksheets per unit)
  - Extra reading and writing worksheets (two worksheets per unit)
  - Grammar practice worksheets (two worksheets per unit)

There are also nine *Letters to parents* (one per unit) which you can print out and send home with the children whenever you start a new unit.

The Tests and Photocopiable Resources Pack also contains a CD with all the audio for the listening activities in the tests and exams.

Digital Book: This is comprised of the digital Pupil's Book and the digital Activity Book. The zoom-in facility allows teachers to focus on individual tasks and also story frames. The digital Activity book includes answers, facilitating whole class correction.

Website: The website address is www.macmillanenglish.com/younglearners.

3 Description of the course materials

The syllabus

The syllabus of *Footprints 1* is specified under the following headings: Structures and grammar, Vocabulary, Main receptive language, Communicative competence, Content links, Learning strategies and thinking skills, Children's culture, and Values and attitudes.

Vocabulary is divided into 'core', which includes the ten target productive vocabulary items for the unit; 'other', which includes additional productive vocabulary introduced in e.g. songs or the episode of the story; 'content / culture', which includes vocabulary in the unit related to these two areas; and 'recycled', which includes vocabulary previously introduced.

Following the CEF, Communicative competence is expressed in terms of 'can do' statements and further sub-divided into 'Understanding', including Listening and Reading; 'Speaking', including Spoken interaction and Spoken production; and 'Writing'.

The syllabus is designed to develop language skills in conjunction with meta-cognitive, cognitive and social skills, and to integrate learning content from other areas of the curriculum, as well as children's culture, through English. Key features of the syllabus include the focus on the development of active vocabulary, the carefully sequenced introduction of language structures, the integration of learning strategies and thinking skills, and regular, systematic recycling of language. This is vital in aiding recall and helps to develop children's long-term memory. It also builds up children's confidence and competence in using language in a range of different contexts.

The teaching programme

The Pupil's Book and Activity Book in *Footprints 1* contain material for 120–150 hours and are suitable for children studying 4–5 hours' English a week.

A suggested plan for teaching *Footprints 1* during the school year is:

Term 1: Units 1, 2 and 3, Christmas

Term 2: Units 4, 5 and 6, Easter, Father's Day*

Term 3: Units 7, 8 and 9, Mother's Day*

* The date of Mother's Day and Father's Day varies in different countries, so you need to check your country's calendar before finalising your teaching programme for the year.

The organisation of the units

There is a one-to-one correspondence between units, lessons and pages in the Pupil's Book and the Activity Book. Children do the activities in the Pupil's Book first, and this is followed by further language practice in the Activity Book.

Introduction

This comprises two lessons and consists of a double-page spread in the Pupil's Book and the Activity Book. In Lesson 1, children meet the course characters (two children, Alex and Katie; two miniature fairy- / pixie-like characters, Pip and Squeak; and Frodo the frog) through a song, and practise and revise some basic classroom vocabulary. In Lesson 2, children are introduced to some of the fairytale characters in the level 1 *Footprints* story, which is a quest to follow the footprints in order to find the treasure at the end of the rainbow. Children sing a song, practise and revise naming colours and put on the first treasure clue sticker of the story.

The Introduction is followed by nine units, each consisting of eight lessons and eight corresponding pages in the Pupil's Book and Activity Book (excluding the cut-out pages).

The units follow the same general pattern throughout as follows:

Lesson 1 – Vocabulary presentation

Children are introduced to the ten target vocabulary items in the unit using the flashcards. They then listen and *Follow the footprints* vocabulary trail in the Pupil's Book, first with their fingers and then drawing a line. As they do this, they stop by each picture and listen and repeat the words. They then identify the word cards and match them to the flashcards on the board. In the second Pupil's Book activity, children listen and sing a song or say a rhyme which contextualises the new vocabulary with a recycled structure or other familiar language. This is followed by a vocabulary activity which engages them cognitively e.g. drawing, sequencing or matching pictures, and focuses on production and saying the words correctly. Two activities in the Activity Book provide reading and writing practice of the new vocabulary introduced.

Lesson 2 – Language input and story

The key language structure(s) and / or grammar point of the unit is presented through an episode of the *Footprints* story. Before listening to the story, children re-cap on the previous episode with their books closed and answer questions to predict what happens next. They then listen and follow the story on the Pupil's Book page to find out. The teacher asks the questions again and children compare what happens in the story with their predictions. Children then listen again and repeat the story. They also answer more detailed questions which check understanding of the story and the new language introduced. Children then put on the treasure clue sticker for this episode of the story. This shows the next fairytale character that Alex, Katie, Pip and Squeak must find in their quest to follow the footprints and find the treasure at the end of the rainbow. After listening to the story, children act it out, taking the roles of the characters in groups. Individual children also act out the story to the rest of the class. Two follow-up activities in the Activity Book focus on comprehension of the story and the key language that it contains.

Lesson 3 – Communication and grammar

Children do an initial activity which practises key language structures introduced in the story together with the vocabulary introduced in Lesson 1. Children then make the cut-out for the unit, which is found at the back of the Activity Book, and play a communication game. In Lesson 3 of Unit 1, children make paper finger puppets of the course characters, Alex, Katie, Pip, Squeak and Frodo. In subsequent units, children make either picture / word cards of the target vocabulary or personalised 'little books' relating to the theme of the unit and using key language structures. Two activities in the Activity Book provide further practice and consolidation of the language used.

Lesson 4 – Communication, grammar and pronunciation

Children listen to a rhyme, chant, rap or song which develops and builds on the key language practised in Lesson 3. They then do a communication activity based on this. This is followed by a pronunciation activity, *Frodo's word fun*, which focuses on individual sounds or word stress and takes the form of tongue-twisters, simple sound discrimination games or clapping stress patterns. Two activities in the Activity Book provide further practice and consolidation of language in the rhyme, chant, rap or song and communication activity.

Lesson 5 – Content input

Lessons 5 and 6, *Learn about the world around you!*, provide an opportunity for children to learn content from other areas of the curriculum through English. In Lesson 5, children read a short text which links the topic and / or language of the unit to content from other subject areas such as Science or Social sciences. In the second part of this activity, children do a listening activity which frequently encourages them to predict, hypothesise and apply the content to what they already know. This is followed by a whole-class game which uses mime, movement or drama, and gives children an opportunity to assimilate and respond to the content input in an enjoyable way. Two activities in the Activity Book check comprehension of the content-based reading text and get children to show and apply their understanding using some of the language it contains.

Lesson 6 – Content and personalisation

This lesson extends the content-based learning in Lesson 5 and provides opportunities for personalisation. The first activity, which is either a listening activity or a game, prepares children to be able to apply and relate the content to their own lives in a personalised way. The second activity in the Pupil's Book and the activities in the Activity Book give children an opportunity to show understanding and respond to the content in ways that are personal to them. These activities also provide further

practice and consolidation of the content-related language and vocabulary that children use.

Lesson 7 – Children's culture

Frodo's *Culture corner* introduces children to traditional or well-known songs, rhymes and games from children's culture in the English-speaking world which relate to the theme of the unit. Frodo's citizenship box, *Remember!*, draws children's attention to personal, social and civic responsibilities, and positive values and attitudes in an enjoyable and light-hearted way. Two follow-up activities in the Activity Book provide further practice of the language in the children's culture activities.

Lesson 8 – Unit review

This lesson provides a review of the main learning points in the unit. In the first activity in the Pupil's Book, children listen to short exchanges using the key language structures and vocabulary. They put full-colour vocabulary stickers on the *Footprints* learning trail and write the words. In the second activity, children listen, read and complete or match short exchanges and sentences using the key language structures and vocabulary. In the Activity Book, children do a further listening and writing activity to check their understanding of what they've learnt. At the end of this lesson, children assess their work in the unit by colouring the picture of Frodo which corresponds to how they think they have done (*My work is OK / My work is good / My work is excellent*).

Children can colour in any pictures they have drawn or any of the pictures in the Activity Book if there is time at the end of an activity.

The organisation of lessons

Every lesson has a clear *Aim* and this is stated together with *Key language* and *Materials* in the lesson overviews for each unit. Lessons follow the same general pattern throughout as outlined below:

Starting out
Greetings and opening routine

Lessons begin with greetings both with the teacher and using the Pip and Squeak finger puppets. This is followed by singing *either* the *Hello song* (Introduction and Units 1–3), *I'm ready for English* (Units 4–6) or *I like English* (Units 7–9), depending on the unit, *or* the Lesson 1 or Lesson 4 song or chant, depending on the lesson. Once children are familiar with the lyrics and words of the songs and chants, the karaoke versions can be used.

Revision activity

This is a short, whole-class activity which re-caps on learning in every lesson (apart from Lesson 1, which introduces a new unit). The revision activities provide a link between lessons and an enjoyable reminder and check-up on recent learning.

Setting objectives

The lesson objectives are expressed in the detailed teaching notes in the form of brief *Today we're going to …* statements. If appropriate, you may wish to elaborate on these or, for example, write a menu of activities that the children are going to do in the lesson on the board, eliciting or giving the reasons for each one. Setting objectives is important in providing a clear structure to lessons and in helping children recognise the importance of having learning goals.

On the learning trail

This is the main part of the lesson and contains a variety of enjoyable and carefully sequenced activities designed to ensure that the learning objective(s) for the lesson is / are met. Throughout the lessons in each unit, there is a range and balance of activity types, involving different skills and multiple intelligences, which are designed to ensure systematic language practice as well as affective and cognitive engagement. After doing the activities on the Pupil's Book page for each lesson, children complete the activities which are designed to consolidate learning and provide further reading and writing practice in the Activity Book.

Ending the lesson
Lesson review

Children are asked to briefly reflect on and identify what they can now do as a result of the lesson. This links back to the objective(s) set at the start of the lesson (and the menu of activities on the board if you wrote this). The lesson review also relates to the 'can do' statements in the syllabus and in the *All About Me* booklet. If you like, children can colour the corresponding 'can do' statement in the *All About Me* booklet as part of the lesson review. If appropriate, you may like to extend the lesson review by encouraging children to think in more detail about the ways in which the activities helped them personally to learn, what they found easy or difficult and why (in L1 if necessary). Following Lesson 8 at the end of the units, you may also like to use the *Learning-to-learn reflection sheet* as part of the Tests and photocopiable resources pack. As part of lesson reviews, it is important to praise children for their efforts as appropriate, and you may also like to use the finger puppets to do this. By conducting regular lesson reviews, you help to develop children's awareness of learning strategies and encourage responsible, positive attitudes towards their own learning.

Goodbye and closing routine

At the end of lessons, children say goodbye to the teacher and finger puppets and, optionally if time, sing the *Goodbye song* (Introduction Unit 1–3), *Shake your head* (Units 4–6) or *Are you ready to finish?* (Units 7–9), depending on the unit. Once children are familiar with the lyrics and words of the routine songs for ending lessons, the karaoke versions can be used.

All About Me Portfolio Booklet

At the end of or during each unit, children complete the corresponding double-page spread in the *All About Me* Portfolio Booklet. When introducing children to the *All About Me* booklet for the first time, you need to explain that the purpose of the booklet is for children to build up a personalised record of their learning and what they can do in English in relation to each unit. If you like, you can explain that the booklet shows the children's personal 'learning journey' during *Footprints 1*, with each unit as a 'footprint' along the way. When children complete the *My portrait* and *My passport* pages, you need to read the text while children follow in the booklet. Be ready to explain and clarify how to complete these pages, including providing the names in English of languages children speak and learn at home and at school. You may want to write these on the board for children to copy. Children can *either* stick in photos of themselves, their home and their school *or* draw and colour pictures on these pages.

As a general procedure for completing the *All About Me* pages for each unit, you need to read the text and speech bubbles on the first page, while children follow in the booklet, and check that they understand how to complete the page. This part of the *All About Me* booklet can be done either in lessons or for homework.

In the case of the 'can do' statements, you also need to read these while children follow in the booklet and use the illustrations to clarify meaning and check understanding. Either the 'can do' statements can be coloured at the end of the corresponding lessons, e.g. 'can act out the story' can be coloured at the end of Lesson 2 in each unit, or the 'can do' statements can be coloured altogether as part of an overall learning review at the end of the unit. As some parts of the 'can do' statements are expressed in language beyond the children's reading level, children need to colour and complete them under your supervision.

It is important to clarify that the children should only colour the statements they think they can do and should leave the others blank if, for example, they were absent during the corresponding lessons. It is up to you whether you think it will be helpful for the children to introduce a colour code for colouring the statements, e.g. green = I can do this well; orange = I can do this OK; red = I can do this but I need more practice.

Once children have completed colouring the 'can do' statements, you may like to ask them to sign this page. You can then endorse that you agree with their assessment of their work (if you do) by adding your own signature and the date. If you have available a fun rubber stamp for achievement, you may like to use this too. If possible, it is also important to create regular opportunities to talk to children individually about their work based on their own assessments in the *All About Me* booklet as this will be invaluable in building up their self-esteem and positive attitudes towards learning.

4 Key features of *Footprints 1*

Episodic story with treasure clue stickers

There is an enjoyable episodic story running through *Footprints 1* which appears in Lesson 2 of each unit. This story is a quest by the main characters (two children, Alex and Katie, and their two miniature, mischievous friends, Pip and Squeak), to follow the footprints and find the treasure at the end of the rainbow.

In the Introduction, we see Alex and Katie poring over the magical world of a compendium of fairy tales, where the other main course characters, Pip, Squeak and Frodo the frog, are from. In Unit 1, the two children enter the book of fairy tales and join in the celebrations for Squeak's birthday. They also meet Frodo the frog and discover the first treasure clue which sets them off on their adventure. In each subsequent episode of the story, Alex, Katie, Pip and Squeak meet different characters from the book of fairy tales: Little Red Riding Hood and the wolf (Unit 2), Pinocchio (Unit 3), Jack and the giant (Unit 4), Hansel and Gretel (Unit 5), Aladdin (Unit 6), Baby Bear and Goldilocks (Unit 7), the three billy goats and the troll (Unit 8), and have a series of exciting and humorous adventures in each one. These eventually lead them to meeting up again with Frodo the frog and finding the treasure at the end of the rainbow in Unit 9. Each episode is a self-contained story in itself. The episodes lead on to each other as a result of the characters finding a treasure clue at the end of each one which leads them to the next fairytale character. The treasure clues are also colourful stickers which children stick on the story page at the end of each episode in the Pupil's Book.

The *Footprints 1* story provides for rich language input as well as introducing the key language structures of each unit. The story motivates children through joining in the ongoing quest of the characters to get to the end of the rainbow. The story also draws on a cultural background of traditional tales that many children share. Children who are already familiar in their own language with the traditional fairytale characters that Alex, Katie, Pip and Squeak meet in the *Footprints 1* story will delight in meeting them in a new context, although this familiarity is neither necessary nor assumed.

Communicative competence from the outset

The integrated approach to language and skills development, which is also reflected in the syllabus, places an emphasis on the development of communicative competence from the outset. There are frequent opportunities for communicative activities, interactive listening and games as well as acting out songs, rhymes, episodes of the story, dialogues and role-plays, and re-telling or re-constructing short texts. Children are given lots of practice in repeating and using language within clearly defined frameworks, in order to help develop memory, recall and good pronunciation. There are also frequent opportunities for children to communicate in contexts which encourage them to draw on the whole of their productive repertoire thereby promoting fluency and confidence in using chunks of language from the start.

Clear presentation of language structures and grammar

The contexts in which children meet and practise new language structures or are introduced to aspects of grammar are designed to be clear, accessible and motivating. Key language of the unit is highlighted in the story in Lesson 2 and children have an opportunity to comprehend, repeat and use this language in the context of the story before moving on to practise it more intensively and in ways which are more personalised in Lessons 3 and 4. As children work through the units, this clear and systematic approach to the presentation and practice of language structures and grammar gives children a sense of constant progress and achievement. It also helps to foster children's positive beliefs in their own ability to learn and succeed in English.

Development of active vocabulary

Footprints 1 places emphasis on the development of children's active vocabulary and this is also reflected in the syllabus. There are ten core vocabulary items in every unit. These are presented orally and in written form using the flashcards and word cards as well as the *Follow the footprints* trail and song in Lesson 1. There are frequent opportunities throughout the unit for children to practise and review the core vocabulary. In addition, children learn a range of other useful and relevant vocabulary items which are either introduced as part of the story episode or form part of the content or culture-based lessons of each unit. The development of active vocabulary provides a sense of pace and progress to children's learning and also helps to boost confidence and train memory skills.

Solid foundations in reading and writing skills

The development of initial reading and writing skills is integrated into every lesson and built up in a systematic way from the start. In Lessons 1–4 of each unit, the focus is on recognising and writing core vocabulary and language which has been introduced through the songs or chants and episode of the story. In Lesson 5, reading is extended to include a short text which provides content-based input. In Lesson 6, writing activities provide opportunities for children to personalise the content and apply it to their own lives. In Lesson 7, children are also exposed to wider language input through traditional or well-known cultural activities such as rhymes, songs and games which relate to the theme of the unit. These also provide opportunities for reading and writing which extend beyond the main language learning points for each unit.

In this way, each unit presents a variety of contexts for children to begin to develop global and specific reading and writing skills. As a support in the development of initial reading skills, children frequently listen at the same time as following in their books. As a support in the development of initial writing skills, children have models to follow and are also motivated through opportunities for personalised writing.

Learning through content

The inclusion of content from other areas of the primary curriculum, such as Science and Social sciences, reflects the increasing trend and importance given to content and language integrated learning (CLIL) in many countries. In *Footprints 1* two lessons in each unit (Lessons 5 and 6, *Learn about the world around you!*) are devoted to learning through content from another area of the curriculum which relates to the theme and language of the unit. The inclusion of content-based learning provides opportunities for children to use English as a vehicle to develop their knowledge and understanding of the real world. It also extends and enriches their language development and their cognitive and conceptual understanding of real issues, and provides an opportunity to apply what they are learning to their own lives.

Intercultural learning

The role of intercultural learning as a way for children to feel secure about their own identity and culture, and to show interest, tolerance and respect towards people of other cultures, is a key feature of *Footprints*. In *Footprints 1*, one lesson in each unit (Lesson 7, Frodo's *Culture corner*) focuses on introducing children to elements of traditional children's culture, such as rhymes, songs and games, from the English-speaking world. Through participating in enjoyable cultural activities, children develop positive attitudes towards learning English. They also become aware of similarities in the kinds of activities that exist in English-speaking children's culture and their own. As part of these lessons, the citizenship *Remember!* boxes are a feature which integrate socio-cultural aspects of learning and foster the development of positive values and attitudes towards self and others in a light-hearted and enjoyable way.

Learning strategies, thinking skills and multiple intelligences

In *Footprints* there is recognition that all children have different strengths, aptitudes, preferences and emerging learning styles and that they need opportunities to develop these in diverse ways in order to become effective, independent learners. For this reason, there is an emphasis on linking language learning to the development of learning strategies, thinking skills and multiple intelligences (linguistic, visual–spatial, musical, kinaesthetic, logical–mathematical, naturalist, interpersonal, intrapersonal) throughout the course. This is reflected in the syllabus of *Footprints 1* and in the balance and variety of activity types used in different lessons which are designed to appeal to children with different individual intelligence profiles and learning styles, thereby helping to ensure success for everyone.

Learning how to learn

Learning how to learn is vital in helping children to become responsible, reflective, independent learners. In *Footprints 1* learning how to learn is integrated into the course materials in a number of ways. Through setting objectives at the start of lessons and lesson reviews at the end as suggested in the detailed teaching notes, children are helped to recognise the importance of learning goals and become increasingly self-aware of what and how they have learnt. At the end of each unit in the Activity Book, children assess their work by colouring a picture of Frodo to show whether their work is excellent, good or OK. In the *All About Me* Portfolio Booklet, children reflect on whether learning goals have been met by colouring 'can do' statements which relate to the learning points of each unit. There is also a *Learning-to-learn reflection sheet* included as part of the Tests and photocopiable resources pack which gets children to identify activities they enjoy and how they help them to learn as well as assessing their level of effort. Learning how to learn is also integrated into the materials through the wide range of meta-cognitive, cognitive and socio-affective strategies and skills that are developed as part of the activities and incorporated in the detailed teaching notes for each unit.

Straightforward and supportive methodology

The course methodology is designed to be straightforward and supportive and includes clear guidelines to follow at every stage. In *Footprints 1*, there is a combination of whole-class activities which engage all the learners and pair-work activities which are short and set up carefully within closely defined frameworks. The main aim is to provide a methodological approach that helps you to manage your classes effectively at the same time as enabling you to teach in a lively, communicative way.

Assessment

There are a range of formative and summative assessment instruments included in the Tests and photocopiable resources pack for *Footprints 1*. Formative assessment allows you to observe children and collect data and evidence in order to measure and monitor their progress and / or performance against specified objectives. Instruments for formative assessment in *Footprints 1* include *Child assessment sheets* for individual children. These detail 'can do' statements in relation to communicative competence and other attainment levels and can be completed using either a tick / cross system or a three-point colour-coded scale at the end of each unit. It also includes *Class assessment sheets* which detail a summary of 'can do' statements for each area of competence and each unit. These can also be completed at the end of each unit using a tick / cross system or three-point colour-coded scale and allows you to compare the progress of children in the class at a glance. There is also an *Observation of speaking activity* sheet which uses a three-point scale to assess children's performance in a speaking activity. This may be particularly useful if you are preparing children for an external speaking exam.

There is also a range of summative assessment instruments in *Footprints 1*. These include a *Diagnostic test* to administer before starting the course in order to assess the children's current level, nine *Unit tests*, three *Term tests* and one *End-of-year test*. All the tests include listening tasks and these are included together with detailed teacher's notes and answer keys in the Tests and photocopiable resources pack.

Support for external Young Learners of English exams and tests

In *Footprints*, it is recognised that many children are entered for external young learners exams and tests and need specific preparation for these in order to perform successfully. The syllabus of *Footprints 1–6* broadly reflects the language and skills requirements of Cambridge ESOL Young Learners English Tests (*Starters*, *Movers* and *Flyers*) and Trinity General Examinations in Spoken English (grades 1–6) and these are also matched to CEF attainment levels. By the end of *Footprints 1*, children will be approximately at the level of Trinity grade 1 and mid-way towards attaining the level of *Starters* (A1.1). The exams practice material included in the *Footprints 1* Tests and photocopiable resources pack prepares children for taking these exams by including a range of practice listening, reading and writing, and speaking activities which familiarise them with the kind of test formats used in the exams. The exams practice material is linked to the *Footprints 1* units and written to match the level the children have currently attained rather than the actual exam. Through familiarising children with the kinds of tasks they are expected to do, the exams practice material steadily builds up children's competence and confidence in doing external tests.

Variety of flexible components and photocopiable resources

A feature of *Footprints 1* is the variety of components and photocopiable resources (see Components of *Footprints 1* on page 14). These enable you to respond flexibly and appropriately to the diverse needs of individual children and classes. The Tests and photocopiable resources pack includes *Mixed ability worksheets*, *Reading and writing worksheets* and *Grammar practice worksheets* linked to each unit. These are intended to be used with either the whole class or individual children and done whenever appropriate either in lesson time or for homework. There are also letters which can optionally be sent home to parents at the start of each unit outlining the approach, learning objectives and suggested ways that parents can support their children's learning. In the Teacher's Book there is also optional photocopiable material to use with the festivals (Christmas, Easter, Father's Day and Mother's Day) (see pages 261–264) and a photocopiable Achievement Certificate to give children when they have completed *Footprints 1* (see page 265).

5 Classroom language

Since for most children the classroom is the only context in which they are exposed to English, it is important to establish this as the main means of communication during lessons from the outset. In *Footprints 1* it is suggested that you build up a core of simple language (e.g. for instructions, praise, classroom management) which children understand and respond to, as well as encourage children to use simple classroom language themselves as, for example, in greetings and goodbyes, asking for things and asking for help. Through continual exposure to English, natural opportunities for use and gentle insistence that children should try and use English as much as possible, you will find that communicating mainly in English during lessons will quickly become the norm.

The following is a list of suggested core teacher and child classroom language for *Footprints 1*.

Teacher language

Good morning / afternoon! / Hello! / How are you?

Stand … up / in a line / in a circle / together / facing this way.

Sit … down / on the floor / with your partner.

Today / In this lesson / unit we're going to … learn … / practise … / read about … / listen to … / review …, etc.

I'm going to … divide you into two groups / show you what to do / explain the game, etc.

I want / I'd like you to … listen / look carefully / talk to your partner / put up your hands, etc.

Open your books on page … / Close your books.

…, please. / Thank you.

Get out / Put away … your books / crayons / pens, etc.

Put your … book / pencils / crayons, etc. on your desk / in your bag.

Put up your hands!

Point to …! / Touch …! / Find …! Show me …! / Tell me …!

Here's … a paper / a pen, etc. for you.

Here are … some scissors / the crayons, etc. for you.

Go to … the board / the door / the back / front of the class.

Look at … the picture / the board / the flashcards / the word cards / me.

Listen to the … song / rhyme / chant / story / exchange / dialogue.

Repeat / Say … the words / the sentences / the chant / the dialogue.

Ask … the questions / your friend / Pip, etc.

Match / Number the … words / sentences / pictures.

Read … the words / the sentences / about …

Write … the words / the answers.

Complete … the sentences / the questions / the answers / the pictures.

Draw / Colour the picture.

Cut out … / Stick … / Fold … like this!

Let's … play a game / sing a song / say a rhyme / do the actions / do it again / tidy up, etc.

Work … in pairs / together / in groups / on your own.

Can you … remember the story? / guess what happens next? / come to the front? / collect the books? / give out the papers? / hold up the flashcard? / clean the board? / put waste paper in the bin?, etc.

Who'd like to … help? / have the next turn? / play the part of …? / act out the dialogue? / stick the flashcards on the board?

Do you like the … song / rhyme / chant / game / story / little book?

I think you need to … finish your picture / look at the spelling / complete the sentence / answer the question.

Quiet / Silence / Sssh everyone!

Calm down / Settle down!

Whisper! / Keep your voices down! / Not a word!

Have you finished? / Are you ready?

One / two minutes to go! Hurry now!

It's time to … finish / stop / clear up / end the lesson.

That's all for … now / today / this week.

What can you do after today's lesson?

Well done! / That's … great / excellent / brilliant / lovely / really good!

Goodbye! / See you soon / tomorrow / on …

Child language

Hello! / Good morning / afternoon!

Goodbye!

How are you? I'm fine.

…, please. / Thank you.

Here you are.

Can I … have the crayons? / go to the toilet? / have a drink? / open the window?

Can you … repeat? / help me? / show me?

What's this?

This is … a cat / my sister, etc.

Here's … my book / my picture / the flashcard.

Is this right?

I don't understand.

I think … / Perhaps … / I don't know.

Sorry I'm late.

I've finished. What now?

I can … say the rhyme / sing the song / write the words.

I like … the song / the game / the story.

It's … easy / difficult / fun.

6 Twenty ways to use the finger puppets

Guidelines for using the two finger puppets, Pip and Squeak, are given in the detailed teaching notes for each unit. The following are additional ideas to provide extra language practice and to help you manage your classes effectively.

1 Follow the finger puppets' instructions

Use the finger puppets to give the children instructions, e.g. **Stand up! / Sit down! / Jump to the board! / Hop to the door!** etc. and the children respond. You can also use the finger puppets to give instructions using flashcards stuck on different walls, e.g. **Go and stand by the plane, Vanessa and David / Touch the socks, Pamela and Cristina,** etc. Children listen and do what the finger puppets say.

2 Repeat what the finger puppets say

Divide the class into two groups (Pip and Squeak). Use the finger puppets to say vocabulary or sentences which the children are familiar with, varying the pitch, volume and pace. Children listen and repeat what their puppet says, imitating pronunciation as closely as possible.

3 Correct the puppet

Stick the flashcards of key vocabulary children are learning on the board. Establish that one of the puppets, e.g. Pip, is feeling a bit confused about the words and that you want the children to help and correct him. For example, use the puppet to point to the flashcard of the hamster and say **This is a guinea pig!** Shake your head and get the children to call out to the puppet in chorus *No, Pip! It's a hamster!*

4 Guess what the finger puppets are thinking about

Stick the unit flashcards on the board. Hold up one of the puppets, e.g. Squeak, and use mime to convey that she's thinking about one of the flashcards. Encourage children to guess which one by asking, *Is it the coat?* etc. Make Squeak fly around and shake her head or nod and say **No, it isn't** or **Yes, it is** as children guess. Repeat the procedure with Pip.

5 Pip or Squeak says …

Use the finger puppets to play a version of the traditional game 'Simon says'. Hold up the finger puppets. Establish that when Pip gives an instruction the children should respond; when Squeak gives an instruction the children should stand still and fold their arms. Explain that the children have three 'lives' in the game. Use the finger puppets to give instructions using any familiar language, e.g. **Pip says touch your nose! / Squeak says point to the door!** Increase the speed as children become familiar with the game. Stop the game before any children have lost all three 'lives'. The children who still have three lives at the end of the game are the winners.

6 Creating dialogues

Use the finger puppets to create and build up simple dialogues using any familiar language, e.g. Pip: **Hello, Squeak. How are you?** Squeak: **Hello, Pip. I'm hungry.** Pip: **Do you like bananas?** Squeak: **Yes, I do.** Pip: **Here's a banana for you!** Squeak: **Oh, thank you. Mmm! It's delicious!** Divide the class into two groups (Pip and Squeak) and children repeat the dialogue with the puppets. Children then pretend to be Pip and Squeak and practise the dialogue in pairs (if you like, children can use the paper finger puppets of Pip and Squeak they make in Unit 1, Lesson 3 (see Activity Book page 79) to do this).

7 Yes! / No!

Hold up the finger puppets. Establish that, e.g, Squeak always says 'yes' and Pip always says 'no'. Divide the class into two groups (Pip and Squeak), ask questions and children respond in role, e.g. T: **Are you happy, Squeak?** PP: *Yes, I am.* / T: **Do you like pizza, Pip?** PP: *No, I don't.* / T: **Is this your pencil, Squeak?** PP: *Yes, it is.*, etc. Note that it will usually be appropriate to ask questions using one language structure only rather than mixing these.

8 Pass the finger puppets

Children stand or sit in a circle. Give the finger puppets to two children on opposite sides of the circle. Play music and children pass the finger puppets the same way round the circle. Whenever you pause the music, the children who have the puppets hold them up and use them either to ask each other a question, e.g. *Do you like apples? / No, I don't* or to say a sentence, e.g. *I've got blue shoes* depending on the language the class is practising.

9 Guess what's in Pip and Squeak's bag

Have available a non-transparent bag (e.g. a cotton bread bag) that 'belongs' to Pip and Squeak. Put several different classroom objects, toys or flashcards in the bag without the children seeing. Use the finger puppets to hold up the bag. Invite individual children to take turns to put their hand in the bag, feel an object or hold one of the flashcards and guess what it is, e.g. *(I think) it's a rubber.* The child then takes the object or flashcard out of the bag to check whether or not they're right. Use the finger puppets to ask the rest of the class, e.g. **Is he / she right?** and to praise the children when they guess correctly.

10 Picture card games with the finger puppets

Use the finger puppets to play simple whole-class games with the picture cards children make in Units 2, 4, 6 and 8 as a way of revising and recycling familiar language. For example, use one of the finger puppets to choose a picture card from the set you are using, without the children seeing, e.g. computer game. Get individual children to ask questions in turn, e.g. *Do you like cars, Squeak?* and the finger puppet responds **Yes, I do** or **No, I don't** depending what's on the card. The child who guesses correctly 'wins' the card. Either this child has the next turn choosing a card or the game continues with the finger puppets taking turns to do this. Children can then also play in pairs.

11 Pips and Squeaks!

Establish that Pip and Squeak make little high-pitched pixie- or fairy-like noises: **Pip, pip, pip** and **Squeak, squeak, squeak.** Use the finger puppets to take turns to say sentences using familiar language and substituting their little noises for key words, e.g. **My cat's got long pip-pip-pip.** Children listen and say the missing word(s), e.g. *Whiskers!*

12 Finger puppet riddles

Use the finger puppets to say little riddles which relate to vocabulary children are learning, e.g. **It's a rectangle. It's brown. It isn't good for you** (*chocolate*). **You walk in them. They aren't cotton or wool** (*shoes*). Children listen to the riddles and say the answers. If you like, this can be turned into a game, with the class scoring points if they guess the riddles, and Pip and Squeak scoring points if they don't.

13 Musical conductors

Put the finger puppets on your index fingers and use them as musical conductors when children sing a song they know, using either the CD track with the lyrics or the karaoke version. Establish that children should sing louder as you raise the puppets in the air to conduct them and softer as you lower them. Once children are familiar with the procedure, you can ask individual children to wear the finger puppets and conduct the singing instead of you.

14 Team games with the finger puppets

Use the finger puppets to organise and lead simple team games with the class divided into 'Pip's team' and 'Squeak's team'. For example, in a team game of board pelmanism, stick a set of flashcards and word cards in jumbled order on the board. Use the finger puppet for each team to point to the flashcards and word cards and ask, e.g. **Do you want this one? / What's this?** as well as to take the flashcards and word cards off the board when children match them and praise the children as they score points for their team.

15 Story with the finger puppets

Use the finger puppets and flashcards to invent a very simple story. Give out the flashcards you are going to use in the story to individual children or pairs. An example of a story using the finger puppets and flashcards of classroom objects in Unit 2 is as follows: **One day Pip and Squeak are late for school** (use mime to convey meaning). **They put their file, notebook, pen, crayons** (naming all the classroom objects on the flashcards) **in their school bag and fly to school as fast as they can. But – oh dear – the school bag has got a hole** (use gesture to show meaning) **and out falls** (use gesture to convey meaning) **the file, the pen, the crayons,** etc. (naming all the objects again). **When they get to school, Pip and Squeak see their school bag is empty** (use gesture and facial expression). **They fly back** (use the finger puppets to show this) **to look for their pen, file, crayons** (name all the objects again). **Phew! – luckily they find them all. Pip and Squeak are late for school but they're happy, too.** Children listen and hold up the flashcards when they hear the corresponding words in the story. Repeat, and children join in naming all the objects and telling the story.

16 Hide the finger puppets

Choose two children to close their eyes or to go out of the classroom for a moment. Hide one of the finger puppets somewhere where it's visible without having to move things. Get the children to open their eyes or call them back into the classroom. Ask, e.g. **Where's Pip?** As the two children look for the finger puppet, get the rest of the class to help by saying *No, no, no! Pip's not here!* softly if they are far away and *Yes, yes, yes! Pip's here!* more loudly as they get close to finding the puppet. Once children have done Unit 6, they can also ask and answer questions as part of the game, e.g. *Is Pip in / on / under …? No, he isn't. / Yes, he is.*

17 True or false?

Use the finger puppets to say true and false sentences about the content in Lessons 5 and 6, e.g. **Germs are big! / Germs are everywhere!** Children respond by saying *Yes!* and waving their arms in the air if the sentences are true, and *No!* and folding their arms if they are false.

18 Using the finger puppets during activities

If you like, you can teach whole lessons wearing the finger puppets, one on each index finger, as this allows you to use them frequently and easily. Alternatively, when you're not using the finger puppets directly, you can put them somewhere where they can be seen by all the children, e.g. on the end of two pencils in a jar on your desk. As part of your classroom management, it can be effective to refer to the finger puppets during activities, e.g. **Let's sing the song again for Pip and Squeak! / Let's show Pip and Squeak we know the names of all the toys! / Let's count again so Pip and Squeak can check we're right!** If you're wearing the finger puppets you can also make them fly about and whisper things to you which you then tell the children, e.g. **Squeak thinks that's very good! / Pip says he'd love you to act out the story again!** This helps to maximise children's attention and engagement.

19 Demonstrating and modelling what to do

Use the finger puppets to demonstrate games and pair work activities, e.g. **Look! Pip is going to choose one of the picture cards and Squeak is going to guess which one it is.** You can also use the finger puppets to demonstrate instructions, e.g. **I want you to draw a picture like Squeak's** (as you draw on the board with the puppet on your finger), and to model out loud thinking processes in order to carry out activities, e.g. **Pip can see that the car has got wheels so he writes a tick here. The ball hasn't got wheels so no tick here.**

20 That's great!

Use the finger puppets from time to time to look at and praise the children's work. Get them to comment and interact with the children about their work, e.g. **Well done! / Very good! / What a lovely …! / I like the … / That's beautiful / fantastic / great!**, etc. You can also use the puppets to gently encourage the children to check and correct their work, e.g. **Pip says have a look again at this word here. / Squeak says find the word in your book and copy it here.**

Introduction

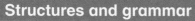

Structures and grammar

- *What's your name? I'm …*
- *Who's this? It's …*
- Recycled: *How are you? I'm fine.*

Vocabulary

- Core: *window, chair, floor, door, book, board, clock, desk*
- Other: *friends, rainbow, tell, come, look,*
- Recycled: *Hello / Hi / Goodbye, please,* colours, numbers 1–5

Main receptive language

- *follow, footprints, find, treasure, clue*

Communicative competence

Understanding

Listening:
- Can understand greetings
- Can understand when someone asks your name
- Can identify key items in the classroom
- Can recognise numbers 1–5
- Can recognise colours

Reading:
- Can recognise words for items in the classroom
- Can recognise colours
- Can recognise two questions to find out names

Speaking

Spoken interaction:
- Can exchange greetings
- Can ask and say your name
- Can ask about and identify others

Spoken production:
- Can name key items in the classroom
- Can sing the *Hello song*
- Can sing the song *What's your name?*
- Can name colours
- Can say numbers 1–5
- Can sing the *Goodbye song*

Writing

- Can copy and write words for items in the classroom
- Can copy and write colour words

Learning strategies and thinking skills

- Following a model
- Imitating and repeating
- Associating pictures and characters
- Associating music with greetings
- Associating rhythm and actions with vocabulary
- Taking turns
- Activating previous knowledge

Children's culture

- Identifying fairytale characters

Values and attitudes

- Interest in learning English
- Pleasure in exchanging greetings and asking and saying your name in English
- Enjoyment in meeting the course characters
- Awareness that fairytale characters exist in English

Introduction

Lesson 1

Aims:
- To meet the course characters
- To identify key items in the classroom

Key language:
- *What's your name? I'm ...*
- *window, chair, floor, door, book, board, clock, desk*
- *friends*

Materials:
- Pupil's Book page 4
- Activity Book page 2
- Finger puppets (Pip and Squeak)
- Flashcards: Alex, Katie, Frodo
- Word cards: Alex, Katie, Frodo, Pip, Squeak
- CD 1

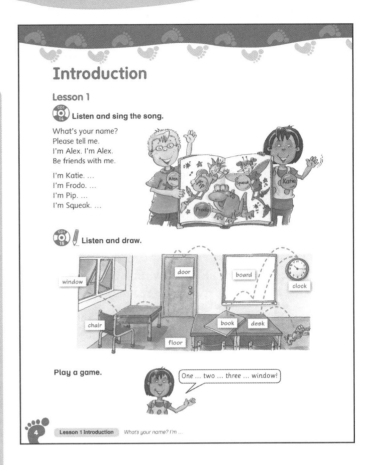

Starting out

Greetings and opening routine

- Greet the children. Hold up the finger puppets on the index fingers of your hands and say **Look. This is Pip. And this is Squeak.** Use the puppets to say **Hello, children** and encourage the children to respond *Hello ...* in chorus to each puppet in turn.

- Say **Let's sing the *Hello* song.** Play the CD (CD 1, track 2). Hold up the puppets on your index fingers. Move them and encourage the children to join in doing the actions as they listen.

- Play the song again and the children sing and do the actions.

 Hello song

Hello.	(wave)
Hello.	(wave)
How are you today?	(put arms out)
I'm fine, thank you.	(move from side to side)
And I'm OK!	(raise arms in the air)

Setting objectives

- Say **Today we're going to meet the characters who are going to help you learn English this year. We're also going to learn words for things in our classroom.** Use mime, gesture and / or L1 to clarify what you mean.

On the learning trail

Listen and sing the song. (PB page 4) (books closed)

- Pretend you have forgotten the puppets' names. Hold up one of them and ask **What's your name?** Use the puppet to reply **I'm ... (Pip / Squeak).**

- Repeat with the other puppet.

- Use the puppets in turn to ask yourself your name and say **I'm ....** Then use the puppets to ask individual children their names in the same way.

- Hold up the flashcards of Alex, Katie and Frodo in turn. Ask **What's your name?** to each character and encourage the children to say this with you. Answer as if you're the character and say **I'm ...** for each one. Stick the flashcards on the board.

- Ask the children to open their Pupil's Books at page 4. Point to the pictures of the characters.

Say **Look. Pip ... Squeak ... Alex ... Katie and Frodo the frog!**

- Say **Listen to the song. Point to the pictures** and demonstrate what you mean.
- Play the CD (CD 1, track 14). The children listen and point to the appropriate character for each verse.
- Use mime, gesture and / or L1 to convey the meaning of **Please tell me** and **Be friends with me** and check the children understand.
- Play the CD again and the children point to the pictures and sing.
- Divide the class in half. Explain and demonstrate that one half should sing the first two lines of each verse and the other half the second two lines.
- Play the CD again. Hold up the finger puppet or flashcard for each verse as the children sing.
- The children then change roles and repeat.

 What's your name?

What's your name?
Please tell me.
I'm Alex. I'm Alex.
Be friends with me.

Verse 2: ... Katie
Verse 3: ... Frodo
Verse 4: ... Pip
Verse 5: ... Squeak

- *Either* ask the children to choose one of the characters' names and pretend to be that character *or* if you and the children don't know each other's names, use real names instead.
- Hold up one of the finger puppets or flashcards and get the rest of the class to ask in chorus *What's your name?* and individual children to respond *I'm ...*, saying their real name or naming the character they have chosen.
- The children ask and say their own names or the names they have chosen in the same way to other children sitting near them.

Listen and draw. (PB page 4)

- Hold up your book. Say **Look. Frodo is a frog. Frodo is jumping to the window ... chair ... floor ... door ... book ... board ... clock ... desk!** Listen and follow Frodo with your finger and demonstrate what you mean.
- Play the CD (CD 1, track 16). The children listen and follow Frodo's jumping lines to each place in the classroom with their fingers.
- Play the CD again. The children draw over the jumping lines to each object and repeat the words.

 Listen and draw.

window ... chair ... floor ... door ... book ... board ... clock ... desk

Play a game. (PB page 4)

- Hold up one of the finger puppets. Make a big circle with your arm as you say **One ... two ... three ...**, and then suddenly point to and name one of the items in the classroom, e.g. **... window!**
- Repeat this several times, getting the children to join in making circles with their arms and pointing to the things you name as fast as they can. As they become familiar with the game, get them to join in saying the numbers and words.

Match, draw and write. (AB page 2) (books closed)

- Stick the flashcards of Alex, Katie and Frodo on the board. Point to each one in turn and ask **What's your name?** The children reply as if they are each character, e.g. *I'm Katie.* Hold up the finger puppets in turn and repeat the procedure.
- Stick the five character word cards on the board in jumbled order (at the children's height and away from the flashcards).
- Point to one word card, e.g. Alex, and read it. Say **Look for the picture of Alex.**
- Ask a child to come to the front of the class and stick the word card for Alex by its flashcard. Ask the rest of the class **Is this right?** and get them to say the name.
- Repeat for Katie and Frodo. For the finger puppets, say e.g. **Look for Pip** and the children find the right word card and hand it to the puppet (which is on your index finger). Ask the children to open their Activity Books at page 2. Read the sentences while the children follow in their books.
- The children work individually and match the sentences and pictures.
- Check the answers.

- Ask the children to draw a picture of themselves and complete the sentence with their name.

  Key: 1 I'm Frodo. 2 I'm Pip. 3 I'm Alex.
  4 I'm Katie. 5 I'm Squeak.

Look, write and say. (AB page 2)

- Read the words at the start of the activity. The children point to the pictures as you read.
- Say **Now write the words.** Draw the children's attention to the example.
- The children work individually and write the words.
- Check the answers by asking the children to point to the pictures and say the words in turn.

  Key: Children match the sentences and pictures.
  1 window 2 door 3 clock 4 chair 5 book 6 desk

Ending the lesson

Lesson review

- Briefly ask the children what they can do as a result of the lesson (sing the song *What's your name?*, name the course characters, name things in the classroom). Praise the children for their efforts and / or use the finger puppets to do this.

Goodbye and closing routine

- Say **Let's sing the *Goodbye song*.** Play the CD (CD 1, track 4). Hold up the finger puppets on your index fingers as the children sing and do the actions.

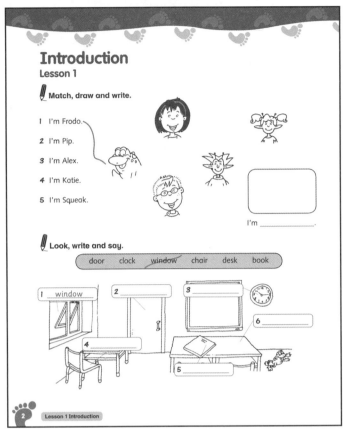

Goodbye song

Goodbye, goodbye (wave)
See you another day! (make marching
movements with arms)
Goodbye, goodbye (wave)
See you soon! Hurray!
(wave both hands in the air)

- Say goodbye to the children yourself and using the finger puppets. Say e.g. **Goodbye everyone. See you on ....** Ask a few individual children to say goodbye to the finger puppets in turn.

Introduction

Lesson 2

Aims:

- To identify fairytale characters in the story
- To review colours
- To review numbers 1–5

Key language:

- *What's your name? I'm ...*
- *Who's this? It's ...*
- *window, chair, floor, door, book, board, clock, desk*
- *red, orange, yellow, blue, green, purple*
- numbers 1–5

Materials:

- Pupil's Book page 5
- Activity Book page 3
- *All About Me* Portfolio Booklet pages 2–5
- Finger puppets (Pip and Squeak)
- Treasure clue sticker for the Introduction
- CD 1

Starting out

Greetings and opening routine

- Greet the children yourself and using the finger puppets, as in Lesson 1.
- Use the finger puppets to ask a few children **What's your name?** and encourage the children to ask the puppets the same question.
- Play the *Hello song* (CD 1, track 2). The children sing and do the actions as in Lesson 1.

Revision activity

- Hold up the Pip finger puppet and play *Pip says ...* Explain and demonstrate that when you say e.g. **Pip says *Point to the clock!***, the children should point to the clock as fast as they can. When you say e.g. **Point to the clock!**, without preceding it by **Pip says**, they should fold their arms and do nothing. Explain that the children have three 'lives' each. They lose a life if they respond incorrectly to an instruction.
- Play the game several times (naming the door, window, board, book, floor, clock, desk, chair in random order). Stop before any child has lost all three lives. The children with most lives left at the end of the game are the winners.

Setting objectives

- Say **Today we're going to identify fairytale characters and get ready for the *Footprints* story.** Use L1 to clarify what you mean.

On the learning trail

Listen and point. (PB page 5)

- Say **Look at Alex and Katie. They're looking at a book of fairy tales.** Explain or ask the children to guess the meaning of *fairy tales* from the picture.
- Ask **Can you find Pip / Squeak / Frodo in the book of fairy tales?** The children find these characters and point to and name them in turn.
- Say **Let's count the other characters!** Hold up your book, point to the pictures in turn and the children count to five with you in chorus.

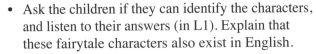

- Ask the children if they can identify the characters, and listen to their answers (in L1). Explain that these fairytale characters also exist in English.

- Point to the pictures again. Get the children to say the numbers and you say the names (*1* **Little Red Riding Hood** *2* **Pinocchio** *3* **Jack** *4* **Aladdin** *5* **Goldilocks**).

- Say **Listen to Alex and Katie asking about the fairytale characters. Point to the pictures.** Play the CD (CD 1 track 17). The children listen and point to the characters in turn. Use the pause button and check they are doing this correctly.

- Repeat what the voice says at the end of the CD (**Follow the footprints! Find the treasure at the end of the rainbow!**).

- Use the picture to clarify meaning. Explain that this is the start of the adventure story which runs through every unit of the book.

- Play the CD again (until the end of the questions and answers only). Use the pause button, and the children point to the pictures and repeat the names of the characters.

- Say e.g. **Little Red Riding Hood is number …** and the children say the number *(… one)*. Repeat for the other characters.

- Then ask e.g. **Number one. Who's this?** and the children name the character. Say e.g. **Yes. Very good. It's Little Red Riding Hood.** Repeat for the other numbers.

- Say **Now listen and repeat what Alex and Katie say.** Play the CD (until the end of the questions and answers only) again. Use the pause button to give the children time to repeat the questions and answers.

- Say the numbers and ask individual children to take turns to ask and answer *Who's this? It's …* for each character. Be ready to help with the names as they do this.

 Listen and point.

Alex: *Wow! A book of fairy tales!*
Katie: *Fantastic! Number one. Who's this?*
Alex: *It's Little Red Riding Hood.*
Katie: *Number two. Who's this?*
Alex: *It's Pinocchio!*
Katie: *Number three. Who's this?*
Alex: *It's Jack.*
Katie: *Number four. Who's this?*
Alex: *It's Aladdin.*
Katie: *Number five. Who's this?*
Alex: *It's Goldilocks!*
Katie: *Listen!*
Voice: *Follow the footprints. Find the treasure at the end of the rainbow!*
Katie and Alex: *Oh, wow!*

Listen and sing the song. (PB page 5)

- Briefly revise colours by pointing to different things in the classroom and asking the children to name the colours.

- Say **Look at the rainbow** and ask the children to identify the colours.

- Say **Listen to the song and point to the colours in the rainbow**. Play the CD (CD 1, track 18).

- Play the CD again. The children point to the colours and sing the song.

 Rainbow song

Red, orange, yellow
Green, purple, blue
Look for the rainbow
Please come too!

Put on the treasure clue sticker.

- Read the treasure clue again. Ask the children to point in turn to the footprints, rainbow and treasure in the picture. Explain in L1 that this is the start of the adventure story in which the characters follow the footprints and 'treasure clues' to find the treasure at the end of the rainbow.

- Say **Find the treasure clue sticker for the Introduction and stick it here.** Point to the treasure clue frame in your book and demonstrate what you mean.

- The children look for the treasure clue sticker for the Introduction and stick it in their books.

Listen and number. (AB page 3)

- Hold up your book and point to the pictures of the fairytale characters in turn. Ask **Who's this?** and the children identify the characters in English or L1. If they answer in L1, recast the names in English, e.g. **Yes, very good. It's Goldilocks.**

- Say **Listen and number the pictures.** Play the CD (CD 1, track 20). Use the pause button to give the children time to write the numbers.

- Check the answers by saying the numbers and getting the children to name the characters.

  Key: 1 Jack 2 Little Red Riding Hood 3 Aladdin 4 Pinocchio 5 Goldilocks

 Listen and number.

1 Who's this?
   It's Jack.
2 Who's this?
   It's Little Red Riding Hood.
3 Who's this?
   It's Aladdin.
4 Who's this?
   It's Pinocchio.
5 Who's this?
   It's Goldilocks.

Write and colour. (AB page 3)

- Read the words at the top of the activity while the children follow in their books.
- Say **Write the words and colour the rainbow.** Draw the children's attention to the example and to the initial letters, which act as prompts.
- Check the answers by getting the children to name the colours on the rainbow in order.

  Key: red; orange; yellow; green; purple; blue

Ending the lesson

Lesson review

- Briefly ask the children what they can do as a result of the lesson (identify fairytale characters, recognise numbers, name colours and sing the *Rainbow song*). Praise the children for their efforts and / or use the finger puppets to do this.

Goodbye and closing routine

- Say **Let's sing the *Goodbye song*.** Play the karaoke version of the song (CD 1, track 5 – see Lesson 1). Hold up the finger puppets and the children sing and do the actions as in Lesson 1.

All About Me Portfolio Booklet

The children complete *My portrait, My passport* and the Introduction unit of their personal *All About Me* Portfolio Booklets. The children complete the *My portrait, My passport* pages with their personal information. In the Introduction unit, children complete their learning journey by colouring the sections on the path to show what they can do. If you like, the children can also sign this page and you can endorse this by adding your own signature and date.

1 My birthday

Structures and grammar

- *How old are you? / I'm ...*
- *Are you ...?*
  Yes, I am. / No, I'm not.
- *Here's a ... (for you)!*
- *The ... is a ...*
- *This is a ...*
- Recycled: *What's your name? I'm ...*

Vocabulary

- Core: *cake, candle, present, balloon, hat, card, biscuit, sandwich, plate, cup*
- Other: *birthday, mat, party, late, boy, girl*
- Content / culture: *circle, rectangle, triangle, square, happy, dear*
- Recycled: *Thank you, door, window, board, book, clock, desk, chair;* numbers 1–10, colours

Main receptive language

- *shape, object, different*
- *recognise*
- *How many ...?*

Communicative competence

Understanding

Listening:

- Can recognise words related to birthdays and birthday parties
- Can understand when someone asks your age
- Can understand the episode of the story
- Can recognise numbers to ten
- Can follow instructions in a game

Reading:

- Can recognise words related to birthdays and birthday parties
- Can recognise words for numbers to ten
- Can read questions and answers related to age
- Can read sentences about the shape of objects

Speaking

Spoken interaction:

- Can ask and say your age
- Can ask and respond to questions to check age
- Can offer things and say *Thank you*

Spoken production:

- Can sing the *Hello song*
- Can name objects related to birthdays and birthday parties
- Can count to ten
- Can say your age
- Can say the shapes of objects
- Can sing the song *A card, a balloon*
- Can say the rap *One, two, three*
- Can sing *Happy birthday*
- Can sing the *Goodbye song*

Writing

- Can copy and write words related to birthdays and birthday parties
- Can copy and write words for numbers to 10
- Can copy and write words for shapes
- Can complete short sentences

Content links

- *Maths:* recognition of shapes

Learning strategies and thinking skills

- Recognising learning objectives
- Following simple instructions
- Using mime and gesture
- Associating rhythm with a language pattern
- Making logical deductions
- Observing shapes in pictures and in the classroom
- Classifying objects according to their shape
- Reflecting on learning

Children's culture

- Singing *Happy birthday*
- Playing a version of a traditional birthday party game: *Pass the present!*

Pronunciation

- Difference between /æ/ and /eɪ/

Values and attitudes

- Pleasure in celebrating a birthday in English
- Interest in recognising and identifying shapes
- Awareness that it's polite to say *Thank you*

1 My birthday

Lesson 1
Vocabulary presentation

Aim:
- To name things related to a birthday

Key language:
- *card, present, hat, balloon, cake, candle, biscuit, sandwich, cup, plate*
- *birthday, mat, party, late*

Materials:
- Pupil's Book page 6
- Activity Book page 4
- Finger puppets (Pip and Squeak)
- Flashcards: Alex, Katie, Frodo, card, present, hat, balloon, cake, candle, biscuit, sandwich, cup, plate
- Word cards: card, present, hat, balloon, cake, candle, biscuit, sandwich, cup, plate
- CD 1

Starting out

Greetings and opening routine

- Greet the children yourself and using the finger puppets. Say e.g. **Hello, children. Hello … How are you today?** *I'm fine, thank you.* Ask a few individual children to greet the puppets in turn.
- Say **Let's sing the *Hello song*.** Play the CD (CD 1, track 2). Hold up the puppets on your index fingers. Move them as the children sing and you do the actions.

 Hello song

Hello.	(wave)
Hello.	(wave)
How are you today?	(put arms out)
I'm fine, thank you.	(move from side to side)
And I'm OK!	(raise arms in the air)

Revision activity

- Hold up the finger puppets and pretend they have forgotten the children's names. Use them to ask a few children **What's your name? I'm …**
- Get the children to ask the finger puppets their names and respond **I'm Pip / Squeak** for each one.
- Hold up the flashcards of the other characters in turn and ask **Who's this?** *It's … Alex … Katie … Frodo.* Stick the flashcards on the board.
- Point to the flashcards or hold up the finger puppets in random order, ask **Who's this?** and the children say the names. Increase the speed as the children respond with increasing confidence.

Setting objectives

- Say **Today we're going to learn words related to a birthday and we're going to sing a song.** Elicit or explain the meaning of *birthday*.

On the learning trail

Vocabulary presentation (books closed)

- Show the children one of the flashcards, e.g. cake, very quickly. The children identify what it is in L1. Say e.g. **Yes. Very good. It's a cake.**
- Point to the flashcard. Say **cake** several times and get the children to repeat the word with you in chorus.
- Stick the flashcard of the cake on the board.
- Repeat the procedure for all the other object flashcards.
- Divide the class in half. Hold up the Pip finger puppet and say to one half **Say the words with Pip.** Use the puppet to point to the flashcards in turn and the children say the words with you. Make the puppet fly around to praise the children.
- Repeat the procedure with the Squeak puppet and the other half of the class.

Follow the footprints. (PB page 6) (books open)

- Hold up the flashcard of Frodo. Say **Listen and follow the footprints with Frodo the frog. Use your finger** and demonstrate this.
- Play the CD (CD 1, track 21). The children listen and follow the footprints with their fingers. They

stop by each picture as they hear the word and repeat the word.

- Say **Now listen and draw a line following the footprints** and demonstrate this. Play the CD again. The children draw a line, stop by each picture and repeat the words as previously.

 Follow the footprints.

card ... present ... hat ... balloon ... cake ... candle ... biscuit ... sandwich ... cup ... plate

- Stick the word cards on the board in jumbled order (at the children's height and away from the flashcards).

- Point to one word card e.g. *present* and read the word. Say **Look for the picture of the present.** Give the children time to do this.

- Ask a child to come to the front of the class and stick the word card for *present* by the corresponding flashcard. Ask the rest of the class **Is this right?** and get them to say the word.

- Repeat the procedure with the rest of the word cards.

- Take the flashcards and word cards off the board.

Listen and sing the song. (PB page 6)

- Say **Look at the picture.** Point to Pip and Squeak in turn and ask **Who's this?** The children identify the characters.

- Ask **What else can you see in the picture?** and the children identify the objects.

- Say **Listen to the song. Point to the pictures.** Play the CD (CD 1 track 22). The children listen to the song and point to the objects in the picture in turn as they hear them.

- Explain the meaning of *mat* by pointing to the mat in the picture. Use mime and gesture to convey the meaning of *Come to the party. Don't be late!*

- Ask five (or ten) children to come to the front of the class. Give them one (or two) flashcard(s) each.

- Play the CD again. The children at the front hold up their flashcard(s) as they hear them in the song and the rest of the class sings.

- Ask the children to guess whose birthday it is, e.g. Pip, Squeak, Alex or Katie. Tell them they will find out in the next lesson.

 A card, a balloon

A card, a balloon
A present and a hat
A cake with candles
On the mat!

A biscuit, a sandwich
A cup and a plate
Come to the party
Don't be late!

Draw, colour and say. (PB page 6)

- Ask the children if they can identify the objects in each half picture and listen to their responses. Say e.g. **Number one?** *It's a hat.*

- Ask the children to complete the pictures. Explain

and demonstrate that they should copy each half as closely as they can. Draw their attention to the example. If appropriate, use L1 to explain that the pictures are based on the idea of symmetry, i.e. the lines on both sides of the dotted line should mirror each other.

- If there is time, ask the children to colour in the pictures.

- Check the answers by asking e.g. **What's number one?** *It's a hat.*

   Key: 1 hat 2 present 3 cup 4 plate 5 balloon 6 cake

Read, match and say. (AB page 4)

- Read the words and the children point to the objects.

- The children work individually and match the words and pictures.

- Check the answers by asking e.g. **What's number one?** and individual children say *It's a ...* for each picture.

   Key: Children match the sentences and pictures.
   1 a card 2 a present 3 a cake 4 a candle
   5 a biscuit 6 a sandwich

Find, colour and write. (AB page 4)

- Read the words at the top of the activity while the children follow in their books.

- Ask the children to find the objects in the puzzle picture, colour them and write the words. Draw their attention to the example.

- The children work individually to find and colour the objects, and write the words.

- Check the answers by asking e.g. **What's number one?** and the children say the word *It's a ...* .

   Key: 1 present 2 cake 3 plate 4 hat 5 balloon 6 cup

Ending the lesson

Lesson review

- Briefly ask the children what they can do as a result of the lesson (name things related to a birthday, sing the song *A card, a balloon*). Praise the children for their efforts and / or use the finger puppets to do this.

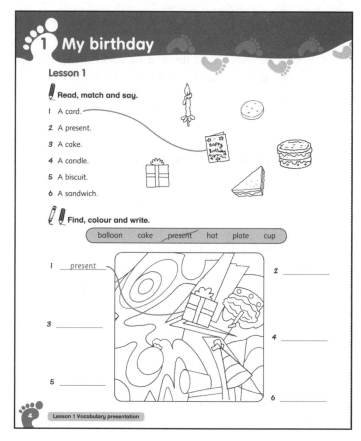

Goodbye and closing routine

- Say **Let's sing the *Goodbye song*.** Play the CD (CD 1, track 4). Hold up the finger puppets on your index fingers as the children sing and do the actions.

 Goodbye song

Goodbye, goodbye (wave)
See you another day! (make marching movements with arms)
Goodbye, goodbye (wave)
See you soon! Hurray!
(wave both hands in the air)

- Say goodbye to the children yourself and using the finger puppets. Say e.g. **Goodbye everyone. See you on ...** Ask a few individual children to say goodbye to the finger puppets in turn.

1 My birthday

Lesson 2
Language input and story

Aim:
- To understand and act out episode 1 of the story

Key language:
- *How old are you? I'm ...*
- *Are you ...? Yes, I am. / No, I'm not.*
- *Here's a ... for you! Thank you!*
- *card, present, balloon, hat, cake, candle, biscuit, sandwich, cup, plate*

Materials:
- Pupil's Book page 7
- Activity Book page 5
- Finger puppets (Pip and Squeak)
- Flashcards: Alex, Katie, Frodo, card, present, balloon, hat, cake, candle, biscuit, sandwich, cup, plate
- Treasure clue sticker for Unit 1
- CD 1

Starting out

Greetings and opening routine

- Greet the children yourself and using the finger puppets.
- Play the karaoke version of the *Hello song* (CD 1, track 3 – see Lesson 1). The children sing and do the actions as in Lesson 1.

Revision activity

- Hold a piece of paper over the flashcard of the birthday card and gradually reveal the picture. The children say the word as soon as they recognise the picture. Stick the flashcard on the board.
- Repeat with the rest of the birthday flashcards in the order of the song *A card, a balloon* (see Lesson 1).
- Say **Let's sing the song** *A card, a balloon.* Play the CD (CD 1, track 22 – see Lesson 1). The children sing the song and point to the flashcards.
- Repeat with the karaoke version (CD 1, track 23).

Setting objectives

- Say **Today, we're going to listen to and act out episode 1 of the story. It's called** *The birthday cake.* Use L1 to clarify what you mean, if necessary.

On the learning trail

Listen and act out the story.
Episode 1: The birthday cake (PB page 7)

Before the story (books closed)

- Stick the flashcards of Alex, Katie and Frodo on the board. Point to them as you recap on the Introduction. Say e.g. **Alex and Katie look at a book of fairy tales with pictures of … Little Red Riding Hood, Pinocchio, Jack and the beanstalk, Aladdin and Goldilocks. Frodo invites them to follow the footprints and find the treasure at the end of the rainbow.**
- Hold up page 5 of the Pupil's Book, point to the treasure clue sticker and read *Follow the footprints! Find the treasure at the end of the rainbow!* as a reminder.
- Ask the following questions in turn. Use mime and gesture to clarify meaning and encourage

35

the children to predict the answers: **1) Whose birthday is it? 2) Who brings the cake? 3) What's in the cake?**

During the story (books open)

- Say **Now listen to the story and find out.** Explain to the children that they will hear a 'beep' noise on the CD to tell them when to move to the next picture in the story.

- Play the CD (CD 1, track 24) and the children follow in their books.

- Ask the three questions in turn again and check the answers, recasting L1 answers in English, if necessary. *(1 Squeak's 2 Frodo 3 a treasure clue)*

- Say **Listen again and repeat the story.** Play the CD again. Pause after each sentence and the children repeat it.

- **Note:** There is more story text on the CD than appears on the Pupil's Book page. This additional text is marked with an asterisk* in the audio script below. The children repeat the whole story, including the language which does not appear in their books.

 Follow the footprints, Episode 1: The birthday cake

Picture 1	
Alex:	*Look! We're in Fairyland!*
Katie:	*Let's follow the footprints!*

Picture 2	
Alex:	*Hello. What's your name?*
Pip:	*I'm Pip.*
Squeak:	*And I'm Squeak. It's my birthday! What's your name?**
Alex:	*I'm Alex.**
Katie:	*And I'm Katie.**
Pip and Squeak:	*Hello, Alex and Katie. Welcome to Fairyland!**

Picture 3	
Katie:	*Who's this?**
Pip:	*It's Frodo the frog.**
Frodo:	*Happy birthday, Squeak! Here's a card for you!*
Squeak:	*Thank you!*
Frodo:	*And here's a present for you!**
Squeak:	*Oh, thank you!**

Frodo:	*And here's a cake for you!**
Squeak:	*Oh, thank you!**

Picture 4	
Alex:	*How old are you?*
Squeak:	*I'm seven.*
Katie:	*Are you seven, too?*
Pip:	*No, I'm not.*
Alex:	*Are you six?**
Pip:	*Yes, I am.**

Picture 5	
Frodo:	*Let's eat the cake!*
Pip:	*Yes! Agh!*
Alex, Katie and Squeak:	*Oh, no!*
Squeak:	*Oh, my cake!**

Picture 6	
Pip:	*Look! Follow the footprints! Find Little Red Riding Hood!*
Frodo:	*It's a treasure clue! Good luck! See you at the end of the rainbow!*
Squeak:	*Come on! Let's go!**
All:	*Thank you, Frodo. Goodbye!**

After the story

- Ask questions about each picture as follows (recast L1 answers): **1) Where are Alex and Katie?** *(in Fairyland)* **What do they follow?** *(pointing to the picture) (the footprints)* **2) Who do Alex and Katie meet?** *(Pip and Squeak)* **Whose birthday is it?** *(Squeak's)* **3) What does Frodo bring?** *(pointing to each object in turn) (a card, a present, a cake)* **4) How old is Squeak?** *(seven)* **How old is Pip?** *(six)* **5) Who falls in the cake?** *(use gesture to convey meaning) (Pip)* **6) What's in the cake?** *(point to the treasure clue) (a treasure clue)*

Put on the treasure clue sticker.

- Say **The treasure clue says *Follow the footprints! Find Little Red Riding Hood!*** Elicit or explain the meaning and remind the children of the character of Little Red Riding Hood from the Introduction, if necessary.

- Say **Find the treasure clue sticker for Unit 1 and stick it here.** Demonstrate what you mean.

- The children look for the treasure clue sticker for Unit 1 and stick it in their books. Use L1 to explain that in every episode of the story from now on, Alex, Katie, Pip and Squeak follow a clue to find a fairytale character and / or a place in Fairyland to help them in their quest to find the treasure at the end of the rainbow.

Act out the story.

- Divide the class into five groups and assign a role to each group: Alex, Katie, Pip, Squeak or Frodo. Give a finger puppet or character flashcard to one child in each group to hold up during the story.

- Read the story speech bubbles on the Pupil's Book page. Point to or stand by each group and join in miming and saying their part with them every time their character speaks.

- Repeat the procedure, this time encouraging the groups to say their parts and mime more independently.

- Ask five confident children to come to the front of the class (one from each group). Give the Pip and Squeak finger puppets and the Alex, Katie and Frodo flashcards to the children playing the parts. The children act out a short version of the story to the rest of the class. Prompt them by reading the story if necessary and encourage them to join in saying their parts with you as you do this. Encourage everyone to clap and say e.g. *Fantastic!* at the end.

Option: The children can act out their parts *either* with *or* without their books, depending on how confident and familiar they are with this episode. If you wish to make the activity more challenging, the children can act out the whole story by joining in their character's part as you replay the CD.

Look, write and say. (AB page 5)

- Read the words at the top of the activity.
- Say **Here's a … for you!** for each picture and the children say the missing word.
- Say **Now write the words.** Draw the children's attention to the example.
- The children work individually and write the words.
- Check the answers by asking the children to say *Here's a … for you!* for each picture.

  Key: 1 card 2 present 3 hat 4 cake

Draw and count. (AB page 5)

- Ask **Whose birthday is it?** *(Squeak's)* **How old is Squeak?** *(seven)*
- Say **Draw seven candles on the cake.** Draw the children's attention to the example candle in dashed outline.
- The children work individually and draw six more candles on the cake to make a total of seven. They draw over the dashed outline as their first candle.
- Check by getting the children to point to and count in chorus the candles they have drawn.

Ending the lesson

Lesson review

- Briefly ask the children what they can do as a result of the lesson (understand and act out the story *The birthday cake*). Praise them for their efforts and / or use the finger puppets to do this.

Goodbye and closing routine

- Say **Let's sing the *Goodbye song*.** Play the karaoke version of the song (CD 1, track 5 – see Lesson 1). Hold up the finger puppets and the children sing and do the actions as in Lesson 1.

1 My birthday

Lesson 3
Communication and grammar

Aim:
- To practise asking and saying how old you are

Key language:
- *How old are you? I'm ...*
- numbers 1–10

Materials:
- Pupil's Book pages 7 and 8
- Activity Book pages 6 and 79
- Finger puppets (Pip and Squeak)
- Flashcards: Alex, Katie, Frodo, card, present, balloon, hat, cake, candle, biscuit, sandwich, cup, plate
- CD 1
- Scissors and glue / stapler
- A prepared set of Unit 1 puppets (AB page 79)

Starting out

Greetings and opening routine

- Greet the children yourself and using the finger puppets.
- *Either* play the karaoke version of the *Hello song* (CD 1, track 3 – see Lesson 1) and the children sing and do the actions as in Lesson 1 *or* stick the birthday flashcards on the board and play the karaoke version of *A card, a balloon* (CD 1, track 23 – see Lesson 1). The children sing and point to the flashcards.

Revision activity

- Hold up the finger puppets and ask **Can you remember who's in the story with Pip and Squeak?** *(Alex, Katie, Frodo)*. Stick the character flashcards on the board as the children respond.
- Ask the children to open their Pupil's Book at page 7. Briefly reconstruct the story, getting the children to supply key words. Say e.g. **Alex and Katie are in Fairyland. They follow the ...** *footprints* **and meet ...** *Pip and Squeak*. **It's Squeak's birthday. Frodo brings ...** *a card, a present and a cake*. **Squeak is ...** *seven*. **Pip falls in the ...** *cake* **and finds the treasure clue. The treasure clue says Follow the ...** *footprints*. **Find ...** *Little Red Riding Hood*.

- Play the CD (CD 1, track 24 – see Lesson 2). The children listen and follow the story in their books.

Setting objectives

- Say **Today we're going to practise asking and saying how old you are.**

On the learning trail

Listen and circle. (PB page 8)

- Ask the children to identify the character in each picture and say each character's age. Be ready to remind them of these if necessary.

Option: If you feel it is necessary, revise the numbers 1 – 10 with the children by writing the numbers on the board and pointing to them in random order. The children say each number as you point to it.

- Draw the children's attention to the example (they already know Pip is six from the story). Encourage them to guess how old Alex, Katie and Frodo are.
- Say **Listen and circle how old Squeak, Alex, Katie and Frodo are.** Play the CD (CD 1, track 25). Use the pause button to give the children time to circle the answers.
- Check the answers by saying e.g. **Pip is …** *six.* The children say the age.
- Say **Listen again. Repeat the questions and answers.** Play the CD again. Use the pause button to give the children time to repeat.
- Use the finger puppets to ask individual children **How old are you?** *I'm …*
- Get the children to ask the puppets *How old are you?* and use the puppets to answer in the same way. Repeat with the flashcards of the other characters.

  Key: 1 Pip 6; 2 Squeak 7; 3 Alex 8; 4 Katie 7; 5 Frodo 9

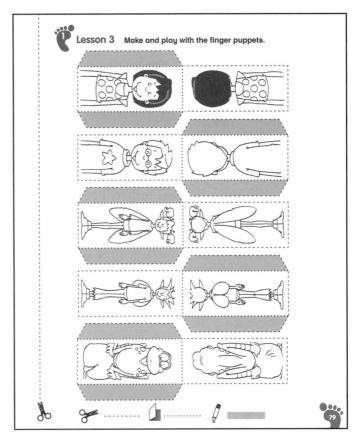

 Listen and circle.

Speaker 1:	*1 How old are you, Pip?*
Pip:	*I'm six.*
Speaker 1:	*2 How old are you, Squeak?*
Squeak:	*I'm seven.*
Speaker 1:	*3 How old are you, Alex?*
Alex:	*I'm eight.*
Speaker 1:	*4 How old are you, Katie?*
Katie:	*I'm seven.*
Speaker 1:	*5 How old are you, Frodo?*
Frodo:	*I'm nine.*

Make the finger puppets. (PB page 8 and AB page 79)

- Hold up your Pupil's Book and point to the pictures of the finger puppets. Say **We're going to make the puppets.** You can show the children the set you have already made. Say **Find page 79 in your Activity Book. Look at the puppets for Unit 1.**
- Point to the puppets. Ask **Who's this?** *(It's …)* for each one.
- Make sure all the children have got scissors and glue (or you can use a stapler).
- Point out the difference between the dashed lines (to be cut) and dotted lines (to be folded). Say **Now cut out the puppets like this. Fold them like this. And stick them (or I'll staple them) like this.** Ask the children to write their names or initials on the back of the puppets.
- When the children are ready, say e.g. **Hold up Frodo! / Hold up Pip!** and the children respond by putting the correct puppets on their fingers and holding them up.

Play with the finger puppets. (PB page 8)

- Ask two pupils to read the first dialogue and two other pupils to read the second dialogue.
- Get the children to hold up a different finger puppet in turn. Ask **How old are you?** and the children answer as if they are the character, according to what they know from the *Listen and circle* activity.
- Change roles and get the children to ask you in chorus about each character in turn as you hold up different finger puppets.
- Divide the children into pairs. Explain and demonstrate that the children should use different finger puppets and take turns to ask each other *How old are you? I'm …*, using what they know about each character from the *Listen and circle* activity.

- If there is time, ask the children to colour their finger puppets.

> **Option:** If you like, the children can also practise asking *What's your name? I'm ...* as part of the activity.

Read, match and colour. (AB page 6)

- Say the numbers 1–10 in turn and the children point to the numbers and words.
- Say **Now match the numbers and words. Colour each number and word the same colour.** Draw the children's attention to the example and explain and demonstrate what you mean.
- The children work individually and match and colour the numbers and words.
- The children compare and check their answers in pairs.

  Key: 1 one 2 two 3 three 4 four 5 five 6 six
  7 seven 8 eight 9 nine 10 ten

Look, write and say. (AB page 6)

- Elicit the age of each character and what each character says, based on the *Listen and circle* activity on page 8 of the Pupil's Book.
- Say **Now write what each character says** and draw the children's attention to the example.
- The children work individually and complete the sentences.
- Check the answers by asking **What does ... say?** for each picture.

  Key: 1 seven 2 eight 3 nine 4 six 5 seven

Ending the lesson

Lesson review

- Briefly ask the children what they can do as a result of the lesson (ask and say how old they are). Praise the children for their efforts and / or use the finger puppets to do this.

Goodbye and closing routine

- Say goodbye to the children yourself and using the finger puppets. If there is time, you can also play the karaoke version of the *Goodbye song* (CD 1, track 5 – see Lesson 1) and the children sing and do the actions as in Lesson 1.

1 My birthday

Lesson 4
Communication, grammar and pronunciation

Aims:
- To ask and answer questions to check how old you are
- To ask and answer questions to guess who you are
- To say words with the sounds /æ/ and /eɪ/

Key language:
- *Are you (a) ...? Yes, I am. / No, I'm not.*
- numbers 1–10

Materials:
- Pupil's Book page 9
- Activity Book page 7
- Finger puppets (Pip and Squeak)
- Flashcards: Alex, Katie and Frodo
- Unit 1 puppets from Lesson 3
- CD 1

Starting out

Greetings and opening routine

- Greet the children yourself and using the finger puppets.
- *Either* play the karaoke version of the *Hello song* (CD 1, track 3 – see Lesson 1) and the children sing and do the actions as in Lesson 1 *or* ask the children to get out the finger puppets they made in Lesson 3. Play the song *What's your name?* (CD 1, track 14 – see Introduction). The children sing and hold up the appropriate finger puppet for each verse.

Revision activity

- Get the children to count to ten with you, using their fingers.
- Say a number, e.g. **Four**. Explain and demonstrate that the children should hold up four fingers as fast as they can.
- Repeat several times saying different numbers to ten in random order.
- Invite different children to choose and say numbers in turn and the rest of the class holds up fingers in the same way.

Setting objectives

- Say **Today we're going to practise asking questions to check how old you are. We're also going to practise pronunciation.** Use L1 to clarify meaning if necessary.

On the learning trail

Listen and say the rap. (PB page 9)

- Give out or ask the children to get out the finger puppets of Alex and Squeak they made in Lesson 3. Either use the cut-out finger puppets you prepared for Lesson 3 or use the flashcard of Alex and the finger puppet of Squeak to demonstrate the activity.
- Ask the children to put on the finger puppets. Explain that Alex asks the questions and Squeak answers in the rap.

- Say **Listen to the rap.** Hold up the puppets as they speak and demonstrate what you mean. Play the CD (CD 1, track 26).
- Divide the class into two groups: Alex and Squeak. Explain that the groups should take turns to ask the question and respond. Play the CD again.
- The groups change roles and repeat.
- Use the finger puppet of Squeak to ask the children **Are you a boy / girl / seven / eight?**, etc. and encourage them to respond *Yes, I am* or *No, I'm not.*
- Get the children to ask the puppets questions in chorus in the same way.

 One, two, three

Alex:	One, two, three.
	Guess with me.
	Are you a boy?
Squeak:	No, I'm not.
Alex:	Are you a girl?
Squeak:	Yes, I am.
Alex:	Are you six?
Squeak:	No, I'm not.
Alex:	Are you seven?
Squeak:	Yes, I am.
	Yes, yes, yes! Yes, I am.

Play a game. (PB page 9)

- Secretly choose one of the characters (except Frodo), e.g. Katie. Get the children to ask you questions to guess which character you are, e.g.

P1:	Are you a boy?
T:	**No, I'm not.**
P2:	Are you a girl?
T:	**Yes, I am.**
P3:	Are you seven?
T:	**Yes, I am.**
P4:	You're Katie!

- Repeat once or twice with the whole class. If you like, you can also choose a child in the class instead of one of the characters.
- Ask a few individual children to take turns to come to the front of the class and choose (or you can assign them) a character or another child in the class. The rest of the class asks questions in the same way.
- Divide the class into pairs. The children take turns to choose a character or another child in the class and play the game with their partner in the same way.

Listen and say: Frodo's word fun. (PB page 9)

- Hold up the flashcard of Frodo. Explain that Frodo is going to use his 'magic' in every unit to help the children pronounce English correctly.
- Say **hat** and draw the children's attention to the vowel sound /æ/.
- Say **cake** and draw the children's attention to the vowel sound /eɪ/.
- Explain and demonstrate that the children should listen and open their hands (like a jaw opening) if the word has a sound /æ/ as in *hat* and move their hands and fingers apart if the word has a sound like /eɪ/ in *cake*.
- Say **Listen to Frodo saying the words.** Play the CD (CD 1, track 28). The children listen and respond with the actions.
- Play the CD again. The children listen, do the actions and repeat the words.

Key: /æ/: hat; candle; sandwich /eɪ/: cake; plate; eight

 Frodo's word fun. Listen and say.

cake ... hat ... candle ... plate ... sandwich ... eight

Listen and tick (✓). (AB page 7)

- Say **Listen and tick the correct picture.** Draw the children's attention to the example.
- Play the CD (CD 1, track 29). Use the pause button to give the children time to tick the correct pictures.
- Check the answers by saying e.g. **Number one is a ...** *boy.* **He's ...** *seven* and the children fill in the correct words.
- Say **Listen again and repeat the questions and answers.** Play the CD again.

Key: 1 boy on right 2 girl on left 3 girl on left 4 boy on right

Listen and tick.

Speaker 1: One.
 Are you a boy?
Boy 1: Yes, I am.
Speaker 1: Are you six?
Boy 1: No, I'm not.
Speaker 1: Are you seven?
Boy 1: Yes, I am.

Speaker 2: Two.
 Are you a boy?
Girl 1: No, I'm not.
Speaker 2: Are you a girl?
Girl 1: Yes, I am.
Speaker 2: Are you nine?
Girl 1: Yes, I am.

Speaker 1: Three.
 Are you six?
Girl 2: Yes, I am.
Speaker 1: Are you a boy?
Girl 2: No, I'm not.
Speaker 1: Are you a girl?
Girl 2: Yes, I am.

Speaker 2: Four.
 Are you eight?
Boy 2: Yes, I am.
Speaker 2: Are you a girl?
Boy 2: No, I'm not.
Speaker 2: Are you a boy?
Boy 2: Yes, I am.

Read, write and act out. (AB page 7)

- Read the dialogue and the children complete the questions orally. Remind them how old Frodo is (he's nine) if necessary.
- The children work individually and complete Katie's questions.
- Check the answers by asking two children to read the dialogue to the class.
- Divide the class into pairs and assign or get the children to choose roles.

- The children act out the dialogue with their partner. They then change roles and repeat. If you like, the children can use the finger puppets they made in Lesson 3 to do this.

Key: 1 seven 2 ten 3 nine

Ending the lesson

Lesson review

- Briefly ask the children what they can do as a result of the lesson (ask questions to check how old they are or guess who someone is, recognise and pronounce words with /æ/ or /eɪ/). Praise the children for their efforts and / or use the finger puppets to do this.

Goodbye and closing routine

- Say goodbye to the children yourself and using the finger puppets. If there is time, you can also play the karaoke version of the *Goodbye song* (CD 1, track 5 – see Lesson 1) and the children sing and do the actions as in Lesson 1.

1 My birthday

Lesson 5
Content input

Aim:
- To recognise and name different shapes and associate them with objects

Key language:
- *This is a …*
- *The … is a … circle / square / rectangle / triangle.*
- *card, present, hat, balloon, cake, candle, biscuit, sandwich, cup, plate*

Materials:
- Pupil's Book page 10
- Activity Book page 8
- Finger puppets (Pip and Squeak)
- Flashcards: Alex, card, present, hat, balloon, cake, candle, biscuit, sandwich, cup, plate
- Word cards: card, present, hat, balloon, cake, candle, biscuit, sandwich, cup, plate
- CD 1

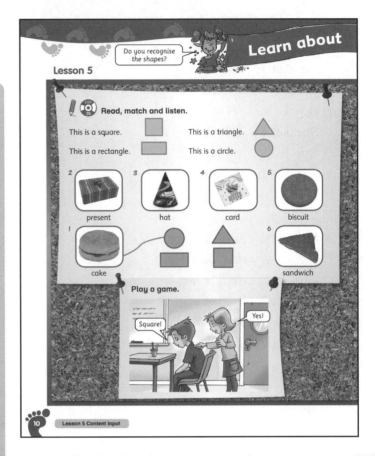

Starting out

Greetings and opening routine

- Greet the children yourself and using the finger puppets.
- *Either* play the karaoke version of the *Hello song* (CD 1, track 3 – see Lesson 1) and the children sing and do the actions as in Lesson 1 *or* hold up the puppet of Squeak and the flashcard of Alex, play *One, two, three* (CD 1, track 26 – see Lesson 4) and the children say the rap in two groups.

Revision activity

- Play a memory game on the board with the Unit 1 flashcards and word cards. Divide the class into two teams.
- Stick the flashcards face down in jumbled order on one side of the board and the word cards face down in jumbled order on the other.
- Ask a child from one team to choose a card from one side of the board. Turn it over and the child names the picture or reads the word. Ask another child from the same team to choose a card from the other side of the board and name the picture or read the word in the same way. If the two cards match, take the cards off the board and put them on your desk nearest to the team.
- Repeat the procedure with the other team.
- Continue playing the game until there are no cards left on the board. The team with most cards at the end of the game wins.

Setting objectives

- Draw a circle, a square, a rectangle and a triangle on the board. Point to each one in turn and say **This is a circle. This is a …**, etc. **They are different shapes.** Check the children understand the meaning.
- Say **Today, we're going to read about shapes and name the shapes of different objects.** Use L1 to clarify what you mean.

On the learning trail

Read, match and listen. (PB page 10)

- Ask the children to open their Pupil's Books at page 10. Read the title **Learn about the world around you!** Hold up the finger puppets and explain that in every unit Pip and Squeak are going to introduce the children to learning something about their world in English.

- Read the question **Do you recognise the shapes?** at the top and the children respond *Yes*.

- Read the text at the start of the activity or play part 1 on the CD (CD 1, track 30) while the children follow in their books.

- Hold up your book and point to the photos. Say **Look at the photos** and read the words. The children point to each photo as you say the word.

- Say **Match the objects and shapes.** Draw the children's attention to the example.

- The children work individually and draw lines matching the pictures and shapes.

- Say **Now listen and check your answers.** Read the sentences in the audio script or play part 2 on the CD. The children listen and check they have matched the pictures and shapes correctly.

- Check the answers by getting individual children to say e.g. *The present is a rectangle.*

    Key: 1 circle 2 rectangle 3 triangle 4 square
    5 circle 6 triangle

 Read, match and listen.

Part 1

This is a square.
This is a triangle.
This is a rectangle.
This is a circle.

Part 2

1 The cake is a circle.
2 The present is a rectangle.
3 The hat is a triangle.
4 The card is a square.
5 The biscuit is a circle.
6 The sandwich is a triangle.

- If appropriate, use L1 to ask the children what differences there are in the shapes and listen to their ideas, e.g. a square has four equal sides; a rectangle has two pairs of equal sides; a triangle has three sides (which may or may not be equal); a circle is a continuous line with no sides; its diameter (the distance across the circle) is the same wherever you measure it from.

Play a game. (PB page 10)

- Ask a (confident) child to the front. Get them to stand with their back to the rest of the class. Use your index finger to draw a shape on the child's back and encourage them to guess what it is, e.g. *Circle!*

- Repeat with several different children.

- Divide the class into pairs. Get the pairs to sit so that one child has their back to their partner. Explain and demonstrate that the other child should draw a shape on their partner's back and their partner should guess what it is. After drawing three shapes, they should change roles and repeat.

- If you like, the children can then change partners and repeat the game.

- At the end, use L1 to ask the children to say briefly which shapes they found easy and which difficult to identify and listen to their response (the square and rectangle are likely to be the most difficult because they have the same number of sides).

Read, draw and say. (AB page 8)

- Read the sentences and draw the children's attention to the example.

- The children work individually. They read the sentences and draw the shapes. It is up to you whether the children either do this freehand or use rulers or protractors, or draw around objects, e.g. a glue stick, to make a circle.

- Check the answers by asking individual children to hold up their books, point to the shapes they have drawn and say e.g. *This is a triangle.*

Look and write. (AB page 8)

- Say **Look at the pictures.** Ask the children to identify orally the shape of each object, e.g. *The biscuit is a circle.*
- The children work individually and complete the sentences.
- If there is time, ask the children to colour the objects.
- Check the answers by asking individual children to read the sentences.

Key: 1 biscuit 2 card 3 sandwich 4 present 5 cake

Ending the lesson

Lesson review

- Briefly ask the children what they can do as a result of the lesson (recognise and name the shapes of objects). Praise the children for their efforts and / or use the finger puppets to do this.

Goodbye and closing routine

- Say goodbye to the children yourself and using the finger puppets. If there is time, you can also play the karaoke version of the *Goodbye song* (CD 1, track 5 – see Lesson 1) and the children sing and do the actions as in Lesson 1.

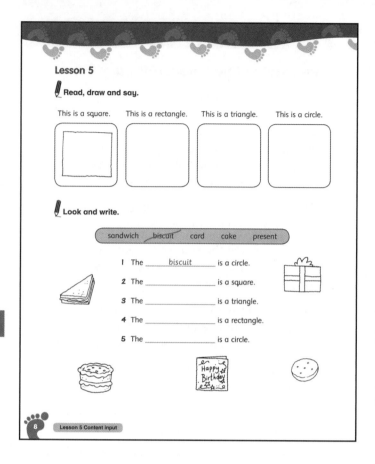

1 My birthday

Lesson 6
Content and personalisation

Aim:
- To identify shapes of objects in our classroom

Key language:
- *The ... is a circle / square / triangle / rectangle.*
- *door, window, board, book, clock, desk, chair*
- *bin, triangle, ball*
- numbers 1–10
- colours

Materials:
- Pupil's Book page 11
- Activity Book page 9
- Finger puppets (Pip and Squeak)
- CD 1

Starting out

Greetings and opening routine

- Greet the children yourself and using the finger puppets.
- *Either* play the karaoke version of the *Hello song* (CD 1, track 3 – see Lesson 1) and the children sing and do the actions as in Lesson 1 *or* hold up the finger puppet of Squeak and the flashcard of Alex, play the karaoke version of *One, two, three* (CD 1, track 27 – see Lesson 4) and the children say the rap in two groups.

Revision activity

- Use one of the finger puppets to draw a shape in the air, e.g. a circle. Ask **What's the shape?** and the children name the shape. Repeat for the other shapes.
- Use the finger puppets to give the children instructions, e.g. **Draw a square!** and the children draw the shapes in the air as the puppets say them.
- If you like, invite a few individual children to take turns to give instructions and the rest of the class responds in the same way.

Setting objectives

- Say **In this lesson we're going to name the shapes of things in our classroom.**

On the learning trail

Play a game. (PB page 11)

- Point to things in the classroom (door, window, board, book, clock, desk, chair) and elicit or remind the children of the words. If possible, include the words *bin*, *ball* and *triangle* (percussion instrument), in preparation for the next activity.

Option: If the children do not know *bin, ball, triangle,* then point to each object in turn, say the word and get the children to repeat it after you. Then name each object and the children point to it.

- Demonstrate the game by pointing to and naming an object, e.g. **The board.** and the children respond in chorus by identifying the shape, e.g. *Rectangle!* Explain that if the class identifies the shape correctly, they score a point. If not, you score a point.
- Play the game by naming things in the classroom in random order and the children respond by saying the shapes. At first, point to the objects you name and go slowly. As the children become familiar with the game, stop pointing to the objects and increase the speed. Keep a score of the points on the board. Stop the game e.g. after you

have named each object twice. Get the children to count up the scores (the class should easily win!).

Look, count and write. (PB page 11)

- Say **Look at the picture and the different shapes.** Ask **How many squares / triangles / rectangles / circles can you see?** Give the children time to count the shapes and respond, e.g. *Two triangles*. If the children's responses vary, don't tell them the correct answers yet.

- Say **Now look at the picture again carefully. Count the shapes and write the numbers in the boxes.** Draw their attention to the example.

- The children work individually, counting the shapes and writing the numbers.

- Check the answers by asking e.g. **How many squares?** *(four)* Ask the children to count and identify the objects they know of each shape, e.g. *One ... two windows, One ... two chairs.*

    Key: 4 squares (2 windows, 2 chairs); 2 triangles (1 hat, 1 triangle); 6 rectangles (door, board, desk, 2 books, bookcase); 4 circles (clock, 2 balls, bin)

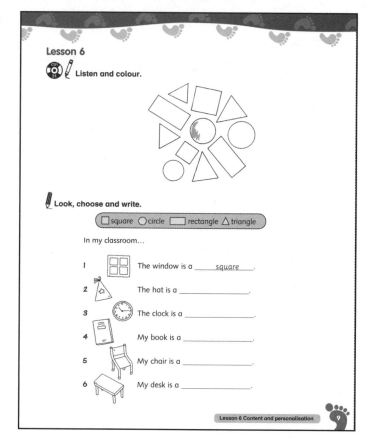

Listen and colour. (AB page 9)

- Ask the children to look at the pattern and identify the shapes (circles, squares, rectangles, triangles).

- Make sure the children have crayons available.

- Say **Listen and colour the shapes.** Explain that the children should just colour one or two shapes as they listen and then finish colouring the whole pattern at the end.

- Play the CD (CD 1, track 31). Use the pause button, if necessary, to give the children time to colour one or two examples of each shape.

- The children finish colouring the pattern.

- Ask the children to name the colours of each shape, e.g. *The circles are red.*

 Listen and colour.

Colour the circles red. Colour the rectangles green. Colour the triangles blue. Colour the squares yellow.

Look, choose and write. (AB page 9)

- Ask the children to say sentences about different objects in their classroom, e.g. *The window is a square.*

- Read the sentences and the children complete them orally. Draw their attention to the example. Explain that they need to look at the pictures to complete sentences 1–3. They then complete sentences 4–6 with words that are true for their own classroom. Explain that they will need to use some of the shape words more than once.

- The children complete the sentences.

- Check the answers by asking individual children to take turns to read their sentences to the class.

    Key: 1 square 2 triangle 3 circle 4–6 children's own answers.

Ending the lesson

Lesson review

- Briefly ask the children what they can do as a result of the lesson (name the shapes of things in the classroom). Praise the children for their efforts and / or use the finger puppets to do this.

Goodbye and closing routine

- Say goodbye to the children yourself and using the finger puppets. If there is time, you can also play the karaoke version of the *Goodbye song* (CD 1, track 5 – see Lesson 1) and the children sing and do the actions as in Lesson 1.

1 My birthday

Lesson 7
Children's culture

Aims:

- To sing *Happy birthday*, say *Thank you!* and play a version of a traditional party game
- To be aware of how to respond appropriately when people give you a present

Key language:

- *Happy birthday*
- *Here's a ... for you! / Thank you!*
- *card, present, hat, balloon, cake, candle, biscuit, sandwich, cup, plate*
- *square, circle, rectangle, triangle*

Materials:

- Pupil's book page 12
- Activity Book page 10
- Finger puppets (Pip and Squeak)
- Flashcards: card, present, hat, balloon, cake, candle, biscuit, sandwich, cup, plate, Frodo
- CD 1

Starting out

Greetings and opening routine

- Greet the children yourself and using the finger puppets.
- *Either* play the karaoke version of the *Hello song* (CD 1, track 3 – see Lesson 1) and the children sing and do the actions as in Lesson 1 *or* stick the flashcards in a row on the board in the same order as the song *A card, a balloon* (CD 1, track 22 – see Lesson 1) and the children sing and point to the pictures.

Revision activity

- Point to the Unit 1 flashcards on the board in turn (put them on the board if they weren't used in the opening routine) and the children say the words with you.
- Remove the flashcard of the plate.
- Point to the flashcards and to the place where the plate was and the children say all the words. Remove the flashcard of the cup.
- Repeat in the same way until the children are saying all the words (or e.g. six of them, if this is too hard) from memory.

Setting objectives

- Hold up the flashcard of Frodo. Explain that in every unit Frodo is going to introduce the children to an aspect of children's culture in English.
- Say **In this lesson we're going to sing** *Happy birthday,* **say** *Thank you* **for things and play a version of a traditional birthday party game.**

On the learning trail

Listen and sing the song. (PB page 12) (books closed)

- Say **Can you remember the story? Whose birthday is it?** *(Squeak's)*
- Hold up the finger puppet of Squeak. Say **Let's sing** *Happy birthday* **to Squeak.**
- Play the CD (CD 1, track 32). The children join in singing *Happy birthday.*

Happy birthday

Happy birthday to you
Happy birthday to you
Happy birthday, dear Squeak
Happy birthday to you!

- Hold up the flashcard of the present in your other hand. Say **Let's sing** *Happy birthday* **again and give Squeak a present**.
- Play the karaoke version of the song on the CD (CD 1, track 33).
- At the end, give the flashcard of the present to Squeak and say **Here's a present for you!** Use the puppet to say **Thank you!**
- Repeat with the flashcards of the card, the cake, the balloon and the hat.
- Give each flashcard to a different child and ask the class to sing the karaoke version of *Happy birthday*.
- At the end, the children give the flashcards to Squeak and say *Here's a ... for you!* Squeak says **Thank you!**
- Give the flashcards to different children in the class and repeat.
- Ask the children to open their Pupil's Books at page 12. Say **Let's sing** *Happy birthday* **to Squeak again. Follow in your books.**
- The children sing and follow in their books either with or without the CD.

 Citizenship box: Remember!

Say **Look at the picture. Who gives a present to Squeak?** *(Frodo)* **What does Squeak say?** *(Thank you.)*

Hold up the flashcard of Frodo, read the *Remember!* note and check understanding. Use L1 to explain that it's polite to say *Thank you* when people give you a present.

Say **Thank you** and get the children to repeat this a few times.

Listen and play *Pass the present!*
(PB page 12)

- Say **Let's play a game that English children play at birthday parties!** If you like, explain that the game is called *Pass the present!* (or traditionally, *Pass the parcel*) and that this is an adapted version for the classroom.
- Either get the children sitting or standing in a circle or, if this is not possible, ask half or all the children to stand in a line at the front facing the class. Alternatively, the children can remain seated at their desks.
- Explain and demonstrate that the children should listen to the music and pass the flashcard of the present round the circle (or along the line, or from child to child seated at their desks). As they do this, they should say *Here's a present! / Thank you!* When the music stops, the children should listen to the instruction on the CD and the child who has got the flashcard should respond. The child who has got the flashcard when the music finishes at the end of the game is the winner.
- Play the CD (CD 1, track 34). The children pass the flashcard and respond to the instructions. Be ready to prompt and / or help them do this as necessary.
- At the end, if you like, use L1 to explain that in the traditional game, the children pass round a real parcel wrapped in many layers of paper. When the music stops, the child who has the parcel unwraps one layer, reads an instruction and does the action. The child who unwraps the last layer of paper wins a small prize.

 Listen and play *Pass the present!*

How old are you?
Count to ten!
Draw a rectangle!   (in the air or on the board)
What's your name?
Draw a circle!   (in the air or on the board)
Point to the door!
Draw a triangle!   (in the air or on the board)
Point to the window!
Draw a square!   (in the air or on the board)
Point to the board!

Look, write and say. (AB page 10)

- Read the words at the top of the activity.
- Read the exchanges and the children say the missing words.
- The children work individually and write the missing words.
- Check the answers by asking individual children to read the exchanges.
- The children act out the exchanges in pairs.

Key: 1 card 2 cake 3 present 4 balloon

Option: From now on, you can actively encourage the children to say *Thank you* whenever appropriate in class.

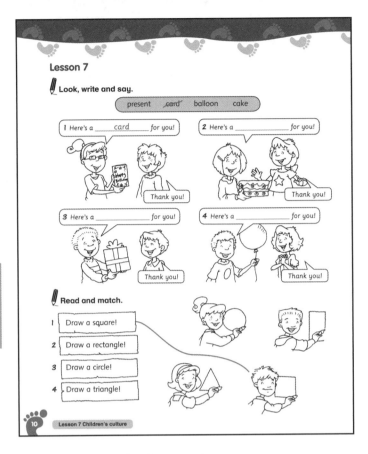

Read and match. (AB page 10)

- Read the instructions and the children point to the correct pictures.
- Say **Read and match the instructions and pictures.** Draw their attention to the example.
- The children work individually and match the pictures and instructions.
- The children compare and check their answers in pairs.
- Check the answers by giving individual children instructions to come and draw different shapes on the board.

Key: Children's own drawings. 1 square 2 rectangle 3 circle 4 triangle

Goodbye and closing routine

- Say goodbye to the children yourself and using the finger puppets. If there is time, you can also play the karaoke version of the *Goodbye song* (CD 1, track 5 – see Lesson 1) and the children sing and do the actions as in Lesson 1.

Ending the lesson

Lesson review

- Briefly ask the children what they can do as a result of the lesson (sing *Happy birthday*, say *Thank you!* for things, play a version of a party game). Praise the children for their efforts and / or use the finger puppets to do this.

1 My birthday

Lesson 8
Unit review / All About Me Portfolio Booklet

Aim:
- To review learning in Unit 1

Key language:
- *How old are you? I'm ...*
- *Are you ...? Yes, I am. / No, I'm not.*
- *Here's a ... for you! / Thank you!*
- *The ... is a circle / square / rectangle / triangle.*
- *card, present, hat, balloon, cake, candle, biscuit, sandwich, cup, plate*
- numbers 1–10

Materials:
- Pupil's book page 13
- Activity book page 11
- *All About Me* Portfolio Booklet pages 6 and 7
- Finger puppets (Pip and Squeak)
- Flashcards: card, present, hat, balloon, cake, candle, biscuit, sandwich, cup, plate, Frodo
- Stickers for Unit 1
- CD 1

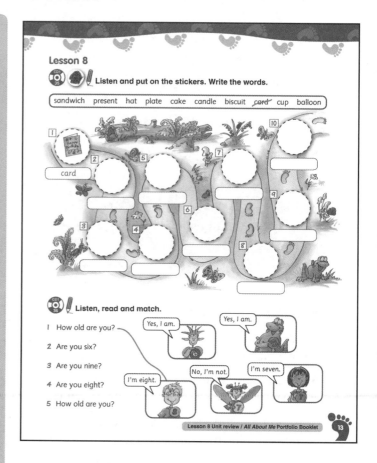

Starting out

Greetings and opening routine

- Greet the children yourself and using the finger puppets.
- *Either* play the karaoke version of the *Hello song* (CD 1, track 3 – see Lesson 1) and the children sing and do the actions as in Lesson 1 *or* stick the unit flashcards in a row on the board in the same order as the song *A card, a balloon* and play the karaoke version (CD 1, track 23 – see Lesson 1). The children sing and point to the flashcards.

Revision activity

- Ask six children to the front. Give five children a flashcard each (card, cake, present, hat and balloon) and one child the finger puppet of Squeak.
- Say **Let's sing *Happy birthday* to Squeak and give him a card, a cake, a present, a hat and a balloon!**
- Play the karaoke version of *Happy birthday* on the CD (CD 1, track 33 – see Lesson 7). The children with the flashcards give them to Squeak and say *Here's a ... for you!* Squeak says *Thank you!*

Setting objectives

- Say **Today we're going to review what we've learnt in Unit 1.** Use L1 to clarify what you mean, if necessary.

On the learning trail

Listen and put on the stickers. Write the words. (PB page 13)

- Make sure the children have the stickers for Unit 1 ready.
- Say **Listen and put on the stickers.** Draw the children's attention to the example.
- Play the CD (CD 1, track 35). Use the pause button to give the children time to put on the stickers.
- Say **Now write the words.** Draw the children's attention to the example.

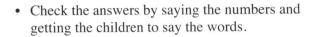

- Check the answers by saying the numbers and getting the children to say the words.

  Key: 1 card 2 balloon 3 cup 4 biscuit 5 cake 6 candle 7 hat 8 plate 9 sandwich 10 present

 Listen and put on the stickers.

1 Here's a card for you! / Thank you!
2 Here's a balloon for you! / Thank you!
3 Here's a cup for you! / Thank you!
4 Here's a biscuit for you. / Mmm! Thank you!
5 Look at the cake!
6 Look at the candle!
7 Look at the hat!
8 The plate is a circle.
9 The sandwich is a triangle.
10 The present is a square.

Listen, read and match. (PB page 13)

- Read the first line of each exchange and ask the children to predict and find the response.
- Say **Now listen, read and match the questions and answers.** Draw the children's attention to the example.
- Play the CD (CD 1, track 36). The children listen and match the questions and answers. Use the pause button to give them time to do this, if necessary.
- Check the answers by asking individual children to read the exchanges.
- Play the CD again as a final check.
- The children read the exchanges in pairs.

  Key: 1 (Alex) I'm eight. 2 (Pip) Yes, I am. 3 (Frodo) Yes, I am. 4 (Squeak) No, I'm not. 5 (Katie) I'm seven.

 Listen, read and match.

1 Speaker 1: How old are you?
   Alex: I'm eight.
2 Speaker 1: Are you six?
   Pip: Yes, I am.
3 Speaker 1: Are you nine?
   Frodo: Yes, I am.
4 Speaker 1: Are you eight?
   Squeak: No, I'm not.
5 Speaker 1: How old are you?
   Katie: I'm seven.

Listen and circle. (AB page 11)

- Say **Listen and find out how old the children are. Circle the numbers.** Draw the children's attention to the example.
- Play the CD (CD 1, track 37). Pause, if necessary, to give the children time to circle the numbers.
- Check the answers by saying e.g. **This boy / girl is …** and the children complete the sentences.

  Key: 1 six 2 eight 3 seven 4 nine

 Listen and circle.

1 How old are you?
   I'm six.
2 Are you eight?
   Yes, I am.
3 How old are you?
   I'm seven.
4 Are you ten?
   No, I'm not.
   Are you nine?
   Yes, I am.

Look and write. (AB page 11)

- Elicit or remind the children of the words for shapes.
- Name the objects in turn and the children say the shapes, e.g.

  T: **Candle!**

  PP: *Circle!*

- Say **Now write the words in the correct list.** Draw the children's attention to the example.
- The children work individually and write each word in the correct list.
- The children compare their lists in pairs.
- Check the answers by asking individual children to say sentences, e.g. *The present is a square.*

  Key: circle: candle, cake, cup, plate, biscuit, balloon

  square: present

  rectangle: card

  triangle: hat, sandwich

Colour Frodo. (AB page 11)

- Hold up the flashcard of Frodo. Use L1 to explain to the children that in this activity they assess their work in the unit by choosing and colouring the picture of Frodo which corresponds best to how they think they have done.
- Explain the key by pointing to the three pictures of Frodo in turn and saying **Colour this picture if your work is OK but you think you need to try harder or need more practice. Colour this picture of Frodo if you think your work is good. Colour this picture of Frodo with a big smile and jumping very high if you think your work is excellent.** Make sure the children understand that there are no right answers and that it is their own opinion of the work they have done which is important. Be ready to encourage the children to have a positive view if they are too hard on themselves.

Ending the lesson

Lesson review

- Briefly ask the children what they can do as a result of the lesson (use the language and vocabulary they've learnt in Unit 1). Praise the children for their efforts and / or use the finger puppets to do this.

Goodbye and closing routine

- Say goodbye to the children yourself and using the finger puppets. If there is time, you can also play the karaoke version of the *Goodbye song* (CD 1, track 5 – see Lesson 1) and the children sing and do the actions as in Lesson 1.

All About Me **Portfolio Booklet**

The children complete Unit 1 of their personal *All About Me* Portfolio Booklets. They complete their learning journey by colouring the sections on the path to show what they can do. If you like, the children can also sign this page and you can endorse this by adding your own signature and the date.

2 My classroom

Structures and grammar

- *What's this? It's a ...*
- *Can I have the ..., please? Here you are.*
- *This / My ... is ...*
- *Me, too.*
- Recycled: *It's ..., Here ..., The / A ...*

Vocabulary

- Core: *school bag, file, notebook, pen, pencil, crayon, rubber, pencil sharpener, pencil case, ruler*
- Other: *wolf, hungry, Mum,.. Dad, school*
- Content / culture: *plastic, wood, natural, trees, hard, soft, paper, stone, scissors, hurry, late, close*
- Recycled: *yes, no, thank you, chair, door, come, numbers, colours*

Main receptive language

- classroom objects, *difference between ..., made of ...*

Communicative competence

Understanding

Listening:
- Can recognise words for classroom objects
- Can understand the episode of the story
- Can understand questions and answers to identify things
- Can understand requests and responses
- Can understand simple statements about classroom objects

Reading:
- Can recognise words for classroom objects
- Can read short exchanges about classroom objects
- Can read requests and responses
- Can read sentences about plastic and wood

Speaking

Spoken interaction:
- Can ask and respond to questions about classroom objects
- Can make and respond to requests
- Can use *please* and *thank you* appropriately

Spoken production:
- Can sing the *Hello song*
- Can name classroom objects
- Can say whether objects are plastic or wood
- Can sing the song *A pencil! A pencil!*
- Can sing the song *Can I have the rubber, please?*
- Can say the rhyme *One, two, three, four*
- Can say a tongue-twister with /p/
- Can sing the *Goodbye song*

Writing

- Can copy and write words for classroom objects
- Can copy and complete sentences about what classroom objects are made of

Content links

- *Science:* differences between plastic and wood

Learning strategies and thinking skills

- Recognising learning objectives
- Using music and rhythm to memorise language
- Sequencing
- Making use of prior knowledge
- Using visual and other clues to make predictions and guesses
- Associating shape and touch with vocabulary
- Classifying classroom objects according to whether they are plastic or wood
- Reflecting on learning

Children's culture

- Saying a traditional rhyme: *One, two, three, four*
- Playing a traditional children's game: *Paper, stone, scissors!*

Pronunciation

- Tongue-twister with /p/

Values and attitudes

- Interest in being able to talk about classroom objects in English
- Recognition that classroom objects are made of different materials
- Awareness that it's polite to say *sorry* if you're late

2 My classroom

Lesson 1
Vocabulary presentation

Aim:
- To name classroom objects

Key language:
- *school bag, file, notebook, pencil case, pencil, pen, rubber, ruler, pencil sharpener, crayon*

Materials:
- Pupil's Book page 14
- Activity Book page 12
- Finger puppets (Pip and Squeak)
- Flashcards: school bag, file, notebook, pencil case, pencil, pen, rubber, ruler, pencil sharpener, crayon, Frodo
- Word cards: school bag, file, notebook, pencil case, pencil, pen, rubber, ruler, pencil sharpener, crayon
- CD 1

Starting out

Greetings and opening routine

- Greet the children yourself and using the finger puppets. Say e.g. **Hello, children. Hello … How are you today?** *Fine, thank you.* Ask a few individual children to greet the puppets in turn.
- Say **Let's sing the *Hello song*.** Play the CD (CD 1, track 2). Hold up the puppets on your index fingers. Move them as the children sing and do the actions.

 Hello song

Hello.	(wave)
Hello.	(wave)
How are you today?	(put arms out)
I'm fine, thank you.	(move from side to side)
And I'm OK!	(raise arms in the air)

Setting objectives

- Ask the children what things we use in the classroom and listen to their response (in L1).
- Say **Today we're going to learn how to name things we use in the classroom.**

On the learning trail

Vocabulary presentation (books closed)

- Hold up one of the flashcards, e.g. pencil. Ask **Have you got a pencil?** and use gesture to convey what you mean. Demonstrate that the children should say *yes* and hold up a pencil if they have one and say *no* if they don't.
- Point to the flashcard. Say **pencil** several times and get the children to repeat the word with you in chorus.
- Stick the flashcard of the pencil on the board.
- Repeat the procedure for all the other object flashcards.
- Divide the class in half. Hold up the Pip finger puppet and say to one half **Say the words with Pip.** Use the puppet to point to the flashcards in turn and the children say the words with you. Make the puppet fly around to praise the children.
- Repeat the procedure with the Squeak puppet and the other half of the class.

Follow the footprints. (PB page 14) (books open)

- Hold up the flashcard of Frodo. Say **Listen and follow the footprints with Frodo the frog. Use your finger** and demonstrate this.
- Play the CD (CD 1, track 38). The children listen and follow the footprints with their fingers. They stop by each picture as they hear the word and they repeat the word.
- Say **Now listen and draw a line following the footprints** and demonstrate this. Play the CD again. The children draw a line, stop by each picture and repeat the words as previously.

 Follow the footprints.

school bag … file … notebook … pencil case … pencil … pen … rubber … ruler … pencil sharpener … crayon

- Stick the word cards on the board in jumbled order (at the children's height and away from the flashcards).
- Point to one word card, e.g. *school bag*, and read the word. Say **Look for the picture of the school bag.** Give the children time to do this.
- Ask a child to come to the front of the class and stick the word card for *school bag* by the corresponding flashcard. Ask the rest of the class **Is this right?** and get them to say the word.
- Repeat the procedure with the rest of the word cards.
- Take the flashcards and word cards off the board.

Listen and sing the song. (PB page 14)

- Say **Look at the picture.** Point to Pip and Squeak in turn and ask **Who's this?** The children identify the characters.
- Say **Pip has got a …** *(pencil)* **and a …** *(rubber).* **Squeak has got a …** *(notebook)* **and a …** *(pen)* and the children identify the objects each character is holding.
- Say **Listen to the song. Point to the pictures.** Play the CD (CD 1, track 39). The children listen to the song and point to the object in each verse.
- Ask four children to come to the front of the class. Give them each a flashcard for one of the verses.
- Play the CD again. The children at the front hold up the flashcards for each verse in turn and the rest of the class sings the song.

 A pencil! A pencil!

Listen, listen
Look and see
A pencil! A pencil!
One, two, three!

Verse 2: *A notebook!*
Verse 3: *A rubber!*
Verse 4: *A pen!*

Look, draw and say. (PB page 14)

- Ask the children to look and say the words in each sequence and to name the two missing items.
- Say **Draw the pictures** and draw the children's attention to the example.
- The children work individually and draw the missing items in each sequence.
- Check the answers by getting the children to point to the pictures and say the words in each sequence in a rhythmic way, e.g. *Pencil, rubber, pencil, rubber, pencil, rubber.*

Key: 1 pencil, rubber 2 ruler, pen 3 school bag, notebook

Read, colour and say. (AB page 12)

- Use objects and clothes to check that the children remember the colours brown, pink, blue, green and red.
- Read the descriptions while the children follow in their books. Ask them to point to the objects on the page as you read.
- Say **Now read and colour the pictures.**
- The children work individually and colour the pictures.
- Check the answers by pointing to the pictures in turn and asking individual children to tell you the correct description for each one.

Key: 1 brown school bag 2 blue pen 3 red notebook 4 green pencil sharpener 5 pink pencil case

Look and write. (AB page 12)

- Ask the children to identify the object in each picture orally.
- Draw their attention to the example and the words in the box. The children write the words.
- Check the answers.

Key: 1 rubber 2 pencil 3 ruler 4 crayon

Ending the lesson

Lesson review

- Briefly ask the children what they can do as a result of the lesson (name classroom objects, sing the song *A pencil! A pencil!*). Praise the children for their efforts and / or use the finger puppets to do this.

Goodbye and closing routine

- Say **Let's sing the *Goodbye song*.** Play the CD (CD 1, track 4). Hold up the finger puppets on your index fingers as the children sing and do the actions.

Goodbye song

Goodbye, goodbye (wave)
See you another day! (make marching movements with arms)
Goodbye, goodbye (wave)
See you soon! Hurray!
(wave both hands in the air)

- Say goodbye to the children yourself and using the finger puppets. Say e.g. **Goodbye everyone. See you on …** Ask a few individual children to say goodbye to the finger puppets in turn.

2 My classroom

Lesson 2
Language input and story

Aim:
- To understand and act out episode 2 of the story

Key language:
- *What's this? It's a ...*
- *Can I have my ..., please?*
- *Here you are. Thank you.*
- *school bag, file, pen, pencil, crayon, rubber, pencil sharpener, pencil case, notebook, ruler*
- *wolf*

Materials:
- Pupil's Book page 15
- Activity Book page 13
- Finger puppets (Pip and Squeak)
- Flashcards: Alex, Katie, school bag, file, pen, pencil, crayon, rubber, pencil sharpener, pencil case, notebook, ruler
- Treasure clue sticker for Unit 2
- CD 1

Starting out

Greetings and opening routine
- Greet the children yourself and using the finger puppets.
- Play the karaoke version of the *Hello song* (CD 1, track 3 – see Lesson 1). The children sing and do the actions as in Lesson 1.

Revision activity
- Stick the flashcards of the pencil, pen, notebook and rubber on different walls in the classroom.
- Say **Let's sing the song *A pencil! A pencil!*** Point to the flashcards and demonstrate what you mean.
- Play the CD (CD 1, track 39 – see Lesson 1). The children sing the song and point to the appropriate flashcard in each verse.
- Choose two different flashcards and sing the karaoke version of the song (CD 1, track 40).
- Repeat the procedure once or twice.

Setting objectives
- Say **Today we're going to listen to and act out episode 2 of the story.**

On the learning trail

Listen and act out the story.
Episode 2: The hungry wolf (PB page 15)

Before the story (books closed)
- Hold up the finger puppets and stick the flashcards of Alex and Katie on the board. Recap on the last episode of the story: **Alex and Katie go to Fairyland. They meet Pip and Squeak. It's Squeak's birthday. Frodo brings a cake. Pip falls in the cake and finds a treasure clue.**
- Ask **Can you remember the clue from Unit 1?** Hold up page 7 of the Pupil's Book and point to the treasure clue sticker.
- Hold up page 5 of the Pupil's Book, point to the picture of Little Red Riding Hood and ask or remind the children of her name.
- Ask **What animal do you think of with Little Red Riding Hood?** and pre-teach the word *wolf*. If the children are not familiar with the story, explain that in this episode of the story there's a wolf.

- Say **Alex, Katie, Pip and Squeak follow the footprints to find Little Red Riding Hood.** Ask the following questions and encourage the children to predict the answers: **1) Where's Little Red Riding Hood going? 2) What does the wolf find? 3) Who does Little Red Riding Hood meet?**

During the story (books open)

- Say **Now listen to the story and find out.** Explain to the children that they will hear a 'beep' noise on the CD to tell them when to move to the next picture in the story.
- Play the CD (CD 1, track 41) and the children follow in their books.
- Ask the questions in turn again and check the answers *(1 school 2 a pencil case, a notebook, 3 the wolf)*
- Say **Listen again and repeat the story.** Play the CD again. Pause after each sentence and the children repeat the story.
- **Note:** There is more story text on the CD than appears on the Pupil's Book page. This additional text is marked with an asterisk* in the audio script below. The children repeat the whole story, including the language which does not appear in their books.

 Follow the footprints, Episode 2: The hungry wolf

Picture 1	
Narrator:	*Alex, Katie, Pip and Squeak follow the footprints to find Little Red Riding Hood.**
Alex:	*Look! It's Little Red Riding Hood!*
Little Red Riding Hood (LRRH):	*I'm ready for school. Goodbye, Mum and Dad.*
Mum and Dad:	*Goodbye, Little Red Riding Hood!**

Picture 2	
Squeak:	*Oh, no! A wolf!*
Wolf:	*What's this? Oh! It's a pencil case.*

Picture 3	
Wolf:	*What's this? Oh! It's a notebook.*

Picture 4	
Wolf:	*Aha. Little Red Riding Hood.**

LRRH:	*Hello, wolf. Can I have my pencil case, please?*
Wolf:	*No. I'm hungry! Grr!*

Picture 5	
LRRH:	*Help!*
Alex and Katie:	*Stop wolf!*

Picture 6	
LRRH:	*Oh, thank you! Here you are.*
Katie and Alex:	*Wow! The next treasure clue. Follow the footprints! Find Pinocchio!*
Pip and Squeak:	*Come on. Let's go! Goodbye, Little Red Riding Hood.**
LRRH:	*Goodbye and good luck!**

After the story

- Ask questions about each picture as follows: **1) Is Little Red Riding Hood going to see her grandma?** (you may have to remind the children of the word *grandma*) *(no)* **Is she going to school?** *(yes)* **Who says goodbye to Little Red Riding Hood?** *(Mum and Dad)* **2) Who's here?** (pointing to the picture) *(the wolf)* **What's this?** (pointing to the pencil case) *(a pencil case)* **3) What's this?** (pointing to the notebook) *(a notebook)* **4) What does Little Red Riding Hood ask the wolf for?** *(her pencil case)* **Does the wolf give it to her?** *(no)* **5) Who helps Little Red Riding Hood?** *(Alex, Katie, Pip and Squeak)* **6) What does Little Red Riding Hood give them?** (pointing to the treasure clue) *(the next treasure clue)*

Put on the treasure clue sticker.

- Say **The treasure clue says *Follow the footprints! Find ...* (*... Pinocchio*).** Elicit the meaning and remind the children of the character of Pinocchio from the Introduction, if necessary.
- Say **Find the treasure clue sticker for Unit 2 and stick it here.** Demonstrate what you mean.
- The children look for the treasure clue sticker for Unit 2 and stick it in their books.

Act out the story.

- Divide the class into six groups and assign a role to each group: Alex, Katie, Pip, Squeak, Little Red Riding Hood or the wolf. Give a finger puppet or character flashcard to one child in each group to hold up during the story.
- Read the story speech bubbles on the Pupil's Book page. Point to or stand by each group and join in

miming and saying their part with them every time their character speaks.

- Repeat the procedure, this time encouraging the groups to say their parts and mime more independently.

- Ask six confident children to come to the front of the class (one from each group). Give the finger puppets and flashcards to the children playing the parts. The children act out a short version of the story to the rest of the class. Prompt them by reading the story if necessary and encourage them to join in saying their parts with you as you do this. Encourage everyone to clap and say e.g. *Fantastic!* at the end.

Option: The children can act out their parts *either* with *or* without their books, depending on how confident and familiar they are with this episode. If you wish to make the activity more challenging, the children can act out the whole story by joining in their character's part as you replay the CD.

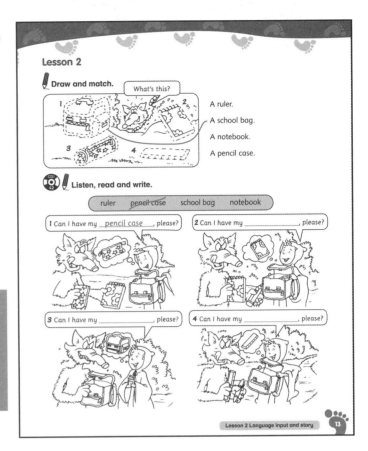

Draw and match. (AB page 13)

- Hold up the Activity Book and point to the pictures. Ask **What's this?** for each picture, using the voice of the wolf. The children identify the objects. Say **Draw the objects and match them to the words.** Draw the children's attention to the example.

- The children work individually and draw round the dashed outlines of the pictures and match them to the words.

- Check the answers.

- Ask individual children to take turns to be the wolf and identify the objects. They say e.g. *What's this? It's a pencil case.*

  Key: 1 a school bag 2 a notebook 3 a pencil case 4 a ruler

Listen, read and write. (AB page 13)

- Read the questions and ask the children to predict what Little Red Riding Hood says in each one.

- Say **Listen to Little Red Riding Hood's questions to the wolf.** Play the CD (CD 1, track 42) while the children follow in their books.

- Say **Now listen and write the words.** Draw the children's attention to the example.

- Play the CD again. Use the pause button to give the children time to write the missing words.

- Check the answers by asking individual children to read the questions.

  Key: 1 pencil case 2 notebook 3 school bag 4 ruler

 Listen, read and write. (AB page 13)

1 Can I have my pencil case, please?
2 Can I have my notebook, please?
3 Can I have my school bag, please?
4 Can I have my ruler, please?

Ending the lesson

Lesson review

- Briefly ask the children what they can do as a result of the lesson (understand and act out *The hungry wolf*). Praise the children for their efforts and / or use the finger puppets to do this.

Goodbye and closing routine

- Say **Let's sing the *Goodbye song.*** Play the karaoke version of the song (CD 1, track 5 – see Lesson 1). Hold up the finger puppets and the children sing and do the actions as in Lesson 1.

2 My classroom

Lesson 3
Communication and grammar

Aim:
- To practise asking and saying what things are

Key language:
- *What's this? / It's a ...*
- *Yes / No*
- *school bag, file, pen, pencil, crayon, rubber, pencil sharpener, pencil case, notebook, ruler*

Materials:
- Pupil's Book pages 15 and 16
- Activity Book pages 14 and 81
- Finger puppets (Pip and Squeak)
- Flashcards: Alex, Katie
- CD 1
- Scissors for each child
- A prepared set of Unit 2 picture cards (AB page 81)

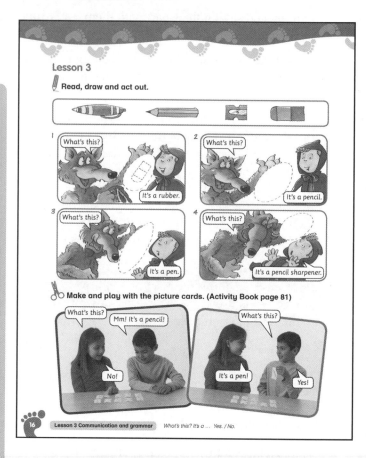

Starting out

Greetings and opening routine

- Greet the children yourself and using the finger puppets.
- *Either* play the karaoke version of the *Hello song* (CD 1, track 3 – see Lesson 1) and the children sing and do the actions as in Lesson 1 *or* play the karaoke version of *A pencil! A pencil!* (CD 1, track 40 – see Lesson 1) and the children sing and hold up a different classroom object in each verse.

Revision activity

- Hold up the finger puppets and stick the character flashcards on the board. Ask **Can you remember who's in the story with Pip, Squeak, Alex and Katie?** *(Little Red Riding Hood, the wolf)*
- Ask the children to open their Pupil's Books at page 15. Briefly reconstruct the story, getting the children to supply key words. Say e.g. **Alex, Katie, Pip and Squeak see ...** *Little Red Riding Hood.* **Little Red Riding Hood is going to ...** *school.* **In Little Red Riding Hood's school bag is a ...** *notebook and a pencil case.* **The wolf sees Little Red Riding Hood's ...** *pencil case and notebook.* **The wolf asks ...** *What's this? It's a ... pencil case. It's a ... notebook.* **Silly wolf! Little Red Riding Hood says** *Can I have my ... pencil case, please?* **The wolf says** *I'm ... hungry.* **Alex and Katie say ...** *Stop, wolf!* **Little Red Riding Hood gives them the next ...** *treasure clue.*

- Play the CD (CD 1, track 41 – see Lesson 2). The children listen and follow the story in their books.

Setting objectives

- Say **Today we're going to practise asking and saying what things are.**

On the learning trail

Read, draw and act out. (PB page 16)

- Say **The wolf is asking Little Red Riding Hood about the things in her pencil case.**
- Draw the children's attention to the pictures at the top of the activity.
- Read the exchanges in turn and the children point to the correct pictures.

- Say **Now draw the pictures.** Draw the children's attention to the example.
- The children work individually and draw the pictures.
- The children compare their answers in pairs.
- Read the question **What's this?** (using the wolf's voice) for each exchange and the children answer (using Little Red Riding Hood's voice).
- Change roles and repeat the procedure.
- Ask a confident child to the front of the class. Demonstrate acting out a short dialogue between the wolf and Little Red Riding Hood using classroom objects, e.g.

    T: **Hello, Little Red Riding Hood.**

    P: *Hello, wolf.*

    T: (taking a pencil out of a pencil case) **What's this?**

    P: *It's a pencil.*

    T: (taking out a rubber) **What's this?**

    P: *It's a rubber.*

    T: **Mmm. I'm hungry.** (pretends to pounce)

    P: *Goodbye, wolf!* (pretends to run away)

- Ask one or two other children to come to the front of the class and act out a similar dialogue using different classroom objects.
- The children act out a dialogue between the wolf and Little Red Riding Hood in pairs.

Make the picture cards. (PB page 16 and AB page 81)

- Hold up your Pupil's Book and point to the pictures. Say **We're going to make the picture cards and play the game.** You can show the children the set you have already made.
- Say **Find page 81 in your Activity Book. Look at the picture cards for Unit 2.** Point to the picture cards in turn. Get individual children to take turns to ask and answer *What's this? / It's a ...* for each one.
- Make sure all the children have got scissors.
- Point to the dashed lines and say **Now cut out the cards like this.** Ask the children to write their names or initials on the back of the cards.
- When the children are ready, say e.g. **Hold up the file! / Hold up the pencil case!** and the children respond by holding up the correct cards.

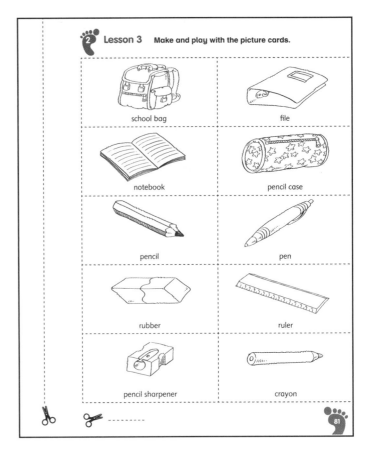

Play with the picture cards. (PB page 16)

- Hold up your Pupil's Book and point to the pictures. Ask two pupils to read the first dialogue and two other pupils to read the second dialogue.
- Use the finger puppets to demonstrate the game. Lay out a set of picture cards face down on your desk. Use Pip to point to one of the cards and ask **What's this?** Use Squeak to pretend to guess the answer, e.g. **Mm ... It's a pencil sharpener!** Turn over the card and hold it up. Use Pip to say **Yes!** if it is a pencil sharpener and **No!** if it isn't a pencil sharpener.
- Ask a few individual children to take turns to come to the front of the class and play the game in the same way.
- Divide the class into pairs. The children take turns to ask their partner three questions about the cards and guess in the same way. At the end, ask the pairs to tell you how many times they guessed correctly.
- If there is time, the children can colour the picture cards.

Read, match and say. (AB page 14)

- Read the sentences and the children point to the pictures.

- The children work individually and match the sentences and pictures.
- Check the answers. Point to the pictures or hold up the picture cards and the children say the sentences.

  Key: Children match the sentences and pictures.
  1 It's a pen. 2 It's a school bag. 3 It's a pencil.
  4 It's a file. 5 It's a notebook. 6 It's a pencil case.

Look and write. (AB page 14)

- Ask **What's this?** (using the wolf's voice) for each picture and the children answer (using Little Red Riding Hood's voice).
- Say **Now write the answers.** Draw the children's attention to the example.
- The children work individually and write the answers.
- Check the answers by asking **What's this?** for each picture.

  Key: 1 rubber 2 pencil 3 ruler 4 crayon

Ending the lesson

Lesson review

- Briefly ask the children what they can do as a result of the lesson (ask and say what things are). Praise the children for their efforts and / or use the finger puppets to do this.

Goodbye and closing routine

- Say goodbye to the children yourself and using the finger puppets. If there is time, you can also play the karaoke version of the *Goodbye song* (CD 1, track 5 – see Lesson 1) and the children sing and do the actions as in Lesson 1.

2 My classroom

Lesson 4
Communication, grammar and pronunciation

Aims:

- To ask for and give things to someone
- To say a tongue-twister with the sound /p/

Key language:

- *Can I have the ..., please?*
- *Yes. Here you are.*
- *Thank you.*
- *school bag, file, pen, pencil, crayon, rubber, pencil sharpener, pencil case, notebook, ruler*

Materials:

- Pupil's Book page 17
- Activity Book page 15
- Finger puppets (Pip and Squeak)
- Flashcards: school bag, file, notebook, pencil case, pencil, pen, rubber, ruler, pencil sharpener, crayon, Frodo
- Unit 2 picture cards from Lesson 3
- CD 1

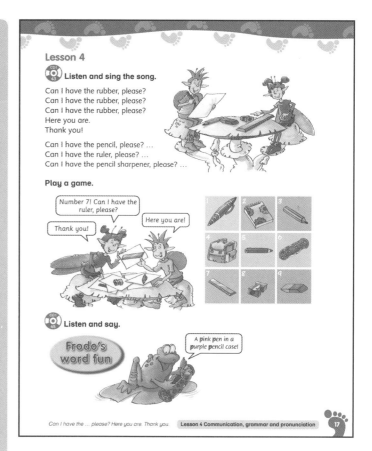

Starting out

Greetings and opening routine

- Greet the children yourself and using the finger puppets.
- *Either* play the karaoke version of the *Hello song* (CD 1, track 3 – see Lesson 1) and the children sing and do the actions as in Lesson 1 *or* play the karaoke version of *A pencil! A pencil!* (CD 1, track 40 – see Lesson 1) and the children sing and hold up a different classroom object in each verse.

Revision activity

- Ask **What's this?** Show the class one of the flashcards very quickly and the children respond, e.g. *It's a pencil case.*
- Repeat with all the flashcards.

Setting objectives

- Say **Today we're going to practise asking for and giving things to someone. We're also going to practise pronunciation.**

On the learning trail

Listen and sing the song. (PB page 17)

- Give out or ask the children to get out the picture cards they made in Lesson 3.
- Ask the children to lay the cards face up on their desks.
- Say **Listen and sing the song. Hold up the pictures to show what Squeak asks for** and demonstrate what you mean. Play the CD (CD 1, track 43). The children sing the song and hold up their picture cards. Pause after each verse to check that the children are holding up the correct cards.

- Hold up the finger puppets and divide the class into two groups: Pip and Squeak. Explain that the groups should take turns to ask the question and respond in each verse. Play the CD again.
- Play the karaoke version (CD 1, track 44) and the children sing the song in the same way naming other objects. Hold up one of the picture cards to show what they should ask for.

 Can I have the rubber, please?

Can I have the rubber, please?
Can I have the rubber, please?
Can I have the rubber, please?
Here you are.
Thank you!

Verse 2: Can I have the pencil, please? ...
Verse 3: Can I have the ruler, please? ...
Verse 4: Can I have the pencil sharpener, please? ...

Play a game. (PB page 17)

- Say the numbers in the grid on the Pupil's Book page in random order and the children ask you for the objects, e.g.

  T: **Number six!**

  P: *Can I have the pencil case, please?*

  T: **Here you are.** (pretend to give something)

  P: *Thank you.*

- Draw a grid on the board with nine numbered squares and stick a Unit 2 flashcard in each square as on the Pupil's Book page. Divide the class into two teams and assign noughts or crosses to each team. Explain and demonstrate that the teams should take turns to choose a number in the grid and ask for the item on the flashcard. If they can do this correctly, you write a nought or a cross in the corresponding square on the board. The first team to make a row of three wins. The row can be horizontal, vertical or diagonal.
- Play once or twice with the whole class in two teams, using the grid and flashcards on the board.
- Divide the class into pairs. The children play with their partner in the same way, lightly drawing noughts or crosses on the squares in the game in their books with a pencil.

Listen and say: Frodo's word fun. (PB page 17)

- Write the letter 'p' on the board and make the sound /p/ as in *paper*, *pencil* and *pen*.
- Get the children to put their hand in front of their mouths and to experiment saying words with /p/ and feeling the breath on their hands.
- Hold up the flashcard of Frodo. Say **Listen to Frodo and say the tongue-twister.** Play the CD (CD 1, track 45).
- Ask pairs of children to say the tongue-twister in turns.
- The children practise saying the tongue-twister with a partner.

 Frodo's word fun. Listen and say.

A pink pen in a purple pencil case!
A pink pen in a purple pencil case!
A pink pen in a purple pencil case!

Listen and circle. (AB page 15)

- Say **Look at the pictures** and ask the children to identify the objects.
- Say **Listen and circle what Pip asks Squeak for in each picture.** Draw the children's attention to the example.
- Play the CD (CD1, track 46). Use the pause button to give the children time to circle the pictures.
- Check the answers by asking the children to say what Pip asks for in each picture.
- Divide the class into two groups (Pip and Squeak). Hold up the finger puppets and play the CD again. The children repeat the exchange for each picture in their groups.
- The children act out the exchanges in pairs.

Key: The following objects should be circled:
1 rubber 2 pencil 3 ruler 4 pen

 Listen and circle.

1 Pip: *Can I have the rubber, please?*
  Squeak: *Here you are.*
  Pip: *Thank you.*

2 Pip: *Can I have the pencil, please?*

Squeak: *Here you are.*
Pip: *Thank you.*

3 Squeak: *Can I have the ruler, please?*
Pip: *Here you are.*
Squeak: *Thank you.*

4 Squeak: *Can I have the pen, please?*
Pip: *Here you are.*
Squeak: *Thank you.*

Read, write and colour. (AB page 15)

- Read the numbers at the start of each exchange and the children identify what Alex asks for in the grid.

- Say **Now write and colour what Alex asks for in the game. Circle the line of three.** Draw the children's attention to the example and demonstrate what you mean by *Circle the line of three,* using the grid on the board.

- The children complete the exchanges and colour the pictures.

- Check the answers by asking different pairs of children to read the exchanges and identify the line of three.

Key: 1 crayon 2 rubber 3 pen

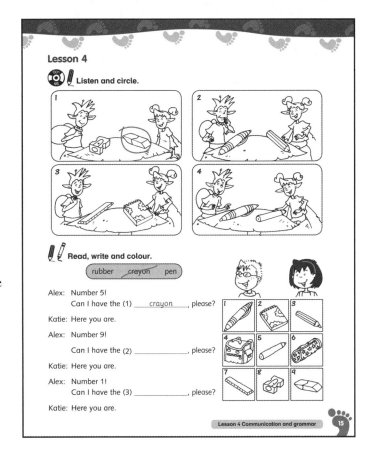

Goodbye and closing routine

- Say goodbye to the children yourself and using the finger puppets. If there is time, you can also play the karaoke version of the *Goodbye song* (CD 1, track 5 – see Lesson 1) and the children sing and do the actions as in Lesson 1.

Ending the lesson

Lesson review

- Briefly ask the children what they can do as a result of the lesson (ask for and give things to someone, say a tongue-twister with /p/). Praise the children for their efforts and / or use the finger puppets to do this.

2 My classroom

Lesson 5
Content input

Aims:

- To understand the difference between plastic and wood
- To identify classroom objects made of plastic and wood

Key language:

- *This is ...*
- *This ... is plastic / wood.*
- *school bag, file, pen, pencil, crayon, rubber, pencil sharpener, pencil case, notebook, ruler, desk, chair*
- *hard, soft, natural, trees*
- colours

Materials:

- Pupil's Book page 18
- Activity Book page 16
- Finger puppets (Pip and Squeak)
- Flashcards: school bag, file, notebook, pencil case, pencil, pen, rubber, ruler, pencil sharpener, crayon
- Word cards: school bag, file, notebook, pencil case, pencil, pen, rubber, ruler, pencil sharpener, crayon
- CD 1
- Classroom objects and / or furniture made of plastic and wood
- Brown and red crayons

Starting out

Greetings and opening routine

- Greet the children yourself and using the finger puppets.
- *Either* play the karaoke version of the *Hello song* (CD 1, track 3 – see Lesson 1) and the children sing and do the actions as in Lesson 1 *or* hold up flashcards, play the karaoke version of *Can I have the rubber, please?* (CD 1, track 44 – see Lesson 4) and the children sing two or three verses of the song in two groups as in Lesson 4.

Revision activity

- Play a memory game on the board with the flashcards and word cards. Divide the class into two teams.
- Stick the flashcards face down in jumbled order on one side of the board and the word cards face down in jumbled order on the other.
- Ask a child from one team to choose a card from one side of the board. Turn it over and the child names the picture or reads the word. Ask another child from the same team to choose a card from the other side of the board and name the picture or read the word in the same way. If the two cards match, get the second child to ask *Can I have the ..., please?* Say **Here you are**, take the cards off the board and pretend to give them to the team.
- Repeat the procedure with the other team.
- Continue playing the game until there are no cards left on the board. The team with most cards at the end of the game wins.

Setting objectives

- Hold up or point to different objects and / or furniture in the classroom made of plastic and wood. Say **This is plastic. And this is wood.** Check the children understand the meaning of both words.
- Hold up the finger puppets. Say **Let's learn about the world around you! Today we're going to read about the difference between plastic and wood and name classroom objects made of plastic and wood.** Use L1 to clarify what you mean, if necessary.

On the learning trail

Read, circle and listen. (PB page 18)

- (Books closed) Say **What's the difference between wood and plastic?**
- Hold up two objects to compare, e.g. a pencil case (soft plastic) and a ruler (wood). Ask the children to name the objects and say which one is plastic and which one is wood.

- Ask the children what they think the differences are between plastic and wood and listen to their ideas (in L1). Use their suggestions to introduce vocabulary, e.g. *natural*, *trees*, *hard*, *soft*. Use objects around the classroom to help their understanding.

- Ask the children to open their Pupil's Books at page 18. Read the text at the start of the activity or play part 1 on the CD (CD 1, track 47). Use the photos to reinforce the meaning of *natural* and *trees*, and classroom objects to demonstrate the difference between *hard* and *soft*.

- Say **Look at photos 1 – 4 and read the sentences. Circle** *plastic* **if you think the object is plastic, or** *wood* **if you think the object is wood.** Draw the children's attention to the example.

- The children work individually and read and circle the words.

- Ask questions about the photos in turn, e.g. **Is the pencil case plastic, do you think?** *Yes, it is.* **Why? Is it soft or hard? Is the chair wood, do you think?** *Yes, it is.* **Why? Is it soft or hard?** Listen to the children's ideas but don't tell them the answers yet.

- Say **Now listen and find out.** Play the CD (CD 1, track 47). Use the pause button to allow the children time to compare their answers with the CD.

- Check the answers by asking individual children to read the sentences with the correct options.

- Play the CD again as a final check.

  Key: 1 plastic 2 wood 3 wood 4 plastic

 Read, circle and listen.

Part 1

Wood is from trees. Wood is natural. Wood is brown. Wood is hard.

Plastic is not natural. Plastic is different colours. Plastic is hard or soft.

Part 2

1 This pencil case is plastic.
2 This chair is wood.
3 This pencil is wood.
4 This ruler is plastic.

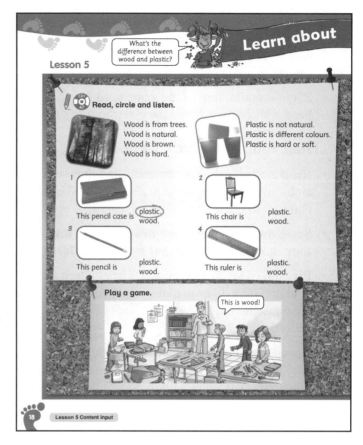

- Ask the children what other things we use wood and plastic for in our daily lives, e.g. for furniture, to keep food in, for toys. Make the point that both plastic and wood are very useful materials.

- Tell the children that there is another important difference between plastic and wood and ask if they know what this is. Use L1 to explain that if wood is thrown away, it rots down into the soil whereas plastic does not (in other words, wood is biodegradable and most plastic is not). Point out that for this reason we need to be very careful about how we throw plastic away as it spoils the environment.

Play a game. (PB page 18)

- Ask a few individual children to take turns to stand up and identify different things in the classroom which are wood or plastic, such as their chair, desk, the door, shelves, crayon tray, etc. Encourage them to say e.g. *This desk is wood* or *This is plastic* (if they don't know the word for the object) as they do this, and ask the rest of the class if they agree.

- Say **Stand up!** Explain that the children should walk slowly round the classroom in a clockwise direction. When you say **Touch wood!** or **Touch plastic!** they should touch or hold up something that is wood or plastic, depending on what you say, as fast as they can, and then freeze in position.

Choose three children to report back, e.g. *This chair is wood* or simply *This is wood* if they don't know the word, before the whole class can 'unfreeze' and continue the game in the same way.

- Play several rounds of the game until the children have walked once round the classroom.

Listen, read and match. (AB page 16)

- Read the two example sentences and draw the children's attention to the joining lines. Ask the children to predict the other sentences.
- Say **Now listen, read and draw lines to make four more sentences about wood and plastic.**
- Play the CD (CD 1, track 48). The children listen, read and draw lines to make sentences. Use the pause button to give them time to do this if necessary.
- Check the answers by asking individual children to read the sentences they have made. If you like, play the CD again as a final check.

Key: Wood is hard. Wood is brown. Wood is natural. Plastic is hard or soft. Plastic is different colours. Plastic is not natural.

 Listen, read and match.

Wood is hard. Plastic is hard or soft.
Wood is brown. Plastic is different colours.
Wood is natural. Plastic is not natural.

Listen, colour and write. (AB page 16)

- Make sure the children have brown and red crayons available.
- Draw the children's attention to the key at the top of the activity. Say **Listen and colour the pictures. Colour brown the things that are wood. Colour red the things that are plastic.**
- Play the CD (CD 1, track 49) once. Use the pause button. The children listen and colour the pictures red or brown.
- The children complete the sentences following the colour key. Play the CD again if necessary.
- Check the answers by asking individual children to tell you about each picture, e.g. *This pen is plastic.*

Key: 1 plastic (red) 2 wood (brown) 3 wood (brown) 4 plastic (red)

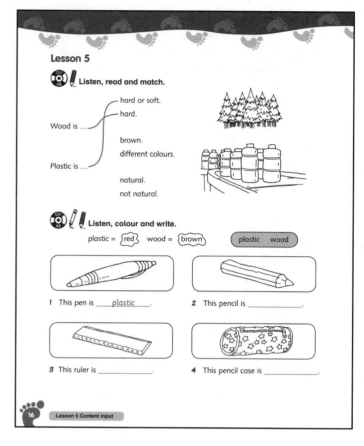

 Listen, colour and write.

1 This pen is plastic.
2 This pencil is wood.
3 This ruler is wood.
4 This pencil case is plastic.

Ending the lesson

Lesson review

- Briefly ask the children what they can do as a result of the lesson (identify classroom objects made of wood and plastic). Praise the children for their efforts and / or use the finger puppets to do this.

Goodbye and closing routine

- Say goodbye to the children yourself and using the finger puppets. If there is time, you can also play the karaoke version of the *Goodbye song* (CD 1, track 5 – see Lesson 1) and the children sing and do the actions as in Lesson 1.

2 My classroom

Lesson 6
Content and personalisation

Aim:
- To describe and classify your classroom objects

Key language:
- *What's this? / It's a ...*
- *It's plastic / wood.*
- *My ... is plastic / wood.*
- *Me, too!*
- *school bag, file, pen, pencil, crayon, rubber, pencil sharpener, pencil case, notebook, ruler, desk, chair*
- colours

Materials:
- Pupil's Book page 19
- Activity Book page 17
- Finger puppets (Pip and Squeak)
- Blindfolds (optional)

Starting out

Greetings and opening routine

- Greet the children using the finger puppets.
- *Either* play the karaoke version of the *Hello song* (CD 1, track 3 – see Lesson 1) and the children sing and do the actions as in Lesson 1 *or* play the karaoke version of *Can I have the rubber, please?* (CD 1, track 44 – see Lesson 4) and the children sing in two groups as previously.

Revision activity

- Use one of the finger puppets to point to or hold up a plastic or wooden object in the classroom. Say a true or false sentence about the object, e.g. **The chair is wood / plastic.** Explain and demonstrate that the children should repeat the sentence if it's true or fold their arms and stay silent if it isn't.
- Repeat several times naming different objects.
- If you like, you can also ask individual children to say a true / false sentence and the rest of the class listen and respond in the same way.

Setting objectives

- Say **In this lesson we're going to describe and classify our own classroom objects.** Use L1 to clarify what you mean.

On the learning trail

Play a game. (PB page 19)

- Ask a child to come to the front of the class. Either blindfold them or get them to stand facing away from you with their hands behind their back.
- Give the child a classroom object made of wood or plastic to feel but not look at. Ask **What's this?** Explain that the child should name the object and say if it's plastic or wood, e.g. *It's a pencil. It's wood.*
- Repeat the game once or twice with different children and objects.
- Ask a child to take over your role and repeat the game again once or twice.
- Divide the class into pairs. Either use blindfolds, if you have these, or ask one child in each pair to sit facing away from their partner and with their hands behind their back. The other child gives

their partner an object from their pencil case to feel and asks *What's this?* as previously. Once the child has guessed the object and the material (if it's plastic or wood), they change roles.

Draw and say. (PB page 19)

- Pretend to look in your pencil case or hold up objects on your desk. Say e.g. **Look. My pen is plastic. / My pencil is wood.**

- Hold up the Pupil's Book, point to the frames and say **Draw two of your things which are plastic here. Draw two of your things which are wood here.**

- The children work individually and draw their pictures.

- Ask individual children to take turns to show and tell the class, e.g. *My ruler is plastic*.

Look, write and say. (AB page 17)

- Draw the children's attention to the pictures and words on the left and right.

- Say **Write about your things** and draw the children's attention to the example.

- The children work individually and complete the sentences with words that are true for them.

- Invite individual children to take turns to tell the class, e.g. *My pen is plastic.* If another child has the same sentence, explain that they should say *Me, too!* and have the next turn.

Look, choose and write. (AB page 17)

- Use different classroom objects to elicit or remind the children of words for colours, e.g. *blue*, *red*, *green*, *brown* and *black*, and write these on the board.

- Hold up different objects and say e.g. **a red pencil / brown ruler**. The children repeat the object and colour each time.

- Hold up other objects and elicit similar descriptions from the children.

- Read the headings on the page and draw the children's attention to the examples.

- Ask the children to choose three things from their school bags and pencil cases to go in each column and to write the colours and words. Give them time to do this and be ready to help if necessary.

- Once they are ready, ask individual children to show and talk about the things they have chosen to go in each column.

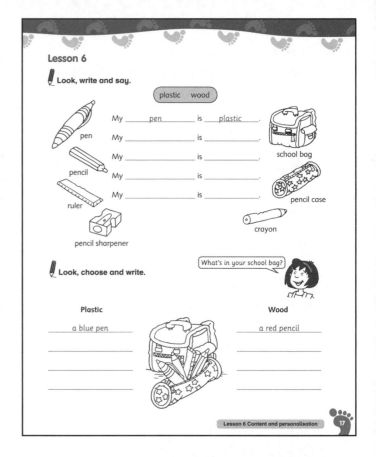

Ending the lesson

Lesson review

- Briefly ask the children what they can do as a result of the lesson (say if their own classroom objects are wood or plastic). Praise the children for their efforts and / or use the finger puppets to do this.

Goodbye and closing routine

- Say goodbye to the children yourself and using the finger puppets. If there is time, you can also play the karaoke version of the *Goodbye song* (CD 1, track 5 – see Lesson 1) and the children sing and do the actions as in Lesson 1.

2 My classroom

Lesson 7
Children's culture

Aim:
- To learn a rhyme and play a traditional children's game

Key language:
- *Please come in.*
- *Close the door.*
- *Sorry I'm late.*
- *paper, stone, scissors*
- numbers 1–8

Materials:
- Pupil's Book page 20
- Activity Book page 18
- Finger puppets (Pip and Squeak)
- Flashcard: Frodo
- CD 1
- Paper, scissors, a stone (optional)

Setting objectives

- Hold up the flashcard of Frodo. Say **In this lesson we're going to learn a traditional rhyme and play a traditional game.**

Starting out

Greetings and opening routine

- Greet the children yourself and using the finger puppets.
- *Either* play the karaoke version of the *Hello song* (CD 1, track 3 – see Lesson 1) and the children sing and do the actions as in Lesson 1 *or* play the karaoke version of *A pencil! A pencil!* (CD 1, track 44 – see Lesson 1) and the children sing and hold up a different classroom object in each verse.

Revision activity

- Play a chain game. Say e.g. **My pen is blue.** Explain and demonstrate that the next person has to say a sentence that either includes the word *blue*, e.g. *My pencil case is blue*, or includes the word *pen*, e.g. *My pen is plastic*.
- Continue in the same way until all or most children have contributed a sentence to the 'chain'.

On the learning trail

Listen and act out the rhyme. (PB page 20) (books closed)

- Say **This is a rhyme about Alex, who arrives late in the classroom.** Use mime, e.g. tapping your watch, to convey the meaning of *late* and check the children understand.
- Ask **What numbers do you hear in the rhyme?** and give examples, e.g. **one, two**.
- Play the CD (CD 1, track 50). Ask the question again and check the answer. *(one, two, three, four, five, six, seven, eight)*
- Ask the pupils to open their Pupil's Book at page 20. Say **Look at the pictures.** Point to Alex and the teacher and ask **Who's this?** *(Alex)* **Who's this?** *(the teacher)*
- Play the CD again. The children follow in their books and join in saying the rhyme. Check they understand the meaning of lines 2 and 4.

- Choose a child to go to the door. Play the CD again. The other children say and act out the rhyme. Encourage the child to say *Sorry I'm late* at the end.

- Repeat once or twice with different children, either with or without the CD. Play the karaoke version of the song on the CD (CD 1, track 51).

 One, two, three, four

One, two, three, four
Please come in and close the door
Five, six, seven, eight
Hurry now. You're very late!

 Citizenship box: Remember!

Say **Look at the picture. Alex is late to class** and tap your watch to convey meaning.

Hold up the flashcard of Frodo, read Frodo's *Remember!* note and check understanding. Use L1 to explain that it's polite to say *Sorry* if you arrive late to class, even if it isn't your fault.

Say **Sorry I'm late** and get the children to practise repeating this a few times.

Option: From now on, actively encourage the children to say *Sorry I'm late* whenever appropriate.

Play *Paper, stone, scissors!* (PB page 20)

- Say **Let's play a game that English children play!** Explain that the children may also be familiar with the game in their own culture.

- Pre-teach the words and actions for the game: for *scissors*, make a cutting action with your index and third finger; for *paper*, hold out your hand flat; for *stone*, make your hand into a fist.

- Say the words in turn several times. Get the children to repeat the word you say and do the action.

- Ask a child to come to the front of the class to demonstrate the game with you. Hold out your right fist, move it up and down three times as you say rhythmically **One, two, three ...** and get the child to do the same. After you say **three**, choose one of the objects (paper, scissors or stone), say the word and do the action, e.g. **... scissors** (make a cutting action with your fingers). Get the child to also choose one of the objects simultaneously and do the action whilst saying the word, e.g. *stone* (make hand into a fist).

- Use L1 and mime to explain that you or the child wins depending on the objects you both choose, as follows:

  scissors – wins with paper because you can cut it; loses with stone because a stone can blunt scissors

  paper – wins with stone because you can wrap it up; loses with scissors because scissors can cut it

  stone – wins with scissors because a stone can blunt scissors; loses with paper because paper can wrap up a stone.

- Invite children to take turns to come to the front of the class and play the game with you. The rest of the class watches and names the winning object each time.

- Divide the class into pairs. The children play the game three times with their partner.

Write, listen and say. (AB page 18)

- Say **Write the missing numbers in the rhyme.** Draw the children's attention to the example.

- The children work individually and write the missing numbers.

- Say **Listen to the rhyme and check your answers.** Play the CD (CD 1, track 52). Use the pause button to check that the children have written the numbers correctly.

- The children say the rhyme once or twice. If you like, you can also ask one child to pretend to be late and say *Sorry I'm late* each time.

Option: From now on, if appropriate, you may like to get the children to say this rhyme (in a light-hearted, fun way) whenever a child arrives late for class.

Key: two, four, five, seven

Write, listen and say.

One, two, three, four
Please come in and close the door
Five, six, seven, eight
Hurry now. You're very late!

Look and write. (AB page 18)

- Ask the children to look at the pictures and write the object that wins in each turn of the game. Draw their attention to the example.
- The children work individually and write the words.
- Check the answers. If there is time, the children can play a few more rounds of the game in pairs.

Key: 1 scissors 2 paper 3 stone

Ending the lesson

Lesson review

- Briefly ask the children what they can do as a result of the lesson (say and act out the rhyme *One, two, three, four*, say *Sorry I'm late*, play *Paper, stone, scissors!*). Praise the children for their efforts and / or use the finger puppets to do this.

Goodbye and closing routine

- Say goodbye to the children yourself and using the finger puppets. If there is time, you can also play the karaoke version of the *Goodbye song* (CD 1, track 5 – see Lesson 1) and the children sing and do the actions as in Lesson 1.

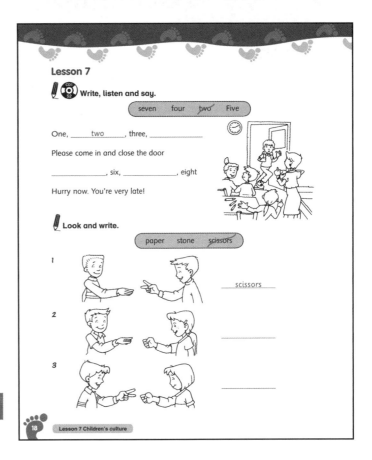

2 My classroom

Lesson 8
Unit review / *All About Me* Portfolio Booklet

Aim:
- To review learning in Unit 2

Key language:
- *What's this? / It's a ...*
- *Can I have the ..., please?*
- *Here you are. / Thank you.*
- *The ... is plastic / wood.*
- *school bag, pen, pencil, crayon, rubber, pencil sharpener, pencil case, notebook, ruler*

Materials:
- Pupil's Book page 21
- Activity Book page 19
- *All About Me* Portfolio Booklet pages 8 and 9
- Finger puppets (Pip and Squeak)
- Flashcards: school bag, file, notebook, pencil case, pencil, pen, rubber, ruler, pencil sharpener, crayon, Frodo
- Stickers for Unit 2
- CD 1

Starting out

Greetings and opening routine
- Greet the children (but without using the finger puppets).
- *Either* play the karaoke version of the *Hello song* (CD 1, track 3 – see Lesson 1) and the children sing and do the actions as in Lesson 1 *or* play the karaoke version of *Can I have the rubber, please?* (CD 1, track 44 – see Lesson 4), hold up a different flashcard for each verse and the children sing in two groups as in Lesson 4.

Revision activity
- Hold up the Pip finger puppet by the door and say **Oh, dear. Pip is very late today. Can you remember the rhyme?**
- Play the CD (CD 1, track 52 – see Lesson 7). The children say the rhyme to the puppet as you bring him into the classroom and close the door.
- Repeat with the Squeak puppet. Play the CD (CD 1, track 52) again.

Setting objectives
- Say **Today we're going to review what we've learnt in Unit 2.**

On the learning trail

Listen and put on the stickers. Write the words. (PB page 21)
- Make sure the children have the stickers for Unit 2 ready.
- Say **Listen and put on the stickers.** Draw the children's attention to the example.
- Play the CD (CD 1, track 53). Use the pause button to give the children time to put on the stickers.
- Say **Now write the words.** Draw the children's attention to the example.
- Check their answers by saying the numbers and getting the children to say the words.

Key: 1 pencil case 2 school bag 3 notebook 4 file 5 rubber 6 ruler 7 crayon 8 pencil 9 pen 10 pencil sharpener

Listen and put on the stickers.

1 What's this? It's a pencil case.
2 What's this? It's a school bag.
3 What's this? It's a notebook.
4 What's this? It's a file.
5 Can I have the rubber, please? Here you are. Thank you.
6 Can I have the ruler please? Here you are. Thank you.
7 Can I have the crayon, please? Here you are. Thank you.
8 The pencil is wood.
9 The pen is plastic.
10 The pencil sharpener is plastic.

Listen, read and match. (PB page 21)

- Read the first line of each exchange and ask the children to predict and find the response.
- Say **Now listen, read and match the questions and answers.** Draw the children's attention to the example.
- Play the CD (CD 1, track 54). The children work individually and match the questions and answers. Use the pause button to give them time to do this if necessary.
- Check the answers by asking individual children to read the exchanges.
- Play the CD again as a final check.
- The children read the exchanges in pairs.

  Key: 1 Yes! Here you are. 2 It's a school bag.
  3 It's a chair. It's wood. 4 It's a ruler. It's plastic.
  5 Yes! Here you are.

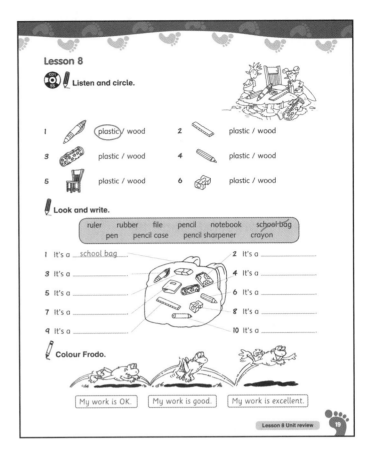

 Listen, read and match.

1 Can I have the rubber, please. Yes! Here you are.
2 What's this? It's a school bag.
3 What's this? It's a chair. It's wood.
4 What's this? It's a ruler. It's plastic.
5 Can I have the pencil case, please? Yes! Here you are.

Listen and circle. (AB page 19)

- Hold up the finger puppets. Say **Pip is telling Squeak about the objects. Listen and circle if they're plastic or wood.** Draw the children's attention to the example.
- Play the CD (CD 1, track 55). Pause, if necessary, to give the children time to circle the words.
- Check the answers by saying e.g. **The pen is …** and the children complete the sentences.

  Key: 1 plastic 2 wood 3 plastic 4 wood 5 wood
  6 plastic

Listen and circle.

1. The pen is plastic.
2. The ruler is wood.
3. The pencil case is plastic.
4. The pencil is wood.
5. The chair is wood.
6. The pencil sharpener is plastic.

Look and write. (AB page 19)

- Say **Look at the things in the school bag and write the answers.** Demonstrate what you mean and draw the children's attention to the example.

- The children work individually. They look at the objects, find the right word(s) in the box and write the answers.

- In pairs, the children take turns to point to their completed pictures and ask *What's this? / It's a …*

- Check the answers by asking individual children questions in the same way.

Key: 1 school bag 2 notebook 3 pen 4 pencil case 5 rubber 6 pencil 7 file 8 pencil sharpener 9 ruler 10 crayon

Colour Frodo. (AB page 19)

- Hold up the flashcard of Frodo. Remind the children that in this activity they assess their work in the unit by choosing and colouring the picture of Frodo which corresponds best to how they think they have done.

- Explain the key by pointing to the three pictures of Frodo and saying **Colour this picture if your work is OK but you think you need to try harder or need more practice. Colour this picture of Frodo if you think your work is good. Colour this picture of Frodo with a big smile and jumping very high if you think your work is excellent.** Make sure the children understand that there are no right answers and that it is their own opinion of the work they have done which is important. Be ready to encourage the children to have a positive view if they are too hard on themselves.

Ending the lesson

Lesson review

- Briefly ask the children what they can do as a result of the lesson (use the language and vocabulary they've learnt in Unit 2). Praise the children for their efforts and / or use the finger puppets to do this.

Goodbye and closing routine

- Say goodbye to the children yourself and using the finger puppets. If there is time, you can also play the karaoke version of the *Goodbye song* (CD 1, track 5 – see Lesson 1) and the children sing and do the actions as in Lesson 1.

All About Me Portfolio Booklet

The children complete Unit 2 of their personal *All About Me* Portfolio Booklets. They complete their learning journey by colouring the sections on the path to show what they can do. If you like, the children can also sign this page and you can endorse this by adding your own signature and the date.

3 My body

Structures and grammar

- *This is my ... / These are my ...*
- *eye / eyes*
- *I brush / wash / have ...*
- *We ...*
- *Our ...*
- Recycled: *I'm ..., Are you ...?, Yes, I am / No, I'm not, my / your*

Vocabulary

- Core: *head, ears, eyes, nose, mouth, chin, arms, legs, fingers, toes*
- Other: *happy, sad, tired, scared*
- Content / culture: *germs, hands, teeth, hair, shower, every day / week, before / after meals*
- Recycled: *please, hungry,* numbers 1–10

Main receptive language

- *noise, lie, tiny, everywhere, ill, body, strong, fight, germs*

Communicative competence

Understanding

Listening:
- Can recognise words for parts of the body
- Can understand words for feelings
- Can understand the episode of the story
- Can understand statements about parts of the body
- Can recognise singular and (regular) plural words
- Can understand some personal daily routines

Reading:
- Can recognise words for parts of the body
- Can read statements about feelings and parts of the body
- Can recognise singular and plural words
- Can read sentences about germs and personal daily routines

Speaking

Spoken interaction:
- Can ask about and respond to questions about feelings
- Can respond to a question about personal daily routines

Spoken production:
- Can sing the *Hello song*
- Can name parts of the body
- Can say the rap *One head*
- Can say sentences to describe parts of the body
- Can sing the song *These are my eyes*
- Can sing the song *This is the way*
- Can say sentences to describe some personal daily routines
- Can say singular and (regular) plural words
- Can sing the *Goodbye song*

Writing

- Can copy and write words for parts of the body
- Can complete short sentences with singular or plural words

Content links

- *Social sciences:* germs and personal hygiene

Learning strategies and thinking skills

- Recognising learning objectives
- Following simple instructions
- Associating vocabulary with touch
- Relating parts to the whole
- Associating sounds with meaning
- Using mime and gesture
- Reflecting on learning

Children's culture

- Singing a song: *This is the way ...*
- Playing a dice game: *Body dice!*

Pronunciation

- Recognising and saying (regular) plural words

Values and attitudes

- Interest in being able to name parts of the body in English
- Awareness of the importance of personal hygiene
- Awareness of the importance of washing your hands

3 My body

Lesson 1
Vocabulary presentation

Aim:
- To name parts of the body

Key language:
- *head, mouth, nose, ears, eyes, chin, arms, legs, fingers, toes*

Materials:
- Pupil's Book page 22
- Activity Book page 20
- Finger puppets (Pip and Squeak)
- Flashcards: head, mouth, nose, ears, eyes, chin, arms, legs, fingers, toes, Frodo
- Word cards: head, mouth, nose, ears, eyes, chin, arms, legs, fingers, toes
- CD 1

Starting out

Greetings and opening routine

- Greet the children yourself and using the finger puppets. Say e.g. **Hello, children. Hello … How are you today?** *Fine, thank you.* Ask a few individual children to greet the puppets in turn.

- Say **Let's sing the *Hello song*.** Play the CD (CD 1, track 2). Hold up the puppets on your index fingers. Move them as the children sing and do the actions.

 Hello song

Hello.	(wave)
Hello.	(wave)
How are you today?	(put arms out)
I'm fine, thank you.	(move from side to side)
And I'm OK!	(raise arms in the air)

Setting objectives

- Say **Today we're going to learn how to name parts of the body and we're going to say a rap.** Click your fingers to suggest the rhythm of a rap and / or use L1 to clarify what you mean.

On the learning trail

Vocabulary presentation (books closed)

- Point to different parts of your body in turn and say the words, e.g. **head, eyes.**

- Repeat, getting the children to do the actions and repeat the words with you.

- Hold up the flashcards in turn. The children point to the parts of their bodies in each picture and say the words with you in chorus.

- Stick the flashcards on the board.

- Divide the class in half. Hold up the Pip finger puppet and say to one half **Say the words with Pip.** Use the puppet to point to the flashcards in turn and the children say the words with you. Make the puppet fly around to praise the children.

- Repeat the procedure with the Squeak puppet and the other half of the class.

Follow the footprints. (PB page 22) (books open)

- Hold up the flashcard of Frodo. Say **Listen and follow the footprints with Frodo the frog. Use your finger** and demonstrate this.

- Play the CD (CD 1, track 56). The children listen and follow the footprints with their fingers. They stop by each picture as they hear the word and repeat the word.

- Say **Now listen and draw a line following the footprints** and demonstrate this. Play the CD again. The children draw a line, stop by each picture and repeat the words as previously.

Follow the footprints.

head ... mouth ... nose ... ears ... eyes ... chin ... arms ... legs ... fingers ... toes

- Stick the word cards on the board in jumbled order (at the children's height and away from the flashcards).

- Point to one word card, e.g. *mouth*, and read the word. Say **Look for the picture of the mouth.** Give the children time to do this.

- Ask a child to come to the front of the class and stick the word card for *mouth* by the corresponding flashcard. Ask the rest of the class **Is this right?** and get them to say the word.

- Repeat the procedure with the rest of the word cards.
- Take the flashcards and word cards off the board.

Listen and say the rap. (PB page 22)

- Say **Look at the picture.** Ask **Who's this?** and the children identify Pip and Squeak.
- Say **Listen to the rap. Point to the parts of the body on Squeak.** Play the CD (CD 1, track 57). The children listen to the rap and point to the parts of the body on Squeak.
- **Note:** For *legs* and *toes,* they will have to point to their own legs and toes.
- Ask the children to stand up. Say **Touch or wave the parts of your body** and demonstrate what you mean (e.g. touch your nose, wave your arms).
- Play the CD again. The children do the actions and say the rap.

 One head

One head, one mouth
One nose, one chin
Two ears, two eyes
Two arms, two legs
Ten fingers and ten toes!

Look, draw and say. (PB page 22)

- Ask the children to look at Pip and to name the missing parts of the body. Say **Draw the missing parts of the body.** Draw the children's attention to the example (*hand*).
- Ask individual children to point to and name the parts of the body they have drawn and how many there are of these parts.
- Draw the children's attention to the singular form *ear, eye, arm* and *leg,* and the plural form *ears, eyes, arms* and *legs*.

  Key: one nose, two eyes, two ears, one mouth, two arms, ten fingers, two legs, ten toes

Look, match and say. (AB page 20)

- Say e.g. **One …** and the children respond by naming the parts of the body which they have one of, i.e. *… head, mouth, nose*.
- Repeat with the numbers **two** and **ten**.

- Say **Match the parts of the body and the numbers.** Draw the children's attention to the example.
- The children work individually and match the parts of the body and the numbers.
- Check the answers by asking individual children to say e.g. *One head, two eyes*.

  Key: 1: head, mouth, nose, chin; 2: eyes, ears, arms, legs; 10: fingers, toes

Look and write. (AB page 20)

- Read the words at the top of the activity. The children point to the parts of the body on the picture as you do this.
- Say **Now write the words.** Draw their attention to the example.
- The children work individually and write the words.
- Check the answers by saying e.g. **Number one is …** and the children point to the parts of the body in the picture and say the words.

  Key: 1 head 2 ears 3 eyes 4 nose 5 mouth 6 chin 7 arms 8 fingers 9 legs 10 toes

Ending the lesson

Lesson review

- Briefly ask the children what they can do as a result of the lesson (name parts of the body, say the rap *One head*). Praise the children for their efforts and / or use the finger puppets to do this.

Goodbye and closing routine

- Say **Let's sing the *Goodbye song*.** Play the CD (CD 1, track 4). Hold up the finger puppets on your index fingers as the children sing and do the actions.

 Goodbye song

Goodbye, goodbye	(wave)
See you another day!	(make marching movements with arms)
Goodbye, goodbye	(wave)
See you soon! Hurray!	
	(wave both hands in the air)

- Say goodbye to the children yourself and using the finger puppets. Say e.g. **Goodbye everyone. See you on …** Ask a few individual children to say goodbye to the finger puppets in turn.

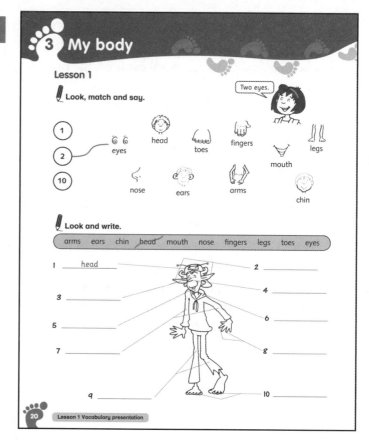

3 My body

Lesson 2
Language input and story

Aim:
- To understand and act out episode 3 of the story

Key language:
- *This is my ... / These are my ...*
- *head, mouth, nose, chin, ears, eyes, arms, legs, fingers, toes*
- *I'm tired / hungry / scared / sad / happy.*

Materials:
- Pupil's Book page 23
- Activity Book page 21
- Finger puppets (Pip and Squeak)
- Flashcards: Alex, Katie, head, mouth, nose, chin, ears, eyes, arms, legs, fingers, toes
- Treasure clue sticker for Unit 3
- CD 1

Starting out

Greetings and opening routine

- Greet the children yourself and using the finger puppets.
- Play the karaoke version of the *Hello song* (CD 1, track 3 – see Lesson 1). The children sing and do the actions as in Lesson 1.

Revision activity

- Hold up the body flashcards in turn and the children say the words.
- Stick the flashcards on the board in the order of the rap *One head* (head, mouth, nose, chin, ears, eyes, arms, legs, fingers, toes).
- Say **Let's say the rap *One head*. Point to the flashcards** and demonstrate what you mean.
- Play the CD (CD 1, track 57 – see Lesson 1). The children say the rap and point to the flashcards.
- Repeat with the karaoke version (CD 1, track 58).

Setting objectives

- Say **Today we're going to listen to and act out episode 3 of the story.**

On the learning trail

Listen and act out the story.
Episode 3: The long nose (PB page 23)

Before the story (books closed)

- Hold up the finger puppets and stick the flashcards of Alex and Katie on the board. Recap on the last episode of the story using mime and gesture and / or L1 as necessary: **Alex, Katie, Pip and Squeak see Little Red Riding Hood going to school. They see a wolf. The wolf finds Little Red Riding Hood's pencil case and notebook. The wolf wants to eat Little Red Riding Hood. Alex, Katie, Pip and Squeak stop the wolf. Little Red Riding Hood gives them the next treasure clue.**

- Ask **Can you remember the clue from Unit 2?** Hold up page 15 of the Pupil's Book and point to the treasure clue sticker. Read *Follow the footprints! Find Pinocchio!* as a prompt if necessary.

- Hold up page 5 of the Pupil's Book, point to the picture of Pinocchio and ask or remind the children of his name.

- Explain that Katie, Alex, Pip and Squeak are looking for Pinocchio. Ask the following questions in turn. Use mime and gesture to clarify meaning and encourage the children to predict the

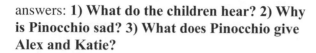

answers: **1) What do the children hear? 2) Why is Pinocchio sad? 3) What does Pinocchio give Alex and Katie?**

During the story (books open)

- Say **Now listen to the story and find out.** Explain to the children that they will hear a 'beep' noise on the CD to tell them when to move to the next picture in the story.

- Play the CD (CD 1, track 59) and the children follow in their books.

- Ask the questions in turn again and check the answers, using mime and gesture to clarify meaning. Recast them in English as necessary. *(1 a noise 2 He hasn't got arms, legs or a nose. 3 the (next) treasure clue)*

- Say **Listen again and repeat the story.** Play the CD again. Pause after each sentence and the children repeat the story.

- **Note:** There is more story text on the CD than appears on the Pupil's Book page. This additional text is marked with an asterisk* in the audio script below. The children repeat the whole story, including the language which does not appear in their books.

 Follow the footprints, Episode 3: The long nose

Picture 1	
Narrator:	*Alex, Katie, Pip and Squeak follow the footprints to find Pinocchio.**
Pip:	*Where's Pinocchio?*
Katie:	*I'm tired!*
Alex:	*I'm hungry!*

Picture 2	
Katie:	*Listen! What's the noise?*
Pip:	*I'm scared!*
Squeak:	*Me, too!*

Picture 3	
Katie:	*Look! It's Pinocchio!*
Pinocchio:	*No arms, no legs, no nose. I'm sad!*
Man:	*Wait, Pinocchio! Be patient!*

Picture 4	
Man:	*Here are your arms, your legs, and your nose. Oh, yes! And the treasure clue!*

Picture 5	
Pinocchio:	*Hello. Look! This is my nose. And these are my arms and my legs. I'm happy now!*

Picture 6	
Squeak:	*Is this the treasure clue?*
Pinocchio:	*No!*

Picture 7	
Man:	*Yes, it is. Don't tell lies, Pinocchio! Be a good boy!*
Pinocchio:	*Sorry! Here you are.*
Squeak:	*Follow the footprints! Find Jack and the beanstalk!*
All:	*Oh, thank you! Goodbye!*

After the story

- Ask questions about each picture as follows: **1) Who's tired?** (use mime to convey meaning) *(Katie)* **Who's hungry?** *(Alex)* **2) Who's scared?** *(Pip and Squeak)* **What do the children hear?** *(a noise)* **3) Is Pinocchio sad?** *(yes)* **4) What does the man give Pinocchio?** (recast the children's answers) *(his arms, legs and nose, and the treasure clue)* **5) Is Pinocchio happy now?** *(yes)* **6) Is Pinocchio's nose long or short?** *(long)* **Why?** *(because he tells a lie)* **7) What does he give Alex, Katie, Pip and Squeak? The next …** *(treasure clue).*

Put on the treasure clue sticker.

- Say **The treasure clue says *Follow the footprints! Find …*** *(... Jack and the beanstalk).* Elicit or explain the meaning of *beanstalk* (a very tall bean plant) and remind the children of Jack from the Introduction, if necessary.

- Say **Find the treasure clue sticker for Unit 3 and stick it here.** Demonstrate what you mean.

- The children look for the treasure clue sticker for Unit 3 and stick it in their books.

Act out the story.

- Divide the class into five groups and assign a role to each group: Alex, Katie, Pip, Squeak or Pinocchio. Give a finger puppet or character flashcard to one child in each group to hold up during the story.

- Follow the procedure for *Act out the story* on page 37 of the Teacher's Book.

Option: The children can act out their parts *either* with *or* without their books, depending on how confident and familiar they are with this episode. If you wish to make the activity more challenging, the children can act out the whole story by joining in their character's parts as you replay the CD.

Read, match and say. (AB page 21)

- Read the sentences in turn. Use mime to convey the meaning of each one and ask the children to do the same by saying e.g. **Show me you're tired!**

- Read the sentences again and ask the children to identify the correct picture for each one.

- Say **Now match the sentences and pictures.** Draw the children's attention to the example.

- The children work individually and match the sentences and pictures.

- Check the answers by asking e.g. **Who says *I'm tired!*?**

  Key: 1 Katie 2 Alex 3 Pinocchio (without nose, arms, legs) 4 Squeak 5 Pinocchio (with nose, arms, legs)

Listen, read and write. (AB page 21)

- Read the sentences and ask the children to predict what Pinocchio says in each one.

- Say **Listen to what Pinocchio says.** Play the CD (CD 1, track 60) while the children follow in their books.

- Say **Now listen and write the words.** Draw the children's attention to the example.

- Play the CD again. Use the pause button to give the children time to write the missing words.

- Check the answers by asking individual children to read the sentences.

  Key: 1 head 2 nose 3 arms 4 legs

 Listen, read and write.

1 This is my head.
2 This is my nose.
3 These are my arms.
4 These are my legs.

Ending the lesson

Lesson review

- Briefly ask the children what they can do as a result of the lesson (understand and act out *The long nose*). Praise the children for their efforts and / or use the finger puppets to do this.

Goodbye and closing routine

- Say **Let's sing the *Goodbye song*.** Play the karaoke version of the song (CD 1, track 5 – see Lesson 1). Hold up the finger puppets and the children sing and do the actions as in Lesson 1.

3 My body

Lesson 3
Communication and grammar

Aim:
- To say sentences about parts of your body

Key language:
- *This is my ... / These are my ...*
- *head, mouth, nose, chin, ears, eyes, arms, legs, fingers, toes*

Materials:
- Pupil's Book pages 23 and 24
- Activity Book pages 22 and 83
- Finger puppets (Pip and Squeak)
- Flashcards: head, mouth, nose, chin, ears, eyes, arms, legs, fingers, toes, Alex, Katie
- CD 1
- Scissors and stapler
- A prepared little book for Unit 3 (AB page 83)

Starting out

Greetings and opening routine

- Greet the children yourself and using the finger puppets.
- *Either* play the karaoke version of the *Hello song* (CD 1, track 3 – see Lesson 1) and the children sing and do the actions as in Lesson 1 *or* stick the flashcards on the board in the order of the rap *One head* (see Lesson 1), play the karaoke version (CD 1, track 58) and the children say the rap and point to the parts of their body.

Revision activity

- Hold up the finger puppets and stick the character flashcards on the board. Ask **Can you remember who's in the story with Pip, Squeak, Alex and Katie?** *(Pinocchio)*
- Ask the children to open their Pupil's Books at page 23. Briefly reconstruct the story, getting the children to supply key words. Say e.g. **Alex, Katie, Pip and Squeak look for ...** *Pinocchio.* **Katie is ...** *tired.* **Alex is ...** *hungry.* **Katie hears ...** *a noise.* **The children see ...** *Pinocchio.* **Pinocchio is ...** *sad.* **The man gives Pinocchio his ...** *nose, arms and legs and the treasure clue.* **Pinocchio is ...** *happy.* **Pinocchio gives Alex, Katie, Pip and Squeak the next ...** *treasure clue.*

- Play the CD (CD 1, track 59 – see Lesson 2). The children listen and follow the story in their books.

Setting objectives

- Say **Today we're going to practise saying sentences about different parts of our bodies.** Use L1 to clarify what you mean if necessary.

On the learning trail

Play a game. (PB page 24)

- Demonstrate the game. Say e.g. **This is my nose** and point to your nose. Demonstrate that the children should repeat the sentence and action.
- Say e.g. **This is my nose** and point to your arm. Demonstrate that the children should fold their arms and stay silent.
- Play the game by saying true or false sentences using *This is my ... / These are my ...* and naming and pointing to different parts of the body. The children listen and repeat the sentences and

actions if they are true, and fold their arms and stay silent if they are not. The class scores a point every time they respond correctly, and you score a point every time they don't. Keep a record of the score on the board. Go slowly at first and speed up as the children become familiar with the sentences and actions. Stop the game once the children are so familiar with the sentences and actions that they are winning easily.

Make *My Little Body Book*. (PB page 24 and AB page 83)

- Hold up your Pupil's Book and point to the pictures. Say **We're going to make the *My Little Body Book* and play the game.**

- Hold up your Activity Book and say **Find page 83 in your Activity Book. Look at the *My Little Body Book*.** Say **Let's make the *My Little Body Book*** and show the children the book you have prepared.

- Say **Cut and fold the pages like this** and demonstrate what you mean. Point out the difference between the dashed lines (cutting lines) and the dotted lines (folding lines).

- Staple the children's books together as soon as they have folded the pages correctly. Then say **Now cut here** and demonstrate cutting along the dotted line at the top to separate the pages.

- **Note:** This is the only dotted line that the children should cut.

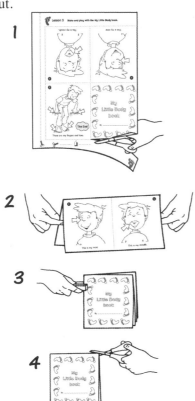

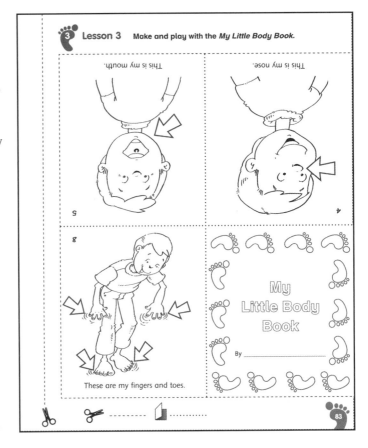

- Go through the little book page by page. Read the text while the children follow.

- Explain that the children should colour the body part named in the text and indicated by an arrow on each page.

- The children work individually and colour their little books.

Play with *My Little Body Book*. (PB page 24)

- Ask two pupils to read the first exchange and two other pupils to read the second exchange.

- Explain and demonstrate the game with one child. Open your little book randomly at any page and get the child to simultaneously do the same. Read the sentence on the page you have opened. If the child has opened their book at the same page, they say *Yes!* and repeat the sentence. If they have opened their book at a different page, they say *No!* and read the sentence they have got.

- Divide the class into pairs. Explain that the children should have six tries in the game. Ask them to predict how many times they think they will open the book at the same page before they begin, e.g. *three, one*.

- The children play the game with their partner.

- At the end, ask them to report back how many times they opened their little book at the same page and whether this was more or less than they had predicted.

Listen, circle and say. (AB page 22)

- Say **Look at the pictures of Alex and Katie. Listen to what Alex and Katie say and circle the correct pictures.** Draw the children's attention to the example.
- Play the CD (CD 1, track 61). The children listen and circle the pictures.
- Check the answers by getting children to name the parts of the body they have circled.
- Say **Now listen and repeat what Alex and Katie say.** Play the CD again. Use the pause button to give the children time to repeat the sentences.
- Ask individual children e.g. **What does Alex say in number one?** and the children say the sentences.

Key: 1 picture on right (eyes) 2 picture on left (mouth) 3 picture on left (arms) 4 picture on right (toes)

 Listen, circle and say.

1 These are my eyes.
2 This is my mouth.
3 These are my arms.
4 These are my toes.

Look and write. (AB page 22)

- Read the sentences and the children say the missing words according to the pictures.
- Say **Now write the words** and draw the children's attention to the example.
- The children work individually and complete the sentences.
- Check the answers by asking individual children to read the sentences.

Key: 1 nose 2 eyes 3 mouth 4 arms 5 chin 6 toes

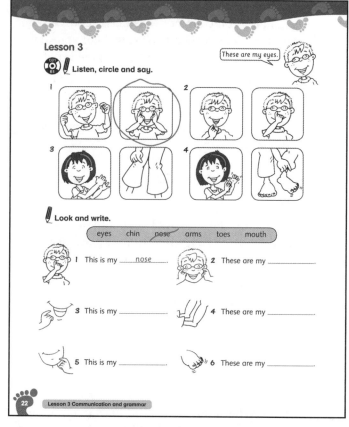

Ending the lesson

Lesson review

- Briefly ask the children what they can do as a result of the lesson (say sentences about parts of the body). Praise the children for their efforts and / or use the finger puppets to do this.

Goodbye and closing routine

- Say goodbye to the children yourself and using the finger puppets. If there is time, you can also play the karaoke version of the *Goodbye song* (CD 1, track 5 – see Lesson 1) and the children sing and do the actions as in Lesson 1.

3 My body

Lesson 4
Communication, grammar and pronunciation

Aims:

- To practise saying *This is ... / These are ...*
- To recognise the difference between singular and (regular) plural words
- To practise saying plural words

Key language:

- *This is my ... / These are my ...*
- *head, mouth, nose, chin, ears, eyes, arms, legs, fingers, toes*

Materials:

- Pupil's Book page 25
- Activity Book page 23
- Finger puppets (Pip and Squeak)
- Flashcards: head, mouth, nose, chin, ears, eyes, arms, legs, fingers, toes, Frodo
- Unit 3 little books from Lesson 3
- CD 1

Starting out

Greetings and opening routine

- Greet the children yourself and using the finger puppets.
- *Either* play the karaoke version of the *Hello song* (CD 1, track 3 – see Lesson 1) and the children sing and do the actions as in Lesson 1 *or* stick the flashcards on the board in the order of the rap *One head* (see Lesson 1), play the karaoke version (CD 1, track 58) and the children say the rap and point to the parts of their body.

Revision activity

- Give out or ask the children to get out the little books they made in Lesson 3.
- The children read their little books with you in chorus.

Setting objectives

- Say **Today we're going to practise saying *This is ... / These are ...* We're also going to learn to recognise, pronounce and write plural words.**

On the learning trail

Listen and sing the song. (PB page 25)

- Ask the children to stand in a circle or line. Teach them the actions for the song as follows: *eyes* – take a step forward and make two round circles with your index fingers in front of your eyes; *ears* – take a step forward and put your open palms to your ears; *mouth* – take a step forward and gesture to extend your mouth in a big smile; *nose* – take a step forward and gesture to make a long nose; *arms* – take a step forward and shake your arms; *legs* – take a step forward, bend your knees and slap your thighs; *fingers* – take a step forward, hold up and shake your fingers; *toes* – take a step forward, hold out your foot and wiggle your toes.

- Say the words in random order and the children respond by doing the actions. They take a step back into the line or circle after each one.
- Say **Listen to the song and do the actions.** Play the CD (CD 1, track 62).
- Play the CD again. The children do the actions and sing the song.

 These are my eyes

These are my eyes and ears
This is my mouth and nose
These are my arms and legs
And these are my fingers and toes!

Draw, point and say. (PB page 25)

- Point to the pictures of parts of the body at the top of the activity and the children say the words.
- Read the two headings. Explain that *or more* here means any number higher than two, e.g. five or ten.
- Ask the children to draw pictures of the parts of the body in the frames, depending on whether they have one, or two or more. Draw their attention to the examples.
- The children work individually and draw pictures in the correct frames.
- Check the answers by asking children to name the parts of the body they have drawn in each frame.
- Read the sentences in the speech bubbles. Ask the children if they can tell you why we say *This is ...* for some words and *These are ...* for others. Listen to their ideas and guide them to an understanding that we use *This is ...* when we are talking about one thing and *These are ...* when we are talking about two or more.
- Elicit sentences from the children about all the pictures they have drawn to illustrate this.

   Key: One: head, mouth, nose, chin; Two or more: eyes, ears, arms, legs, fingers, toes

Listen and say: Frodo's word fun. (PB page 25)

- Say the parts of the body in the *Two or more* frame in the previous activity.
- Ask the children what sound they notice at the end of the words, i.e. /z/.
- Explain that when we hear the sound /z/ or /s/ at the end of words for things (i.e. nouns), it usually means that there are two or more (i.e. it's plural).
- Hold up the flashcard of Frodo. Say **Listen to Frodo.** Explain and demonstrate that the children should wave one hand if they hear a singular word such as *head* and wave both hands if they hear a plural word such as *fingers*.
- Play the CD (CD 1, track 64) and the children respond by doing the actions.
- Play the CD again. The children do the actions and repeat the words.
- If you like, you can point out that for a word like *nose* the plural is *noses*, i.e. with /ɪz/.

 Frodo's word fun. Listen and say.

head ... fingers ... toes ... arm ... leg ... eye ... ears ... door ... books ... crayons ... pencil ... pens

Look, write and say. (AB page 23)

- Read the headings. Elicit or remind the children of the meaning of *Two or more*.
- Read the words at the top of the activity. Get the children to respond *One* or *Two or more*, depending on the list they should go in.
- Say **Now write the words in the correct list.** Draw the children's attention to the examples.
- The children work individually and write the words in the correct lists.
- Check the answers by asking the children to say the words in both lists.

   Key: One: head, mouth, chin, nose; Two or more: ears, arms, legs, eyes, fingers, toes

Look, read and circle. (AB page 23)

- Ask the children to look at the pictures and read the correct word underneath each one, according to whether the pictures show one or more of each item.
- Say **Now look, read and circle the correct words.** Draw the children's attention to the example.
- The children work individually and circle the words.
- Check the answers by asking individual children to read the word they have circled for each picture.

Key: 1 head 2 fingers 3 toes 4 arm 5 pencil 6 books 7 cake 8 biscuits 9 rubber 10 crayons

Ending the lesson

Lesson review

- Briefly ask the children what they can do as a result of the lesson (say sentences using *This is my ... / These are my ...*, recognise and pronounce (regular) plural words). Praise the children for their efforts and / or use the finger puppets to do this.

Goodbye and closing routine

- Say goodbye to the children yourself and using the finger puppets. If there is time, you can also play the karaoke version of the *Goodbye song* (CD 1, track 5 – see Lesson 1) and the children sing and do the actions as in Lesson 1.

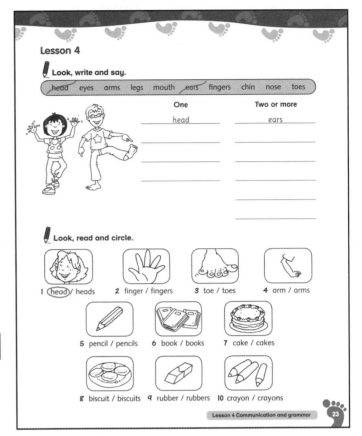

3 My body

Lesson 5
Content input

Aims:

- To read about germs
- To understand ways you can help your body fight germs

Key language:

- *wash your hair / hands, brush your hair / teeth, have a shower*
- *please*
- *germs, tiny, everywhere, ill*

Materials:

- Pupil's Book page 26
- Activity Book page 24
- Finger puppets (Pip and Squeak)
- Flashcards: head, mouth, nose, chin, ears, eyes, arms, legs, fingers, toes
- Word cards: head, mouth, nose, chin, ears, eyes, arms, legs, fingers, toes
- CD 1

Starting out

Greetings and opening routine

- Greet the children yourself and using the finger puppets.
- *Either* play the karaoke version of the *Hello song* (CD 1, track 3 – see Lesson 1) and the children sing and do the actions as in Lesson 1 *or* play the karaoke version of *These are my eyes* (CD 1, track 63 – see Lesson 4) and the children sing and do the actions as in Lesson 4.

Revision activity

- Play a memory game on the board with the flashcards and word cards. Divide the class into two teams.
- Stick the flashcards face down in jumbled order on one side of the board and the word cards face down in jumbled order on the other side.
- Ask a child from one team to choose a card from one side of the board. Turn it over and the child points to the part of their body shown or written on the flashcard or word card and says *This is my ...* or *These are my ...* Ask another child from the same team to choose a card from the other side of the board and say a sentence in the same way. If the two cards match, take the cards off the board and put them on your desk nearest the team.
- Repeat the procedure with the other team.
- Continue playing the game until there are no cards left on the board. The team with most cards at the end of the game wins.

Setting objectives

- Hold up the finger puppets. Say **Let's learn about the world around you! Today we're going to read about what we can do to fight germs.** Use L1 to explain that *germs* are bacteria (or micro-organisms) in the environment, and mime to convey the meaning of *fight*.

On the learning trail

Read, listen and number. (PB page 26)

- (Books closed) Read the question **What do you do to fight germs?** using gesture to convey meaning.
- Listen to the children's ideas (in L1). Use their suggestions to introduce vocabulary, e.g. *wash, brush, hands, teeth, shower*. Use mime and gesture to help understanding.
- Ask the children to open their Pupil's Books at page 26. Read the text at the top of the activity or play part 1 on the CD (CD 1, track 65). Use the illustration to convey the meaning of *strong*. Use mime to reinforce the meaning of *fight* and convey the meaning of *everywhere,* and ask the children to guess the meaning of *ill*.
- Say **Look at the photos of things you can do to fight germs.** Read the sentences below the pictures while the children follow in their books. Compare them with the ideas that the children suggested at the start of the activity.
- Say **Now listen and number in order the things you can do to fight germs.** Draw the children's attention to the example.
- Play the CD (CD 1, track 65). The children listen and number the pictures in order. Use the pause button to give them time to do this if necessary.
- Check the answers by saying e.g. **Number one is ...** and the children read the correct sentence.

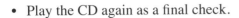

- Play the CD again as a final check.

  Key: 1 Have a shower. 2 Wash your hands. 3 Brush your teeth. 4 Brush your hair. 5 Wash your hair.

 Read, listen and number.

Part 1

Germs are tiny. Germs are everywhere. Germs can make you ill.

Your body is strong. You can help your body fight germs!

Part 2

1 Have a shower.
2 Wash your hands.
3 Brush your teeth.
4 Brush your hair.
5 Wash your hair.

Play a game. (PB page 26)

- Teach the children a mime for all the actions above, e.g. for *have a shower* – pretend to hold a shower head and spray water over your body.

- Explain and demonstrate that when you give an instruction and say *please*, the children should mime the action, and when you give an instruction but don't say *please*, the children should fold their arms and do nothing.

- Say **Stand up!** Say e.g. **Wash your hair, please!** The children respond by miming the action.

- Repeat, giving different instructions in random order and saying *please* or not. The children respond by either miming the action or folding their arms and doing nothing. If all the children respond correctly, they win a point; if not, you win a point. Keep a score on the board. Go slowly at first and speed up as the children become familiar with the instructions. Stop the game once the children are winning easily.

Listen, read and circle. (AB page 24)

- Read the sentences and options. Pre-teach *big* and *small*, using classroom objects.

- The children predict the answers by saying *Yes* to the words that they think are correct to complete the sentences.

- Say **Now listen, read and circle the words.** Draw the children's attention to the example.

- Play the CD (CD 1, track 66). The children work individually and circle the correct words.

- Check the answers by reading the sentences and options and the children say *Yes* to the words they have circled.

  Key: 1 tiny 2 everywhere 3 ill 4 strong

 Listen, read and circle.

1 Germs are tiny.
2 Germs are everywhere.
3 Germs can make you ill.
4 Your body is strong.

Read, draw and say. (AB page 24)

- Read the sentences in turn. Ask the children to look at the pictures and identify what's missing in each one. *(1 shower 2 hair 3 hair 4 hands 5 teeth)*. Be ready to recast their answers in English if necessary.

- The children work individually and draw what's missing in the pictures.

- Check the answers by asking individual children to read a sentence and say what they have drawn in the picture above it.

  Key: The following should be drawn in:
  1 shower 2 hair 3 hair 4 hands 5 teeth

Ending the lesson

Lesson review

- Briefly ask the children what they can do as a result of the lesson (understand what germs are and identify ways you can help your body to fight them). Praise the children for their efforts and / or use the finger puppets to do this.

Goodbye and closing routine

- Say goodbye to the children yourself and using the finger puppets. If there is time, you can also play the karaoke version of the *Goodbye song* (CD 1, track 5 – see Lesson 1) and the children sing and do the actions as in Lesson 1.

3 My body

Lesson 6
Content and personalisation

Aim:
- To say what you do to help your body fight germs

Key language:
- *I wash / brush my ... hair / hands / teeth.*
- *I have a shower every day / week.*
- *before meals, after I go to the toilet*

Materials:
- Pupil's Book page 27
- Activity Book page 25
- Finger puppets (Pip and Squeak)
- CD 1

Starting out

Greetings and opening routine

- Greet the children yourself and using the finger puppets.
- *Either* play the karaoke version of the *Hello song* (CD 1, track 3 – see Lesson 1) and the children sing and do the actions as in Lesson 1 *or* play the karaoke version of *These are my eyes* (CD 1, track 63 – see Lesson 4) and the children sing and do the actions as previously.

Revision activity

- Say true and false sentence about germs, e.g. **Germs are big / Germs can make you ill** (use the first activity in Lesson 5 of the Activity Book for more ideas). The children respond by saying *Yes!* in chorus if the sentences are true and *No!* if they're not.

Setting objectives

- Say **In this lesson we're going to say what we do to help our body fight germs.**

On the learning trail

Play a game. (PB page 27)

- Say **Here are some things we can do to fight germs.** Mime an action, e.g. brush your teeth, and encourage the children to guess and say what it is.
- Repeat, miming several different actions from Lesson 5, and the children guess in the same way.
- Invite pairs of children to the front of the class and *either* they choose an action *or* you whisper an action to them. They do a mime and the rest of the class guesses.
- Divide the class into pairs. The children take turns to mime and guess actions with their partner. Stop when the children have had three turns each.

Listen, match and say. (PB page 27)

- Ask the children to look at the pictures and identify the actions in each one, e.g. *wash hands*. Use the pictures to introduce phrases they will listen to, e.g. *before meals / after I go to the toilet*. Use a calendar to introduce the phrases *every day* and *every week* or write days and dates on the board and point to them to pre-teach these phrases.
- Say **Alex and Katie are talking about what they do to fight germs. Listen and match the pictures to Alex or Katie.** Draw the children's attention to the example.
- Play the CD (CD 1, track 67). The children listen and match the pictures to Katie or Alex. Use the pause button to give them time to do this.

- Check the answers by asking e.g. **Who says I have a shower every day?** *(Katie)*
- Say **Now listen and repeat what Alex and Katie say.** Play the CD again. Use the pause button to give the children time to repeat what Alex and Katie say. You can do this in two groups, with the boys saying what Alex says and the girls saying what Katie says. Then change roles.

  Key: Katie: washing hands before meals, having a shower every day, brushing hair every day.
  Alex: brushing teeth after meals, washing hands after going to the toilet, washing hair every week

 Listen, match and say. (PB page 27)

Alex: *What do you do to fight germs, Katie?*
Katie: *I wash my hands before meals! I have a shower every day. And ... mmm, I brush my hair every day. What about you, Alex?*
Alex: *Well, I brush my teeth after meals. I wash my hands after I go to the toilet. And ... mmm ... I wash my hair every week.*

Listen, read and match. (AB page 25)

- Say **Let's listen to and read what Katie and Alex say they do to fight germs.** Play the CD (CD 1, track 68). The children follow in their books.
- Say **Listen, read and match the two parts of each sentence.** Draw the children's attention to the example.
- Play the CD again. The children draw lines to match the two parts of each sentence. Use the pause button to give them time to do this.
- Check the answers by inviting individual children to read one of the sentences to the class.

  Key: 1 I wash my hands before meals. 2 I have a shower every day. 3 I brush my teeth after meals. 4 I wash my hair every week.

 Listen, read and match.

1 I wash my hands before meals. 2 I have a shower every day. 3 I brush my teeth after meals. 4 I wash my hair every week.

Read, write and tick (✓). (AB page 25)

- Read the sentences and the children say the missing words.

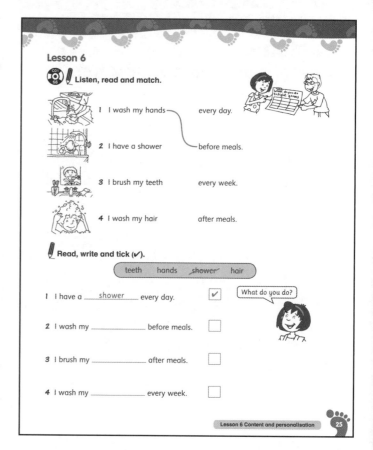

- Ask the children to write the missing words and to put a tick in the box at the end of each sentence if it is true for them. Draw their attention to the example.
- The children complete the sentences and tick the boxes if the sentences are true for them.
- Once they are ready, ask individual children to tell the class one sentence that is true for them.
- If you like, use L1 to ask the children to identify other things they can do to fight germs, e.g. wash your hands after going to the toilet / playing with a pet / playing with sand or earth, wash fruit before you eat it, don't eat food if it falls on the floor, cover your nose with a tissue if you sneeze.

Ending the lesson

Lesson review

- Briefly ask the children what they can do as a result of the lesson (say what they do to fight germs). Praise the children for their efforts and / or use the finger puppets to do this.

Goodbye and closing routine

- Say goodbye to the children yourself and using the finger puppets. If there is time, you can also play the karaoke version of the *Goodbye song* (CD 1, track 5 – see Lesson 1) and the children sing and do the actions as in Lesson 1.

3 My body

Lesson 7
Children's culture

Aim:
- To sing a version of a traditional song and play a game

Key language:
- *This is the way we ...*
- *wash / brush our ... hands / teeth / hair*
- *have a shower*
- *head, arm, leg, eye, ear*
- numbers 1–6

Materials:
- Pupil's Book page 28
- Activity Book page 26
- Finger puppets (Pip and Squeak)
- Flashcard: Frodo
- Dice (one for you – ideally large, and one for each pair – optional)
- CD 1

Starting out

Greetings and opening routine

- Greet the children yourself and using the finger puppets.
- *Either* play the karaoke version of the *Hello song* (CD 1, track 3 – see Lesson 1) and the children sing and do the actions as in Lesson 1 *or* play the karaoke version of *These are my eyes* (CD 1, track 63 – see Lesson 4) and the children sing and do the actions as previously.

Revision activity

- Explain that you are going to say sentences about what you do to fight germs and the children should repeat the sentences if they are true for them.
- Say sentences, e.g. **I have a shower every day** (see the first activity in Lesson 6 of the Activity Book for other sentences). If you like, keep a score on the board of all the sentences that are true for the whole class (although this may be a sensitive area and it is important not to be judgemental about the children's responses).

Setting objectives

- Hold up the flashcard of Frodo. Say **In this lesson we're going to sing a version of a traditional song and play a game.** Use gesture to convey the meaning of this.

On the learning trail

Listen and sing the song. (PB page 28) (books closed)

- Ask **What actions can you hear in the song?** and give an example, e.g. **wash our hands.**
- Play the CD (CD 1, track 69). Ask the question again and check the answers *(wash our hands, brush our teeth, have a shower, wash our hair)*.
- Ask the children to open their Pupil's Books at page 28. Play verse 1 of the song again. The children follow in their books and sing the first verse of the song. Check they understand the meaning of lines 1 and 5. Explain that *we* and *our* refer to all of us doing the actions together.
- Ask the children to stand in a circle or by their desks. Say **Let's sing the song again and mime the actions.** Demonstrate what you mean.
- Play the CD again. The children sing and mime the action for each verse. If the children are

standing in a circle, they hold hands and skip clockwise to the music between each verse. If they are standing by their desks, they can skip or dance on the spot.

 This is the way

This is the way we wash our hands
Wash our hands
Wash our hands
This is the way we wash our hands
To keep the germs away!

Verse 2: *Brush our teeth ...*
Verse 3: *Have a shower ...*
Verse 4: *Wash our hair ...*

 Citizenship box: Remember!

Say **The song is about things we do to keep germs away.**

Hold up the flashcard of Frodo, read the *Remember!* note and check understanding. Use L1 to ask the children for other examples of when they should wash their hands, e.g. after going to the toilet, after playing with a pet or with sand. Emphasise the importance of the children taking responsibility for their own personal hygiene.

Option: From now on, remind the children to wash their hands when appropriate, e.g. if you teach them the lesson before lunch.

Play *Body dice!* (PB page 28)

- Show the children the dice and say **Look. This is a dice.** Say **Let's play a game with the dice that English children sometimes play!** Explain that the children may also be familiar with a similar game in their own culture.

- Ask **How many numbers are there on the dice?** *(six)*. Write the numbers 1 – 6 on the board and a body word by each number, as in the game in the Pupil's Book (*1 head 2 arm 3 leg 4 ear 5 eye 6 ?*). Explain that the question mark by number 6 means any body part.

- Draw two simple outlines of a torso and neck on the board, as on the Pupil's Book page. Explain that the aim of the game is to draw a full picture of a person. Each player takes turns to throw the dice and to draw the body part which corresponds to the number thrown. If they throw a 1 and the picture already has a head, then they don't draw anything; if they throw a 6, they can choose what they want to draw on the picture, e.g. hair or nose, or a leg if their picture only has one. The person with the most complete picture after ten throws of the dice is the winner.

- Demonstrate the game by playing against the whole class. Throw the dice yourself first. Show it to the class and say e.g. **Three! A leg! Oh, good** and draw a leg on one of the torsos on the board. Then ask a child to come and throw the dice and draw a body part on the other picture on the board in the same way.

- Continue in the same way for several turns and at the end ask the class to decide which picture is the most complete and who is the winner.

- Depending on whether or not you have dice for the children, *either* divide the class into pairs, give out the dice and the children play again using the picture in their books *or* divide the class into two teams and play again using pictures on the board in the same way as previously and inviting different children from each team to have a turn each time. In this case, the children also draw the picture built up by their team in their books as they play.

- At the end, if the children have played in pairs, ask some pairs to show their winning pictures to the class and name the parts of the body. If the children have played in teams, get them to decide the winner and name the parts of the body on each picture.

Listen, draw and say. (AB page 26)

- Say **Listen to the numbers on the dice and draw the parts of the body.** Draw the children's attention to the example.

- Play the CD (CD 1, track 71). Use the pause button to give the children time to draw the parts of the body.

- Check the answers by asking individual children to name the parts of the body they have drawn on the picture.

    Key: an arm, a head, an ear, hair, an eye, a leg

- Ask the children to complete their pictures by drawing the parts of the body which are still missing. If you like, they can also colour their pictures.

 Listen, draw and say.

Two! An arm! Oh, great!
One! A head! Oh, good!
Four! An ear! Oh, great!
Six! Free choice! This is the hair!
Five! An eye! Oh, good!
Three! A leg! Oh, great!

Read, write and draw. (AB page 26)

- Read the sentences and the children suggest possible words to complete them. Make sure they realise that there are different possible answers for numbers 2, 3 and 4, e.g. for number 2, they can write *hair* or *teeth*.

- Ask the children to choose words to complete the sentences and draw a picture of themselves doing each action. Draw their attention to the example.

- The children work individually and complete the sentences and draw pictures.

- At the end, ask individual children to show their pictures and say the appropriate sentences, e.g. *This is the way I brush my hair.*

    Key: 1 hair 2 hair / teeth 3 hair / hands 4 hair / teeth

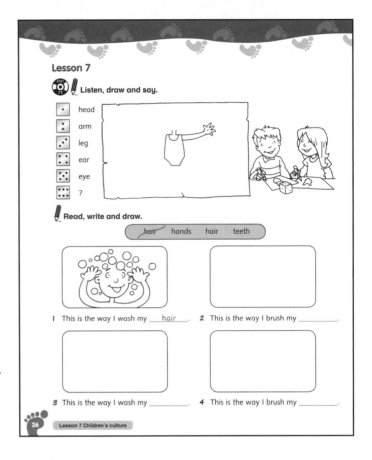

Ending the lesson

Lesson review

- Briefly ask the children what they can do as a result of the lesson (sing a version of a traditional song, play a dice game). Praise the children for their efforts and / or use the finger puppets to do this.

Goodbye and closing routine

- Say goodbye to the children yourself and using the finger puppets. If there is time, you can also play the karaoke version of the *Goodbye song* (CD 1, track 5 – see Lesson 1) and the children sing and do the actions as in Lesson 1.

3 My body

Lesson 8
Unit review / *All About Me Portfolio Booklet*

Aim:
- To review learning in Unit 3

Key language:
- *This is my ... / These are my ...*
- *head, mouth, nose, chin, ears, eyes, arms, legs, fingers, toes*
- *I wash / brush my hair / teeth ...*
- *I wash my hands*
- *every day / week, before / after meals*

Materials:
- Pupil's Book page 29
- Activity Book page 27
- *All About Me* Portfolio Booklet pages 10 and 11
- Finger puppets (Pip and Squeak)
- Flashcards: head, mouth, nose, chin, ears, eyes, arms, legs, fingers, toes, Frodo
- Stickers for Unit 3
- CD 1

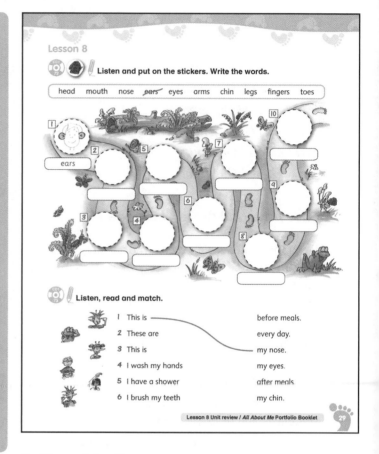

Starting out

Greetings and opening routine

- Greet the children (but without using the finger puppets).
- *Either* play the karaoke version of the *Hello song* (CD 1, track 3 – see Lesson 1) and the children sing and do the actions as in Lesson 1 *or* stick the flashcards on the board in the order of the rap *One head* (see Lesson 1) and the children say the rap and do the actions.

Revision activity

- Say **This is the way we ...** and mime the following actions in turn (wash our hands, brush our teeth, have a shower, wash our hair). The children identify the actions.
- Say **Stand up! Let's sing the song** *This is the way.* Play the karaoke version (CD 1, track 70 – see Lesson 7). The children sing the song and mime the actions.

Setting objectives

- Say **Today we're going to review what we've learnt in Unit 3.**

On the learning trail

Listen and put on the stickers. Write the words. (PB page 29)

- Make sure the children have the stickers for Unit 3 ready.
- Say **Listen and put on the stickers.** Draw the children's attention to the example.
- Play the CD (CD 1, track 72). Use the pause button to give the children time to put on the stickers.
- Say **Now write the words.** Draw the children's attention to the example.
- Check the answers by saying the numbers and the children say the words.

Key: 1 ears 2 legs 3 head 4 fingers 5 arms 6 nose 7 eyes 8 mouth 9 chin 10 toes

Listen and put on the stickers.

1 These are my ears.
2 These are my legs.
3 This is my head.
4 These are my fingers.
5 These are my arms.
6 This is my nose.
7 These are my eyes.
8 This is my mouth.
9 This is my chin.
10 These are my toes.

Listen, read and match. (PB page 29)

- Read the first part of each sentence and ask the children to predict and find the second part by looking at the pictures.
- Say **Now listen, read and match the parts of each sentence.** Draw the children's attention to the example.
- Play the CD (CD 1, track 73). The children work individually and match the parts of the sentences. Use the pause button to give them time to do this if necessary.
- Check the answers by asking individual children to read the sentences.
- Play the CD again as a final check.
- The children read the sentences in pairs.

  Key: 1 This is my nose. 2 These are my eyes.
  3 This is my chin. 4 I wash my hands before meals.
  5 I have a shower every day. 6 I brush my teeth after meals.

 Listen, read and match.

1 This is my nose.
2 These are my eyes.
3 This is my chin.
4 I wash my hands before meals.
5 I have a shower every day.
6 I brush my teeth after meals.

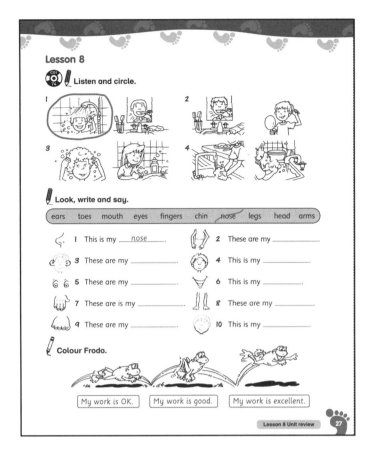

Listen and circle. (AB page 27)

- Say **Look at the pictures. Listen and circle what they say they do to fight germs.** Draw the children's attention to the example.
- Play the CD (CD 1, track 74). Pause if necessary to give the children time to circle the pictures.
- Check the answers by saying e.g. **The child in number one says …** and the children finish the sentence by repeating what the child on the CD says.

  Key: 1 picture on the left 2 picture on the left
  3 picture on the left 4 picture on the right

 Listen and circle.

1 I have a shower every day.
2 I brush my teeth after meals.
3 I wash my hair every week.
4 I wash my hands after I go to the toilet.

Look, write and say. (AB page 27)

- Draw the children's attention to the words at the start of the activity. Say **Write the words** and draw the children's attention to the example.

- The children work individually and complete the sentences.
- Check the answers by asking individual children to say one of the sentences. The children point to their own parts of the body and say the sentences in pairs.

Key: 1 nose 2 arms 3 ears 4 head 5 eyes
6 mouth 7 fingers 8 legs 9 toes 10 chin

Colour Frodo. (AB page 27)

- Hold up the flashcard of Frodo. Remind the children that in this activity they assess their work in the unit by choosing and colouring the picture of Frodo which corresponds best to how they think they have done.
- Remind the children of the key by pointing to the three pictures of Frodo and saying **Colour this picture if your work is OK but you think you need to try harder or need more practice. Colour this picture of Frodo if you think your work is good. Colour this picture of Frodo with a big smile and jumping very high if you think your work is excellent.** Make sure the children understand that there are no right answers and that it is their own opinion of the work they have done which is important. Be ready to encourage the children to have a positive view if they are too hard on themselves.

Ending the lesson

Lesson review

- Briefly ask the children what they can do as a result of the lesson (use the language and vocabulary they've learnt in Unit 3). Praise the children for their efforts and / or use the finger puppets to do this.

Goodbye and closing routine

- Say goodbye to the children yourself and using the finger puppets. If there is time, you can also play the karaoke version of the *Goodbye song* (CD 1, track 5 – see Lesson 1) and the children sing and do the actions as in Lesson 1.

All About Me Portfolio Booklet

The children complete Unit 3 of their personal *All About Me* Portfolio Booklets. They complete their learning journey by colouring the sections on the path to show what they can do. If you like, the children can also sign this page and you can endorse this by adding your own signature and the date.

4 My clothes

Structures and grammar

- *I've got a ..., (too).*
- *Is this your ...? Yes, it is. / No, it isn't.*
- *Are these your ...? Yes, they are. / No, they aren't.*
- Recycled: *This ... / These ..., It's ..., Can I ...?, Your / My ...*

Vocabulary

- Core: *coat, gloves, trousers, shirt, t-shirt, dress, skirt, shoes, jumper, socks*
- Other: *shorts, everybody, put on, giant, beanstalk, castle, new*
- Content / culture: *jeans, tracksuit, wool, cotton, warm, cool, bed, cross, river, crocodile*
- Recycled: *hat*, colours, numbers

Main receptive language

- *material, clothes, pocket*
- *plant, sheep*
- *natural, new*
- *take care*

Communicative competence

Understanding

Listening:
- Can recognise clothes words
- Can recognise words for two materials used to make clothes
- Can understand the episode of the story
- Can understand statements about clothes
- Can understand questions and answers about clothes
- Can discriminate between the sounds /s/ and /ʃ/ at the start of words

Reading:
- Can recognise clothes words
- Can read statements about clothes
- Can read questions and answers about clothes
- Can read sentences about wool and cotton

Speaking

Spoken interaction:
- Can ask about and respond to questions about clothes
- Can ask for permission in a game

Spoken production:
- Can sing the song *I'm ready for English*
- Can name clothes
- Can say the chant *Everybody put on your coat*
- Can say sentences about clothes
- Can say the chant *Is this your hat?*
- Can say the rhyme *Diddle, diddle, dumpling*
- Can sing the song *Shake your head*

Writing
- Can copy and write words for clothes
- Can complete questions and sentences with words for clothes

Content links

- *Science:* wool and cotton

Learning strategies and thinking skills

- Recognising learning objectives
- Following simple instructions
- Associating colours and materials with clothes
- Associating vocabulary with touch
- Classifying
- Making logical deductions
- Using mime and gesture
- Reflecting on learning

Children's culture

- Saying a version of a traditional rhyme: *Diddle, diddle, dumpling*
- Playing a version of a traditional game: *Mr Crocodile!*

Pronunciation

- Discriminating between words which start with /s/ and /ʃ/

Values and attitudes

- Enjoyment in being able to talk about your clothes in English
- Interest in materials used to make clothes
- Awareness of the importance of taking care of your clothes

4 My clothes

Lesson 1
Vocabulary presentation

Aim:
- To name clothes

Key language:
- *coat, gloves, trousers, skirt, dress, shirt, t-shirt, jumper, socks, shoes*
- *Put on your ...*
- *everybody*

Materials:
- Pupil's Book page 30
- Activity Book page 28
- Finger puppets (Pip and Squeak)
- Flashcards: coat, gloves, trousers, skirt, dress, shirt, t-shirt, jumper, socks, shoes, Frodo
- Word cards: coat, gloves, trousers, skirt, dress, shirt, t-shirt, jumper, socks, shoes
- CD 1 and CD 2

Starting out

Greetings and opening routine

- Greet the children yourself and using the finger puppets. Say e.g. **Hello, children. Hello ... How are you today?** *Fine, thank you.* Ask a few individual children to greet the puppets in turn.

- Say **Let's sing the song** *I'm ready for English.* Play the CD (CD 1, track 6). Hold up the puppets on your index fingers. Move them and pick up classroom objects as the children sing and do the actions.

 I'm ready for English

Hello, hello, hello.
            (wave hello to teacher and friends)
I'm ready for English. Look!
            (hold out your arms)
Here's my pencil and rubber
            (hold out objects in turn)
And here's my notebook!
            (hold up notebook)
I'm ready! I'm ready! Hurray!
            (wave arms in the air)

Setting objectives

- Say **Today we're going to learn how to name clothes** (point to your clothes to convey meaning) **and we're going to say a chant.**

On the learning trail

Vocabulary presentation (books closed)

- Show the children one of the flashcards, e.g. shirt, very quickly. The children identify what it is in L1. Say e.g. **Yes. Very good. It's a shirt.**

- Point to the flashcard. Say **shirt** several times and get the children to repeat the word with you in chorus.

- Stick the flashcard of the shirt on the board.

- Repeat the procedure for all the other clothes flashcards.

- Divide the class in half. Hold up the Pip finger puppet and say to one half **Say the words with Pip.** Use the puppet to point to the flashcards in turn and the children say the words with you. Make the puppet fly around to praise the children.

- Repeat the procedure with the Squeak puppet and the other half of the class.

Follow the footprints. (PB page 30) (books open)

- Hold up the flashcard of Frodo. Say **Listen and follow the footprints with Frodo the frog. Use your finger** and demonstrate this.

- Play the CD (CD 2, track 1). The children listen and follow the footprints with their fingers. They stop by each picture as they hear the word and they repeat the word.

- Say **Now listen and draw a line following the footprints** and demonstrate this. Play the CD again. The children draw a line, stop by each picture and repeat the words as previously.

 Follow the footprints.

coat ... gloves ... trousers ... skirt ... dress ... shirt ... t-shirt ... jumper ... socks ... shoes

- Stick the word cards on the board in jumbled order (at the children's height and away from the flashcards).

- Point to one word card, e.g. *coat*, and read the word. Say **Look for the picture of the coat.** Give the children time to do this.
- Ask a child to come to the front of the class and stick the word card for *coat* by the corresponding flashcard. Ask the rest of the class **Is this right?** and get them to say the word.
- Repeat the procedure with the rest of the word cards.
- Take the flashcards and word cards off the board.

Listen and say the chant. (PB page 30)

- Say **Look at the picture.** Say **Pip's putting on a …** *(coat)*, using mime to clarify meaning and eliciting the word from the children. Say **Squeak's putting on …** *(shoes)*.
- Say **Stand up! Listen to the chant. Mime putting on the clothes** and demonstrate what you mean. Play the CD (CD 2, track 2). The children listen to the chant and mime putting on the clothes in each verse.
- Play the CD again. The children mime putting on clothes and say the chant.

 Everybody put on your coat

Everybody put on your coat	(gesture to include everybody, and do the mime)
Put on your coat	(repeat the mime)
Put on your coat	(repeat the mime)
Everybody put on your coat	(as above)
Just like me!	(point to yourself three times)

Verse 2: … *shoes* …

Verse 3: … *gloves* …

Look, match and say. (PB page 30)

- Ask the children to look at the pictures and to identify the clothes in the numbered puzzle pieces, e.g.

    T: **Number one?**

    P: *A t-shirt.*

- Ask the children to draw lines to match the puzzle pieces. Draw their attention to the example.
- The children work individually and match the puzzle pieces.
- Check the answers by getting individual children to point to and name all the clothes.

Key: 1 t-shirt 2 trousers 3 jumper 4 coat 5 shoes 6 gloves

Read and draw. (AB page 28)

- Read Frodo's instructions in turn and the children identify the clothes in the pictures at the top of the activity.
- Say **Now read and draw the clothes.** Draw the children's attention to the example. The children work individually and draw the clothes in each picture.
- Check the answers by reading the instructions again and getting different children to mime putting on the clothes they have drawn.

Key: 1 shoes 2 coat 3 jumper 4 gloves

Find, colour and write. (AB page 28)

- Read the words at the top of the activity.
- Say **Look at the puzzle picture. Find and colour the clothes. Then write the words.** Draw the children's attention to the example.
- The children work individually. They follow the lines to the clothes, colour them and write the words.

- Check the answers by saying e.g. **Number one is …** and the children point to the clothes in the picture and say the words.

  Key: 1 skirt 2 trousers 3 t-shirt 4 dress 5 socks 6 shoes 7 coat 8 jumper 9 shirt 10 gloves

Ending the lesson

Lesson review

- Briefly ask the children what they can do as a result of the lesson (name clothes, say the chant *Everybody put on your coat*). Praise the children for their efforts and / or use the finger puppets to do this.

Goodbye and closing routine

- Say **Let's sing the song** *Shake your head.* Play the CD (CD 1, track 8). Hold up the finger puppets on your index fingers as the children sing and do the actions.

 Shake your head

Shake your head   (shake head)
Wave your arms   (wave arms in the air)
Touch your ears and eyes   (point to ears and eyes)
It's the end of the lesson now (tap real or imaginary watch)
Goodbye! Goodbye! Goodbye!   (wave goodbye)

- Say goodbye to the children yourself and using the finger puppets, e.g. say **Goodbye everyone. See you on …** Ask a few individual children to say goodbye to the finger puppets in turn.

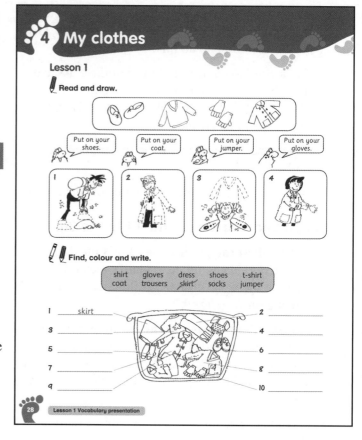

4 My clothes

Lesson 2
Language input and story

Aim:
- To understand and act out episode 4 of the story

Key language:
- *coat, trousers, shirt, t-shirt, skirt, dress, jumper, socks, shoes, gloves, hat*
- *I've got ...*
- *Is this ...? Yes, it is.*
- *Are these ...? Yes, they are.*
- *castle, giant, beanstalk*

Materials:
- Pupil's Book page 31
- Activity Book page 29
- Finger puppets (Pip and Squeak)
- Flashcards: Alex, Katie, coat, gloves, trousers, shirt, t-shirt, skirt, dress, jumper, socks, shoes
- Treasure clue sticker for Unit 4
- CD 1 and CD 2

Setting objectives

- Say **Today we're going to listen to and act out episode 4 of the story.**

Starting out

Greetings and opening routine

- Greet the children yourself and using the finger puppets.
- Play *I'm ready for English* (CD 1, track 6 – see Lesson 1). The children sing and do the actions as in Lesson 1.

Revision activity

- Hold up the clothes flashcards in turn and the children say the words.
- Say **Stand up! Let's say the chant *Everybody put on your coat.* Mime putting on the clothes** and demonstrate what you mean.
- Play the CD (CD 2, track 2 – see Lesson 1). The children say the chant and mime putting on clothes.
- Repeat with the karaoke version (CD 2, track 3). Hold up different flashcards, e.g. trousers, jumper, shirt, in each verse and the children say the chant and mime putting on the clothes.

On the learning trail

Listen and act out the story.
Episode 4: The hungry giant (PB page 31)

Before the story (books closed)

- Hold up the finger puppets and stick the flashcards of Alex and Katie on the board. Recap on the last episode of the story using mime and gesture as necessary: **Alex, Katie, Pip and Squeak look for Pinocchio. Katie is tired. Alex is hungry. Pip and Squeak are scared. They see Pinocchio with a man. Pinocchio is sad. The man gives Pinocchio his nose, arms and legs. Pinocchio is happy. Pinocchio gives Alex, Katie, Pip and Squeak the next treasure clue.**
- Ask **Can you remember the clue from Unit 3?** Hold up page 23 of the Pupil's Book and point to the treasure clue sticker. Read *Follow the footprints! Find Jack and the beanstalk!* as a prompt if necessary.
- Ask **Who's Jack?** *(a boy)* and explain that *a beanstalk* is a plant. Explain that in the traditional

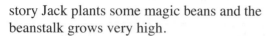

story Jack plants some magic beans and the beanstalk grows very high.

- Explain that in this episode Katie, Alex, Pip and Squeak follow the footprints to find Jack and the beanstalk. Ask the following questions in turn. Use mime and gesture to clarify meaning and encourage the children to predict the answers: **1) What's at the top of the beanstalk? 2) Where's the next treasure clue? 3) Who gets the treasure clue?**

During the story (books open)

- Say **Now listen to the story and find out.**
- Play the CD (CD 2, track 4) and the children follow in their books.
- Ask the questions in turn again and check the answers, using mime and gesture to clarify meaning. Recast them in English as necessary. *(1 a castle and a hungry giant 2 in the giant's pocket 3 Jack)*
- Say **Listen again and repeat the story.** Play the CD again. Pause after each sentence and the children repeat the story.
- **Note:** Additional text is marked with an asterisk* below. The children repeat the whole story, including the language which does not appear in their books.

 Follow the footprints, Episode 4: The giant

Picture 1	
Narrator:	*Alex, Katie, Pip and Squeak follow the footprints to find Jack and the beanstalk.**
Alex:	*Hello. What's your name?**
Jack:	*I'm Jack.**
Katie:	*Is this the beanstalk, Jack?*
Jack:	*Yes, it is.*
Pip:	*Jack and the beanstalk!**
Alex, Katie, Pip and Squeak:	*Hurray!**

Picture 2	
Katie:	*Let's climb the beanstalk!*
Jack:	*Are you sure? At the top is a castle and a hungry giant ...*
Alex, Katie, Pip and Squeak:	*Oh, no!**

Picture 3	
Jack:	*... and it's very cold. I've got a coat.*
Pip:	*I've got socks.*
Squeak:	*I've got a jumper.*
Alex:	*I've got a hat.**
Katie:	*And I've got gloves.**
Jack:	*Come on then. Let's go!**

Picture 4	
Pip:	*Is this the giant's hat?*
Jack:	*Yes, it is.*
Alex:	*Are these the giant's shoes?*
Jack:	*Yes, they are.*
Squeak:	*Oh, no! Here's the giant!**

Picture 5	
Giant:	*Fee, fi, fo, foy. I smell a girl. I smell a boy.*
Pip:	*I'm scared.**
Squeak:	*Help!**
Jack:	*I've got the clue!*

Picture 6	
Jack:	*Quick! Come on!*
Alex:	*Hurry!*

Picture 7	
All:	*Phew!**
Jack:	*Here's the next clue!*
Katie:	*Fantastic! Thank you, Jack!*
Alex:	*Follow the footprints! Find a house of food! Yum ...**
Jack:	*Goodbye and good luck!**
All:	*Goodbye, Jack!**

After the story

- Ask questions about each picture as follows: **1) What's the boy's name?** *(Jack)* **Is this the beanstalk?** *(yes)* **2) What's at the top of the beanstalk?** *(a castle and a hungry giant)* **3) Is it cold?** (use mime to convey meaning) *(yes)* **What's Jack got?** *(a coat)* **What's Pip got?** *(socks)* **What's Squeak got?** *(a jumper)* **What's Alex got?** *(a hat)* **What's Katie got?** *(gloves)* **4)** (point to the pictures and ask about each item of clothing in turn) **Is this the giant's hat?** *(yes)* **Are these the giant's shoes?** *(yes)* **Who's here?** *(the giant)* **What's in the giant's pocket?** (use gesture to convey meaning) *(the treasure clue)* **5) What does the giant say?** *I smell ...* (sniff to demonstrate meaning) *(a girl / boy)* **Who gets the clue?** *(Jack)* **6) Do Alex, Katie, Pip and Squeak escape from the giant?** (use gesture to convey meaning) *(yes)* **7) What does Jack give them?** *(the next treasure clue)*

Put on the treasure clue sticker.

- Say **The treasure clue says *Follow the footprints! Find a house of food!*** Elicit or explain the meaning of *house* and *food*.

- Say **Find the treasure clue sticker for Unit 4 and stick it here.** Demonstrate what you mean.

- The children look for the treasure clue sticker for Unit 4 and stick it in their books.

Act out the story.

- Divide the class into six groups and assign a role to each group: Alex, Katie, Pip, Squeak, Jack or the giant. Give a finger puppet or character flashcard to one child in each group to hold up during the story.

- Follow the procedure for *Act out the story* on page 37 of the Teacher's Book.

> **Option:** The children can act out their parts *either* with *or* without their books. If you wish to make the activity more challenging, they can act out the whole story by joining in their character's part as you replay the CD.

Read, match and say. (AB page 29)

- Read the sentences in turn. The children point to the correct clothes as you do this.

- Say **Now match the sentences and the clothes.** Draw the children's attention to the example.

- The children work individually and match the sentences and the clothes.

    Key: Children match the sentences and pictures.
    1 jumper 2 coat 3 socks 4 gloves 5 hat

Listen, write and act out. (AB page 29)

- Say **Look at the pictures. Listen to Pip asking Jack about the giant's clothes.** Play the CD (CD 2, track 5) while the children follow in their books.

- Read the words at the top of the activity.

- Say **Now listen again and write the words.** Draw the children's attention to the example.

- Play the CD again. The children listen and write the missing words. Use the pause button to give them time to do this if necessary.

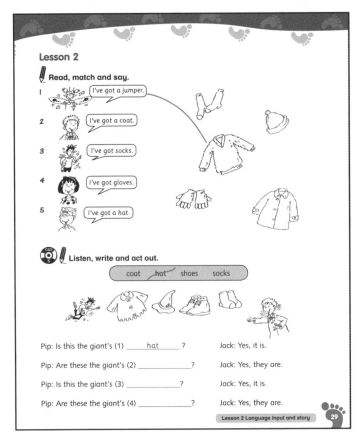

- Check the answers by asking pairs of children to read the question and answer to the class.

- The children act out the dialogue in pairs.

    Key: 1 hat 2 shoes 3 coat 4 socks

 Listen, write and act out.

1 Pip: *Is this the giant's hat?*
  Jack: *Yes, it is.*

2 Pip: *Are these the giant's shoes?*
  Jack: *Yes, they are.*

3 Pip: *Is this the giant's coat?*
  Jack: *Yes, it is.*

4 Pip: *Are these the giant's socks?*
  Jack: *Yes, they are.*

Ending the lesson

Lesson review

- Briefly ask the children what they can do as a result of the lesson (understand and act out *The giant*). Praise the children for their efforts and / or use the finger puppets to do this.

Goodbye and closing routine

- Say **Let's sing *Shake your head*.** Play the CD (CD 1, track 8 – see Lesson 1). Hold up the finger puppets and the children sing and do the actions as in Lesson 1.

4 My clothes

Lesson 3
Communication and grammar

Aim:
- To practise saying what clothes you've got

Key language:
- *I've got ..., (too).*
- *Snap!*
- *coat, trousers, shirt, t-shirt, skirt, dress, jumper, socks, shoes, gloves, hat*
- *shorts*
- *colours*

Materials:
- Pupil's Book pages 31 and 32
- Activity Book pages 30 and 85
- Finger puppets (Pip and Squeak)
- Flashcards: Alex, Katie, coat, trousers, shirt, t-shirt, skirt, dress, jumper, socks, shoes, gloves, hat
- CD 1 and CD 2
- Scissors
- A prepared set of Unit 4 picture cards (AB page 85)

Starting out

Greetings and opening routine

- Greet the children yourself and using the finger puppets.
- *Either* play the karaoke version of *I'm ready for English* (CD 1, track 7 – see Lesson 1) and the children sing and do the actions as in Lesson 1 *or* play the karaoke version of *Everybody put on your coat* (CD 2, track 3 – see Lesson 1). Hold up a flashcard for each verse. The children say the chant and mime putting on the clothes.

Revision activity

- Hold up the finger puppets and stick the character flashcards on the board. Ask **Can you remember who's in the story with Pip, Squeak, Alex and Katie?** *(Jack, the giant)*
- Ask the children to open their Pupil's Book at page 31. Briefly reconstruct the story, getting the children to supply key words. Say e.g. **Alex, Katie, Pip and Squeak find ...** *Jack and the beanstalk.* **Katie, Alex, Pip and Squeak climb the ...** *beanstalk.* **It's cold. Jack's got ...** *a coat,* **Pip's got ...** *socks,* **Squeak's got ...** *a jumper,* **Alex has got ...** *a hat,* **Katie's got ...** *gloves.* **At the top of the beanstalk is ...** *a castle* **and a hungry ...** *giant.* **The giant comes and Jack gets the ...** *treasure clue* **from the giant's pocket. Alex, Katie, Pip and Squeak escape. Jack gives them the next ...** *treasure clue.*
- Play the CD (CD 2, track 4 – see Lesson 2). The children listen and follow the story in their books.

Setting objectives

- Say **Today we're going to practise saying sentences about clothes we've got.**

On the learning trail

Play a game. (PB page 32)

- If necessary, revise the colours needed for the game by pointing to objects of different colours in the classroom and asking the children to say the colours.
- Say the numbers of the squares in order and demonstrate that the children should respond by

naming the colours and clothes in chorus, e.g.

T: **Number one!**

PP: *A red shirt!*

- Repeat, this time saying the numbers in random order and asking individual children to name the colours and clothes.

- Ask the children to choose six squares. Explain and demonstrate that they should put a light cross (in pencil if you want to play the game more than once) on the squares they choose.

- Once the children are ready, play the game by saying sentences in turn, e.g. **I've got a purple t-shirt.** Explain and demonstrate that if the purple t-shirt is one of the six squares a child has chosen, they should say *I've got a purple t-shirt, too!* and draw a light cross through the whole square. Continue saying sentences (keeping a note so that you know which sentences you have said) and the children respond in the same way. The first child to say sentences about all six of their squares says *Bingo!* and is the winner.

- If you like, ask the children to rub out the crosses in their books. Ask them to choose six more squares and play the game again. Alternatively, the children can work in pairs and take turns to say e.g. *I've got a red shirt. / No!* or *I've got a red shirt, too*, according to what they have crossed. They can find out how many squares they chose that are the same as their partner.

Make the picture cards. (PB page 32 and AB page 85)

- Hold up your Pupil's Book and point to the picture cards. Say **We're going to make the picture cards.** You can show the children the set you have already made.

- Say **Find page 85 in your Activity Book. Look at the picture cards.** Point to the picture cards in turn. The children say the words.

- Make sure all the children have scissors.

- Point to the dashed cutting lines and say **Now cut out the cards like this.** Ask the children to write their names or initials on the back of the cards.

- When the children are ready say e.g. **Hold up the dress! / Hold up the gloves!** and the children respond by holding up the correct cards.

Play with the picture cards. (PB page 32)

- Hold up your Pupil's Book and point to the

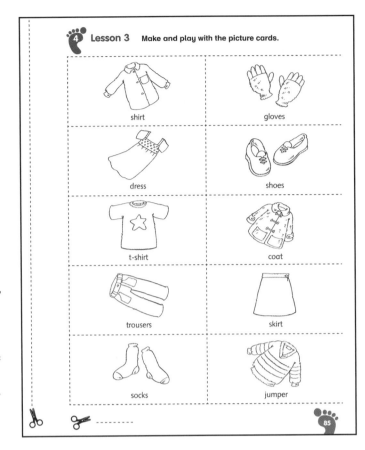

pictures. Ask two pupils to read the first dialogue and two other pupils to read the second dialogue.

- Ask a child to the front to demonstrate the game. Hold your set of picture cards face down in a pack and get the child to do the same. Demonstrate turning over one card, laying it down on the table and saying e.g. **I've got a skirt.** Get the child to do the same. If the card they lay down is different from yours, the child says e.g. *I've got gloves.* If the card is the same, the child says *I've got a skirt, too. Snap!* The child wins these cards, takes them out of the game and has the next turn to lay down a card first. The person with most cards at the end of the game is the winner.

- Divide the class into pairs. The children play the game with their partner.

- At the end, ask the children to shuffle their cards (demonstrate this) and play the game again or, alternatively, they can change partners.

- The children can colour the picture cards.

Read and colour. (AB page 30)

- Read what Katie and Alex say while the children follow in their books.

- Say **Now read and colour the clothes.**

- The children work individually and colour the

clothes.

- Check the answers by asking, e.g **What colour's Katie's t-shirt?** *(yellow)*

    Key: Katie: purple skirt, yellow t-shirt, orange socks
    Alex: blue trousers, red shirt, black shoes

Draw, colour and write about your clothes. (AB page 30)

- Read and complete the sentences, giving examples of your own clothes, e.g. **I've got a blue jumper.**
- Elicit examples from the children for each sentence about their own clothes.
- Ask the children to draw and colour pictures of their own clothes and complete the sentences. Draw their attention to the example and the colour words in the box.
- The children work individually. They draw and colour pictures and complete the sentences.
- The children compare and check their answers in pairs.
- Ask individual children to take turns to show their pictures and say sentences about their clothes to the rest of the class, e.g. *I've got black shoes. / I've got a red dress.*

    Key: Children's own answers.

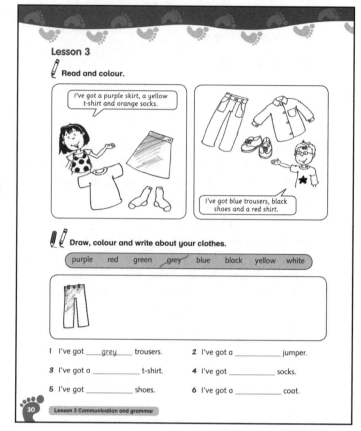

Ending the lesson

Lesson review

- Briefly ask the children what they can do as a result of the lesson (say sentences about clothes they've got). Praise the children for their efforts and / or use the finger puppets to do this.

Goodbye and closing routine

- Say goodbye to the children yourself and using the finger puppets. If there is time, you can play the karaoke version of *Shake your head* (CD 1, track 9 – see Lesson 1). Hold up the finger puppets on your index fingers as the children sing and do the actions as in Lesson 1.

4 My clothes

Lesson 4
Communication, grammar and pronunciation

Aims:
- To practise asking and answering questions about clothes
- To discriminate between words which start with /s/ and /ʃ/

Key language:
- *Is this your …? Yes, it is. / No it isn't.*
- *Are these your …? Yes, they are. / No they aren't.*
- *coat, trousers, shirt, t-shirt, skirt, dress, jumper, socks, shoes, gloves, hat*
- *new*

Materials:
- Pupil's Book page 33
- Activity Book page 31
- Finger puppets (Pip and Squeak)
- Flashcards: coat, trousers, shirt, t-shirt, skirt, dress, jumper, socks, shoes, gloves, hat, Frodo
- Unit 4 picture cards from Lesson 3
- CD 1 and CD 2

Starting out

Greetings and opening routine

- Greet the children yourself and using the finger puppets.
- *Either* play the karaoke version of *I'm ready for English* (CD 1, track 7 – see Lesson 1) and the children sing and do the actions as in Lesson 1 *or* play the karaoke version of *Everybody put on your coat* (CD 2, track 3 – see Lesson 1) and hold up flashcards of different clothes. The children say the chant and mime putting on clothes.

Revision activity

- Give out or ask the children to get out the picture cards they made in Lesson 3. Have your own set ready.
- Hold up one picture card and say e.g. **I've got a shirt.** Demonstrate that the children should respond by holding up their picture of a shirt and saying in chorus *I've got a shirt, too!*
- Repeat with the rest of the picture cards.

Setting objectives

- Say **Today we're going to practise asking and answering questions about clothes. We're also going to practise pronunciation.**

On the learning trail

Listen and say the chant. (PB page 33)

- (Books closed) Pre-teach the word *new*. If necessary, demonstrate the meaning by pointing to two similar objects – one that is new and one that is old.
- Say **Listen to the chant with Katie and Jack. What clothes does Katie ask Jack about?**
- Play the CD once (CD 2, track 6) and check the answer. *(hat, shoes)*
- Ask the children to open their Pupil's Books at page 33. Play the CD again. The children follow in their books and say the chant.

- Divide the children into two groups: one for the questions (Katie) and one for the answers (Jack).
- Play the CD again (CD 2, track 6). The children say the chant in their groups.
- The groups change roles and repeat.

Is this your hat? (CD 2, 6)

Is this your hat?	No, it isn't. My hat is new.
Is this your hat?	Yes, it is. Thank you!
Are these your shoes?	No, they aren't. My shoes are blue.
Are these your shoes?	Yes, they are. Thank you!

Look, ask and answer. (PB page 33)

- Say **Look at Squeak asking Pip about his clothes!** Hold up the finger puppets and read the two questions and answers at the start of the activity. Point out to the children that the cross through a picture means that item of clothing doesn't belong to Pip.
- Say **Let's ask Pip about all the clothes!** Hold up the Squeak puppet and get the children to repeat the question for each picture after you in chorus.
- Repeat, this time getting individual children to ask the questions as Squeak and encouraging everyone else to answer as Pip.
- Ask individual children to take turns to pretend to be Squeak and Pip and to ask and answer the question for each picture.
- Divide the class into pairs. The children act out the exchanges with their partner and then change roles.
- At the end, you may like to ask one or two pairs to the front to act out the exchanges to the class.

Key: 1 Is this your hat? Yes, it is. 2 Are these your gloves? No, they aren't. 3 Is this your coat? Yes, it is. 4 Are these your shoes? Yes, they are. 5 Is this your jumper? No, it isn't. 6 Are these your socks? No, they aren't.

Listen, circle and say: Frodo's word fun. (PB page 33)

- Hold up the flashcard of Frodo. Say **Listen and circle the pictures of clothes which begin with the sound 'sh'** /ʃ/ and demonstrate what you mean.

- Play the CD (CD 2, track 8) and the children circle the pictures. Use the pause button to give them time to do this if necessary.
- Check the answers by getting the children to tell you the numbers and say the words for the items beginning with /ʃ/.
- Play the CD again. The children listen and repeat the words.

Key: 1 shirt 5 shorts 9 shoes

Frodo's word fun. Listen, circle and say. (CD 2, 8)

1 shirt 2 skirt 3 socks 4 socks 5 shorts
6 skirt 7 skirt 8 socks 9 shoes

Listen and circle. (AB page 31)

- Ask the children to name the items in the pictures by asking e.g. **Number one?** *(It's a coat.)*
- Say **Katie, Alex, Pip and Squeak are asking Jack questions. Listen and circle the things that are Jack's.** Draw their attention to the example.
- Play the CD once or twice (CD 2, track 9). The children listen and circle the items that are Jack's. Use the pause button to give them time to do this if necessary.

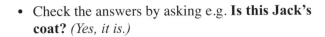

- Check the answers by asking e.g. **Is this Jack's coat?** *(Yes, it is.)*

  Key: 1 coat 2 gloves 3 book 4 crayons 5 jumper 6 shoes 7 pencil case 8 pencil sharpener

 Listen and circle.

1 Katie: *Is this your coat?*
  Jack: *Yes, it is.*
2 Katie: *Are these your gloves?*
  Jack: *Yes, they are.*
3 Katie: *Is this your book?*
  Jack: *No, it isn't.*
4 Katie: *Are these your crayons?*
  Jack: *Yes, they are.*
5 Katie: *Is this your jumper?*
  Jack: *Yes, it is.*
6 Katie: *Are these your shoes?*
  Jack: *No, they aren't.*
7 Katie: *Is this your pencil case?*
  Jack: *No, it isn't.*
8 Katie: *Is this your pencil sharpener?*
  Jack: *Yes, it is.*

Look, write and say. (AB page 31)

- Hold up the finger puppets and read the exchanges. The children say the missing words.
- Say **Now look and write the missing words.** Draw the children's attention to the example.
- The children work individually and write the words.
- Check the answers by asking individual children to read the exchanges.
- The children act out the exchanges, taking turns to be Pip and Squeak in pairs.

  Key: 1 hat 2 gloves 3 coat 4 shoes 5 jumper 6 socks

Ending the lesson

Lesson review

- Briefly ask the children what they can do as a result of the lesson (ask and answer questions about clothes, recognise and say words which begin with the sound 'sh' /ʃ/). Praise the children for their efforts and / or use the finger puppets to do this.

Goodbye and closing routine

- Say goodbye to the children yourself and using the finger puppets. If there is time, you can also play the karaoke version of *Shake your head* (CD 1, track 9 – see Lesson 1) and the children sing and do the actions as in Lesson 1.

4 My clothes

Lesson 5
Content input

Aim:

- To read and understand where cotton and wool are from

Key language:

- *Wool / Cotton is from sheep / the cotton plant.*
- *This ... is ... / These ... are ...*
- *jumper, jeans, tracksuit, t-shirt, coat, gloves*
- *warm, cool*

Materials:

- Pupil's Book page 34
- Activity Book page 32
- Finger puppets (Pip and Squeak)
- Flashcards: coat, trousers, shirt, t-shirt, skirt, dress, jumper, socks, shoes, gloves, hat
- Word cards: coat, trousers, shirt, t-shirt, skirt, dress, jumper, socks, shoes, gloves, hat
- CD 1 and CD 2
- Examples of wool and cotton clothes (optional)

Starting out

Greetings and opening routine

- Greet the children yourself and using the finger puppets.
- *Either* play the karaoke version of *I'm ready for English* (CD 1, track 7 – see Lesson 1) and the children sing and do the actions as in Lesson 1 *or* play the karaoke version of *Is this your hat?* (CD 2, track 7 – see Lesson 4) and the children say the chant in two groups as in Lesson 4.

Revision activity

- Play a memory game on the board with the flashcards and word cards. Divide the class into two teams.
- Stick the flashcards face down in jumbled order on one side of the board and the word cards face down in jumbled order on the other.
- Ask a child from one team to choose a card from one side of the board. Turn it over and the child points and says *This is a ...* or *These are ...* Ask another child from the same team to choose a card from the other side of the board and say a sentence in the same way. If the two cards match, take the cards off the board and put them on your desk nearest to the team.
- Repeat the procedure with the other team.
- Continue playing the game until there are no cards left on the board. The team with most cards at the end of the game wins.

Setting objectives

- Hold up the finger puppets. Say **Let's learn about the world around you! Today we're going to read about materials we use to make clothes.** Feel your own clothes to convey the meaning.

On the learning trail

Read, circle and listen. (PB page 34)

- (Books closed) Read the question **What do we use to make clothes?**
- Listen to the children's ideas (in L1). Use their suggestions to introduce vocabulary, e.g. *cotton, wool*. If you have examples of cotton and wool clothes, show these to the children and allow them to feel the texture.
- Ask the children to open their Pupil's Books at page 34. Read the text at the start of the activity or play part 1 on the CD (CD 2, track 10). Use the photos to clarify the meaning of *plant* and *sheep*. Use mime to convey the meaning of *warm* and *cool*. Use the photos in part 2 or clothes the children are wearing to explain the meaning of *jeans* and *tracksuit*.
- Say **Look at the photos and read the sentences. Circle** *cotton* **if you think the clothes are cotton, and** *wool* **if you think the clothes are wool.**
- The children work individually and read and circle the words.
- Ask questions about the photos in turn, e.g. **Is the t-shirt cotton, do you think?** *(Yes, it is.)* **Why? Are the gloves wool, do you think?** *(Yes, they are.)* **Why?** Listen to the children's ideas in L1 (e.g. t-shirts are for sport and cotton is cool / gloves keep you warm and wool is warm) but don't tell them the answers yet.
- Say **Now listen and find out.** Play part 2 on the CD (CD 2, track 10). Use the pause button to

allow the children time to compare their answers with the CD.

- Check the answers by asking individual children to read the sentences with the correct options.
- Play the CD again as a final check. Make the point that wool and cotton are both natural materials, whereas other materials such as acrylic or nylon are not natural.

Key: 1 cotton 2 wool 3 cotton 4 wool

 Read, circle and listen.

Part 1

Cotton is from the cotton plant.
Cotton is cool.
Jeans, tracksuits and t-shirts are cotton.

Wool is from sheep.
Wool is warm.
Jumpers, coats and gloves are wool.

Part 2

1 This t-shirt is cotton.
2 These gloves are wool.
3 These jeans are cotton.
4 This jumper is wool.

Listen and play a game. (PB page 34)

- Explain and demonstrate that the children should listen to the music and dance on the spot. When the music stops, they should listen to the clothes instruction, e.g. *Cotton socks!* They should sit down as fast as they can if they are wearing the clothes mentioned. Explain and demonstrate that the children should then be ready to show and tell the class why they have sat down, e.g. they should say *These socks are cotton!* Explain that the children have three lives in the game. They lose a life if they sit down when they haven't got the clothes they hear on the CD or if they don't sit down when they have got the clothes.

- **Note:** accept if children respond with clothes which are, for example, a mixture of cotton and nylon as the game is only intended to focus on the general difference between wool and cotton rather than other materials.

- Say **Stand up!** Play the CD (CD 2, track 11) and the children respond depending on whether or not they are wearing the clothes. Get two or three

children who sit down each time to report back using *This ... is ...* or *These ... are ...* between each turn. Be generous with the lives and do not worry if, for example, a child responds to *wool jumper* when their jumper is in fact acrylic or a mixture of the two. The children with three lives left at the end of the game are the winners.

 Listen and play a game.

Cotton socks!
Wool jumper!
Cotton shirt!
Cotton dress!
Wool socks!
Cotton trousers!
Cotton tracksuit!
Cotton t-shirt!
Wool trousers!
Wool skirt!

117

Read and circle. (AB page 32)

- Read the sentences and the children say *Yes* or *No* depending on whether they are true or false.
- Say **Now read and circle *Yes* or *No*.** Draw their attention to the example.
- The children work individually and circle *Yes* or *No*.
- Check the answers by reading the sentences and the children saying *Yes* or *No*. If you like, you can also ask the children to correct the sentences that are wrong, e.g. *1 No. Cotton is from a plant.*

Key: 1 No 2 Yes 3 No 4 Yes

Look, write and say. (AB page 32)

- Draw the children's attention to the key at the top of the activity.
- Read the sentences and the children complete them by saying *wool* or *cotton,* depending on the little picture by each item of clothing and following the key.
- Say **Now write *wool* or *cotton*.** Draw their attention to the example.
- The children work individually and complete the sentences.
- Check the answers by asking individual children to take turns to say a sentence.

Key: 1 cotton 2 cotton 3 wool 4 wool 5 cotton 6 wool

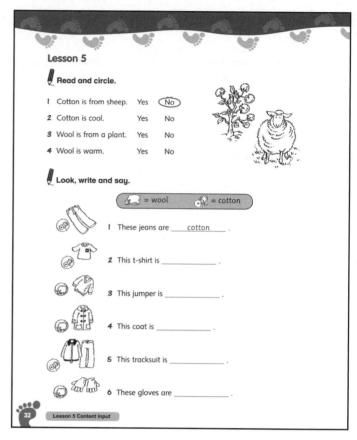

Ending the lesson

Lesson review

- Briefly ask the children what they can do as a result of the lesson (read and understand where wool and cotton are from, name clothes that are wool or cotton). Praise the children for their efforts and / or use the finger puppets to do this.

Goodbye and closing routine

- Say goodbye to the children yourself and using the finger puppets. If there is time, you can also play the karaoke version of *Shake your head* (CD 1, track 9 – see Lesson 1) and the children sing and do the actions as in Lesson 1.

4 My clothes

Lesson 6
Content and personalisation

Aims:

- To identify wool and cotton by touch
- To talk about your own clothes

Key language:

- *Is this ...?*
- *Are these ...?*
- *It's / They're ...*
- *wool, cotton*
- *I've got (a) ... Me, too!*
- *warm, cool*
- *jumper, jeans, tracksuit, t-shirt, coat, gloves, shirt, skirt, dress, trousers, gloves, socks*

Materials:

- Pupil's Book page 35
- Activity Book page 33
- Finger puppets (Pip and Squeak)
- CD 1 and CD 2
- Examples of wool and cotton clothes or small pieces of wool and cotton
- Blindfolds (optional)

Starting out

Greetings and opening routine

- Greet the children yourself and using the finger puppets.
- *Either* play the karaoke version of *I'm ready for English* (CD 1, track 7 – see Lesson 1) and the children sing and do the actions as in Lesson 1 *or* play the karaoke version of *Is this your hat?* (CD 2, track 7 – see Lesson 4) and the children say the chant in two groups as previously.

Revision activity

- Show the children an example of something made of wool and something made of cotton. Say e.g. **This is ...** and elicit or remind the children of the words *cotton* and *wool*.
- Say sentences about wool and cotton in turn. Either whistle or say a nonsense word, e.g. **bleep!** and the children supply the missing word, e.g.

Wool is *bleep*! *(warm)* Cotton is *bleep*! *(cool)*. (Use the text on page 34 of the Pupil's Book for more ideas).

Setting objectives

- Say **In this lesson we're going to play a game to identify cotton and wool by touch** (use gesture to convey meaning) **and talk about our own clothes.**

On the learning trail

Play a game. (PB page 35)

- Ask a child to the front of the class. Either blindfold them or get them to stand facing away from you with their hands behind their back.
- Give the child a piece of wool or cotton or an item of clothing to feel but not look at. Ask **Is this / Are these wool or cotton?** Encourage them to guess, e.g. *It's / They're wool!*
- Repeat the game once or twice with different children and clothes.
- Ask a child to take over your role and repeat the game again once or twice.
- Divide the class into pairs. Either use blindfolds, if you have these, or ask one child in each pair to

sit facing away from their partner and with their hands behind their back. The other child gives their partner a piece of wool or cotton or an item of clothing to feel and asks *Is this wool or cotton?*, etc. as previously. The children then change roles.

Option: As in Lesson 5, wool or cotton clothes which include some other material such as nylon or acrylic can also be used, as it is intended to focus only on the general differences in texture.

Draw and say. (PB page 35)

- Point to your own clothes and say e.g. **Look. I've got a cotton t-shirt. / I've got a wool jumper.**

- Hold up your Pupil's Book, point to the two circles in turn and say **Draw three of your clothes which are cotton here. Draw three of your clothes which are wool here.**

- **Note:** be flexible about the children drawing clothes which include another material as well as cotton and wool.

- The children work individually and draw pictures.

- Ask individual children to take turns to show their pictures and tell the class, e.g. *I've got cotton trousers. / I've got a wool coat.*

Listen and match. (AB page 33)

- Say **Listen and match the children to the clothes.** Draw the children's attention to the example.

- Play the CD once (CD 2, track 12). Use the pause button if necessary to give them time to match the children and clothes.

- Check the answers by saying e.g. **The boy in number one says …** and the children complete what the children say on the CD.

   Key: 1 coat 2 jeans 3 tracksuit 4 gloves

 Listen and match.

   1 I've got a wool coat. 2 I've got cotton jeans. 3 I've got a cotton tracksuit. 4 I've got wool gloves.

Look, write and say. (AB page 33)

- Say **Write about your clothes** and draw the children's attention to the example.

- The children work individually and complete the sentences about their own clothes. They can use the words at the top to help them.

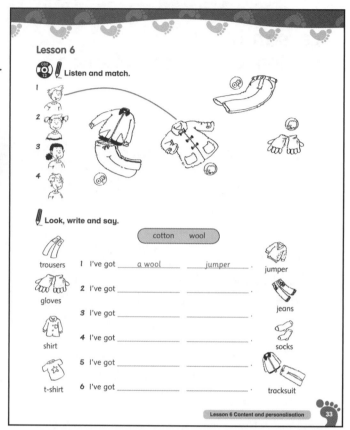

Option: As above, be flexible if the children write about clothes which include other materials as well as cotton and wool.

- Invite individual children to take turns to tell the class one of their sentences, e.g. *I've got a cotton dress.* If another child has the same, explain that they should say *Me, too!* and have the next turn.

Ending the lesson

Lesson review

- Briefly ask the children what they can do as a result of the lesson (identify cotton and wool by touch, talk about their own clothes). Praise the children for their efforts and / or use the finger puppets to do this.

Goodbye and closing routine

- Say goodbye to the children yourself and using the finger puppets. If there is time, you can also play the karaoke version of *Shake your head* (CD 1, track 9 – see Lesson 1) and the children sing and do the actions as in Lesson 1.

4 My clothes

Lesson 7
Children's culture

Aim:
- To say a version of a traditional rhyme and play a traditional game

Key language:
- *coat, trousers, shirt, t-shirt, socks, shoes, skirt, dress, jumper, jeans, tracksuit, gloves, hat*
- *friend, bed, crocodile, river, cross*
- *Can I ...?*
- colours

Materials:
- Pupil's Book page 36
- Activity Book page 34
- Finger puppets (Pip and Squeak)
- Flashcard: Frodo
- CD 1 and CD 2

Starting out

Greetings and opening routine

- Greet the children yourself and using the finger puppets.
- *Either* play the karaoke version of *I'm ready for English* (CD 1, track 7 – see Lesson 1) and the children sing and do the actions as in Lesson 1 *or* play the karaoke version of *Is this your hat?* (CD 2, track 7 – see Lesson 4) and the children say the chant in groups as previously.

Revision activity

- Explain that you are going to say sentences about clothes you've got and the children should repeat the sentences if they are true for them, too.
- Say sentences, e.g. **I've got a cotton t-shirt / I've got wool gloves** and the children respond. If you like, keep a score on the board of all the sentences that are true for the whole class.

Setting objectives

- Hold up the flashcard of Frodo. Say **In this lesson we're going to learn about children's culture with Frodo. We're going to say a version of a traditional rhyme and play a game.** Use gesture to convey the meaning of this.

On the learning trail

Listen and say the rhyme. (PB page 36) (books closed)

- Say **We're going to listen to a version of a traditional rhyme. This rhyme is about a boy – my friend John – who goes to bed** (use mime to convey meaning) **with clothes on. Listen to the rhyme and tell me the clothes.**
- Play the CD (CD 2, track 13). Ask the children to name the clothes they hear in the rhyme *(trousers, shoe)*, although don't expect them to understand *one shoe off / on* yet.
- Ask the children to open their Pupil's Books at page 36. Say **Look. John's got one shoe off and one shoe on** and use the picture to clarify meaning.
- Explain that *Diddle, diddle, dumpling* are nonsense words. They don't mean anything but are fun to

say and give rhythm to the rhyme. You may like to ask the children if they know any rhymes in their own language which use rhythmic nonsense words in a similar way.

- Say **Now listen, follow in your books and say the rhyme.** Play the CD again.

- Divide the class into two groups. The groups take turns to say alternate lines of the rhyme. Play the CD again.

- Change roles and repeat.

 Diddle, diddle, dumpling

Diddle, diddle, dumpling
My friend John
Goes to bed with his trousers on
One shoe off and one shoe on
Diddle, diddle, dumpling
My friend John!

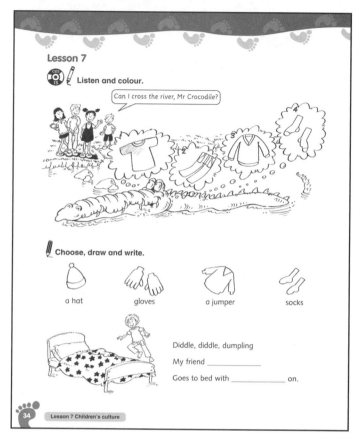

 Citizenship box: Remember!

Say e.g. **Look at John in bed with his trousers on. That's not a very good way to take care of his clothes!**

Hold up the flashcard of Frodo, read the *Remember!* note and explain the meaning of *take care of*. Ask the children for examples of how they can take care of their clothes, e.g. put them away when they're not using them, fold them, try not to lose them. Emphasise the importance of the children taking responsibility for their own clothes at school.

Play *Mr Crocodile!* (PB page 36)

- Ask the children to stand in a line on one side of the classroom. Explain that the classroom is a river and you are a crocodile! The children can only cross the river if they've got the clothes you say!

- Teach the children the question to ask in the game: **Can I cross the river, Mr (Mrs or Miss) Crocodile?** and get them to repeat it several times in chorus.

- Demonstrate the game by getting the children to ask you the question and respond by saying e.g. **Yes, if you've got … a blue shirt.** Explain that all the children wearing a blue shirt can safely cross the river. The others must wait.

- Play the game, saying different clothes each time. The last child or children left on the bank after six to eight turns are eaten by the crocodile! These children then have the next turn at being the crocodile with your help, e.g. you say **if you've got …**, and the children who are the crocodiles take turns to say the clothes, e.g. *… a wool dress*.

Option: If you have the opportunity to go to the playground or gym, you can play the traditional version of this game with the children. In this, the children who haven't got the item specified by the crocodile have to try and run across the 'river' without the crocodile catching them. If they are caught they become crocodiles as well. The last child to be caught wins and has the next turn being the crocodile.

Listen and colour. (AB page 34)

- Say **Listen to what the crocodile says and colour the clothes.** Draw the children's attention to the partially coloured t-shirt in number one to convey meaning. Explain and demonstrate that the children should only put a spot of colour on the clothes as they listen, and finish colouring at the end.

- Play the CD (CD 2, track 15). Use the pause button to give the children time to put a spot of colour on each picture. They finish colouring them at the end.

- Check the answers by saying e.g. **Number one. The crocodile says if you've got ...** and the children name the colours and clothes.

  Key: The clothes should be coloured as follows:
  1 red 2 green 3 yellow 4 blue

 Listen and colour.

1 Can I cross the river, Mr Crocodile?
   Yes, if you've got a red t-shirt.

2 Can I cross the river, Mr Crocodile?
   Yes, if you've got green trousers.

3 Can I cross the river, Mr Crocodile?
   Yes, if you've got a yellow jumper.

4 Can I cross the river, Mr Crocodile?
   Yes, if you've got blue socks.

Choose, draw and write. (AB page 34)

- Read the words at the top of the activity. Explain that the children are going to choose a friend and some clothes and create their own version of part of the rhyme they learnt earlier in the lesson.

- Say **Diddle, diddle, dumpling, my friend ...** (and name a child in the class) **goes to bed with ... on** (and encourage a different child to name one of the clothes items at the top of the activity).

- Repeat several times, inviting individual children to name different friends and clothes each time. Do this in a light-hearted way and make sure the children realise that the rhyme is humorous and nonsensical rather than serious. Say **Now choose a friend and some clothes. Draw a picture and write the name of your friend and the clothes.**

- The children work individually and draw clothes onto the picture and complete this extract of the rhyme.

- If you like, at the end, ask a few children to show their pictures and read their version of the rhyme to the rest of the class.

Ending the lesson

Lesson review

- Briefly ask the children what they can do as a result of the lesson (say the rhyme *Diddle, diddle, dumpling* and play *Mr Crocodile!*). Praise the children for their efforts and / or use the finger puppets to do this.

Goodbye and closing routine

- Say goodbye to the children yourself and using the finger puppets. If there is time, you can also play the karaoke version of *Shake your head* (CD 1, track 9 – see Lesson 1) and the children sing and do the actions as in Lesson 1.

4 My clothes

Lesson 8
Unit review / *All About Me Portfolio Booklet*

Aim:
- To review learning in Unit 4

Key language:
- *I've got ...*
- *Is this your ...? Yes, it is. / No, it isn't.*
- *Are these your ...? Yes, they are. / No, they aren't.*
- *coat, trousers, shirt, t-shirt, jumper, socks, shoes, skirt, dress, gloves, hat, jeans, tracksuit*
- *cotton, wool*

Materials:
- Pupil's Book page 37
- Activity Book page 35
- *All About Me* Portfolio Booklet pages 12 and 13
- Finger puppets (Pip and Squeak)
- Flashcards: coat, trousers, shirt, t-shirt, skirt, dress, jumper, socks, shoes, gloves, hat, Frodo
- Stickers for Unit 4
- CD 1 and CD 2

Starting out

Greetings and opening routine

- Greet the children yourself and using the finger puppets.
- *Either* play the karaoke version of *I'm ready for English* (CD1, track 7 – see Lesson 1) and the children sing and do the actions as in Lesson 1 *or* hold up flashcards and play the karaoke version of the chant *Everybody put on your coat* (CD 2, track 3 – see Lesson 1) and the children say the chant and mime putting on different clothes.

Revision activity

- Say **Let's say the rhyme *Diddle, diddle, dumpling*.** Play the CD (CD 2, track 13 – see Lesson 7) and the children join in saying the rhyme.
- Play the karaoke version on the CD (CD 2, track 14). Say the first line and get the children to say the second line. Help them to do this at first.

- Continue saying alternate lines of the rhyme with the whole class.
- Change roles and repeat.
- Divide the class into pairs. Play the karaoke version on the CD again. The children take it in turns to say alternate lines of the rhyme with their partner.

Setting objectives

- Say **Today we're going to review what we've learnt in Unit 4.**

On the learning trail

Listen and put on the stickers. Write the words. (PB page 37)

- Make sure the children have the stickers for Unit 4 ready.
- Say **Listen and put on the stickers.** Draw the children's attention to the example.
- Play the CD (CD 2, track 16). Use the pause button to give the children time to put on the stickers.

- Say **Now write the words.** Draw the children's attention to the example.
- Check the answers by saying the numbers and getting the children to say the words.

  Key: 1 coat 2 trousers 3 jumper 4 socks
  5 t-shirt 6 skirt 7 gloves 8 shoes 9 shirt 10 dress

 Listen and put on the stickers.

1 Is this your coat? Yes, it is.
2 Are these your trousers? Yes, they are.
3 Is this your jumper? Yes, it is.
4 Are these your socks? Yes, they are.
5 Is this your t-shirt? Yes, it is.
6 I've got a purple skirt.
7 I've got wool gloves.
8 I've got blue shoes.
9 I've got a cotton shirt.
10 I've got a cotton dress.

Look, write and say. (PB page 37)

- Read the exchanges and sentences and the children say the missing words. They look at the pictures and use the words at the top of the activity.
- Say **Now write the words.** Draw the children's attention to the example.
- The children work individually and write the missing words.
- Check the answers by asking children to say the exchanges and sentences.

  Key: 1 coat 2 gloves 3 t-shirt 4 trousers
  5 socks 6 jumper

Listen, circle and say. (AB page 35)

- Say **Look at the pictures. Listen and circle the clothes they've got.** Draw the children's attention to the example.
- Play the CD (CD 2, track 17). Pause if necessary to give the children time to circle the pictures.
- Check the answers by saying e.g. **The child in number one says …** and the children repeat what they say.

  Key: The following items should be circled:
  1 hat on the right 2 socks on the left 3 trousers on the right 4 dress on the left

 Listen, circle and say.

1 I've got a wool hat.
2 I've got cotton socks.
3 I've got wool trousers.
4 I've got a cotton dress.

Look and write. (AB page 35)

- Ask e.g. **What does Katie / Alex say?** and elicit what the characters say orally, e.g. *I've got a cotton t-shirt.*
- Say **Write what Katie and Alex say** and draw the children's attention to the example.
- The children work individually and complete the sentences. They use the words at the top of the activity.
- Check the answers by asking individual children to say what Alex and Katie say.

  Key: Katie: 1 cotton t-shirt 2 cotton dress
  3 wool jumper; Alex: 4 cotton trousers 5 wool coat
  6 wool gloves

Colour Frodo. (AB page 35)

- Hold up the flashcard of Frodo. Remind the children that in this activity they assess their work in the unit by choosing and colouring the picture of Frodo which corresponds best to how they think they have done.

- Remind the children of the key by pointing to the three pictures of Frodo and saying **Colour this picture if your work is OK but you think you need to try harder or need more practice. Colour this picture of Frodo if you think your work is good. Colour this picture of Frodo with a big smile and jumping very high if you think your work is excellent.** Make sure the children understand that there are no right answers and that it is their own opinion of the work they have done which is important. Be ready to encourage the children to have a positive view if they are too hard on themselves.

Ending the lesson

Lesson review

- Briefly ask the children what they can do as a result of the lesson (use the language and vocabulary they've learnt in Unit 4). Praise the children for their efforts and / or use the finger puppets to do this.

Goodbye and closing routine

- Say goodbye to the children yourself and using the finger puppets. If there is time, you can also play the karaoke version of *Shake your head* (CD 1, track 9 – see Lesson 1) and the children sing and do the actions as in Lesson 1.

All About Me Portfolio Booklet

The children complete Unit 4 of their personal *All About Me* Portfolio Booklets. They complete their learning journey by colouring the sections on the path to show what they can do. If you like, the children can also sign this page and you can endorse this by adding your own signature and the date.

5 Food I like

Structures and grammar

- *I like … / I don't like …*
- *Do you like …? Yes, I do. / No, I don't.*
- *Is / Are … good for you?.*
- Recycled: *What's this? It's …, Yes, it is / No, it isn't., Yes, they are. / No, they aren't, I'm …, too! Me, too!*

Vocabulary

- Core: *hamburger, chicken, chips, salad, pizza, ice cream, chocolate, yogurt, apple, banana*
- Other: *delicious, horrible, house, food, witch, key*
- Content / culture: *good for you, water, sweet, coffee, tea, apple pie, roast beef, cheese*
- Recycled: *boy, girl, table, biscuit, sandwich, cake, hungry,* colours

Main receptive language

- *body, need, food, drink, snack, lunch, train, pot, important*
- *my friend*

Communicative competence

Understanding

Listening:
- Can recognise food words
- Can understand the episode of the story
- Can understand when people say they like or don't like food
- Can understand questions about food you like
- Can understand questions and answers about whether food is good for you

Reading:
- Can recognise food words
- Can read statements about food people say they like and don't like
- Can read questions and answers about food you like
- Can understand questions and answers about whether food is good for you

Speaking

Spoken interaction:
- Can ask about and respond to questions about food you like
- Can ask and answer questions about whether food is good for you

Spoken production:
- Can name food
- Can sing the song *I'm ready for English*
- Can sing the song *Delicious for me, delicious for you!*
- Can say sentences about food you like and don't like
- Can say the chant *Do you like yogurt?*
- Can say the chant *The lunch train*
- Can say a skipping game rhyme
- Can say a tongue-twister with /tʃ/
- Can sing the song *Shake your head*

Writing

- Can copy and write words for food
- Can complete questions and sentences about food you like and don't like

Content links

- *Social sciences:* food that is good for you

Learning strategies and thinking skills

- Recognising learning objectives
- Associating vocabulary with personal preferences
- Completing a chart
- Cooperating with others
- Classifying
- Using rhythm to memorise vocabulary and language patterns
- Reflecting on learning

Children's culture

- Saying a chant: *The lunch train*
- Playing a traditional skipping game: *Coffee and tea!*

Pronunciation

- Tongue-twister with 'ch' /tʃ/

Values and attitudes

- Pleasure in expressing personal likes and dislikes
- Interest and respect for other people's opinions
- Awareness that it is important to eat food that is good for you
- Awareness of the importance of eating a good lunch

5 Food I like

Lesson 1
Vocabulary presentation

Aim:
- To name food

Key language:
- *chicken, hamburger, salad, chips, pizza, chocolate, ice cream, apple, banana, yogurt*
- *delicious for me / you*

Materials:
- Pupil's Book page 38
- Activity Book page 36
- Finger puppets (Pip and Squeak)
- Flashcards: chicken, hamburger, salad, chips, pizza, chocolate, ice cream, apple, banana, yogurt, Frodo
- Word cards: chicken, hamburger, salad, chips, pizza, chocolate, ice cream, apple, banana, yogurt
- CD 1 and CD 2

Starting out

Greetings and opening routine

- Greet the children yourself and using the finger puppets. Say e.g. **Hello, children. Hello … How are you today?** *Fine, thank you.* Ask a few individual children to greet the puppets in turn.

- Say **Let's sing the song *I'm ready for English*.** Play the CD (CD 1, track 6). Hold up the puppets on your index fingers. Move them as the children sing and do the actions.

 I'm ready for English

Hello, hello, hello.
　　　　　(wave hello to teacher and friends)
I'm ready for English. Look!
　　　　　(hold out your arms)
Here's my pencil and rubber
　　　　　(hold out objects in turn)
And here's my notebook! (hold up notebook)
I'm ready! I'm ready! Hurray!
　　　　　(wave arms in the air)

Setting objectives

- Say **Today we're going to learn how to name food** (use gesture to convey meaning) **and we're going to sing a song.**

On the learning trail

Vocabulary presentation (books closed)

- Cover one of the flashcards, e.g. banana, with a piece of paper. Pull down the piece of paper slowly. The children identify the food as soon as they can see what it is. Say e.g. **Yes. Very good. It's a banana.**

- Point to the flashcard. Say **banana** several times and get the children to repeat the word with you in chorus.

- Stick the flashcard of the banana on the board.

- Repeat the procedure for the other food flashcards.

- Divide the class in half. Hold up the Pip finger puppet and say to one half **Say the words with Pip.** Use the puppet to point to the flashcards in turn and the children say the words with you. Make the puppet fly around to praise the children.

- Repeat the procedure with the Squeak puppet and the other half of the class.

Follow the footprints. (PB page 38) (books open)

- Hold up the flashcard of Frodo. Say **Listen and follow the footprints with Frodo the frog. Use your finger** and demonstrate this.

- Play the CD (CD 2, track 18). The children listen and follow the footprints with their fingers. They stop by each picture as they hear the word and repeat the word.

- Say **Now listen and draw a line following the footprints** and demonstrate this. Play the CD again. The children draw a line, stop by each picture and repeat the words as previously.

 Follow the footprints.

chicken … hamburger … salad … chips … pizza … chocolate … ice cream … apple … banana … yogurt

- Stick the word cards on the board in jumbled order (at the children's height and away from the flashcards).

- Point to one word card, e.g. *hamburger,* and read the word. Say **Look for the picture of the hamburger.** Give the children time to do this.

- Ask a child to come to the front of the class and stick the word card for *hamburger* by the corresponding flashcard. Ask the rest of the class **Is this right?** and get them to say the word.

- Repeat the procedure with the rest of the word cards.

- Take the flashcards and word cards off the board.

Listen and sing the song. (PB page 38)

- Say **Look at the picture of Pip and Squeak.** Ask **What food can you see on the table?** and the children name the food in the picture.

- Say **Listen to the song. Point to the food** and demonstrate what you mean. Play the CD (CD 2, track 19). The children listen to the song and point to the food in each verse as they hear it.

- Use facial expression to elicit or explain the meaning of *delicious*.

- Invite four (or eight) children to the front of the class. Give them each one (or two) flashcard(s) and get them to stand facing the class holding up the flashcards in the same order as each verse of the song.

- Explain and demonstrate that the children at the front should wave their flashcard(s) from side to side when they hear the words in the song and the rest of the class should point to the flashcards in turn. The children should gesture to themselves and then to a friend when they sing *Delicious for me, delicious for you!* in each verse.

- Play the CD again. The children point to the flashcards, do the actions and sing the song.

 Delicious for me, delicious for you!

Chicken, pizza, salad, too
Delicious for me, delicious for you!
Apples, bananas, yogurt, too
Delicious for me, delicious for you!
Chocolate and ice cream, too
Delicious for me, delicious for you!

Find, colour and say. (PB page 38)

- Ask the children to look at the puzzle picture and find and name the 'hidden' food, e.g. *banana*.

- Say **Now find and colour the food.** Draw their attention to the example.

- The children work individually and colour the 'hidden' pictures of food.

- Check the answers by getting individual children to point to and name a food they can find. Then ask the children to name the food they can't find in the picture (ask them to look at the pictures in the word trail to identify these if necessary).

Key: ice cream, banana, apple, hamburger, chocolate

Find, match and circle. (AB page 36)

- Stick the word cards for all the foods on the board and get the children to read them with you.

- Say **Look and find the words. Match the words and pictures.** Draw the children's attention to the example. Use gesture to explain that all the words are written horizontally rather than vertically or diagonally.

- The children work individually. They first find the food words in the wordsearch and then match the words and pictures. They circle the words in the wordsearch.

- The children check their answers in pairs. They take turns to read the words in the wordsearch and point to the corresponding pictures.

  Key: Children match the words and pictures.
  1. banana, 2. pizza, 3. chicken, 4. chocolate,
  5. hamburger, 6. ice cream, 7. apple, 8. yogurt,
  9. salad, 10. chicken

Look, write and listen. (AB page 36)

- The children look at the pictures and say the missing words to complete the song *Delicious for me, delicious for you!*

- Say **Now write the words.** Draw the children's attention to the example.

- The children work individually and complete the song.

- Check the answers by asking individual children to take turns to read lines of the song.

- If you like, play the karaoke version of the song (CD 2, track 21) and the children sing the song.

  Key: Chicken, pizza, salad; Apples, bananas, yogurt; Chocolate, ice cream

Ending the lesson

Lesson review

- Briefly ask the children what they can do as a result of the lesson (name food, sing the song *Delicious for me, delicious for you!*). Praise the children for their efforts and / or use the finger puppets to do this.

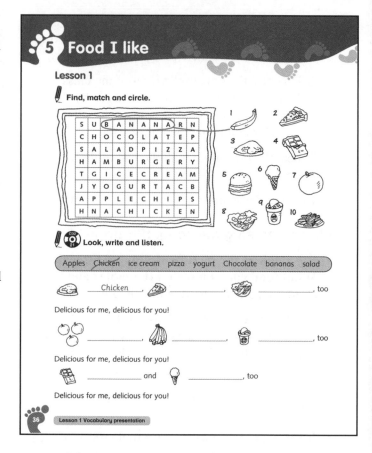

Goodbye and closing routine

- Say **Let's sing the song *Shake your head*.** Play the CD (CD 1, track 8). Hold up the finger puppets on your index fingers as the children sing and do the actions.

Shake your head

Shake your head	(shake head)
Wave your arms	(wave arms in the air)
Touch your ears and eyes	(point to ears and eyes)
It's the end of the lesson now	(tap real or imaginary watch)
Goodbye! Goodbye! Goodbye!	(wave goodbye)

- Say goodbye to the children yourself and using the finger puppets. Say e.g. **Goodbye everyone. See you on …** Ask a few individual children to say goodbye to the finger puppets in turn.

5 Food I like

Lesson 2
Language input and story

Aim:
- To understand and act out episode 5 of the story

Key language:
- *I like ... / I don't like ...*
- *Do you like ...? Yes, I do. / No, I don't.*
- *hamburger, chicken, chips, pizza, salad, ice cream, chocolate, apple, banana, yogurt*
- *house, witch, food*

Materials:
- Pupil's Book page 39
- Activity Book page 37
- Finger puppets (Pip and Squeak)
- Flashcards: Alex, Katie, hamburger, chicken, chips, pizza, salad, ice cream, chocolate, apple, banana, yogurt
- Treasure clue sticker for Unit 5
- CD 1 and CD 2

Starting out

Greetings and opening routine
- Greet the children yourself and using the finger puppets.
- Play the karaoke version of *I'm ready for English* (CD 1, track 7 – see Lesson 1). The children sing and do the actions as in Lesson 1.

Revision activity
- Hold up the food flashcards in turn and the children say the words.
- Stick the flashcards in the same order as the song *Delicious for me, delicious for you!* (see Lesson 1) on the board.
- Play the CD (CD 2, track 19 – see Lesson 1). The children sing the song, point to the flashcards and do the actions as in Lesson 1. Repeat with the karaoke version (CD 2, track 20 – see Lesson 1).

Setting objectives
- Say **Today we're going to listen to and act out episode 5 of the story.**

On the learning trail

Listen and act out the story.
Episode 5: The witch (PB page 39)

Before the story (books closed)
- Hold up the finger puppets and stick the flashcards of Alex and Katie on the board. Recap on the last episode of the story using mime and gesture and / or L1 as necessary: **Alex, Katie, Pip and Squeak find Jack and climb the beanstalk. At the top of the beanstalk is a castle and a hungry giant. Jack gets the treasure clue from the giant's pocket. Jack gives the treasure clue to Alex, Katie, Pip and Squeak.**
- Ask **Can you remember the clue from Unit 4?** Hold up page 31 of the Pupil's Book and point to the treasure clue sticker. Read *Follow the footprints! Find a house of food!* as a prompt if necessary. Elicit or remind the children of the meaning of *house* and *food*.
- Use L1 to ask the children if they know a traditional story with a 'house of food' and listen to their response. If they are familiar with the story of Hansel and Gretel, briefly ask who the main characters are. If they don't know the story,

introduce the characters: a boy called Hansel, a girl called Gretel and a witch.

- Explain that in this episode Katie, Alex, Pip and Squeak find the house of food. Ask the following questions in turn. Use mime and gesture to clarify meaning, and encourage the children to predict the answers: **1) What food is the house made of? 2) Who's in the house? 3) Where's the next treasure clue?**

During the story (books open)

- Say **Now listen to the story and find out.** Explain to the children that they will hear a 'beep' noise on the CD to tell them when to move to the next picture in the story.

- Play the CD (CD 2, track 22) and the children follow in their books.

- Ask the questions in turn again and check the answers, recasting them in English as necessary. *(1 ice cream, chocolate, pizza, salad 2 the witch, a boy and a girl 3 in the witch's pot)*

- Say **Listen again and repeat the story.** Play the CD again. Pause after each sentence and the children repeat the story.

- **Note:** There is more story text on the CD than appears on the PB page. This additional text is marked with an asterisk* in the audio script below. The children repeat the whole story, including the language which does not appear in their books.

 Follow the footprints, Episode 5: The witch

Picture 1	
Narrator:	*Alex, Katie, Pip and Squeak follow the footprints to find the house of food.**
Katie:	*Look! It's the house of food!*
Pip:	*Wow! It's pink, yellow, brown, red, green …*
Alex:	*Mmm. I'm hungry!**
Squeak:	*Come on. Let's go.**

Picture 2	
Alex:	*Mmm! Ice cream!*
Pip:	*I like ice cream. Delicious!*
Squeak:	*Yuk! I don't like ice cream.*
Katie:	*And look! Chocolate! Mmm. I like chocolate.**

Picture 3	
Katie:	*Do you like pizza?*
Squeak:	*Yes, I do.*
Pip:	*No, I don't. It's horrible! Do you like salad?**
Alex:	*Yes, I do.**

Picture 4	
Pip:	*Ssh! Listen!**
Alex:	*Look! A boy and a girl.*
Squeak:	*And a witch!*
Alex:	*Oh, no!**

Picture 5	
Witch:	*Ha! I'm hungry! I like boys and I like girls.*
Hansel and Gretel:	*Oh, no!*

Picture 6	
Hansel:	*Help! Quick!*
Gretel:	*The key's on the table.*

Picture 7	
Gretel:	*Here's the witch!**
Hansel:	*Run everybody!*
Alex:	*Look! Here's the next treasure clue!*
Pip and Squeak:	*Hurray!**
Alex:	*Follow the footprints! Find Aladdin and the lamp! Come on. Let's go.**
Hansel and Gretel:	*Goodbye and good luck!**

After the story

- Ask questions about each picture as follows: **1) What colour is the house?** *(pink, yellow, brown, red, green)* **2) Who says *I like ice cream*?** *(Pip)* **Who says *I don't like ice cream*?** *(Squeak)* **Who says *I like chocolate*?** *(Katie)* **3) Does Pip like pizza?** *(no)* **Does Squeak like pizza?** *(yes)* **Does Alex like salad?** *(yes)* **4) Who's in the house?** *(a boy, a girl, a witch)* **5) What is the witch planning to do?** *(to eat the boy and girl)* **6) Where's the key?** (use gesture to convey meaning) *(on the table)* **7) Who's here?** *(the witch)* **Are the boy and girl free?** (use gesture to convey meaning) *(yes)* **Is the witch happy?** *(no,* *she's very angry)* **Where's the treasure clue?** *(in the witch's pot)* **Who gets the treasure clue?** *(Alex)*

Put on the treasure clue sticker.

- Say **The treasure clue says *Follow the footprints! Find Aladdin and the lamp!*** Elicit or explain the meaning of *lamp*.

- Say **Find the treasure clue sticker for Unit 5 and stick it here.** Demonstrate what you mean.

- The children look for the treasure clue sticker for Unit 5 and stick it in their books.

Act out the story.

- Divide the class into seven groups and assign a role to each group: Alex, Katie, Pip, Squeak, Hansel, Gretel or the witch.

- Follow the procedure for *Act out the story* on page 37 of the Teacher's Book (seven children are needed to act out the story).

Option: The children can act out their parts *either* with *or* without their books, depending on how confident and familiar they are with this episode. If you wish to make the activity more challenging, the children can act out the whole story by joining in their character's part as you replay the CD.

Read, colour and say. (AB page 37)

- Read the sentences while the children follow in their books.

- Say **Now colour the house of food.** The children work individually and colour the picture.

- When they are ready, ask individual children to point to their completed picture and say e.g. *The ice cream is pink.*

Look, write and listen. (AB page 37)

- Read the speech bubbles and the children say the missing words.

- Say **Now write the words.** Draw the children's attention to the example.

- Play the CD (CD 2, track 23).

- The children listen and read the sentences. They work individually and complete the sentences.

- Check the answers by asking e.g. **What does Alex say?**

Key: 1 ice cream 2 chocolate 3 pizza 4 salad

 Look, write and listen

1 I like ice cream.
2 I like chocolate.
3 I like pizza.
4 I like salad.

Ending the lesson

Lesson review

- Briefly ask the children what they can do as a result of the lesson (understand and act out *The witch*). Praise the children for their efforts and / or use the finger puppets to do this.

Goodbye and closing routine

- Say **Let's sing *Shake your head.*** Play the karaoke version of the song (CD 1, track 9 – see Lesson 1). Hold up the finger puppets and the children sing and do the actions as in Lesson 1.

5 Food I like

Lesson 3
Communication and grammar

Aim:
- To practise saying what foods you like and don't like

Key language:
- *I like … / I don't like …*
- *hamburger, chicken, chips, pizza, salad, ice cream, chocolate, apple, banana, yogurt*

Materials:
- Pupil's Book pages 39 and 40
- Activity Book pages 38 and 87
- Finger puppets (Pip and Squeak)
- Flashcards: Alex, Katie, hamburger, chicken, chips, pizza, salad, ice cream, chocolate, apple, banana, yogurt
- Scissors and stapler
- A prepared little book for Unit 5 (AB page 87)

Starting out

Greetings and opening routine

- Greet the children yourself and using the finger puppets.
- *Either* play the karaoke version of *I'm ready for English* (CD 1, track 7 – see Lesson 1) and the children sing and do the actions as in Lesson 1 *or* stick the flashcards on the board in the order of the song *Delicious for me, delicious for you!* and play the karaoke version (CD 2, track 20 – see Lesson 1). The children point to the flashcards, do the actions and sing the song as previously.

Revision activity

- Hold up the finger puppets and stick the character flashcards on the board. Ask **Can you remember who's in the story with Pip, Squeak, Alex and Katie?** *(the witch, a boy / Hansel, a girl / Gretel)*
- Ask the children to open their Pupil's Books at page 39. Briefly reconstruct the story, getting the children to supply key words. Say e.g. **Alex, Katie, Pip and Squeak find the house of …** *food*. **The house is pink …** *yellow, brown, red and green*. **It's made of …** *ice cream, chocolate, pizza and salad*. **In the house is …** *a boy, a girl, a witch*. **The witch is planning to eat** (use gesture to convey meaning) **the …** *boy* **and the …** *girl*. **The key is on the …** *table*. **The children escape. The witch is very angry. Alex finds the next treasure clue in the witch's …** *pot*.
- Play the CD (CD 2, track 22 – see Lesson 2). The children listen and follow the story in their books.

Setting objectives

- Say **Today we're going to practise saying sentences about food we like and don't like.**

On the learning trail

Listen and tick (✔) or cross (✗). (PB page 40)

- Ask the children to look at the pictures and identify the character and food in each one.
- Draw the children's attention to the key and to the example.
- Say **Listen and write a tick if the character says *I like …* and a cross if the character says *I don't like …***

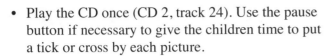

- Play the CD once (CD 2, track 24). Use the pause button if necessary to give the children time to put a tick or cross by each picture.

- Check the answers by asking e.g. **What does Alex say?** *(I like chips.)*

- Say **Now listen again. Repeat what the characters say.** Play the CD again. Use the pause button to give the children time to repeat the sentences.

Key: 1 ✔ 2 ✘ 3 ✔ 4 ✔ 5 ✘ 6 ✘

 Listen and tick or cross.

1 Alex: *I like chips.*
2 Katie: *I don't like yogurt.*
3 Pip: *I like apples.*
4 Squeak: *I like bananas.*
5 Hansel: *I don't like hamburgers.*
6 Gretel: *I don't like chicken.*

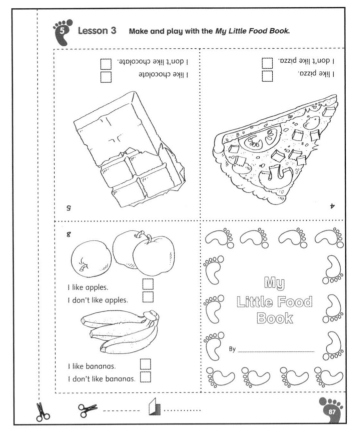

Make the *My Little Food Book*. (PB page 40 and AB page 87)

- Hold up your Pupil's Book and point to the pictures. Say **We're going to make the *My Little Food Book* and play the game.**

- Hold up your Activity Book and say **Find page 87 in your Activity Book. Look at the *My Little Food Book*.** Say **Let's make the *My Little Food Book*** and show the children the book you have prepared.

- Say **Cut and fold the pages like this** and demonstrate what you mean (see page 87 of the Teacher's Book for a diagram of how to make the little book). Point out the difference between the dashed lines (cutting lines) and the dotted lines (folding lines).

- Staple the children's books together as soon as they have folded the pages correctly. Then say **Now cut here** and demonstrate cutting along the dotted line at the top to separate the pages.

- Go through the little book page by page and read the two options for each picture.

- Explain that the children should cross out *like* or *don't like* to make sentences which are true for them and colour the food on each page.

- The children work individually and complete and colour their little books.

Play with the *My Little Food Book*. (PB page 40)

- Hold up your Pupil's Book. Ask two pupils to read the first dialogue and two other pupils to read the second dialogue.

- Explain that you want the children to read their books with a partner and count how many sentences in their little books are the same.

- Demonstrate the activity with one child. Open your little book at the first page and read the sentence you have made, e.g. *I don't like hamburgers.* Then get the child to read the sentence they have made for the same picture. If your sentences are the same (i.e. both *I like ...* or *I don't like ...*), say e.g. **So that's one sentence the same!** Continue taking turns to read the pages of your books in the same way. At the end, count up how many of the sentences about food you and the child like or don't like are the same.

- Divide the class into pairs. Ask the children to predict before they begin how many of their opinions about food (out of ten) they think will be the same as their partner's.

- The children take turns to read their books with their partner.

- At the end, ask them to report back how many

pages were the same and whether this was more or less than they had predicted.

Read, write and say. (AB page 38)

- Ask individual children to say the sentence for one of the characters, filling in the missing words.
- Say **Now read and write the words.** Draw the children's attention to the example.
- The children work individually and complete the sentences.
- Check the answers by asking e.g. **What does Squeak say?** *(I like bananas.)*

   Key: 1 bananas 2 chocolate 3 yogurt 4 pizza
   5 apples 6 chips

Draw and write. (AB page 38)

- Say sentences giving examples of food you like and don't like, e.g. **I like ice cream. / I don't like hamburgers.**
- Ask individual children to say a sentence about food they like or don't like.
- Point to the two frames on the page and say **Draw pictures of food you like here and food you don't like here. Write the words.** Draw their attention to the example.
- The children work individually. They draw pictures and write the words.
- In pairs, the children compare the pictures they have drawn in each frame.
- Ask individual children to take turns to show their pictures and say a sentence about one food they like and one food they don't like to the rest of the class, e.g. *I like apples. / I don't like bananas.*

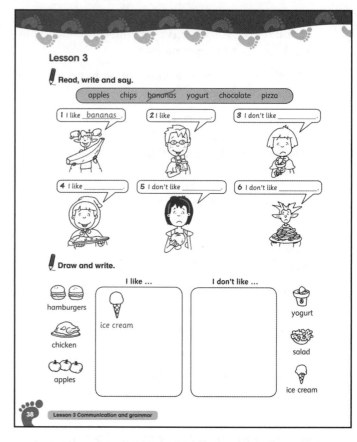

Ending the lesson

Lesson review

- Briefly ask the children what they can do as a result of the lesson (say sentences about food they like and don't like). Praise the children for their efforts and / or use the finger puppets to do this.

Goodbye and closing routine

- Say goodbye to the children yourself and using the finger puppets. If there is time, you can also play the karaoke version of *Shake your head* (CD 1, track 9 – see Lesson 1) and the children sing and do the actions as in Lesson 1.

5 Food I like

Lesson 4
Communication, grammar and pronunciation

Aims:

- To practise asking and answering questions about food you like
- To say a tongue-twister with the sound /tʃ/

Key language:

- *Do you like …? Yes, I do. / No, I don't.*
- *hamburger, chicken, chips, pizza, salad, ice cream, chocolate, apple, banana, yogurt*

Materials:

- Pupil's Book page 41
- Activity Book page 39
- Finger puppets (Pip and Squeak)
- Flashcards: chicken, pizza, salad, apple, banana, yogurt, chocolate, ice cream, Frodo
- Unit 5 little books from Lesson 3
- CD 1 and CD 2

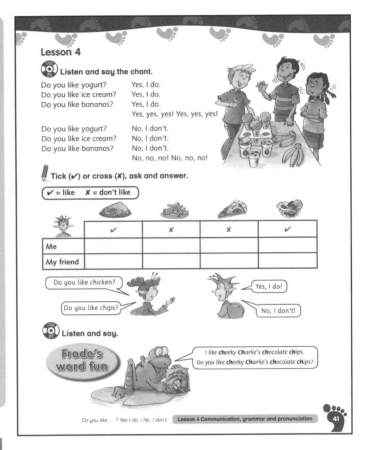

Starting out

Greetings and opening routine

- Greet the children yourself and using the finger puppets.
- *Either* play the karaoke version of *I'm ready for English* (CD 1, track 7 – see Lesson 1) and the children sing and do the actions as in Lesson 1 *or* stick the flashcards in the order of the song *Delicious for me, delicious for you!* on the board and play the karaoke version (CD 2, track 20 – see Lesson 1). The children point to the flashcards, do the actions and sing the song as previously.

Revision activity

- Give out or ask the children to get out the little books they made in Lesson 3.
- Read your little book page by page. Explain and demonstrate that the children should turn the pages of their books at the same time as you read. They should repeat the sentences you say if they are the same as the sentences in their little books, and stay silent if they are not.

Setting objectives

- Say **Today we're going to practise asking and answering questions about food we like. We're also going to practise pronunciation.**

On the learning trail

Listen and say the chant. (PB page 41)

- (Books closed) Say **Listen to the chant. What three foods are the questions about?**
- Play the CD once (CD 2, track 25) and check the answer. *(yogurt, ice cream, bananas)*
- Ask the children to open their Pupil's Books at page 41. Play the CD again. The children follow in their books and say the chant.
- Divide the children into three groups (one for the questions, one for the 'yes' answers in the first verse, and one for the 'no' answers in the second verse).

- Teach actions to each group as follows: question group – hold out arms questioningly; 'yes' group – raise hands in the air every time you say *yes*; 'no' group – wave your index finger from side to side every time you say *no*.
- Play the CD again. The children say the chant and do the actions with their group.
- Repeat twice more. The groups change roles each time.

 Do you like yogurt?

Do you like yogurt?	*Yes, I do.*
Do you like ice cream?	*Yes, I do.*
Do you like bananas?	*Yes, I do.*
	Yes, yes, yes! Yes, yes yes!
Do you like yogurt?	*No, I don't.*
Do you like ice cream?	*No, I don't.*
Do you like bananas?	*No, I don't.*
	No, no, no! No, no, no!

Tick (✔) or cross (✘), ask and answer. (PB page 41)

- Say **Look at the table.** Ask the children to name the food at the top of each column.
- Draw the children's attention to the key and to Pip's answers to the questions in the table. Ask two children to read the dialogue under the table.
- Hold up the finger puppets. Divide the class into two groups: Squeak and Pip.
- Say to the Squeak group **Let's ask Pip about the food!** Get the children to repeat the question after you in chorus for each food in the table. Get the Pip group to answer in chorus, following Pip's answers in the table.
- Change roles and repeat.
- Point to the first column in the table and point to yourself to convey the meaning of *me*. Ask the children to put ticks and crosses in this row in the table to show which food they like and which they don't like. Demonstrate this by pretending to complete the table for yourself and saying e.g. **I don't like chicken so I write a cross here.** Give the children a few moments to do this and be ready to help if necessary.
- Ask a child to the front and say e.g. **Elena is my friend.** Demonstrate the activity by asking the child **Do you like …?** and putting ticks and crosses in the *My friend* row of the table.
- Divide the class into pairs. The children take turns to ask their partner questions and put ticks or crosses in the *My friend* row, depending on their responses.

Key: Children's own answers.

Listen and say: Frodo's word fun. (PB page 41)

- Write the letters *'ch'* on the board and make the sound /tʃ/ as in *ch*ocolate and *ch*ips.
- Read the tongue-twister slowly. Use the picture of Charlie to convey the meaning of *cheeky* (a little bit naughty and lacking in respect but in a lively, attractive way).
- Hold up the flashcard of Frodo. Say **Listen to Frodo and say the tongue-twister.** Play the CD (CD 2, track 27).
- Ask pairs of children to say the tongue-twister in turn.
- The children practise saying the tongue-twister with a partner.

 Frodo's word fun. Listen and say.

I like cheeky Charlie's chocolate chips.
Do you like cheeky Charlie's chocolate chips?

I like cheeky Charlie's chocolate chips.
Do you like cheeky Charlie's chocolate chips?

I like cheeky Charlie's chocolate chips.
Do you like cheeky Charlie's chocolate chips?

Read and circle. (AB page 39)

- Read the questions and invite a few individual children to tell you their personal answers by saying *Yes, I do* or *No, I don't* in response to each question.
- Say **Now read the questions and circle the answers that are true for you.** Draw the children's attention to the example.
- The children read the sentences and circle the answers which are true for them.
- Divide the class into pairs. The children take turns to ask and answer the questions with their partner.

Key: Children's own answers.

Look and write. (AB page 39)

- Read the exchanges and the children say the missing words.

- Say **Now look and write the missing words.** Draw the children's attention to the example.

- The children work individually and write the words. They use the words at the top of the activity.

- Check the answers by asking pairs of children to read the exchanges.

- If you like, the children can also act out the exchanges in pairs.

Key: 1 yogurt 2 hamburgers 3 chocolate 4 salad 5 chips 6 pizza

Ending the lesson

Lesson review

- Briefly ask the children what they can do as a result of the lesson (ask and answer questions about food they like and don't like, say a tongue-twister with /tʃ/). Praise the children for their efforts and / or use the finger puppets to do this.

Goodbye and closing routine

- Say goodbye to the children yourself and using the finger puppets. If there is time, you can also play the karaoke version of *Shake your head* (CD 1, track 9 – see Lesson 1) and the children sing and do the actions as in Lesson 1.

5 Food I like

Lesson 5
Content input

Aims:

- To read and understand that your body needs food and water
- To name food that is good for you and food that isn't good for you

Key language:

- *Is ... good for you? Yes, it is. / No, it isn't.*
- *Are ... good for you? Yes, they are. / No, they aren't.*
- *hamburgers, salad, chips, yogurt, chocolate, sweets, apples, bananas*
- *Hurray!*

Materials:

- Pupil's Book page 42
- Activity Book page 40
- Finger puppets (Pip and Squeak)
- Flashcards: hamburger, chicken, chips, pizza, salad, ice cream, chocolate, apple, banana, yogurt
- CD 1 and CD 2

Starting out

Greetings and opening routine

- Greet the children yourself and using the finger puppets.
- *Either* play the karaoke version of *I'm ready for English* (CD 1, track 7 – see Lesson 1) and the children sing and do the actions as in Lesson 1 *or* divide the class into three groups, play the karaoke version of *Do you like yogurt?* (CD 2, track 26 – see Lesson 4) and the children say and do the actions for the chant as in Lesson 4.

Revision activity

- *Either* get the children to stand or sit in a circle or they can remain seated at their desks.
- Hold up a food flashcard and ask a child **Do you like ...?** Explain and demonstrate that the child should take the flashcard and answer *Yes, I do* or *No, I don't*. They should then ask the same question to the child next to them and pass the flashcard on. That child should answer, and so on.
- Continue the activity in the same way, getting the children to ask and answer the question and pass the flashcard round the circle, or from desk to desk. Once the flashcard is about three children away from you, introduce another one into the circle or row of desks. If you have a big class, you can introduce different flashcards to the rows at the back and front of the class. Stop the activity when the children have had an opportunity to ask two to four questions about different foods.

Setting objectives

- Hold up the finger puppets. Say **Let's learn about the world around you! Today we're going to read about food and find out about food that is or isn't good for you.** Clarify that *good for you* means that it is healthy for you.

On the learning trail

Read, tick (✔) and listen. (PB page 42)

- (Books closed) Ask the question **Is all food good for you?**
- Listen to the children's ideas (in L1). Use their suggestions to introduce or remind them of vocabulary, e.g. *sweets*, *chocolate*.
- Ask the children to open their Pupil's Books at page 42. Read the text at the start of the activity or play part 1 on the CD (CD 2, track 28). Use the photo to clarify the meaning of *water*. Ask **Is all food good for you?** *(no)* **Is it important to eat food which is good for you?** *(yes)* **Is it important to drink water?** *(yes)* and the children respond.
- Say **Look at the photos.** Read the question (*Is this food good for you?*) and the word for each photo while the children follow in their books.
- Say **Put a tick if you think the food is good for you.** Draw their attention to the example.
- The children work individually and put a tick if they think the food is good for them. Ask e.g. **Is salad good for you? / Are hamburgers good for you?** and the children answer *yes* or *no*. Don't tell them the answers yet.
- Say **Now listen and find out.** Play the CD (CD

2, track 28). Use the pause button to allow the children time to compare their answers with the CD.

- Check the answers by asking individual children questions about the photos.
- Play the CD again as a final check.

Key: 1 ✓ 2 ✗ 3 ✗ 4 ✓ 5 ✓ 6 ✗ 7 ✓ 8 ✗

 Read, tick and listen.

Part 1

Your body needs food and water.
Some food is good for you.
Some food isn't good for you.
It is important to eat food that is good for you.
It is also important to drink water.

Part 2

1 Is salad good for you? Yes, it is.
2 Are hamburgers good for you? No, they aren't.
3 Are chips good for you? No, they aren't.
4 Are bananas good for you? Yes, they are.
5 Are apples good for you? Yes, they are.
6 Are sweets good for you? No, they aren't.
7 Is yogurt good for you? Yes, it is.
8 Is chocolate good for you? No, it isn't.

Play a game. (PB page 42)

- Explain and demonstrate that you are going to say the names of food. The children should listen and respond *Hurray!* in chorus if the food is good for you, and fold their arms and stay silent if it isn't good for you. Explain that every time the children respond correctly they score a point and that every time they respond incorrectly you score a point.

- Play the game by saying different words for food and drink in random order. The children respond by saying *Hurray!* or folding their arms and staying silent. Keep a score of the points on the board. Examples of words you can say are: *hamburger, chips, pizza, ice cream, chocolate, apple, banana, yogurt, sweets, biscuit, sandwich, cake, chicken, salad, water.*

- At the end, make the point that it's fine to eat food such as hamburgers, chips, chocolate and ice cream from time to time or as a treat. The important thing is to try mainly to eat food which

is good for you and not to eat too many things, such as sweets, which aren't good for you.

Read and tick (✓) or cross (✗). (AB page 40)

- Read the sentences in turn and the children say if they are true or not.

- Say **Now read and tick the sentences which are true, and cross the sentences which aren't true.** Draw the children's attention to the example.

- The children work individually and tick or cross the sentences.

- Check the answers by reading the sentences again and the children say if they have put a tick or a cross.

Key: 1 ✓ 2 ✗ 3 ✓ 4 ✓

Write and say. (AB page 40)

- Read the headings at the top of the two lists and draw the children's attention to the example.
- The children write the food words in the correct list.
- Check the answers by asking individual children questions about the different foods, e.g. **Are apples good for you?** *Yes, they are.*
- The children can work in pairs and ask and answer questions about the different foods.

Key: Good for you: apples, bananas, salad, yogurt
Not good for you: sweets, hamburgers, chips, chocolate

Ending the lesson

Lesson review

- Briefly ask the children what they can do as a result of the lesson (read and understand that your body needs food and water, name food which is good for you and food which isn't good for you). Praise the children for their efforts and / or use the finger puppets to do this.

Goodbye and closing routine

- Say goodbye to the children yourself and using the finger puppets. If there is time, you can also play the karaoke version of *Shake your head* (CD 1, track 9 – see Lesson 1) and the children sing and do the actions as in Lesson 1.

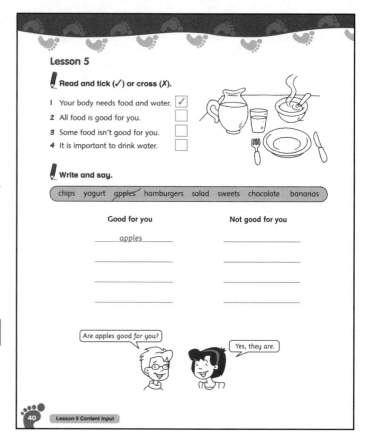

5 Food I like

Lesson 6
Content and personalisation

Aims:
- To recognise snacks that are good for you
- To talk about snacks you like and don't like

Key language:
- *I like ... / I don't like ...*
- *Me, too!*
- *biscuits, sweets, apples, bananas, ice cream, chocolate, sandwiches, yogurt, cake*
- *snack*

Materials:
- Pupil's Book page 43
- Activity Book page 41
- Finger puppets (Pip and Squeak)
- CD 1 and CD 2

Starting out

Greetings and opening routine

- Greet the children yourself and using the finger puppets.
- *Either* play the karaoke version of *I'm ready for English* (CD 1, track 7 – see Lesson 1) and the children sing and do the actions as in Lesson 1 *or* divide the class into three groups, play the karaoke version of *Do you like yogurt?* (CD 2, track 26 – see Lesson 4) and the children say and do the actions for the chant as in Lesson 4.

Revision activity

- Say true and false sentences about food and water in turn, e.g. **Your body needs water. / All food is good for you.** (Use the text on page 42 of the Pupil's Book for more ideas.) The children respond by saying *yes* in chorus if the sentences are true and *no* if they're not.

Setting objectives

- Explain the meaning of *snack*, i.e. a small amount of food and drink you have between meals, e.g. at break time. Say **In this lesson we're going to identify snacks that are good for you and snacks that aren't good for you. We're also going to talk about snacks we like and snacks we don't like.**

On the learning trail

Listen and match. (PB page 43)

- Ask the children to name the food in each snack.
- Say **Listen and match the characters and snacks.** Draw the children's attention to the example.
- Play the CD (CD 2, track 29). Use the pause button if necessary to give the children time to draw matching lines.
- Check the answers by asking e.g. **What does the child in photo one say?** *(I like apples and biscuits.)*

Key: 1 apples and biscuits 2 sweets and sandwiches 3 cake and chocolate 4 yogurt and bananas

Listen and match.

1 I like apples and biscuits.
2 I like sweets and sandwiches.
3 I like cake and chocolate.
4 I like yogurt and bananas.

Draw and say. (PB page 43)

- Read the speech bubbles and draw the children's attention to the example pictures drawn in each frame.

- Ask the children to tell you snacks they like which are good for you, e.g. *I like apples and yogurt,* and snacks they like which aren't good for you, e.g. *I like sweets and chocolate.*

- Hold up your book, point to the frames and say **Draw a snack you like which is good for you here. Draw a snack you like which isn't good for you here.**

- The children work individually and draw their pictures.

- Ask individual children to take turns to show their pictures and tell the class, e.g. *I like bananas and sandwiches. / I like cake and sweets.*

- Use the activity to make the point that it's fine to eat snacks such as cakes from time to time. The important thing is to eat a variety and balance of different food and not to eat too many snacks such as sweets and chocolate which aren't good for you.

Read and write. (AB page 41)

- Read the sentences and the children say the missing words.

- Say **Now write what the characters say.** Draw the children's attention to the example.

- The children work individually and write the missing words.

- Check the answers by asking individual children to read one of the sentences.

    Key: 1 apples 2 sweets 3 chocolate 4 bananas

Choose and write about you. (AB page 41)

- Ask individual children to say a sentence about snacks they like (whether they are good for them or not), e.g. *I like bananas and cakes.*

- Repeat, this time getting children to say a sentence about snacks they don't like, e.g. *I don't like chocolate and apples.*

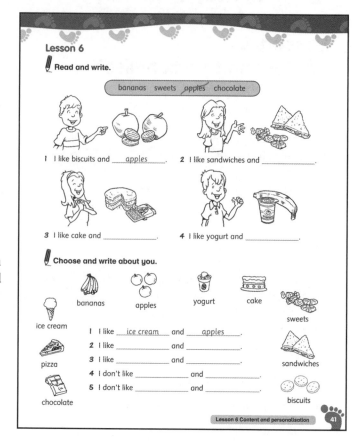

- Ask the children to complete the sentences with snacks they like and snacks they don't like. Draw their attention to the example.

- Invite children to take turns to tell the class about the snacks they like and don't like, e.g. *I like sandwiches and chocolate.* If another child has the same, explain that they should say *Me, too!* and have the next turn.

    Key: Children's own answers.

Ending the lesson

Lesson review

- Briefly ask the children what they can do as a result of the lesson (name snacks which are good for you, say what snacks they like and don't like). Praise the children for their efforts and / or use the finger puppets to do this.

Goodbye and closing routine

- Say goodbye to the children yourself and using the finger puppets. If there is time, you can also play the karaoke version of *Shake your head* (CD 1 track 9 – see Lesson 1) and the children sing and do the actions as in Lesson 1.

5 Food I like

Lesson 7
Children's culture

Aim:

- To say a version of a traditional chant and play a version of a traditional skipping game

Key language:

- *I like … / I don't like …*
- *water, coffee, tea, cheese, biscuits, apple pie, roast beef, soup*

Materials:

- Pupil's Book page 44
- Activity Book page 42
- Finger puppets (Pip and Squeak)
- Flashcard: Frodo
- CD 1 and CD 2
- A skipping rope (optional)

Starting out

Greetings and opening routine

- Greet the children yourself and using the finger puppets.
- *Either* play the karaoke version of *I'm ready for English* (CD 1, track 7 – see Lesson 1) and the children sing and do the actions as in Lesson 1 *or* play the karaoke version of *Do you like yogurt?* (CD 2, track 26 – see Lesson 4) and the children say the chant and do the actions as previously.

Revision activity

- Explain that you are going to say sentences about snacks you like and don't like. The children should repeat the sentences if they are true for them and stay silent if they are not.
- Say sentences, e.g. **I like bananas / I don't like biscuits** and the children respond. If you like, keep a score on the board of all the sentences that are true for the whole class.

Setting objectives

- Hold up the flashcard of Frodo. Say **In this lesson we're going to learn about children's culture with Frodo. We're going to say a chant and play a version of a traditional skipping game.** Use mime to show the meaning of *skipping* and show the children a skipping rope if you have one.

On the learning trail

Listen and say the chant. (PB page 44)

- Elicit or explain the meaning of *lunch* and *train*.
- Hold up your book. Say e.g. **Look at what's for lunch!** Point to the different food and drink in turn and say the words. Be ready to explain the meaning of *pie*, i.e. a dish with pastry, and *roast beef*, i.e. beef cooked in the oven. Explain that these are traditional English dishes.
- Say **Listen to the lunch train and point to the food.** Demonstrate what you mean.
- Play the CD (CD 2, track 30). The children listen to the chant and point to the food and drink.

145

- Say **Stand up, please.** Demonstrate making a train-like movement by moving up and down, bending your arms at the elbow and making circles in a rhythmic way.

- Play the CD again. The children listen and say the chant, moving rhythmically like a train.

 The lunch train

Water, water
Cheese and biscuits
Cheese and biscuits
Apple pie
Apple pie
Roast beef
Roast beef
Soup! Soup!

 Citizenship box: Remember!

Say e.g. **Look at the lunch. Soup, roast beef, apple pie, cheese and biscuits, water. Delicious!**

Hold up the flashcard of Frodo, read the *Remember!* note and check understanding. Ask the children why it is important to eat a good lunch every day, including drinking water. *(to give you energy, to play sport, to keep strong and healthy)*

Play *Coffee and tea!* (PB page 44)

- Explain that the children are going to play a version of a traditional skipping game (and skip on the spot to demonstrate meaning).

- Play the CD (CD 2, track 32) while the children follow in their books. Elicit or explain the meaning of *coffee* and *tea*.

- Explain that in the game the children name a friend in line 3.

- Play the CD again. The children practise saying the rhyme. Give them the name of a child in the class to call in line 3 of each verse, e.g. *Pablo!*

- Ask the children to stand in a circle. Choose a (confident) child (A) to stand in the middle of the circle.

- Explain and demonstrate that the children should skip on the spot. Child A in the centre says the rhyme (with everyone's help) and names a child (B) in line 3 to join them in the circle. The two children hold hands and skip round once on the spot together. Child B then says verse 2 and names child A, who goes out of the circle. Child B then says verse 1 and names a child (C) in line 3 to join them in the circle, and so on.

- Continue the game in the same way. Stop once four to six children have had a turn in the circle.

Option: If you have a skipping rope and the opportunity to go to the playground or gym, you can play this as a real skipping game. Turn the rope with one child; other children take turns to jump in, say the rhyme, name a friend and jump out as above. If you don't have space in the classroom for the children to stand in a circle, the children can simply take turns to come to the front of the class and say the rhyme in the same way.

 Play *Coffee and tea!*

I like coffee
I like tea
I like ... in with me!

I don't like coffee
I don't like tea
I don't like ... in with me!

Look, match and say. (AB page 42)

- Read the words and the children point to the appropriate pictures.

- Say **Look and match the words and pictures.** Draw the children's attention to the example.

- Check the answers by asking the children to point to the pictures and say the words.

- Encourage the children to say e.g. *I like biscuits / I don't like cheese* and / or ask questions, e.g. **Do you like apple pie?** and they respond *Yes, I do* or *No, I don't.*

Key: Children match the words and pictures.
1 water 2 cheese and biscuits 3 apple pie
4 roast beef 5 soup

Draw and write your friend's name. (AB page 42)

- Read the rhyme and the children say the missing words and name a friend in line 3.

- Ask the children to write the missing words and the name of a friend they like in the rhyme. Explain that they should then draw a picture of themselves and the friend playing the skipping game.

- The children work individually. They complete the rhyme and draw a picture.

- Briefly ask individual children to report back and say the friend they like, e.g. *I like Pablo.*

Option: If you're concerned that by allowing the children to name friends freely, some children may be excluded, it's best to divide the class in pairs and the children name their partner.

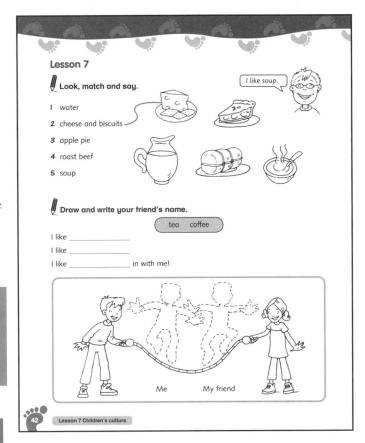

Ending the lesson

Lesson review

- Briefly ask the children what they can do as a result of the lesson (say the chant *The lunch train*, play a version of a skipping game). Praise the children for their efforts and / or use the finger puppets to do this.

Goodbye and closing routine

- Say goodbye to the children yourself and using the finger puppets. If there is time, you can also play the karaoke version of *Shake your head* (CD 1, track 9 – see Lesson 1) and the children sing and do the actions as in Lesson 1.

5 Food I like

Lesson 8
Unit review / *All About Me Portfolio Booklet*

Aim:
- To review learning in Unit 5

Key language:
- *I like ... / I don't like ...*
- *Do you like ...? Yes, I do. / No, I don't.*
- *Is ... good for you? Yes, it is. / No, it isn't.*
- *Are ... good for you? Yes, they are / No, they aren't.*
- *hamburger, chicken, chips, pizza, salad, ice cream, chocolate, apple, banana, yogurt*

Materials:
- Pupil's Book page 45
- Activity Book page 43
- *All About Me* Portfolio Booklet pages 14 and 15
- Finger puppets (Pip and Squeak)
- Flashcards: chicken, hamburger, salad, chips, pizza, chocolate, ice cream, apple, banana, yogurt
- Stickers for Unit 5
- CD 1 and CD 2

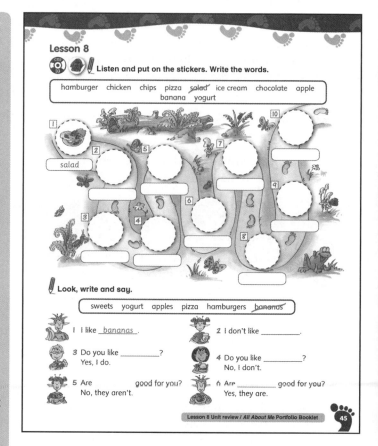

Starting out

Greetings and opening routine

- Greet the children yourself and using the finger puppets.
- *Either* play the karaoke version of *I'm ready for English* (CD 1, track 7 – see Lesson 1) and the children sing and do the actions as in Lesson 1 *or* stick the flashcards on the board in order and play the karaoke version of the song *Delicious for me, delicious for you!* (CD 2, track 20 – see Lesson 1) and the children sing the song and do the actions.

Revision activity

- Say the first word of the *The lunch train* chant (see Lesson 7), moving your arms rhythmically, and get the children to respond by saying the second word in exactly the same way as you, e.g.

  T: **Water ...**

  PP: *Water.*

- Repeat for all the phrases and lines of the chant.
- Ask the children to stand up. Play the karaoke version on the CD (CD 2, track 31 – see Lesson 7). The children say the chant and move rhythmically like a train (as in Lesson 7).

Setting objectives

- Say **Today we're going to review what we've learnt in Unit 5.**

On the learning trail

Listen and put on the stickers. Write the words. (PB page 45)

- Make sure the children have the stickers for Unit 5 ready.
- Say **Listen and put on the stickers.** Draw the children's attention to the example.
- Play the CD (CD 2, track 33). Use the pause button to give the children time to put on the stickers.

- Say **Now write the words.** Draw the children's attention to the example.
- Check the answers by saying the numbers and the children say the words.

  Key: 1 salad 2 hamburger 3 pizza 4 chocolate
  5 chicken 6 apples 7 ice cream 8 bananas
  9 chips 10 yogurt

 Listen and put on the stickers.

1 I like salad.
2 I don't like hamburgers.
3 I like pizza.
4 I don't like chocolate.
5 Do you like chicken? Yes, I do.
6 Do you like apples? Yes, I do.
7 Do you like ice cream? No, I don't.
8 Are bananas good for you? Yes, they are.
9 Are chips good for you? No, they aren't.
10 Is yogurt good for you? Yes, it is.

Look, write and say. (PB page 45)

- Read the sentences and exchanges and the children say the missing words.
- Say **Now write the words.** Draw the children's attention to the example.
- The children work individually and write the missing words.
- Check the answers by asking individual children to say the sentences and exchanges.

  Key: 1 bananas 2 yogurt 3 pizza 4 hamburgers
  5 sweets 6 apples

Listen and tick (✓) or cross (X). (AB page 43)

- Say **Look at the pictures.** Draw the children's attention to the key.
- Say **Listen and write a tick if the child likes the food and a cross if they don't.** Draw the children's attention to the examples.
- Play the CD (CD 2, track 34). Pause if necessary to give the children time to put ticks and crosses.
- Check the answers by saying **Number one. The child says …** and the children say, *I like hamburgers.*

  Key: 1 ✓ 2 X 3 X 4 ✓ 5 ✓ 6 X 7 X 8 X 9 ✓ 10 ✓

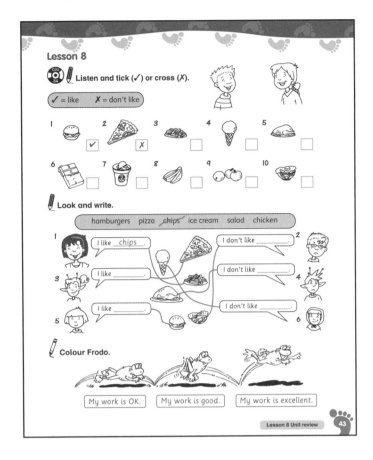

 Listen and tick or cross.

1 I like hamburgers.
2 I don't like pizza.
3 I don't like chips.
4 I like ice cream.
5 I like chicken.
6 I don't like chocolate.
7 Do you like yogurt? No, I don't.
8 Do you like bananas? No, I don't.
9 Do you like apples? Yes, I do.
10 Do you like salad? Yes, I do.

Look and write. (AB page 43)

- Ask e.g. **What does Katie say?** Hold up the book and demonstrate following the puzzle line with your index finger to the picture of chips, and the children say *I like chips.*
- Repeat for the rest of the characters, getting the children to follow the puzzle lines with their fingers in their own books.
- Say **Write what the characters say** and draw the children's attention to the example.
- The children work individually and complete the sentences.

- Check the answers by asking e.g. **What does Alex say?**
- Ask individual children to say sentences about food they like and don't like.

    Key: 1 chips 2 salad 3 pizza 4 chicken
    5 hamburgers 6 ice cream

Colour Frodo. (AB page 43)

- Hold up the flashcard of Frodo. Remind the children that in this activity they assess their work in the unit by choosing and colouring the picture of Frodo which corresponds best to how they think they have done.
- Remind the children of the key by pointing to the three pictures of Frodo and saying **Colour this picture if your work is OK but you think you need to try harder or need more practice. Colour this picture of Frodo if you think your work is good. Colour this picture of Frodo with a big smile and jumping very high if you think your work is excellent.** Make sure the children understand that there are no right answers and that it is their own opinion of the work they have done which is important. Be ready to encourage the children to have a positive view if they are too hard on themselves.

Ending the lesson

Lesson review

- Briefly ask the children what they can do as a result of the lesson (use the language and vocabulary they've learnt in Unit 5). Praise the children for their efforts and / or use the finger puppets to do this.

Goodbye and closing routine

- Say goodbye to the children yourself and using the finger puppets. If there is time, you can also play the karaoke version of *Shake your head* (CD 1, track 9 – see Lesson 1) and the children sing and do the actions as in Lesson 1.

All About Me Portfolio Booklet

The children complete Unit 5 of their personal *All About Me* Portfolio Booklets. They complete their learning journey by colouring the sections on the path to show what they can do. If you like, the children can also sign this page and you can endorse this by adding your own signature and the date.

6 My toys

Structures and grammar

- Where's the ...? It's in / on / under ...
- Where are the ...? They're ...
- How many ...?
- Recycled: I've got ..., What's this? It's ..., Can I have a ...? Here you are.

Vocabulary

- Core: doll, bike, ball, car, train, marbles, skates, plane, robot, computer game, numbers 11–20
- Other: cave, genie, magic, lamp, box, jar, shelf, big, small
- Content / culture: skateboard, scooter, teddy bear, wheel, driver, bus, hoot, chatter, hot, cold
- Recycled: table, chair, children, thank you, numbers 1–10

Main receptive language

- dark
- shape, things, move, have got ...

Communicative competence

Understanding

Listening:
- Can recognise names of toys
- Can understand the episode of the story
- Can understand when people ask and say where things are
- Can understand the question How many ...?
- Can recognise numbers to 20
- Can recognise word stress (in two-syllable words)

Reading:
- Can recognise the names of toys
- Can recognise numbers to 20
- Can read questions and answers about where things are
- Can read sentences about the wheel

Speaking

Spoken interaction:
- Can ask about and respond to questions about where things are
- Can ask and answer questions about how many

Spoken production:
- Can sing the song I'm ready for English
- Can name toys
- Can sing the song I've got a car and a ball
- Can say where things are
- Can say the chant How many marbles are in the jar?
- Can say familiar two-syllable words with the correct stress
- Can count to 20
- Can sing the song The wheels on the bus
- Can sing the song Shake your head

Writing

- Can copy and write words for toys
- Can copy and write words for numbers to twenty
- Can complete questions and sentences about where things are

Content links

- Science: things with wheels

Learning strategies and thinking skills

- Recognising learning objectives
- Associating vocabulary with personal possessions
- Classifying
- Using rhythm to memorise vocabulary and language patterns
- Observing objects and pictures in close detail
- Associating language with spatial positions
- Reflecting on learning

Children's culture

- Singing a traditional song: The wheels on the bus
- Playing a version of a traditional game: Where's the ...?

Pronunciation

- Clapping the stress (in familiar two-syllable words)

Values and attitudes

- Enjoyment in talking about toys in English
- Awareness that many things have got wheels
- Awareness of noise level when you chat with friends

6 My toys

Lesson 1
Vocabulary presentation

Aim:
- To name toys

Key language:
- *ball, doll, bike, car, train, marbles, skates, plane, robot, computer game*
- *I've got a ...*

Materials:
- Pupil's Book page 46
- Activity Book page 44
- Finger puppets (Pip and Squeak)
- Flashcards: ball, doll, bike, car, train, marbles, skates, plane, robot, computer game, Frodo
- Word cards: ball, doll, bike, car, train, marbles, skates, plane, robot, computer game, Frodo
- CD 1 and CD 2

Starting out

Greetings and opening routine

- Greet the children yourself and using the finger puppets. Say e.g. **Hello, children. Hello ... How are you today?** *Fine, thank you.* Ask a few individual children to greet the puppets in turn.

- Say **Let's sing the song *I'm ready for English*.** Play the CD (CD 1, track 6). Hold up the puppets on your index fingers. Move them as the children sing and do the actions.

 I'm ready for English

Hello, hello, hello.
　　　　(wave hello to teacher and friends)
I'm ready for English. Look!
　　　　(hold out your arms)
Here's my pencil and rubber
　　　　(hold out objects in turn)
And here's my notebook! (hold up notebook)
I'm ready! I'm ready! Hurray!
　　　　(wave arms in the air)

Setting objectives

- Say **Today we're going to learn how to name toys** (use L1 to explain what you mean or hold up two or three of the flashcards) **and we're going to sing a song.**

On the learning trail

Vocabulary presentation (books closed)

- Show the children one of the flashcards, e.g. train, very quickly. The children identify what it is in L1. Say e.g. **Yes. Very good. It's a train.**

- Point to the flashcard. Say **train** several times and get the children to repeat the word with you in chorus.

- Stick the flashcard of the train on the board.

- Repeat the procedure for the other toy flashcards.

- Divide the class in half. Hold up the Pip finger puppet and say to one half **Say the words with Pip.** Use the puppet to point to the flashcards in turn and the children say the words with you. Make the puppet fly around to praise the children.

- Repeat the procedure with the Squeak puppet and the other half of the class.

Follow the footprints. (PB page 46) (books open)

- Hold up the flashcard of Frodo. Say **Listen and follow the footprints with Frodo the frog. Use your finger** and demonstrate this.

- Play the CD (CD 2, track 35). The children listen and follow the footprints with their fingers. They stop by each picture as they hear the word and repeat the word.

- Say **Now listen and draw a line following the footprints** and demonstrate this. Play the CD again. The children draw a line, stop by each picture and repeat the words as previously.

 Follow the footprints.

ball ... doll ... bike ... car ... train ... marbles ... skates ... plane ... robot ... computer game

- Stick the word cards on the board in jumbled order (at the children's height and away from the flashcards).

- Point to one word card, e.g. *bike*, and read the word. Say **Look for the picture of the bike.** Give the children time to do this.

- Ask a child to come to the front of the class and stick the word card for *bike* by the corresponding flashcard. Ask the rest of the class **Is this right?** and get them to say the word.

- Repeat the procedure with the rest of the word cards.

- Take the word cards off the board.

Listen and sing the song. (PB page 46)

- Say **Look at the picture of Pip and Squeak.** Ask **What toys can you see?** and the children name the toys in the picture.

- Draw the children's attention to the flashcards on the board. Say **Listen to the song. Point to the toys** and demonstrate what you mean. Play the CD (CD 2, track 36). The children listen to the song and point to the flashcards as they hear them in each verse.

- Invite five children to the front of the class. Give them each two flashcards (for each line of the song) and get them to stand facing the class, holding up the flashcards in the same order as the song (the child with the doll and computer game should stand after the child with the robot and plane, at the end of the line).

- Explain and demonstrate that the children at the front should hold up their flashcards when they hear the words in the song and the rest of the class should point to the flashcards in turn as they sing.

- Play the CD again. The children point to the pictures and sing the song.

- At the end, invite individual children to say sentences about toys they've got, e.g. *I've got a car. / I've got a computer game.*

 I've got a car and a ball

I've got a car and a ball
I've got a bike and a train
I've got skates and marbles
I've got a robot and a plane!

I've got a car and a ball
I've got a bike and a train
I've got skates and marbles
I've got a doll and a computer game!

Match, draw and say. (PB page 46)

- Hold up your book. Point to the missing pieces of toys in turn and say **This goes on the …** and the children name the toy, e.g. *… car.*

- Ask the children to draw matching lines from the missing pieces to the correct pictures and to complete the pictures. Draw their attention to the example.

- The children work individually and match and complete the pictures.

- Check the answers by pointing to the complete pictures and asking **What's this?** and the children respond *It's a …* for each picture.

Key: 1 car: door 2 plane: wing 3 skates: boot
4 robot: leg 5 bike: wheel 6 doll: eyes and nose

Read and match. (AB page 44)

- Read the sentences and the children name the character who has got the toys in each one.
- The children work individually and match the sentences and pictures.
- Check the answers by asking **Who says** *I've got …?* and the children say the names.

   Key: 1 Katie 2 Frodo 3 Alex 4 Pip 5 Squeak

Look, write and say. (AB page 44)

- Read the speech bubbles and the children look at the pictures and say the missing words.
- Say **Now write the words.** Draw the children's attention to the example.
- The children work individually and complete the speech bubbles.
- Check the answers by asking individual children to read what the characters say.

   Key: 1 car 2 train 3 bike 4 computer game 5 doll 6 plane

Ending the lesson

Lesson review

- Briefly ask the children what they can do as a result of the lesson (name toys, sing the song *I've got a car and a ball*). Praise the children for their efforts and / or use the finger puppets to do this.

Goodbye and closing routine

- Say **Let's sing the song** *Shake your head.* Play the CD (CD 1, track 8). Hold up the finger puppets on your index fingers as the children sing and do the actions.

 Shake your head

Shake your head	(shake head)
Wave your arms	(wave arms in the air)
Touch your ears and eyes	(point to ears and eyes)
It's the end of the lesson now	(tap real or imaginary watch)
Goodbye! Goodbye! Goodbye!	(wave goodbye)

- Say goodbye to the children yourself and using the finger puppets. Say e.g. **Goodbye everyone. See you on …** Ask a few individual children to say goodbye to the finger puppets in turn.

6 My toys

Lesson 2
Language input and story

Aim:
- To understand and act out episode 6 of the story

Key language:
- Where's X / the ...?
- He's / It's in / on / under the ...
- doll, ball, bike, car, train, marbles, skates, plane, robot, computer game
- cave, table, shelf, lamp, genie, magic, dark

Materials:
- Pupil's Book page 47
- Activity Book page 45
- Finger puppets (Pip and Squeak)
- Flashcards: Alex, Katie, doll, ball, bike, car, train, marbles, skates, plane, robot, computer game
- Treasure clue sticker for Unit 6
- CD 1 and CD 2

Starting out

Greetings and opening routine
- Greet the children yourself and using the finger puppets.
- Play *I'm ready for English* (CD 1, track 6 – see Lesson 1). The children sing and do the actions as in Lesson 1.

Revision activity
- Hold up the toy flashcards in turn and the children say the words.
- Stick the flashcards on the board in the same order as the song *I've got a car and a ball* (see Lesson 1).
- Play the CD (CD 2 track 36 – see Lesson 1). The children sing the song and point to the flashcards.
- Repeat with the karaoke version (CD 2, track 37 – see Lesson 1).

Setting objectives
- Say **Today we're going to listen to and act out episode 6 of the story.**

On the learning trail

Listen and act out the story.
Episode 6: The genie of the lamp
(PB page 47)

Before the story (books closed)
- Hold up the finger puppets and stick the flashcards of Alex and Katie on the board. Recap on the last episode of the story using mime and gesture and / or L1 as necessary: **Alex, Katie, Pip and Squeak find the house of food. The house is made of ice cream, chocolate, pizza and salad. In the house is a boy, a girl and a witch. The witch wants to eat the boy and girl. Alex and Katie help the children escape. Alex finds the treasure clue in the witch's pot.**
- Ask **Can you remember the clue from Unit 5?** Hold up page 39 of the Pupil's Book and point to the treasure clue sticker. Read *Follow the*

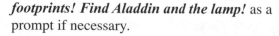

footprints! Find Aladdin and the lamp! as a prompt if necessary.

- Ask the children if they know the traditional story of Aladdin and listen to their response.

- Ask the following questions in turn. Use mime and gesture to clarify meaning, and encourage the children to predict the answers: **1) Where's Aladdin? 2) Is the lamp magic? 3) Who produces the next treasure clue?** Use the children's responses to introduce vocabulary in the story, e.g. *cave, genie*.

- You may also need to pre-teach *shelf* and remind the children of *table*. Use the classroom furniture to do this. You can remind them of *on* and introduce them to *in* and *under* at this point, too. In addition, pre-teach *dark*.

During the story (books open)

- Say **Now listen to the story and find out.** Explain to the children that they will hear a 'beep' noise on the CD to tell them when to move to the next picture in the story.

- Play the CD (CD 2, track 38) and the children follow in their books.

- Ask the three questions in turn again and check the answers, recasting them in English as necessary *(1 in the cave 2 yes 3 the genie)*

- Say **Listen again and repeat the story.** Play the CD again. Pause after each sentence and the children repeat the story.

- **Note:** There is more story text on the CD than appears on the PB page. This additional text is marked with an asterisk* in the audio script below. The children repeat the whole story, including the language which does not appear in their books.

 Follow the footprints, Episode 6: The genie of the lamp

Picture 1	
Narrator:	*Alex, Katie, Pip and Squeak follow the footprints to find Aladdin and the lamp.**
Alex:	*Oh, dear! Where's Aladdin?*
Pip:	*I don't know!*
Katie:	*Look! A cave!**
Squeak:	*Maybe Aladdin is in the cave!**

Picture 2	
Pip:	*Oh, it's dark!**
Squeak:	*I'm scared!**
Katie:	*It's Aladdin!*
Alex:	*Where's the lamp?*
Pip:	*It's on the shelf!*

Picture 3	
Aladdin:	*Hello. I'm Aladdin. And this is my magic lamp!*
Alex:	*Is it really magic?*
Aladdin:	*Oh, yes!*

Picture 4	
Aladdin:	*Rub-a-dub-dub. One, two, three! Magic genie come to me!**
Genie:	*What is your wish?*
Aladdin:	*Mm! Can I have some toys for my friends?*
Genie:	*Yes, of course.**

Picture 5	
Genie:	*Here's a doll ... a car ... a plane ... and a computer game!*
Pip and Squeak:	*Wow!*
Katie:	*Can I try?**
Aladdin:	*Yes! Here you are!**

Picture 6	
Katie:	*Rub-a-dub-dub. One, two, three! Magic genie come to me!**
Genie:	*What is your wish?*
Katie:	*Can we have the next treasure clue, please?*
Genie:	*Yes, of course!**

Picture 7	
Squeak:	*Where's the treasure clue?*
Aladdin:	*Look! It's under the table!*
Katie:	*Oh! Thank you, Aladdin.* Follow the footprints! Find Goldilocks!*
Alex:	*Come on! Hurry! Let's go!**
Aladdin:	*Goodbye and good luck!**
All:	*Goodbye, Aladdin!**

After the story

- Ask questions about each picture as follows (recast L1 answers): **1) What does Katie see?** *(a cave)* **2) What's the cave like?** *(dark)* **Is Aladdin in the cave?** *(yes)* **Where's the lamp?** *(on the shelf)*

3) **Is the lamp magic?** *(yes)* 4) **Who appears from the lamp?** *(a genie)* **What does Aladdin ask the genie for?** *(toys)* 5) **What toys does the genie produce?** *(a doll, a car, a plane, a computer game)* 6) **Who has a turn with the magic lamp?** *(Katie)* **What does Katie ask the magic genie for?** *(the next treasure clue)* 7) **Does the genie produce the next treasure clue?** *(yes)* **Where is the treasure clue? Under the …** *(table)*

Put on the treasure clue sticker.

- Say **The treasure clue says *Follow the footprints! Find Goldilocks!*** Remind the children of the character of Goldilocks from the Introduction, if necessary.

- Say **Find the treasure clue sticker for Unit 6 and stick it here.** Demonstrate what you mean.

- The children look for the treasure clue sticker for Unit 6 and stick it in their books.

Act out the story.

- Divide the class into six groups and assign a role to each group: Alex, Katie, Pip, Squeak, Aladdin or the genie.

- Follow the procedure for *Act out the story* on page 37 of the Teacher's Book.

> **Option:** The children can act out their parts *either* with *or* without their books depending on how confident and familiar they are with this episode. If you wish to make the activity more challenging, the children can act out the whole story by joining in their character's part as you replay the CD.

Look, read and match. (AB page 45)

- Say **Look at the picture.** Ask **Where's Aladdin? Can you find him?** and the children point to the picture of Aladdin. As they do this, say **Yes, here's Aladdin. He's in the cave.**

- Repeat the procedure with the other questions.

- Say **Now read and match the questions and answers.** Draw the children's attention to the example.

- The children match the questions and answers.

- Check the answers by asking individual children to read the questions and answers.

  Key: 1 He's in the cave. 2 It's on the shelf.
  3 He's in the lamp. 4 It's under the table.

Look, write and listen. (AB page 45)

- Read what the genie says and the children say the missing words. Draw their attention to the example.

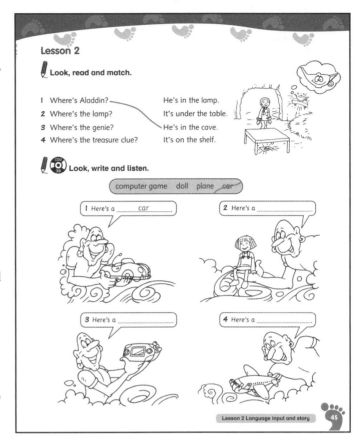

- Play the CD (CD 2, track 39). The children listen and complete the speech bubbles.

- Check the answers by asking e.g. **What does the genie say in number one?**

  Key: 1 car 2 doll 3 computer game 4 plane

 Look, write and listen.

1 Here's a car.
2 Here's a doll.
3 Here's a computer game.
4 Here's a plane.

Ending the lesson

Lesson review

- Briefly ask the children what they can do as a result of the lesson (understand and act out *The genie of the lamp*). Praise the children for their efforts and / or use the finger puppets to do this.

Goodbye and closing routine

- Say **Let's sing *Shake your head*.** Play the karaoke version of the song (CD 1, track 9 – see Lesson 1). Hold up the finger puppets and the children sing and do the actions as in Lesson 1.

6 My toys

Lesson 3
Communication and grammar

Aim:
- To practise asking and saying where things are

Key language:
- *Where's the ...? It's in / on / under ...*
- *Where are the ...? They're in / on / under ...*
- doll, ball, bike, car, train, marbles, skates, plane, robot, computer game
- box, shelf, table

Materials:
- Pupil's Book pages 47 and 48
- Activity Book pages 46 and 89
- Finger puppets (Pip and Squeak)
- Flashcards: Alex, Katie, doll, ball, bike, car, train, marbles, skates, plane, robot, computer game
- CD 1 and CD 2
- Scissors
- A prepared set of Unit 6 picture cards (AB page 89)

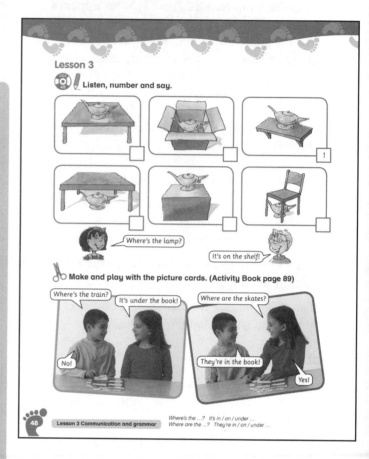

Starting out

Greetings and opening routine

- Greet the children yourself and using the finger puppets.

- *Either* play the karaoke version of *I'm ready for English* (CD 1, track 7 – see Lesson 1) and the children sing and do the actions as in Lesson 1 *or* stick the flashcards in the order of the song *I've got a car and a ball* on the board and play the karaoke version (CD 2, track 37 – see Lesson 1). The children point to the flashcards and sing the song.

Revision activity

- Hold up the finger puppets and stick the character flashcards on the board. Ask **Can you remember who's in the story with Pip, Squeak, Alex and Katie?** *(Aladdin, the genie)*

- Ask the children to open their Pupil's Books at page 47. Briefly reconstruct the story, getting the children to supply key words. Say e.g. **Alex, Katie, Pip and Squeak look for ...** *Aladdin and the lamp.* **Katie sees ...** *a cave.* **Aladdin is in the ... cave and the lamp is on the ... shelf. The lamp is ...** *magic.* **Aladdin rubs the lamp** (use gesture to convey meaning) **and out of the lamp comes a ...** *genie.* **Aladdin asks the genie for ... toys. The genie says Here's a ...** *doll, car, plane, computer game.* **Katie rubs the ...** *lamp* (use gesture again). **Katie asks the ...** *genie* **for the next ...** *treasure clue.* **The treasure clue is under the ...** *table.*

- Play the CD (CD 2, track 38 – see Lesson 2). The children listen and follow the story in their books.

Setting objectives

- Say **Today we're going to practise asking and saying where things are.** Use gesture to explain what you mean.

On the learning trail

Listen, number and say. (PB page 48)

- Ask the children to look at the pictures. Check that the children know the word *chair*. Pre-teach *box*.

- Say a sentence about each picture and the children complete it, e.g. **The lamp's on the …** *(table).* **The lamp's in the …** *(box).* **The lamp's on the …** *(shelf).* As you do this, use gesture to explain and clarify the difference between *in*, *on* and *under*.

- Say **Listen and number the pictures in order.** Draw the children's attention to the example.

- Play the CD (CD 2, track 40) once. Use the pause button, if necessary, to give the children time to number the pictures.

- Check the answers by asking e.g. **Where's the lamp in number one?** *(on the shelf)*

- Say **Now listen and repeat the questions and answers.** Play the CD again. Use the pause button to give the children time to repeat the question and answer in each exchange.

Key: first row, from left to right: 2, 3, 1; second row, from left to right: 5, 6, 4

 Listen, number and say.

1 Where's the lamp? It's on the shelf.
2 Where's the lamp? It's on the table.
3 Where's the lamp? It's in the box.
4 Where's the lamp? It's under the chair.
5 Where's the lamp? It's under the table.
6 Where's the lamp? It's on the box.

Make the picture cards. (PB page 48 and AB page 89)

- Hold up your Pupil's Book and point to the pictures. Say **We're going to make the picture cards and play the game.** You can show the children the set you have already made.

- Say **Find page 89 in your Activity Book. Look at the picture cards for Unit 6.** Point to the picture cards in turn. The children say the words.

- Make sure all the children have scissors.

- Say **Now cut out the cards like this.** Ask the children to write their names or initials on the back of the cards.

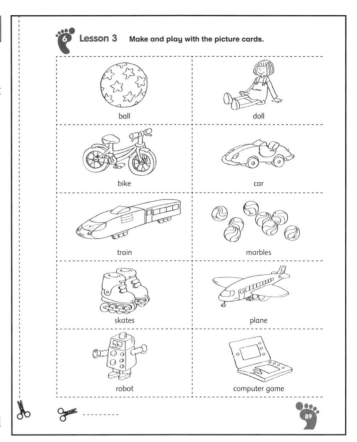

- When the children are ready, say e.g. **Hold up the plane! / Hold up the marbles!** and the children respond by holding up the correct cards.

Play with the picture cards. (PB page 48)

- Hold up your Pupil's Book and point to the pictures. Ask two pupils to read the first exchange and two other pupils to read the second exchange.

- Hold up a book. Put one of the picture cards, e.g. the car, in the book. Get the children to ask you in chorus *Where's the car?* and say **It's in the book.**

- Put another picture card of e.g. the skates, in the book and get the children to ask you *Where are the skates?* in chorus. Draw the children's attention to the way the question is different when we ask about one toy, e.g. a car, from when we ask about two or more, e.g. skates.

- Repeat, putting different picture cards in, on or under the book.

- Ask a (confident) child to the front with their book and their set of picture cards.

- Explain and demonstrate that the child should secretly choose three picture cards to hide under their book, three picture cards to hide in their book and four cards to 'hide' (face down) on the book. Do this yourself as well.

- When both of you are ready, point to your own book and cards and ask e.g. **Where's the train?** Explain and demonstrate that the child has three chances to guess, e.g. *It's in / on / under the book*. If they guess correctly the first or second time, give them the card. If they only guess correctly the third time, then you keep the card. Explain that you and the child alternate asking *Where's the …?* or *Where are the …?* regardless of who won a card in the previous round. The person with the most cards at the end of the game is the winner.

- Divide the class into pairs. The children play the game with their partner.

- If there is time, the children can colour their picture cards.

Read, draw and say. (AB page 46)

- Read the question and the sentences under the pictures. Check that the children understand where to draw the lamp in each picture.

- Say **Now read the sentences and draw the lamp in the correct position in each picture.** Draw the children's attention to the example.

- The children work individually and draw the lamp in each picture.

- The children check their answers in pairs by asking e.g. *Number two: Where's the lamp? It's in the box* for each picture.

Key: Children's own drawings. 1 on the table
2 in the box 3 under the table 4 on the chair

Listen, write and act out. (AB page 46)

- Say **Alex and Katie are playing a guessing game with the picture cards and their book.**

- Explain that the children need to look at the picture and read the questions and answers in order to work out the missing words.

- Read the exchanges in turn and the children say the missing words.

- Say **Now listen and write the words.** Draw the children's attention to the example. Play the CD (CD 2, track 41). The children work individually and write the missing words. Pause the CD if necessary to give them time to do this.

- Check the answers by asking individual children to read the exchanges.

- The children act out the exchanges in pairs.

Key: 1 train 2 bike 3 skates 4 marbles

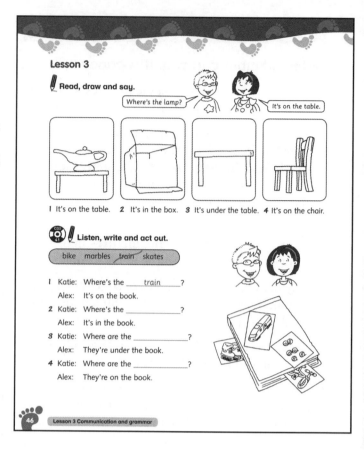

Listen, write and act out.

1 Katie: *Where's the train?*
  Alex: *It's on the book.*
2 Katie: *Where's the bike?*
  Alex: *It's in the book.*
3 Katie: *Where are the skates?*
  Alex: *They're under the book.*
4 Katie: *Where are the marbles?*
  Alex: *They're on the book.*

Ending the lesson

Lesson review

- Briefly ask the children what they can do as a result of the lesson (ask and say where things are). Praise the children for their efforts and / or use the finger puppets to do this.

Goodbye and closing routine

- Say goodbye to the children yourself and using the finger puppets. If there is time, you can also play the karaoke version of *Shake your head* (CD 1, track 9 – see Lesson 1) and the children sing and do the actions as in Lesson 1.

6 My toys

Lesson 4
Communication, grammar and pronunciation

Aims:

- To practise asking *How many ...?*
- To count to 20
- To recognise word stress in familiar two-syllable words

Key language:

- *How many ...?*
- *ball, doll, bike, car, train, marbles, skates, plane, robot, computer game*
- *jar, box*
- numbers 1–20

Materials:

- Pupil's Book page 49
- Activity Book page 47
- Finger puppets (Pip and Squeak)
- Flashcards: ball, doll, bike, car, train, marbles, skates, plane, robot, computer game, Frodo
- Unit 6 picture cards from Lesson 3
- CD 1 and CD 2

Starting out

Greetings and opening routine

- Greet the children yourself and using the finger puppets.
- *Either* play the karaoke version of *I'm ready for English* (CD 1, track 7 – see Lesson 1) and the children sing and do the actions as in Lesson 1 *or* stick the flashcards on the board in the order of the song *I've got a car and a ball* and play the karaoke version (CD 2, track 37 – see Lesson 1). The children point to the flashcards and sing the song.

Revision activity

- Give out or ask the children to get out the picture cards they made in Lesson 3. Have your own set ready.
- Give instructions using different picture cards, e.g. **Put the computer game in your pencil case. / Put the doll under your chair. / Put the marbles on your book.** The children listen and respond.
- Repeat and go faster as the children become familiar with the instructions. If you like, you can turn it into a game and introduce a scoring system, e.g. the class scores a point if everyone responds correctly within (approximately) ten seconds, and you score a point if they don't. Add up the scores at the end of the game (making sure that the class wins!).

Setting objectives

- Say **Today we're going to practise asking *How many ...?* and counting to twenty. We're also going to practise pronunciation.**

On the learning trail

Listen and say the chant. (PB page 49)

- (Books closed) Hold up five fingers and ask **How many?** Use gesture to clarify the meaning of *How many?* Repeat a few times.

- Draw a very simple picture of a jar and a box on the board. Elicit the word *box* and pre-teach *jar*.

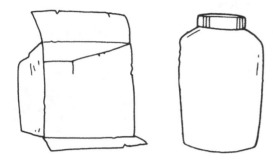

- Say **Listen to the chant. How many marbles are in the jar? How many balls are in the box?** Play the CD once (CD 2, track 42) and check the answer to both questions *(20)*. If you like, draw 20 marbles and / or 20 balls in the jar and box on the board and get the children to count to 20 with you as you do this.

- Ask the pupils to open their Pupil's Books at page 49. Play the CD again. The children count the marbles and balls in the picture and say the chant. Explain that *plenty* means *many* or *a lot*.

- Divide the children into two groups (one to ask the question in line one and say the last two lines of each verse, the other to count to 20 in each verse).

- Play the CD again. The children say the chant with their group.

- Get the groups to change roles and repeat.

 How many marbles are in the jar?

How many marbles are in the jar?
One, two, three, four, five, six, seven,
Eight, nine, ten, eleven, twelve,
Thirteen, fourteen, fifteen, sixteen,
Seventeen, eighteen, nineteen, twenty.
Twenty? That's plenty!
Twenty marbles in the jar!

How many balls are in the box? ...

Ask, count and say. (PB page 49)

- Ask the children e.g. **How many cars are in the box?** Get them to point to the picture of the cars in their books and count the cars with you.

- Repeat with one or more of the other pictures, depending on how much choral counting practice the children need.

- Draw the children's attention to the speech bubbles under the activity.

- Hold up the finger puppets. Divide the class into two groups: Squeak and Pip.

- Say to the Squeak group **Let's ask Pip about the toys!** Get the children to repeat the question for each toy after you in chorus. Get the Pip group to count the toys and answer the questions in chorus.

- Change roles and repeat.

- Divide the class into pairs. The children take turns with their partner to ask, count and say how many there are of each toy.

Key: 1 fifteen cars 2 eleven dolls 3 thirteen robots 4 twelve skates

Listen and say: Frodo's word fun. (PB page 49)

- Use L1 to explain that in English we give more stress to some parts of words than to others when we say them. Demonstrate what you mean by saying familiar words, e.g. **treasure**, **yellow**, **twenty**, and clapping loudly on the stressed syllables and softly on the unstressed syllables.

- Hold up the flashcard of Frodo. Say **Listen to Frodo and clap the stress.** Play the CD (CD 2, track 44). The children clap the stress in the pause after each word and then listen to check they have done this correctly.

- Play the CD again. This time, get the children to repeat the words and stress the correct syllables as they clap.

 Frodo's word fun. Listen and say.

robot ... marble ... treasure ... window ... yellow ... twenty ... purple ... pencil ... ruler ... biscuit ... apple

Look, count and write. (AB page 47)

- Say **Look at the picture.** Ask how many there are of each type of toy, e.g. **How many bikes?**, and the children count and tell you the answers.

- Say **Now count the toys and write the numbers.** Draw the children's attention to the example.

- The children work individually. They count the toys and write the numbers.
- Check the answers by asking e.g. **How many planes?** and the children say the answers.
- Divide the class into pairs. The children take turns to ask and answer *How many ...?* with their partner.

Key: 4 bikes; 15 dolls; 20 marbles; 6 planes; 12 cars; 11 trains

Listen, read and write. (AB page 47)

- Read the chant and the children say the missing numbers.
- Say **Now look and write the missing numbers.** Draw the children's attention to the example.
- The children work individually and write the numbers.
- Check the answers by asking individual children to say the missing numbers.
- Play the first verse of the chant (CD 2, track 45). The children pretend to put 20 marbles in a jar as they say the chant.

Key: eleven; fourteen; sixteen; seventeen; twenty

Ending the lesson

Lesson review

- Briefly ask the children what they can do as a result of the lesson (ask *How many ...?* and count to 20, clap the stress in a word). Praise the children for their efforts and / or use the finger puppets to do this.

Goodbye and closing routine

- Say goodbye to the children yourself and using the finger puppets. If there is time, you can also play the karaoke version of *Shake your head* (CD 1, track 9 – see Lesson 1) and the children sing and do the actions as in Lesson 1.

6 My toys

Lesson 5
Content input

Aims:
- To read and understand that things with wheels can move
- To name toys which have got wheels

Key language:
- *How many ...?*
- *wheel*
- *car, plane, ball, robot, skates, train, doll, bike*
- *scooter, skateboard, teddy bear*
- *big, small*
- numbers 1–20

Materials:
- Pupil's Book page 50
- Activity Book page 48
- Finger puppets (Pip and Squeak)
- Flashcards: ball, doll, bike, car, train, marbles, skates, plane, robot, computer game
- CD 1 and CD 2
- Objects for children to count, e.g. crayons, flashcards

Starting out

Greetings and opening routine

- Greet the children yourself and using the finger puppets.
- *Either* play the karaoke version of *I'm ready for English* (CD 1, track 7 – see Lesson 1) and the children sing and do the actions as in Lesson 1 *or* divide the class into two groups, play the karaoke version of *How many marbles are in the jar?* (CD 2, track 43 – see Lesson 4) and the children say the chant and pretend to drop marbles into a jar and balls into a box and count them.

Revision activity

- Hold up or point to a set of objects (no more than 20) that you want the children to count. Say e.g. **I'm not sure if I've got all the flashcards here. Can you help me count them?**

- The children count the objects with you in chorus as you hold them up (show the reverse side if they are flashcards so the children are not distracted by the pictures) and lay them down in turn on your desk.

Setting objectives

- Hold up the finger puppets. Say **Let's learn about the world around you! Today we're going to read about wheels and name toys which have got wheels.** Explain the meaning of *wheel* by saying e.g. **Cars have got wheels** and either drawing a simple picture on the board or pointing to the wheels on the flashcard of the car.

On the learning trail

Read, tick (✓) and listen. (PB page 50)

- (Books closed) Read the question **What are wheels?**

- Listen to the children's ideas (in L1). Use their suggestions to introduce or remind the children of vocabulary, e.g. *move, shape, circle*.

- Remind the children of the meaning of *big* and *small* using items in the classroom.

- Ask the children to open their Pupil's Books at page 50. Read the text at the start of the activity or play part 1 on the CD (CD 2, track 46).

- Ask questions to check comprehension and clarify meaning, e.g. **Are wheels the shape of a circle?** *(yes)* **Have many things got wheels?** *(yes)* **Can things with wheels move?** *(yes).*

- Say **Look at the pictures.** Read the question (*How many toys have got wheels?*) and the word for each toy while the children follow in their books.

- You can ask the children to repeat the words *scooter*, *skateboard* and *teddy bear* after you as you say them, as they are new words.

- Say **Write a tick by the toys which have got wheels.** Draw their attention to the example.

- The children work individually and tick the toys with wheels.

- Ask **How many of the toys have got wheels?** The children count up and answer *(five)*. Ask the children to name the toys which have got wheels but don't confirm the answers yet.

- Say **Now listen and check your answers.** Play the CD (CD 2, track 46). Use the pause button to allow the children time to compare their answers with the CD.
- Check the answers by getting individual children to name a toy with wheels.
- Play the CD again as a final check.

  Key: car ✓ plane ✓ skates ✓ scooter ✓ skateboard ✓

 Read, tick and listen.

Part 1

Wheels are the shape of a circle.
Many things have got wheels.
Things with wheels can move.
Some wheels are big.
Some wheels are small.

Part 2

How many toys have got wheels?
Five! The car, the plane, the skates, the scooter and the skateboard have got wheels.

Play a game. (PB page 50)

- Explain and demonstrate that you are going to say the names of toys and other objects. The children should make a big circle with their arms and respond *Wheels!* in chorus if they think the object you name has got wheels. They should fold their arms and respond *No wheels!* in chorus if they think the object hasn't got wheels. Explain that every time the children respond correctly they score a point, and that every time they respond incorrectly you score a point.
- Play the game by saying different toys and other objects in random order. The children respond by saying *Wheels!* or *No wheels!* and doing the actions. Keep a score of the points you and the children win on the board. Examples of toys you can say are: *car, plane, ball, skates, train, doll, scooter, skateboard, teddy bear, bike, marble, robot, computer game*. With other words that are ambiguous, e.g. *table, chair, school bag*, i.e. that may have wheels, allow the children to score a point if they themselves point this out.
- At the end, if appropriate, you may like to point out (in L1) that wheels on things such as cars

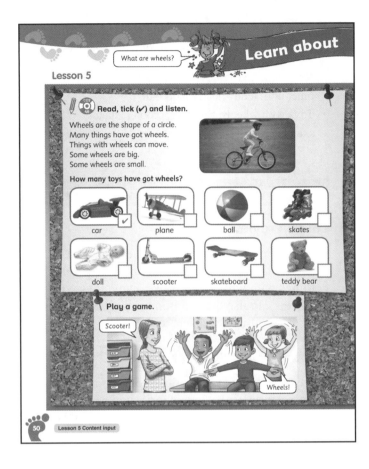

and bikes help to move things along the ground. Wheels are also important for turning objects such as doorknobs or taps and for lifting heavy weights or, for example, water out of a well.

Read and circle. (AB page 48)

- Read each sentence and the children say *Yes* or *No* depending on whether it is true or false.
- The children work individually and circle *Yes* or *No*.
- Check the answers by reading the sentences again and the children saying *Yes* or *No*.

  Key: 1 No 2 Yes 3 Yes 4 No

Look, colour and write. (AB page 48)

- Read the two instructions at the start of the activity and check understanding.
- Say **Colour the toys red or blue. Write a list of the toys with wheels.** Draw the children's attention to the example.
- The children work individually and colour the toys red or blue depending on whether they have got wheels or not. They then write a list of the toys with wheels.

- Check the answers by asking individual children to take turns to name the toys with wheels.

  Key: red: bike, car, scooter, skates, skateboard, plane
  blue: doll, teddy bear, robot, ball
  Toys with wheels: bike, car, scooter, skates, skateboard, plane

Ending the lesson

Lesson review

- Briefly ask the children what they can do as a result of the lesson (read and understand that things with wheels can move, name toys with wheels). Praise the children for their efforts and / or use the finger puppets to do this.

Goodbye and closing routine

- Say goodbye to the children yourself and using the finger puppets. If there is time, you can also play the karaoke version of *Shake your head* (CD 1, track 9 – see Lesson 1) and the children sing and do the actions as in Lesson 1.

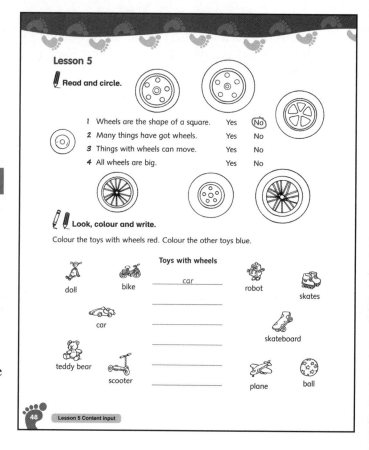

6　My toys

Lesson 6
Content and personalisation

Aims:

- To recognise that many things we use every day have got wheels
- To talk about toys you've got with wheels

Key language:

- *I've got ...*
- *How many ...?*
- *car, plane, bike, scooter, marbles, skates, train, doll, teddy bear, computer game, boat, ball, skateboard*
- numbers 1–20

Materials:

- Pupil's Book page 51
- Activity Book page 49
- Finger puppets (Pip and Squeak)
- CD 1 and CD 2

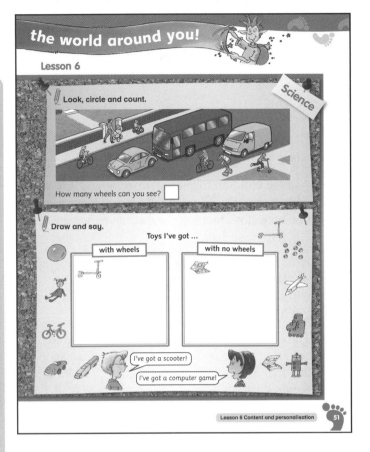

Starting out

Greetings and opening routine

- Greet the children yourself and using the finger puppets.
- *Either* play the karaoke version of *I'm ready for English* (CD 1, track 7 – see Lesson 1) and the children sing and do the actions as in Lesson 1 *or* divide the class into two groups, play the karaoke version of *How many marbles are in the jar?* (CD 2, track 43 – see Lesson 4) and the children say the chant and pretend to drop marbles into a jar and put balls in a box and count them.

Revision activity

- Draw a wheel on the board and elicit or remind the children of the word.
- Say sentences about wheels. Either whistle or say a nonsense word, e.g. **bleep***!*, instead of certain words and the children supply the missing words, e.g. **Wheels are the shape of a *bleep*!** (circle) **Many things have got *bleep*!** (wheels). (Use the text on page 50 of the Pupil's Book for more ideas.)

Setting objectives

- Say **In this lesson we're going to observe and count wheels on things we use every day.** (Use mime, gesture and / or L1 to convey what you mean.) **We're also going to talk about toys we've got with wheels.**

On the learning trail

Look, circle and count. (PB page 51)

- Read the question and check understanding.
- Say **Let's count how many wheels we can see!** Get the children to count to 20 in chorus with you and point to different wheels in the picture as they do this.
- **Note:** just count the wheels you can see in the picture, i.e. although a car has four wheels, you should only count the two wheels you can see.
- Say e.g. **Oh, dear. I'm not sure if 20 is the correct answer! Please can you check!** Divide the class into pairs and ask the children to circle the wheels in their books and count them in English together with their partner.
- Check the answers by getting the children to count the wheels they have circled with you one more time.

- At the end, point out how many things we use every day that have got wheels (you do not need to introduce the words for these in English). If you like, ask the children to name other things with wheels they can think of (in L1), e.g. lorry, tractor, trailer.

Key: 20

Draw and say. (PB page 51)

- Ask the children to tell you toys they've got with wheels, e.g. *I've got a car.* Then ask them to tell you other toys they've got that haven't got wheels, e.g. *I've got a ball.*

- Hold up your book, point to the two frames and say **Draw and colour toys you've got with wheels here. Draw and colour other toys you've got here.**

- The children work individually and draw and colour their pictures. (If you like, you can specify that they should draw a maximum of two or three pictures.)

- Ask individual children to take turns to show their pictures and tell the class about them, e.g. *I've got a plane. / I've got marbles.*

- If appropriate, make the point that the children are lucky to have toys and that it is important to look after these carefully as well as be willing to share them with others when they play.

Look, count and write. (AB page 49)

- Either get the children to count the wheels in each picture in chorus with you first or they can do this in pairs (depending on how confident they are at counting to 20 in English). They then write the number of wheels under each picture. They use the numbers at the top. Draw their attention to the example.

- Check the answers by asking e.g. **How many wheels can you see in picture one?** and the children say the number.

Key: 1 fourteen 2 twelve 3 eighteen 4 twenty

Choose, write and say. (AB page 49)

- Read the words for the toys while the children follow in their books.

- Ask individual children to tell the class a toy they've got with wheels, e.g. *I've got skates,* and another toy they've got without wheels, e.g. *I've got a doll.*

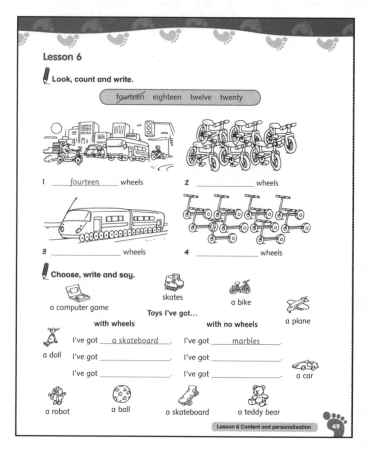

- Say **Write sentences about toys you've got with wheels and other toys.** Draw the children's attention to the example.

- The children work individually and complete the sentences.

- Ask individual children to take turns to tell the class their sentences, e.g. *I've got a train. / I've got a computer game.*

Key: Children's own answers.

Ending the lesson

Lesson review

- Briefly ask the children what they can do as a result of the lesson (count wheels on things we use every day, talk about toys they've got with wheels and other toys). Praise the children for their efforts and / or use the finger puppets to do this.

Goodbye and closing routine

- Say goodbye to the children yourself and using the finger puppets. If there is time, you can also play the karaoke version of *Shake your head* (CD 1, track 9 – see Lesson 1) and the children sing and do the actions as in Lesson 1.

6 My toys

Lesson 7
Children's culture

Aim:
- To sing a traditional song and play a version of a traditional game

Key language:
- *wheels, bus, driver, children, go round, chatter, hoot*
- *Where's the ...?*
- *doll, ball, bike, car, train, marbles, skates, plane, robot, computer game*
- *hot, cold*

Materials:
- Pupil's Book page 52
- Activity Book page 50
- Finger puppets (Pip and Squeak)
- CD 1 and CD 2
- Flashcards: ball, doll, bike, car, train, marbles, skates, plane, robot, computer game, Frodo
- Real toys or thimble (optional)

Starting out

Greetings and opening routine

- Greet the children yourself and using the finger puppets.
- *Either* play the karaoke version of *I'm ready for English* (CD 1, track 7 – see Lesson 1) and the children sing and do the actions as in Lesson 1 *or* play the karaoke version of *How many marbles are in the jar?* (CD 2, track 43 – see Lesson 4) and the children say the chant and pretend to put marbles in the jar and balls in the box as they count, as previously.

Revision activity

- Explain that you are going to say sentences about toys you've got and that the children should repeat them if they are true for them.
- Say sentences, e.g. **I've got a bike / I've got a teddy bear** and the children respond. If you like, keep a score on the board of all the sentences that are true for the whole class.

Setting objectives

- Hold up the flashcard of Frodo. Say **In this lesson we're going to learn about children's culture with Frodo. We're going to sing a traditional song and play a game.**

On the learning trail

Listen and sing the song. (PB page 52) (books closed)

- Say e.g. **Cars and bikes have got wheels. Can you think of other things with wheels?** As soon as the children say *bus* (in L1), recast it in English and say **Yes! Very good. And we're going to sing a song called** *The wheels on the bus*!
- Say **Stand up please! Listen to the song and do the actions.** Play the CD (CD 2, track 47). The children listen to the song and do the actions (see audio script below) with you.
- Play the CD (CD 2, track 47) again. The children do the actions and join in singing the song.
- Ask the children to open their Pupil's Books at page 52. Play the CD again. The children sing and follow in their books. Explain that *chatter* means to talk in an excited and animated way.

The wheels on the bus

The wheels on the bus go round and round
(make circles with your arms)
Round and round, round and round
The wheels on the bus go round and round
All day long!

The driver on the bus goes hoot, hoot, hoot …
(pretend to drive and hoot on horn)
The children on the bus go chatter, chatter, chatter …
(open your fingers and thumb rapidly on both hands to suggest two people chattering)

 Citizenship box: Remember!

Ask the children **Do you like to chat with your friends?** and listen to their response.

Hold up the flashcard of Frodo, read the *Remember!* note and check understanding. Ask the children why it's best not to make a lot of noise when you chat, especially in public places such as on a bus *(so as not to disturb or annoy other people)*.

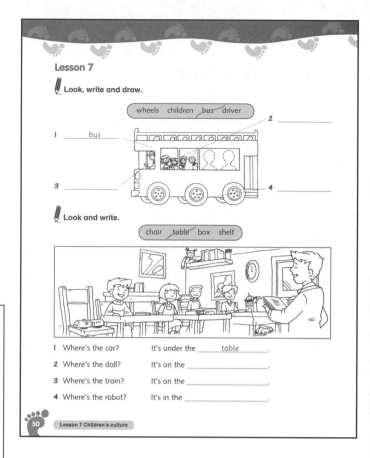

Play *Where's the …?* (PB page 52)

- Say **Let's play a game!** Explain that in the game a pair of children *either* go out of the classroom for a moment *or* stand facing the board with their eyes closed. The rest of the class choose where to 'hide' a toy (either a real toy or a flashcard) in the classroom. The toy or flashcard should be 'hidden' somewhere visible, i.e. the children should not need to touch or move objects in order to find it.

- Once the toy or flashcard is hidden, the pair of children turn round and open their eyes or come back into the classroom. The rest of the class asks them in chorus: *Where's the …?* The pair of children then walk round the classroom looking for the toy. As they do this, the rest of the class chant *Hot, hot, hot!* (use mime to convey meaning) or *Cold, cold, cold!* (again use mime to convey meaning). Explain and demonstrate that this gives a clue to the children whether they are getting closer to or further away from the hidden toy. As soon as one of the children finds the toy, everyone says e.g. *Hurray!* or *Fantastic!*

- Get the children to practise saying *Hot, hot hot!* and *Cold, cold, cold!* in chorus a few times before playing the game.

- Demonstrate the game, asking a pair of confident children to have the first turn.

- Repeat the game several times with different children. Hide a different real toy or flashcard each time.

Option: The traditional version of this game is called *Hunt the thimble* (a thimble is the thing you wear to protect your finger when sewing). If you have a thimble available, you may like to play the game using this instead of real toys or flashcards.

Look, write and draw. (AB page 50)

- Read the words at the top of the activity and the children point to the appropriate parts of the picture.

- Say **Now write the words.** Draw the children's attention to the example.

- Check the answers by asking e.g. **What's number one?** and the children say the words.

- Hold up your book and point to the frame with the outlines. Say **Now draw a picture of you and a friend on the bus.**
- If you like, when the children are ready, say **Let's sing the song.** Play the CD of *The wheels on the bus* (CD 2, track 47) or the karaoke version (CD 2, track 48). The children sing and point to the different parts of the picture in their books.

  Key: 1 bus 2 children 3 driver 4 wheels

Look and write. (AB page 50)

- Say **Look at the picture.** Ask the questions and the children answer orally.
- Say **Now write the answers.** Draw the children's attention to the example.
- The children work individually and complete the answers.
- Check the answers by asking individual children to take turns to ask and answer one of the questions.

  Key: 1 table 2 shelf 3 chair 4 box

Ending the lesson

Lesson review

- Briefly ask the children what they can do as a result of the lesson (sing a traditional song, play a version of a traditional game). Praise the children for their efforts and / or use the finger puppets to do this.

Goodbye and closing routine

- Say goodbye to the children yourself and using the finger puppets. If there is time, you can also play the karaoke version of *Shake your head* (CD 1, track 9 – see Lesson 1) and the children sing and do the actions as in Lesson 1.

6 My toys

Lesson 8
Unit review / All About Me Portfolio Booklet

Aim:
- To review learning in Unit 6

Key language:
- *Where's the ...? It's in / on / under ...*
- *Where are ...? They're ...*
- *How many ...?*
- *doll, ball, bike, car, train, marbles, skates, plane, computer game, robot*
- *driver, wheels, children*
- numbers 10–20

Materials:
- Pupil's Book page 53
- Activity Book page 51
- *All About Me* Portfolio Booklet pages 16 and 17
- Finger puppets (Pip and Squeak)
- Flashcards: doll, ball, bike, car, train, marbles, skates, plane, computer game, robot
- Word cards: doll, ball, bike, car, train, marbles, skates, plane, computer game, robot
- Stickers for Unit 6
- CD 1 and CD 2

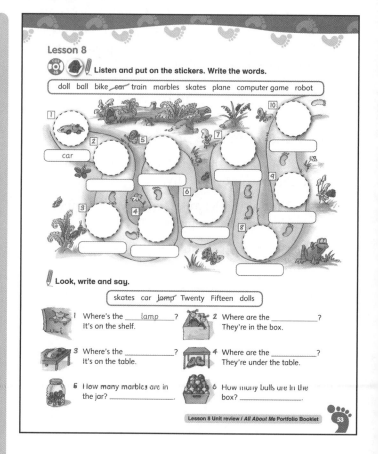

Starting out

Greetings and opening routine
- Greet the children yourself and using the finger puppets.
- *Either* play the karaoke version of *I'm ready for English* (CD 1, track 7 – see Lesson 1) and the children sing and do the actions as in Lesson 1 *or* stick the flashcards on the board in the order of the song *I've got a car and a ball* and play the karaoke version (CD 2, track 37 – see Lesson 1) and the children sing the song and point to the flashcards.

Revision activity
- Say the following words from the song *The wheels on the bus* (see Lesson 7) and the children respond by doing the actions: *wheels* (move arms in circles), *driver* (pretend to drive the bus and / or hoot horn), *children* (move fingers and thumbs to show chattering).
- Repeat a few times, speeding up and saying the words in random order.
- Ask the children to stand up. Play the karaoke version of *The wheels on the bus* on the CD (CD 2, track 48 – see Lesson 7). The children sing the song and do the actions.

Setting objectives
- Say **Today we're going to review what we've learnt in Unit 6.**

On the learning trail

Listen and put on the stickers. Write the words. (PB page 53)
- Make sure the children have the stickers for Unit 6 ready.

- Say **Listen and put on the stickers.** Draw the children's attention to the example.
- Play the CD (CD 2, track 49). Use the pause button to give the children time to put on the stickers.
- Say **Now write the words.** Draw the children's attention to the example.
- Check the answers by saying the numbers and getting the children to say the words.

  Key: 1 car 2 train 3 doll 4 skates 5 marbles
  6 balls 7 plane 8 computer game 9 bike 10 robot

 Listen and put on the stickers.

1 Where's the car? It's on the shelf.
2 Where's the train? It's in the box.
3 Where's the doll? It's under the table.
4 Where are the skates? They're on the box.
5 How many marbles are in the jar? Twenty.
6 How many balls are in the box? Twenty.
7 I've got a plane.
8 I've got a computer game.
9 I've got a bike.
10 I've got a robot.

Look, write and say. (PB page 53)

- Read the exchanges and the children look at the pictures and say the missing words.
- Say **Now write the words.** Draw the children's attention to the example.
- The children work individually and write the missing words.
- Check the answers by asking individual children to read the exchanges.

  Key: 1 lamp 2 dolls 3 car 4 skates 5 Fifteen
  6 Twenty

Listen and draw. (AB page 51)

- Say **Listen and draw the lamp in each picture.** Draw the children's attention to the example.
- Play the CD (CD 2, track 50). Pause to give the children time to draw the lamp in each picture.
- Check the answers by getting individual children to ask *Where's the lamp?* and answer for each picture.

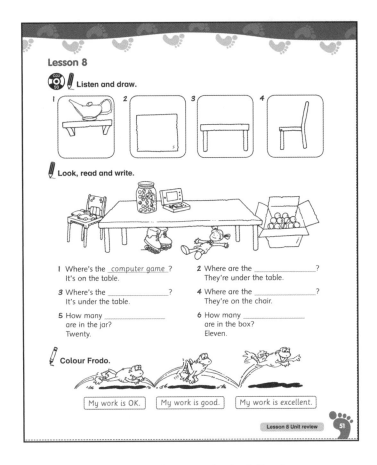

Key: The lamp should be drawn in the following places:
1 on the shelf 2 in the box 3 under the table
4 on the chair

 Listen and draw.

1 Where's the lamp? It's on the shelf.
2 Where's the lamp? It's in the box.
3 Where's the lamp? It's under the table.
4 Where's the lamp? It's on the chair.

Look, read and write. (AB page 51)

- Read the exchanges and the children look at the picture and say the missing words.
- Say **Write the words.** Draw the children's attention to the example.
- The children work individually and complete the exchanges.
- Check the answers by asking individual children to read the exchanges.

  Key: 1 computer game 2 skates 3 doll 4 cars
  5 marbles 6 balls

Colour Frodo. (AB page 51)

- Hold up the flashcard of Frodo. Remind the children that in this activity they assess their work in the unit by choosing and colouring the picture of Frodo which corresponds best to how they think they have done.

- Remind the children of the key by pointing to the three pictures of Frodo and saying **Colour this picture if your work is OK but you think you need to try harder or need more practice. Colour this picture of Frodo if you think your work is good. Colour this picture of Frodo with a big smile and jumping very high if you think your work is excellent.** Make sure the children understand that there are no right answers and that it is their own opinion of the work they have done which is important. Be ready to encourage the children to have a positive view if they are too hard on themselves.

Goodbye and closing routine

- Say goodbye to the children yourself and using the finger puppets. If there is time, you can also play the karaoke version of *Shake your head* (CD 1, track 9 – see Lesson 1) and the children sing and do the actions as in Lesson 1.

> **All About Me** Portfolio Booklet
>
> The children complete Unit 6 of their personal *All About Me* Portfolio Booklets. They complete their learning journey by colouring the sections on the path to show what they can do. If you like, the children can also sign this page and you can endorse this by adding your own signature and the date.

Ending the lesson

Lesson review

- Briefly ask the children what they can do as a result of the lesson (use the language and vocabulary they've learnt in Unit 6). Praise the children for their efforts and / or use the finger puppets to do this.

7 My family

Structures and grammar

- *Who's he / she? He's / She's my ...*
- *His / Her name is ...*
- *He's / She's got ...*
- Recycled: *Who ...?, I've got ..., This is ... / These are ..., my / your, ..., too.*

Vocabulary

- Core: *mother, father, brother, sister, baby, grandmother, grandfather, aunt, uncle, cousin*
- Other: *love, fair, house, soup, name, goat*
- Content / culture: *colour, glasses, clap, fold, lap, nap*
- Recycled: *boy, girl, friend, eyes, hair, brown, blue, red, green, black, hat, hands, arms, fantastic, delicious*, numbers 1–20

Main receptive language

- *similar to, members, family, also, special, Let's ...*

Communicative competence

Understanding

Listening:
- Can recognise words for members of the family
- Can understand the episode of the story
- Can understand questions which ask and say who people are
- Can understand statements about people's hair and eye colour
- Can recognise the difference between /ð/ and /θ/

Reading:
- Can recognise words for members of the family
- Can read sentences that describe the colour of eyes and hair
- Can read questions and answers about who people are
- Can read about ways we are similar to other members of our family

Speaking

Spoken interaction:
- Can ask and respond to questions about who people are

Spoken production:
- Can sing the song *I like English*
- Can name members of the family
- Can sing the song *My mother and father*
- Can say who people are
- Can sing the song *She's my friend*
- Can say words with /ð/ and /θ/ correctly
- Can describe people's hair and eye colour
- Can say the rhyme *These are grandmother's glasses*
- Can sing the song *Are you ready to finish?*

Writing

- Can copy and write words for members of the family
- Can copy and write words for the colour of hair and eyes
- Can complete questions and sentences about who people are

Content links

- *Science:* ways in which we are similar to other members of our family

Learning strategies and thinking skills

- Recognising learning objectives
- Associating vocabulary with people you know
- Using pictures to memorise vocabulary and language patterns
- Observing people in close detail
- Guessing who people are
- Deducing
- Reflecting on learning

Children's culture

- Saying a rhyme: *These are grandmother's glasses*
- Playing a version of a traditional game: *Grandmother's footsteps!*

Pronunciation

- Saying words with /ð/ and /θ/

Values and attitudes

- Pleasure in talking about your family in English
- Recognition that we are similar to other members of our family
- Awareness that your family is special

7 My family

Lesson 1
Vocabulary presentation

Aim:
- To name members of the family

Key language:
- *mother, father, brother, sister, baby, grandmother, grandfather, aunt, uncle, cousin*
- *My ...*
- *You're fantastic.*
- *I love you.*

Materials:
- Pupil's Book page 54
- Activity Book page 52
- Finger puppets (Pip and Squeak)
- Flashcards: Alex, Katie, Frodo, mother, father, brother, sister, baby, grandmother, grandfather, aunt, uncle, cousin
- Word cards: mother, father, brother, sister, baby, grandmother, grandfather, aunt, uncle, cousin
- CD 1 and CD 3

Starting out

Greetings and opening routine

- Greet the children yourself and using the finger puppets. Say e.g. **Hello, children. Hello … How are you today?** *Fine, thank you.* Ask a few individual children to greet the puppets in turn.

- Say **Let's sing the song** *I like English.* Play the CD (CD 1, track 10). Stick the character flashcards of Alex, Katie and Frodo on the board. Hold up the puppets on your index fingers. Move the puppets, use them to point to the other characters and hold each one out when the children sing their names.

 I like English

I like English.	(thumbs up)
And I like you.	(gesture to a friend)
I like Alex, Katie and Frodo.	(point to the flashcards)
I like Pip and Squeak, too!	(wave to the puppets)

Setting objectives
- Say **Today we're going to learn to name members of the family and we're going to sing a song.**

On the learning trail

Vocabulary presentation (books closed)

- Say **I want you to meet my family.**

- Hold up the flashcard of the mother. Say **This is my mother.** Say **mother** several times and get the children to repeat the word with you in chorus.

- Stick the flashcard of mother on the board.

- Repeat the procedure with the other family flashcards. Say **This is the baby** or **This is my little brother. He's the baby.** Clarify the meaning of *aunt* and *uncle* and explain that *cousin* can be either male or female.

- Divide the class in half. Say to one half **Can you name the members of my family?** Point to the flashcards in turn and the children say the words with you. Praise the children.

- Repeat the procedure with the other half

Follow the footprints. (PB page 54) (books open)

- Hold up the flashcard of Frodo. Say Listen and follow the footprints with Frodo the frog. Use your finger and demonstrate this.

- Play the CD (CD 3, track 1). The children listen and follow the footprints with their fingers. They stop by each picture as they hear the word and repeat the word.

- Say **Now listen and draw a line following the footprints** and demonstrate this. Play the CD again. The children draw a line, stop by each picture and repeat the words as previously.

 Follow the footprints.

mother ... father ... brother ... sister ... baby ... grandmother ... grandfather ... aunt ... uncle ... cousin

- Stick the word cards on the board in jumbled order (at the children's height and away from the flashcards).
- Point to one word card, e.g. *sister*, and read the word. Say **Look for my sister.** Give the children time to do this.
- Ask a child to come to the front of the class and stick the word card for *sister* by the corresponding flashcard. Ask the rest of the class **Is this right?** and get them to say the word.
- Repeat the procedure with the rest of the word cards.
- Take the flashcards and word cards off the board.

Listen and sing the song. (PB page 54)

- Say **Look. Pip is showing us photos of his family.** Ask **Who can you see?** and the children name the family members in the picture.
- Say **Listen to the song. Point to the family members in the picture** and demonstrate what you mean. Play the CD (CD 3, track 2). The children listen to the song and point to the family members for each verse. Elicit or clarify the meaning of *You're fantastic* and *I love you*.
- Invite five (or ten) children to the front of the class. Give them each one (or two) flashcard(s) and get them to stand facing the class holding up the flashcards in the same order as the song. Explain and demonstrate that the children at the front should hold up their flashcard(s) when they hear their word(s) in the song. The rest of the class should point to the flashcards in turn as they sing and do actions in the last two lines of each verse (see the audio script below).
- Play the CD again. The children point to the pictures, do the actions and sing the song.
- At the end, briefly ask the children e.g. **Is your family fantastic like Pip's? / Do you love your family like Pip?**

 My mother and father

My mother and father
My brother, sister and baby, too
You're fantastic.   (wave arms in the air)
I love you!   (mime giving a big hug)

My grandmother and grandfather
My uncle, aunt and cousin, too
You're fantastic.   (wave arms in the air)
I love you!   (mime giving a big hug)

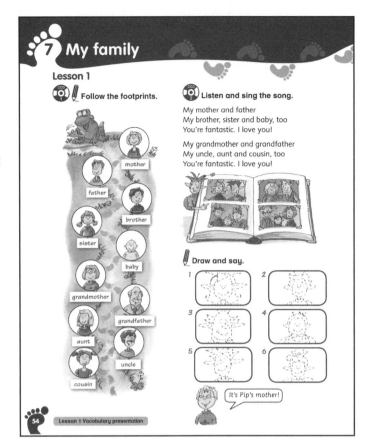

Draw and say. (PB page 54)

- Hold up your book. Point to the outlines in turn and say **This is Pip's …** and the children say the words. If the children need help, point out that the shape of each outline is the same as the pictures in Pip's photo album. Ask the children to draw round the outlines and complete the pictures. Draw their attention to the example.
- The children work individually and complete the pictures.
- Check the answers by asking **Who's this?** and the children respond *It's …* for each picture.

Key: 1 mother 2 brother 3 grandfather 4 baby
5 father 6 sister

Read and match. (AB page 52)

- Read the sentences and the children point to the 'photos' of Pip's family.
- The children work individually and match the sentences and pictures.
- Check the answers by asking individual children to read a sentence and point to the correct picture in their book or to come to the front and hold up the correct flashcard.

Key: 1 bottom left 2 top left 3 top right
4 bottom right

Look and write. (AB page 52)

- Read the words and the children identify the family members.
- Say **Now write the words.** Draw the children's attention to the example.
- The children work individually and write the words under the pictures.
- Check the answers by saying e.g. **Number one is Pip's ...** and the children say the words.

Key: 1 grandmother 2 brother 3 grandfather
4 father 5 mother 6 sister

Ending the lesson

Lesson review

- Briefly ask the children what they can do as a result of the lesson (name members of the family, sing the song *My mother and father*). Praise the children for their efforts and / or use the finger puppets to do this.

Goodbye and closing routine

- Say **Let's sing the song** *Are you ready to finish?* Play the CD (CD 1, track 12). Hold up the finger puppets on your index fingers and move them rhythmically as the children count, sing and do the actions.

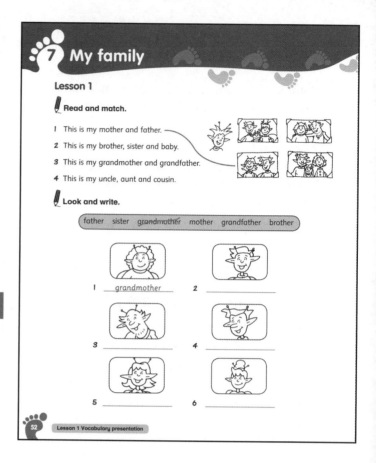

Are you ready to finish?

Are you ready to finish?   (gesture questioningly)
Count to twenty and say goodbye
                              (mime counting fingers)
One, two, three, four, five, six, seven
    (move arms rhythmically as sing each number)
Eight, nine, ten, and now eleven
Twelve, thirteen, fourteen, fifteen, sixteen
Seventeen, eighteen, nineteen, twenty – Hey!
                (make a big circle with arms)
Goodbye! Goodbye!
Goodbye for today!   (wave goodbye)

- Say goodbye to the children yourself and using the finger puppets. Say e.g. **Goodbye everyone. See you on ...** Ask a few individual children to say goodbye to the finger puppets in turn.

7 My family

Lesson 2
Language input and story

Aim:
- To understand and act out episode 7 of the story

Key language:
- *mother, father, brother, sister, baby, grandmother, grandfather, aunt, uncle, cousin*
- *bear, Mummy, Daddy, Baby Bear, friend, soup, delicious, goat*
- *Who's he / she? He's / She's my ...*
- *His / Her name's ...*

Materials:
- Pupil's Book page 55
- Activity Book page 53
- Finger puppets (Pip and Squeak)
- Flashcards: Alex, Katie, mother, father, brother, sister, baby, grandmother, grandfather, aunt, uncle, cousin
- Treasure clue sticker for Unit 7
- CD 1 and CD 3

Starting out

Greetings and opening routine
- Greet the children yourself and using the finger puppets.
- Play *I like English* (CD 1, track 10 – see Lesson 1). The children sing and do the actions as in Lesson 1.

Revision activity
- Hold up the family flashcards in turn and the children say the words.
- Stick the flashcards on the board in the same order as the song *My mother and father* (see Lesson 1).
- Play the CD (CD 3, track 2 – see Lesson 1). The children sing the song, do the actions and point to the flashcards.
- Repeat with the karaoke version (CD 3, track 3 – see Lesson 1).

Setting objectives
- Say **Today we're going to listen to and act out episode 7 of the story.**

On the learning trail

Listen and act out the story.
Episode 7: The soup (PB page 55)

Before the story (books closed)
- Hold up the finger puppets and stick the flashcards of Alex and Katie on the board. Recap on the last episode of the story, using mime and gesture as necessary: **Alex, Katie, Pip and Squeak find Aladdin and the lamp in a cave. Aladdin rubs the lamp and out of the lamp comes a genie. Aladdin asks the genie for toys. Then Katie rubs the lamp and asks the genie for the next treasure clue. The treasure clue is under the table.**
- Ask **Can you remember the clue from Unit 6?** Hold up page 47 of the Pupil's Book and point to the treasure clue sticker. Read *Follow the footprints! Find Goldilocks!* as a prompt if necessary.

- Use L1 to ask the children if they know the story of Goldilocks and listen to their responses. If they are familiar with the story, briefly ask who else is in the story *(three bears)*. If they don't know the story, explain it to them.

- Ask the following questions in turn. Use mime and gesture to clarify meaning, and encourage the children to predict the answers: **1) Who do Alex, Katie, Pip and Squeak meet in the forest? 2) Where's Goldilocks? 3) Where's the next treasure clue?**

During the story (books open)

- Say **Now listen to the story and find out.** Explain to the children that they will hear a 'beep' noise on the CD to tell them when to move to the next picture in the story.

- Play the CD (CD 3, track 4) and the children follow in their books.

- Ask the questions in turn again and check the answers, recasting them in English and using mime and gesture to clarify meaning as necessary. *(1 Baby Bear, Daddy Bear and Mummy Bear 2 in the bears' house 3 in the (bowl of) soup)*

- Clarify and / or remind the children that *Mummy* and *Daddy* (or *Mum* and *Dad*) are the names you call your own mother and father. Use the picture to clarify the meaning of *fair hair* and *blue eyes*.

- Say **Listen again and repeat the story.** Play the CD again. Pause after each sentence and the children repeat the story.

- **Note:** There is more story text on the CD than appears on the Pupil's Book page. This additional text is marked with an asterisk* in the audio script below. The children repeat the whole story, including the language which does not appear in their books.

 Follow the footprints, Episode 7: The soup

Picture 1	
Narrator:	*Alex, Katie, Pip and Squeak follow the footprints to find Goldilocks.**
Katie:	*Oh, I hope we find Goldilocks!*
Alex:	*Me, too!*
Pip:	*Ssh! Listen!*

Picture 2	
Squeak:	*Hello. Who are you?**
Baby Bear:	*I'm Baby Bear.**
Katie:	*Who's he?*
Baby Bear:	*He's my father. His name is Daddy Bear.*
Squeak:	*Who's she?**
Baby Bear:	*She's my mother. Her name is Mummy Bear.**

Picture 3	
Katie:	*Do you know this girl? Her name is Goldilocks.*
Alex:	*She's got fair hair and blue eyes.*
Baby Bear:	*Oh, yes! She's my friend!*

Picture 4	
Baby Bear:	*Goldilocks! Where are you?*

Picture 5	
Baby Bear:	*Oh, dear! Goldilocks isn't here. Let's go to my house!*
Pip:	*Oh, yes.**
Alex:	*Good idea!**

Picture 6	
Baby Bear:	*Oh, look! Here's Goldilocks.**
Goldilocks:	*Hello, everyone! Mmm! This soup is delicious!*
Baby Bear:	*Oh, Goldilocks! Not my soup again!*

Picture 7	
Goldilocks:	*Look! Here's the next treasure clue!*
Pip:	*Thank you! Follow the footprints! Find three goats!*
Goldilocks:	*Goodbye and good luck.**
All:	*Goodbye, Goldilocks. Goodbye, Baby Bear. Thank you!**

After the story

- Ask questions about each picture as follows: **1) Who do Alex and Katie hope to find?** *(Goldilocks)* **Who hears a noise?** (use mime to convey meaning) *(Pip)* **2) Who appears?** *(Baby Bear, Daddy Bear, Mummy Bear)* **3) Does Baby Bear know Goldilocks?** *(yes)* **Goldilocks is his …** *(friend)* **4) Who does Baby Bear call?** *(Goldilocks)* **5) Is Goldilocks here?** *(no)* **Baby Bear says *Let's go to my …*** *(house)* **6) Who's in the bears' house?** *(Goldilocks)* **Does Goldilocks like the soup?** *(Yes, it's delicious.)* **7) Where's the next clue?** *(in the bowl)*

Put on the treasure clue sticker.

- Say **The treasure clue says** *Follow the footprints! Find three goats!* Use the picture to clarify the meaning of *goat*.
- Say **Find the treasure clue sticker for Unit 7 and stick it here.** Demonstrate what you mean.
- The children look for the treasure clue sticker for Unit 7 and stick it in their books.

Act out the story.

- Divide the class into six groups and assign a role to each group: Alex, Katie, Pip, Squeak, Baby Bear or Goldilocks. Follow the procedure for *Act out the story* on page 37 of the Teacher's Book.

Option: The children can act out their parts *either* with *or* without their books, depending on how confident and familiar they are with this episode. If you wish to make the activity more challenging, the children can act out the whole story by joining in their character's part as you replay the CD.

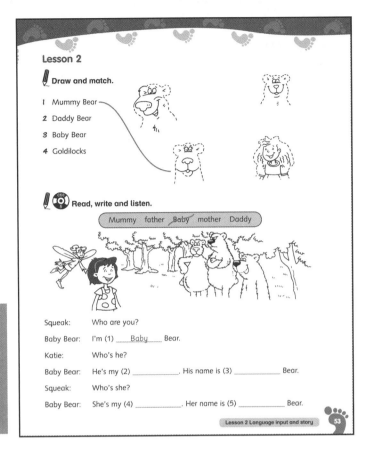

Draw and match. (AB page 53)

- Read the characters' names and the children point to the dashed outline of each one.
- Say **Draw the pictures and match with the names.** Draw the children's attention to the example.
- The children work individually. They can colour the pictures as well.
- Check the answers by asking individual children to point to a picture and name the character.

  Key: 1 Mummy Bear picture bottom left
  2 Daddy Bear picture top left
  3 Baby Bear picture top right
  4 Goldilocks picture bottom right

Read, write and listen. (AB page 53)

- Read the exchanges with Baby Bear and the children say the missing words.
- Say **Now write the words.** Draw the children's attention to the words at the top of the activity.
- The children work individually and complete the exchanges.
- Play the CD (CD 3, track 5) for the children to check their answers.
- The children can act out the exchanges in pairs (one child takes the part of Baby Bear and the other takes the part of Katie and Squeak).

Key: 1 Baby 2 father 4 Daddy 4 mother 5 Mummy

 Read, write and listen.

Squeak:	*Who are you?*
Baby Bear:	*I'm <u>Baby</u> Bear.*
Katie:	*Who's he?*
Baby Bear:	*He's my <u>father</u>. His name is <u>Daddy</u> Bear.*
Squeak:	*Who's she?*
Baby Bear:	*She's my <u>mother</u>. Her name is <u>Mummy</u> bear.*

Ending the lesson

Lesson review

- Briefly ask the children what they can do as a result of the lesson (understand and act out *The Soup*). Praise the children for their efforts and / or use the finger puppets to do this.

Goodbye and closing routine

- Say **Let's sing** *Are you ready to finish?* Play the CD (CD 1, track 12 – see Lesson 1). Hold up the finger puppets and the children sing and do the actions as in Lesson 1.

7 My family

Lesson 3
Communication and grammar

Aim:
- To practise asking and saying who members of your family are

Key language:
- *Who's he / she?*
- *He's / She's my ...*
- *His / Her name is ...*
- *mother, father, brother, sister, baby, grandmother, grandfather, aunt, uncle, cousin*

Materials:
- Pupil's Book pages 55 and 56
- Activity Book pages 54 and 91
- Finger puppets (Pip and Squeak)
- Flashcards: Alex, Katie, mother, father, brother, sister, baby, grandmother, grandfather, aunt, uncle, cousin
- CD 1 and CD 3
- Scissors and stapler
- A prepared little book for Unit 7 (AB page 91)

Starting out

Greetings and opening routine

- Greet the children yourself and using the finger puppets.
- *Either* play the karaoke version of *I like English* (CD 1, track 11 – see Lesson 1) and the children sing and do the actions as in Lesson 1 *or* stick the flashcards in the order of the song *My mother and father* on the board and play the karaoke version (CD 3, track 3 – see Lesson 1). The children point to the flashcards, do the actions and sing the song.

Revision activity

- Hold up the finger puppets and stick the character flashcards on the board. Ask **Can you remember who's in the story with Pip, Squeak, Alex and Katie?** *(Baby Bear, Goldilocks, Daddy Bear, Mummy Bear)*
- Ask the children to open their Pupil's Books at page 55. Briefly reconstruct the story, getting the children to supply key words. Say e.g. **Alex, Katie, Pip and Squeak meet ...** *Baby Bear, Daddy Bear and Mummy Bear* **in the forest. Baby Bear tells them that Goldilocks is his ...** *friend.* **Baby Bear calls ...** *Goldilocks!* **but Goldilocks isn't here. Baby Bear takes Alex, Katie, Pip and Squeak to his ...** *house.* **Goldilocks is in the ...** *house.* **She's eating Baby Bear's ...** *soup.* **The soup is ...** *delicious.* **The next treasure clue is in the bowl of ...** *soup.*
- Play the CD (CD 3, track 4 – see Lesson 2). The children listen and follow the story in their books.

Setting objectives

- Say **Today we're going to practise asking and saying who members of our family are.**

On the learning trail

Listen, number and say. (PB page 56)

- Say **Pip is asking Baby Bear about his family.** Ask the children to name who's in each 'photo', e.g. *brother, aunt,* etc. They will have to guess who some of them are.
- Say **Listen and number the 'photos' in order.** Draw the children's attention to the example.

- Play the CD once (CD 3, track 6). Use the pause button if necessary to give the children time to number the pictures.
- Check the answers by asking e.g. **Who's in photo one?** *(aunt).*
- Say **Now listen again. Repeat the questions and answers.** Play the CD again. Use the pause button to give the children time to repeat the question and answer in each exchange.
- Ask the children to take turns to pretend to be Pip and Baby Bear and ask and say *Who's he? He's my ...* for each picture.

  Key: Aunty Bear 2; Uncle Bear 5; Charlie Bear cousin, 3; Bella Bear sister, 4; Benny Bear brother, 1; Grandmother Bear 6

Listen, number and say.

1	Pip:	Who's he?
	Baby Bear:	He's my brother. His name is Benny Bear.
2	Pip:	Who's she?
	Baby Bear:	She's my aunt. Her name is Aunty Bear.
3	Pip:	Who's he?
	Baby Bear:	He's my cousin. His name is Charlie Bear.
4	Pip:	Who's she?
	Baby Bear:	She's my sister. Her name is Bella Bear.
5	Pip:	Who's he?
	Baby Bear:	He's my uncle. His name is Uncle Bear.
6	Pip:	Who's she?
	Baby Bear:	She's my grandmother. Her name is Grandmother Bear.

Make the *My Little Family* Book. (PB page 56 and AB page 91)

- Hold up your Pupil's Book and point to the pictures. Say **We're going to make the *My Little Family Book* and play the game.**
- Hold up your Activity Book and say **Find page 91 in your Activity Book. Look at the *My Little Family Book*.** Say **Let's make the *My Little Family Book*** and show the children the book you have prepared. (See page 87 of the Teacher's Book for instructions on how to make the little book.)

- Say **Cut and fold the pages like this** and demonstrate what you mean. Point out the difference between the dashed lines (cutting lines) and the dotted lines (folding lines).
- Staple the children's books together as soon as they have folded the pages correctly. Then say **Now cut here** and demonstrate cutting along the dotted line at the top to separate the pages.
- Go through the little book page by page and read the question and answer on each page.
- Explain that the children should draw and colour a picture of the appropriate member of their family and write their (first) name on each page. Use L1 to make the point that all families are different, and if the children haven't got any of the family members mentioned, they should simply leave the page blank. If they have got more than one of the same family member, e.g. two brothers, then they should just choose one to include in their little book.
- The children work individually to draw and colour pictures of their family and write the names in their little books.

Play with the *My Little Family* Book (PB page 56)

- Hold up your Pupil's Book. Ask two pupils to read the first exchange and two other pupils to read the second exchange.
- Explain that you want the children to use their books to play the same guessing game with a partner.

- Demonstrate the game with one child. Get the child to open their little book at any page and cover the text at the bottom either with their hand or with a piece of paper. Get the child to ask you the question at the top of the page, *Who's he?* Mime thinking very hard and say e.g. **He's / She's your cousin!** Get the child to respond *Yes!* or *No!* depending on whether or not you guess correctly. Demonstrate or explain that you have three chances to guess correctly before changing roles. When the answer is *Yes*, get the child to take their hand away from the text and read this to you, e.g. *He's my cousin. His name is David.*

- Play the game several times with the whole class. Ask individual children to take turns to come to the front and show a page of their book to the class, covering the text at the bottom of the page with their hand or a piece of paper. Ask individual children to guess, e.g. *He's your uncle!*, and to have the next turn if they guess correctly.

- Divide the class into pairs. The children play the game with their partner.

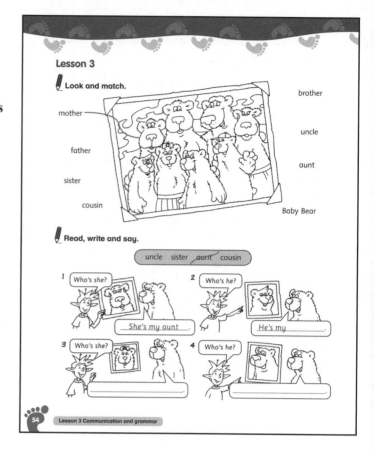

Look and match. (AB page 54)

- Hold up your book, read the words and the children identify all the bear family members in the 'photo'.

- Say **Now match the words to the members of Baby Bear's family.** Draw the children's attention to the example.

- The children work individually and match the words and bears.

- Check the answers by asking **Who's he / she?** for each picture.

  Key: Back row from left to right: mother, father, uncle, aunt
  Front row from left to right: cousin, sister, Baby Bear, brother

Read, write and say. (AB page 54)

- Read the words at the top of the activity.

- Read the exchanges in turn and the children say the missing words and phrases.

- Say **Now write the words.** Draw the children's attention to the example.

- The children work individually and write the missing words.

- Check the answers by asking individual children to read the exchanges.

- The children practise the exchanges in pairs.

  Key: 1 She's my aunt. 2 He's my cousin.
  3 She's my sister. 4 He's my uncle.

Ending the lesson

Lesson review

- Briefly ask the children what they can do as a result of the lesson (ask and name members of their family). Praise the children for their efforts and / or use the finger puppets to do this.

Goodbye and closing routine

- Say goodbye to the children yourself and using the finger puppets. If there is time, you can also play the karaoke version of *Are you ready to finish?* (CD 1, track 13 – see Lesson 1) and the children sing and do the actions as in Lesson 1.

7 My family

Lesson 4
Communication, grammar and pronunciation

Aims:
- To practise saying sentences to describe other people's hair and eyes
- To recognise the difference between /ð/ and /θ/

Key language:
- *He's / She's my friend.*
- *He's / She's got ... hair / eyes.*
- *fair, brown, black, red, blue, green*
- *great*

Materials:
- Pupil's Book page 57
- Activity Book page 55
- Finger puppets (Pip and Squeak)
- Flashcards: mother, father, brother, sister, baby, grandmother, grandfather, aunt, uncle, cousin, Frodo
- Unit 7 little books from Lesson 3
- CD 1 and CD 3

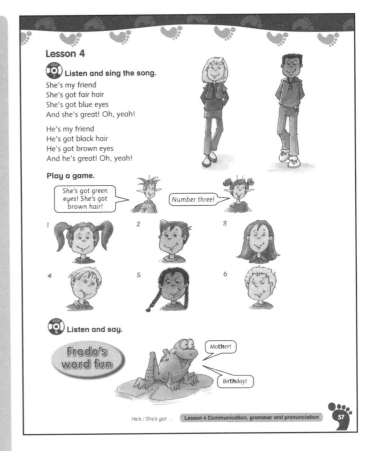

Starting out

Greetings and opening routine

- Greet the children yourself and using the finger puppets.
- *Either* play the karaoke version of *I like English* (CD 1, track 11 – see Lesson 1) and the children sing and do the actions as in Lesson 1 *or* stick the flashcards in the order of the song *My mother and father* (CD 3, track 3 – see Lesson 1) on the board and play the karaoke version. The children point to the flashcards, do the actions and sing the song.

Revision activity

- Give out or ask the children to get out the little books they made in Lesson 3.
- Divide the class into pairs. Explain and demonstrate that the children should take turns to read their little books with their partner. One child looks at their partner's book and reads the question *Who's he / she?* at the top of each page and the child whose book it is should read the answer. They should then change roles.
- The children take turns to read their little family books with their partner.

Setting objectives

- Say **Today we're going to practise saying sentences to describe other people's hair and eyes** (point to your hair and eyes to convey meaning). **We're also going to practise pronunciation.**

On the learning trail

Listen and sing the song. (PB page 57)

- (Books closed) Ask the children if they can remember Goldilocks in the story. Elicit or establish that *She's got fair hair. She's got blue eyes.*

- Say similar sentences about a few children in the class. Use this as an opportunity to elicit and / or revise colours to describe hair and eyes, e.g. *black, brown, blue, green, red.*

- Say **Listen to the song. It's about two friends. What colour hair and eyes has the girl got? What colour hair and eyes has the boy got?**

- Play the CD once (CD 3, track 7) and check the answers. (girl: *fair hair, blue eyes,* boy: *black hair, brown eyes*)

- Ask the children to open their Pupil's Books at page 57. The children look at the pictures to confirm their answers.

- Play the CD again. The children sing the song and point to the hair and eyes of the boy and girl in the picture.

- Divide the children into two groups (one for each verse).

- Play the CD again. The children sing their verse of the song with their group and wave their hands in the air in the last line of the verse.

- Get the groups to change roles and repeat.

 She's my friend

She's my friend
She's got fair hair
She's got blue eyes
And she's great! Oh, yeah!

He's my friend
He's got black hair
He's got brown eyes
And he's great! Oh, yeah!

Play a game. (PB page 57)

- Ask the children to look at the pictures. Say sentences about the characters in random order, e.g. **He's got fair hair. He's got green eyes** and the children say the appropriate numbers, e.g. *Number six!*

- Ask individual children to say sentences about one of the characters and the rest of the class identify the picture in the same way.

- Divide the class into pairs. The children take turns to say sentences and identify the characters with their partner.

Key: 1 blue eyes, brown hair
2 brown eyes, brown hair
3 green eyes, brown hair
4 blue eyes, fair hair
5 brown eyes, black hair
6 green eyes, fair hair

Listen and say: Frodo's word fun. (PB page 57)

- Say the words *mother* and *birthday*. Explain and demonstrate the different positions of the tongue when you say /ð/ and /θ/.

- Hold up the flashcard of Frodo. Say **Listen to Frodo.** Explain and demonstrate that the children should respond by folding their hands together when they hear the /ð/ sound as in *mother*, and put their tongue between their teeth and wave their hands by their face when they hear the /θ/ sound as in *birthday*.

- Play the CD (CD 3, track 9) and the children respond by doing the actions.

- Play the CD again. The children do the actions and repeat the words.

 Frodo's word fun. Listen and say.

mother ... birthday ... mouth ... father ... teeth ... thank you ... grandmother ... three ... brother ... grandfather ... thirteen

Read, write and colour. (AB page 55)

- Read the sentences while the children follow in their books.

- Say **Now read the sentences, write the words and colour the hair and eyes of the boy or girl in each picture.**

- The children work individually. They read and complete the sentences and colour the pictures.

- When they are ready, say e.g. **Tell me about the girl in picture one** and the children say the sentence about each picture.

Key: 1 She's got 2 He's got 3 She's got 4 He's got

Draw, colour and write about your friends. (AB page 55)

- Read the words to describe hair and eyes at the top of the activity. Read the example description under picture 1.

- Ask the children to draw and colour a picture of two friends of their choice (one girl and one boy) and complete the sentences.

- Make sure the children understand that they should choose words from the top of the activity to describe their friends. Explain that they can use a word, e.g. *brown*, more than once if they need to.

- The children work individually. They draw and colour pictures of two friends and complete the sentences.

- When they are ready, ask individual children to take turns to show the picture and read the sentences for one of their friends to the rest of the class.

Key: Children's own answers.

Ending the lesson

Lesson review

- Briefly ask the children what they can do as a result of the lesson (say sentences to describe people's hair and eyes, recognise the difference between /ð/ and /θ/). Praise the children for their efforts and / or use the finger puppets to do this.

Goodbye and closing routine

- Say goodbye to the children yourself and using the finger puppets. If there is time, you can also play the karaoke version of *Are you ready to finish?* (CD 1, track 13 – see Lesson 1) and the children sing and do the actions as in Lesson 1.

7 My family

Lesson 5
Content input

Aims:
- To read and understand that we are similar to other members of our family
- To read and talk about eye and hair colour

Key language:
- ... has got ... eyes / hair.
- mother, father, grandmother, grandfather, boy, girl, colour, fair, brown, black, red, blue, green
- similar, also

Materials:
- Pupil's Book page 58
- Activity Book page 56
- Finger puppets (Pip and Squeak)
- Flashcards: mother, father, brother, sister, baby, grandmother, grandfather, aunt, uncle, cousin
- CD 1 and CD 3

Starting out

Greetings and opening routine

- Greet the children yourself and using the finger puppets.
- *Either* play the karaoke version of *I like English* (CD 1, track 11 – see Lesson 1) and the children sing and do the actions as in Lesson 1 *or* divide the class into two groups, play the song *She's my friend* (CD 3, track 7 – see Lesson 4) and the children sing the song and do the actions in the last line of each verse, as in Lesson 4.
- Repeat with the karaoke version of *She's my friend* (CD 3, track 8).

Revision activity

- Say sentences to describe a child in the class, e.g. **She's got brown hair. She's got blue eyes.** The children ask questions, e.g. *Is it ...?*, and guess who it is.
- Repeat several times. If the children are confident about saying sentences themselves, ask the child who guesses correctly each time to have the next turn.

Setting objectives

- Hold up the finger puppets. Say **Let's learn about the world around you! Today we're going to read about ways we are similar to other members of our family.** Explain the meaning of *similar* by pointing out a similarity between two children in the class, e.g. **Carlos has got black hair. Andrés has got black hair. Their hair is similar.**

On the learning trail

Read, circle and listen. (PB page 58)

- (Books closed) Read the question **Are you similar to other members of your family?** Give examples to clarify what you mean by *other members of your family*.
- Listen to the children's ideas (in L1). Use their suggestions to introduce or remind the children of vocabulary, e.g. colour.
- Ask the children to open their Pupil's Books at page 58. Read the text at the start of the activity or play part 1 on the CD (CD 3, track 10).

- Ask questions to check comprehension and clarify meaning, e.g. **Are we similar to other members of our family?** *(yes)* **Who is the colour of our hair from?** *(our mother, father, grandmother or grandfather)* **Who is the colour of our eyes from?** *(our mother, father, grandmother or grandfather)*.
- Read the question in the next part. Then say **Look at photo number one.** Say **The mother has got …** *(fair hair)*. **The father has got …** *(brown hair)*. Point to the boy and say **The child has got …** *(fair hair)*. **The colour of the boy's hair is from his …** *(mother)*. Draw the children's attention to the word *mother* circled in the example.
- Say **Now look at photos two and three and circle** *mother* **or** *father*.
- The children work individually, look at the photos and circle the words.
- Say **Now listen and check your answers.** Play the CD (CD 3, track 10).
- Check the answers. Elicit sentences about all the photos. Say e.g. **Tell me about the father in photo one.** *(He's got brown hair.)*
- Play the CD again as a final check.

Key: 1 mother 2 father 3 mother

 Read, circle and listen.

Part 1

We are similar to other members of our family.

The colour of our hair is from our mother, father, grandmother or grandfather.

The colour of our eyes is also from our mother, father, grandmother or grandfather.

Part 2

Is the hair colour from the children's mother or father?

1 The mother has got fair hair. The father has got brown hair. The boy has got fair hair. The colour of the boy's hair is from his mother.

2 The mother has got red hair. The father has got black hair. The girl has got black hair. The colour of the girl's hair is from her father.

3 The mother has got red hair. The father has got fair hair. The girl has got red hair. The colour of the girl's hair is from her mother.

Listen and play a game. (PB page 58)

- Ask the children to stand up. Explain and demonstrate that you are going to play a CD with music and the children should dance. When there's a pause and they hear an instruction, e.g. *Blue eyes!*, they should either sit on the floor as fast as they can if they've got blue eyes, or stand still and fold their arms if they haven't got blue eyes. Explain that the children have got three 'lives'. If they are last to respond or if they respond incorrectly, then they lose a 'life'.
- Play the CD (CD 3, track 11). The children dance and respond, following the instructions. Make sure, if possible, that no child loses all three lives before the end of the game. At the end, the children who have still got three 'lives' are the winners.

Option: If you don't want the children to stand up and dance, they can remain seated during the game. In this case, the children move their hands from side to side rhythmically while the music plays and respond either by putting both hands up if they have got the feature named or by folding their arms if they haven't. The system of 'lives' can work in the same way.

 Listen and play a game.

blue eyes … fair hair … brown eyes … brown hair … green eyes … red hair … black hair

Read and colour. (AB page 56)

- Read the descriptions of each family while the children follow in their books.
- Say **Now read and colour the eyes of the mother, father and boy or girl in each picture.**
- The children work individually and read and colour the eyes in the pictures.
- Check the answers. Ask questions about each picture, e.g. **Who is the boy's eye colour from in picture one?** *(the father)*

Key: Children colour the pictures.

1 mother – brown eyes; father – green eyes; boy – green eyes

2 mother – blue eyes; father – brown eyes; girl – brown eyes

Read and write. (AB page 56)

- Read the sentences and the children say the missing words.
- Say **Now write the missing words.** Draw their attention to the example.
- The children work individually and complete the sentences.
- Check the answers by asking individual children to read a sentence.

  Key: father, grandfather, mother, grandmother

Ending the lesson

Lesson review

- Briefly ask the children what they can do as a result of the lesson (read and understand that we are similar to other members of our family, read and talk about eye and hair colour). Praise the children for their efforts and / or use the finger puppets to do this.
- **Note:** Ask the children to have a look when they are at home and to make sure they know the colour of their mother's and father's hair and eyes before doing the next lesson.

Goodbye and closing routine

- Say goodbye to the children yourself and using the finger puppets. If there is time, you can also play the karaoke version of *Are you ready to finish?* (CD 1, track 13 – see Lesson 1) and the children sing and do the actions as in Lesson 1.

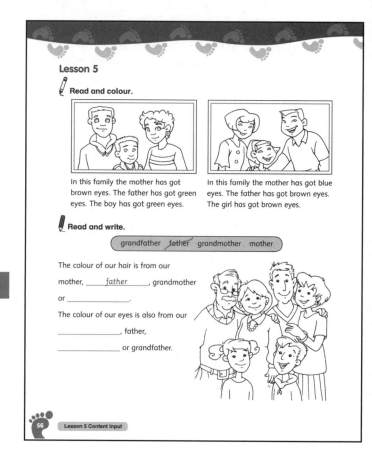

7 My family

Lesson 6
Content and personalisation

Aims:

- To identify mothers, fathers and children from the colour of their hair and eyes
- To identify who the colour of your hair and eyes is from

Key language:

- He's / She's got ..., (too).
- I've got ... hair / eyes.
- My mother's / father's got ...
- mother, father, fair, brown, black, red, blue, green

Materials:

- Pupil's Book page 59
- Activity Book page 57
- Finger puppets (Pip and Squeak)
- CD 1 and CD 3

Starting out

Greetings and opening routine

- Greet the children using the finger puppets.
- *Either* play the karaoke version of *I like English* (CD 1, track 11) and the children sing and do the actions as in Lesson 1 *or* divide the class into two groups, play the karaoke version of *She's my friend* (CD 3, track 8 – see Lesson 4) and the children sing the song and do the actions.

Revision activity

- Recap on Lesson 5 by asking the children **Are you similar to other members of your family?** Listen to their response, recasting their answers in English as necessary.
- Read part of the text on page 58 of the Pupil's Book. Either whistle or say a nonsense word, e.g. **bleep!**, instead of certain words, and the children supply the missing words, e.g. **We are similar to other members of our** *bleep!* (family). **The colour of our** *bleep!* (touch your hair) (hair) **is from our mother, father, grandmother or** *bleep!* (grandfather).

Setting objectives

- Say **In this lesson we're going to identify mothers, fathers and children from the colour of their hair and eyes. We're also going to identify who our hair and eye colour are from.**

On the learning trail

Look, match and say. (PB page 59)

- Say **Look at the photos.** Explain that the three adults in the photos (with numbers) are the mother or father of one of the three children below.
- Say e.g. **Tell me about the father in photo one.** *(He's got black hair. He's got brown eyes.)* Say **Find the child who's got black hair and brown eyes.** The children identify the photo (which is also the example).
- Elicit sentences about the other photos and get the children to identify the child of each mother.
- Say **Now match the photos.** The children work individually and match the photos.
- Check the answers. Ask children to say why they have matched the photos, e.g. *Number two: She's got red hair. He's got red hair, too.*

Key: 1: bottom row, middle photo 2: bottom row, photo on right 3: bottom row, photo on left

Draw, colour and say. (PB page 59)

- Read the heading for each frame. Ask the children to draw and colour a picture in each frame to show the hair and eye colour of their mother, father and themselves. If children want to know the name of other colours to describe their eyes, e.g. *grey, violet*, tell them these.

- When they are ready, ask individual children to take turns to hold up their book and show and tell the class, e.g. *My mother's got blue eyes. My father's got brown eyes. I've got brown eyes.* After each one, either ask the child e.g. **Who is your eye colour from?** or ask the rest of the class **Who is …'s eye colour from?** and the children name the mother, father or both.

Listen and colour. (AB page 57)

- Say **Look at Alex and his mother and father. Listen and colour their eyes and hair.**

- Play the CD (CD 3, track 12). Use the pause button to give the children time to colour the hair and eyes.

- The children compare their pictures in pairs.

- Play the CD again.

- Check the answers by eliciting sentences about the pictures. Say e.g. **Tell me about Alex's mother.** *(She's got brown hair. She's got blue eyes.)*

- Ask questions, e.g. **Who's Alex's hair from?** *(his father)* **Who are Alex's eyes from?** *(his mother and his father)*

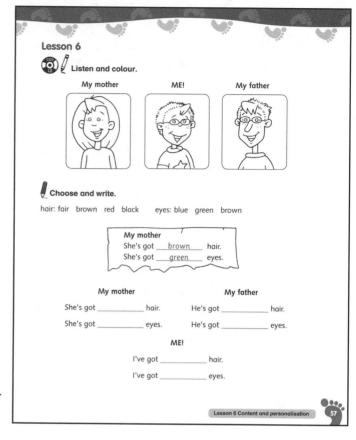

 Listen and colour.

This is my mother. She's got brown hair. She's got blue eyes.

This is my father. He's got fair hair. He's got blue eyes.

This is me. I've got fair hair and blue eyes.

Key: Children colour the pictures.
mother – brown hair, blue eyes; father – fair hair, blue eyes; Alex – fair hair, blue eyes

Choose and write. (AB page 57)

- Read the colours to describe hair and eyes at the top of the activity.

- Read the example. Explain that you want the children to choose words to complete the sentences so that they are true for their mother, father and themselves. If you have introduced colours such as *grey*, write these on the board.

- The children complete the sentences.

- Ask individual children to take turns to tell the class, e.g. *My mother: She's got brown hair. She's got blue eyes.* After each one, either ask the children themselves or ask others in the class, e.g. **Who is your / …'s eye colour from?**

Key: Children's own answers.

Ending the lesson

Lesson review

- Briefly ask the children what they can do as a result of the lesson (identify mothers, fathers and children from the colour of their hair and eyes, say who their hair and eye colour are from).

- Praise the children for their efforts and / or use the finger puppets to do this.

Goodbye and closing routine

- Say goodbye to the children yourself and using the finger puppets. If there is time, you can also play the karaoke version of *Are you ready to finish?* (CD 1, track 13 – see Lesson 1) and the children sing and do the actions as in Lesson 1.

7 My family

Lesson 7
Children's culture

Aim:
- To say a traditional rhyme and play a version of a traditional game

Key language:
- *These are ...*
- *This is grandmother's / grandfather's ...*
- *glasses, hat, clap, hands, fold, arms, lap, nap*
- numbers 1–20

Materials:
- Pupil's Book page 60
- Activity Book page 58
- Finger puppets (Pip and Squeak)
- Flashcards: Frodo, grandmother, grandfather
- CD 1 and CD 3

Starting out

Greetings and opening routine

- Greet the children yourself and using the finger puppets.
- *Either* play the karaoke version of *I like English* (CD 1, track 11 – see Lesson 1) and the children sing and do the actions as in Lesson 1 *or* play the karaoke version of *She's my friend* (CD 3, track 8 – see Lesson 4) and the children sing the song and do the actions.

Revision activity

- Say a sentence about a child in the class, e.g. *Susana's got blue eyes.* Explain and demonstrate that the child you name should then say a sentence about another child, e.g. *David's got brown hair*, and so on round the class. Stop the activity after six to ten children have had a turn, depending on the size of the class.

Setting objectives

- Hold up the flashcard of Frodo. Say **In this lesson we're going to learn about children's culture with Frodo. We're going to say a traditional rhyme and play a version of a traditional game.**

On the learning trail

Listen and say the rhyme. (PB page 60) (books closed)

- Show the children the flashcards of grandmother and grandfather and elicit the words.
- Introduce the word *glasses* either by showing the children a pair or by drawing one on the board. Elicit or remind the children of the word *hat*.
- Sit on a chair in front of the children. Say the rhyme yourself slowly and teach them the actions (see audio script below). If you like, clarify the meaning of *claps her hands*, *puts them in her lap*, *folds his arms* and *has a little nap* (sleep), although the children will have no problem understanding these from the actions.
- Play the CD (CD 3, track 13). The children listen to the rhyme and do the actions with you.
- Play the CD (track 13) again. The children do the actions and join in saying the rhyme.
- Ask the children to open their Pupil's Books at page 60. Play the CD again. The children say the rhyme and follow in their books.

These are grandmother's glasses

These are grandmother's glasses
                (make circles round your eyes
                with thumb and index finger)
And this is grandmother's hat
                (pretend to put on hat)
And this is the way she claps her hands
                (clap hands)
And puts them in her lap!
                (put hands together in lap)

These are grandfather's glasses   (as verse 1)
And this is grandfather's hat   (as verse 1)
And this is the way he folds his arms (fold arms)
And has a little nap!   (put head on one side
                and pretend to go to sleep)

 Citizenship box: Remember!

Ask the children **Does anyone in your family ever have a little nap?** (using gesture to convey meaning) and listen to their responses.

Hold up the flashcard of Frodo, read the *Remember!* note and check understanding. Ask the children why their families are special (e.g. because they take care of them, love them, help them) and recast their answers in English as necessary.

Play *Grandmother's footsteps!* **(PB page 60)**

- Say **Let's play a game that English children play! The name of the game is *Grandmother's footsteps!*** Demonstrate the meaning of *footstep*. Explain that the children may be familiar with a similar game in their own culture.

- Depending on available space and the size of the class, ask *either* all the children *or* half the class *or* a group of six to eight children to stand at the back of the classroom. Ask another child to join you at the front of the class. Explain and demonstrate that you and that child are the 'grandmother' (or 'grandfather') and that you are going to stand facing the board. Explain that the object of the game is for the children at the back of the class to try and reach you without you seeing them. They should take footsteps carefully and silently while you have your back turned. As soon as you turn round, they should freeze in position and call *Hello, grandmother!* or *Hello grandfather!* Explain that as the 'grandmother', you are going to count to a number between three and twenty before you turn round each time. The child who reaches you first taps you on the shoulder and says *Hello, grandmother!* This child is the winner and chooses a friend to be 'grandmother' with them in the next round of the game.

- Play the game by facing the board with the child who is 'grandmother' and secretly agreeing to count up to e.g. ten. When you reach ten, turn round suddenly together. If you see any children moving, encourage the child to say with you *Grandmother can see you! Go back please, ...!* and the child or children you name have to go to the back of the class and start again.

- Repeat several times, counting to different numbers each time, until one of the children reaches you and says *Hello, grandmother!*

- Play the game once or twice again. If you have a large class, make sure all the children have a chance to participate once. When they are not participating directly, ask children *either* to count with 'grandmother' (or 'grandfather') *or* to say e.g. *Come on! Hurry!* to the children who are taking footsteps.

Option: If you have the opportunity to go to the playground or gym, you can play the game with all the children at the same time, even if you have a large class.

Read and colour. (AB page 58)

- Read the sentences above each picture and the children follow in their books.

- Say **Now colour grandmother and grandfather's glasses and hat.**

- Check the answers by asking e.g. **What colour are grandmother's glasses?** and the children name the colours.

- When the children are ready, say **Let's say the rhyme.** Play the CD (CD 3, track 13). The children say the rhyme *These are grandmother's glasses* and point to the pictures in their books.

Key: Children colour the pictures.
Grandmother's glasses – pink, hat – green;
Grandfather's glasses – blue, hat – red

Count and write. (AB page 58)

- Say **Look at the picture. Count the footsteps to get to the grandmother!** Ask the children to point and count the footsteps with you.

- Divide the class into pairs. Say **Now count the footsteps with your partner and write the number.** Draw their attention to the example.

- Check the answers by asking the children to tell you the number of footsteps each child takes.

Key: 1 twelve 2 eight 3 fifteen 4 ten

Ending the lesson

Lesson review

- Briefly ask the children what they can do as a result of the lesson (say a traditional rhyme, play a version of a traditional game). Praise the children for their efforts and / or use the finger puppets to do this.

Goodbye and closing routine

- Say goodbye to the children yourself and using the finger puppets. If there is time, you can also play the karaoke version of *Are you ready to finish?* (CD 1, track 13 – see Lesson 1) and the children sing and do the actions as in Lesson 1.

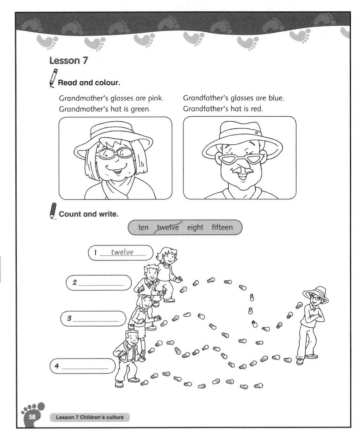

7 My family

Lesson 8
Unit review / All About Me Portfolio Booklet

Aim:
- To review learning in Unit 7

Key language:
- *Who's he / she?*
- *He's / She's my ...*
- *He's / She's got ... eyes / hair.*
- *mother, father, brother, sister, baby, grandmother, grandfather, aunt, uncle, cousin*
- *fair, black, brown, blue, green*

Materials:
- Pupil's Book page 61
- Activity Book page 59
- *All About Me* Portfolio Booklet pages 18 and 19
- Finger puppets (Pip and Squeak)
- Flashcards: mother, father, brother, sister, baby, grandmother, grandfather, aunt, uncle, cousin
- Word cards: mother, father, brother, sister, baby, grandmother, grandfather, aunt, uncle, cousin
- Stickers for Unit 7
- CD 1 and CD 3

Starting out

Greetings and opening routine

- Greet the children yourself and using the finger puppets.
- *Either* play the karaoke version of *I like English* (CD 1, track 11 – see Lesson 1) and the children sing and do the actions as in Lesson 1 *or* stick the flashcards on the board in the order of the song *My mother and father* and play the karaoke version (CD 3, track 3 – see Lesson 1) and the children sing the song and point to the flashcards.

Revision activity

- Say the rhyme *These are grandmother's glasses* (see Lesson 7). Get the children to respond by doing the actions.
- Change roles. Do the actions yourself while the children say the rhyme in chorus.
- Play the karaoke version (CD 3, track 14 – see Lesson 7). The children and you say the rhyme and do the actions together.

Setting objectives

- Say **Today we're going to review what we've learnt in Unit 7.**

On the learning trail

Listen and put on the stickers. Write the words. (PB page 61)

- Make sure the children have the stickers for Unit 7 ready.
- Say **Listen and put on the stickers.** Draw the children's attention to the example.
- Play the CD (CD 3, track 15). Use the pause button to give the children time to put on the stickers.
- Say **Now write the words.** Draw the children's attention to the example.

- Check their answers by saying the numbers and getting the children to say the words.

  Key: 1 grandmother 2 father 3 aunt 4 brother 5 cousin 6 sister 7 baby 8 grandfather 9 mother 10 uncle

 Listen and put on the stickers.

1 Who's she? She's my grandmother.
2 Who's he? He's my father.
3 Who's she? She's my aunt.
4 Who's he? He's my brother.
5 Who's she? She's my cousin.
6 She's got green eyes. She's my sister.
7 He's got blue eyes. He's a baby.
8 He's got brown eyes. He's my grandfather.
9 She's got fair hair. She's my mother.
10 Who's he? He's my uncle.

Look, write and say. (PB page 61)

- Read the exchanges and sentences and the children say the missing words.
- Say **Now write the words.** Draw the children's attention to the example.
- The children work individually and write the missing words.
- Check the answers by asking individual children to read the exchanges and sentences.

  Key: 1 father 2 mother 3 brother 4 friend 5 hair 6 eyes

Listen and match. (AB page 59)

- Say **Alex is showing Katie pictures of his family. Listen and match the sentences and pictures.** Draw the children's attention to the example.
- Play the CD (CD 3, track 16). Pause, if necessary, to give the children time to match the sentences and pictures.
- Check the answers by getting children to ask and answer the question *Who's he / she?* for each picture.

  Key: Children match the sentences and pictures.
  1 cousin 2 mother 3 sister 4 uncle 5 father 6 aunt

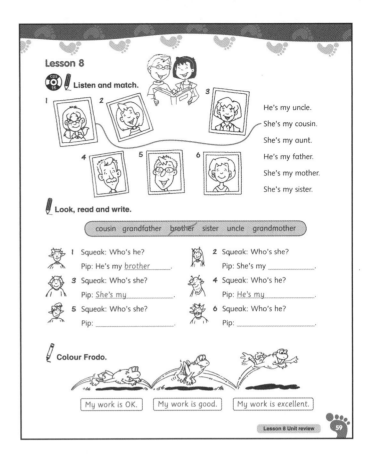

 Listen and match.

1 Katie: *Who's she?*
  Alex: *She's my cousin.*
2 Katie: *Who's she?*
  Alex: *She's my mother.*
3 Katie: *Who's she?*
  Alex: *She's my sister.*
4 Katie: *Who's he?*
  Alex: *He's my uncle.*
5 Katie: *Who's he?*
  Alex: *He's my father.*
6 Katie: *Who's she?*
  Alex: *She's my aunt.*

Look, read and write. (AB page 59)

- Say **Pip is showing Squeak pictures of his family.** Read the exchanges and the children look at the pictures and say the missing words.
- Say **Write the words** and draw the children's attention to the example.
- The children work individually and complete the exchanges.

- Check the answers by asking individual children to read the exchanges.

  Key: 1 brother 2 cousin 3 grandmother
  4 grandfather 5 sister 6 uncle

Colour Frodo. (AB page 59)

- Hold up the flashcard of Frodo. Remind the children that in this activity they assess their work in the unit by choosing and colouring the picture of Frodo which corresponds best to how they think they have done.

- Remind the children of the key by pointing to the three pictures of Frodo and saying **Colour this picture if your work is OK but you think you need to try harder or need more practice. Colour this picture of Frodo if you think your work is good. Colour this picture of Frodo with a big smile and jumping very high if you think your work is excellent.** Make sure the children understand that there are no right answers and that it is their own opinion of the work they have done which is important. Be ready to encourage the children to have a positive view if they are too hard on themselves.

Ending the lesson

Lesson review

- Briefly ask the children what they can do as a result of the lesson (use the language and vocabulary they've learnt in Unit 7). Praise the children for their efforts and / or use the finger puppets to do this.

Goodbye and closing routine

- Say goodbye to the children yourself and using the finger puppets. If there is time, you can also play the karaoke version of *Are you ready to finish?* (CD 1, track 13 – see Lesson 1) and the children sing and do the actions as in Lesson 1.

All About Me **Portfolio Booklet**

The children complete Unit 7 of their personal *All About Me* Portfolio Booklets. They complete their learning journey by colouring the sections on the path to show what they can do. If you like, the children can also sign this page and you can endorse this by adding your own signature and the date.

8 My pets

Structures and grammar

- *It's got ...*
- *What's its name? Its name is ...*
- *What a ...!*
- Recycled: *It's ..., I like ..., I've got ..., I brush my ..., This is ..., my / your, Here's the ..., Hurry!, Can I ...?*

Vocabulary

- Core: *cat, dog, pony, mouse, rabbit, hamster, bird, fish, guinea pig, turtle*
- Other: *goat, troll, cross, bridge, pet, tail, fur, whiskers, long, short, medium*
- Content / culture: *feed, clean, give water, take for walks, little, fly, shiny, curly*
- Recycled: *brush, play, eyes, ears, nose, legs, big, small,* colours

Main receptive language

- *live, home, keep, important, care for, kind*

Communicative competence

Understanding

Listening:
- Can recognise words for pets
- Can understand the episode of the story
- Can understand statements describing pets
- Can understand statements about ways to care for pets

Reading:
- Can recognise words for pets
- Can recognise words to describe pets
- Can read simple statements about pets
- Can read about ways to care for pets

Speaking

Spoken interaction:
- Can ask and say the names of pets

Spoken production:
- Can sing the song *I like English*
- Can identify pets
- Can sing the song *I like pets!*
- Can describe and say the names of pets
- Can say the chant *This is my dog*
- Can say a tongue-twister with /h/
- Can say what you do to care for pets
- Can sing the song *Little Peter Rabbit*
- Can sing the song *Are you ready to finish?*

Writing

- Can copy and write words for pets
- Can copy and write words to describe pets
- Can complete sentences about pets

Content links

- *Social sciences:* ways to care for pets

Learning strategies and thinking skills

- Recognising learning objectives
- Associating vocabulary and pictures
- Using mime to memorise language patterns
- Identifying features of pets
- Deducing from a description
- Expressing personal preferences
- Reflecting on learning

Children's culture

- Singing a song: *Little Peter Rabbit*
- Playing a traditional game: *Cat and mouse!*

Pronunciation

- Saying a tongue-twister with /h/

Values and attitudes

- Pleasure in talking about pets in English
- Awareness of the responsibility of having a pet
- Recognition that it is important to be kind to pets

8 My pets

Lesson 1
Vocabulary presentation

Aim:
- To learn the words for animals we keep as pets

Key language:
- *cat, dog, pony, mouse, turtle, hamster, rabbit, bird, guinea pig, fish*
- *I like ...*
- *Hurray!*

Materials:
- Pupil's Book page 62
- Activity Book page 60
- Finger puppets (Pip and Squeak)
- Flashcards: Alex, Katie, Frodo, cat, dog, pony, mouse, turtle, hamster, rabbit, bird, guinea pig, fish
- Word cards: cat, dog, pony, mouse, turtle, hamster, rabbit, bird, guinea pig, fish
- CD 1 and CD 3

Starting out

Greetings and opening routine

- Greet the children yourself and using the finger puppets. Say e.g. **Hello, children. Hello … How are you today?** *Fine, thank you.* Ask a few individual children to greet the puppets in turn.

- Say **Let's sing the song** *I like English.* Play the CD (CD 1, track 10). Stick the character flashcards of Alex, Katie and Frodo on the board. Hold up the puppets on your index fingers. Move them as the children sing and do the actions. Move the puppets, use them to point to the other characters and hold each one out when the children sing their names.

 I like English

I like English.	(thumbs up)
And I like you.	(gesture to a friend)
I like Alex, Katie and Frodo.	(point to the flashcards)
I like Pip and Squeak, too!	(wave to the puppets)

Setting objectives

- Say **Today we're going to learn the words for animals we keep as pets and we're going to sing a song.**

On the learning trail

Vocabulary presentation (books closed)

- Cover one of the flashcards, e.g. dog, with a piece of paper. Pull down the piece of paper slowly. The children identify the animal (in English or L1) as soon as they can see what it is. Say e.g. **Yes. Very good. It's a dog.**

- Point to the flashcard. Say **dog** several times and get the children to repeat the word with you in chorus.

- Stick the flashcard of the dog on the board.

- Repeat the procedure for the other pet flashcards.

- Divide the class in half. Hold up the Pip finger puppet and say to one half **Say the words with Pip.** Use the puppet to point to the flashcards in turn and the children say the words with you. Make the puppet fly around to praise the children.

- Repeat the procedure with the Squeak puppet and the other half of the class.

Follow the footprints. (PB page 62) (books open)

- Hold up the flashcard of Frodo. Say **Listen and follow the footprints with Frodo the frog. Use your finger** and demonstrate this.

- Play the CD (CD 3, track 17). The children listen and follow the footprints with their fingers. They stop by each picture as they hear the word and repeat the word.

- Say **Now listen and draw a line following the footprints** and demonstrate this. Play the CD again. The children draw a line, stop by each picture and repeat the words as previously.

 Follow the footprints.

cat ... dog ... pony ... mouse ... turtle ... hamster ... rabbit ... bird ... guinea pig ... fish

- Stick the word cards on the board in jumbled order (at the children's height and away from the flashcards).
- Point to one word card, e.g. *mouse* and read the word. Say **Look for the mouse.** Give the children time to do this.
- Ask a child to come to the front of the class and stick the word card for *mouse*, by the corresponding flashcard. Ask the rest of the class **Is this right?** and get them to say the word.
- Repeat the procedure with the rest of the word cards.
- Take the word cards off the board.

Listen and sing the song. (PB page 62)

- Say **Look at the pictures. What pets can you see?** and the children name the animals in the picture.
- Draw the children's attention to the flashcards on the board. Say **Listen to the song.** Point to the pets and demonstrate what you mean. Play the CD (CD 3, track 18). The children listen to the song and point to the appropriate flashcards in each verse.
- Elicit or remind the children of the meaning of *I like …*
- Invite five (or ten) children to the front of the class. Give them one (or two) flashcard(s) each and get them to stand facing the class holding up the flashcards in the same order as the song. Explain and demonstrate that the children at the front should hold up their flashcard(s) when they hear the words in the song. The rest of the class should point to the flashcards in turn as they sing, and do actions (see audio script below).
- Play the CD again. The children point to the flashcards, do the actions and sing the song.
- At the end, ask the children to say sentences naming pets they like, e.g. *I like dogs. / I like hamsters.*

 I like pets!

A dog, a rabbit and a pony
Oh, I like pets! Hurray!
(cross your arms diagonally, hunch your shoulders and move from side to side; wave both arms in the air)
A dog, a rabbit, a pony, a mouse and a turtle
Oh, I like pets! Hurray!
(actions as above)
A dog, a rabbit, a pony, a mouse, a turtle,
a bird and a hamster

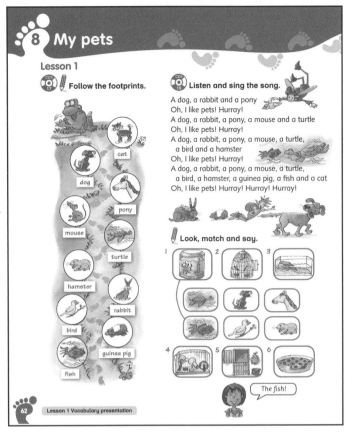

Oh, I like pets! Hurray! (actions as above)
A dog, a rabbit, a pony, a mouse, a turtle, a bird,
a hamster, a guinea pig, a fish and a cat
Oh, I like pets! Hurray!
Hurray! Hurray! (actions as above; wave arms in air three times)

Look, match and say. (PB page 62)

- Hold up your book. Point to the pictures of pets in turn and the children name them.
- Point to the different homes and ask **Who lives here?** The children identify the animal that lives in each home.
- Ask the children to match the pets and homes. Draw their attention to the example.
- Check the answers by asking e.g. **Who lives in number one?** and the children name the pets.

Key: 1 fish 2 bird 3 turtle 4 hamster 5 pony 6 dog

Read, match and say. (AB page 60)

- Read the sentences and the children point to the pets.
- The children work individually and match the speech bubbles and pictures of pets.
- Check the answers by saying e.g. **Pip likes …** and the children name the pets.
- Ask individual children in turn to say *I like …* and name the pet they like. (Be ready to introduce *mice* as the plural for *mouse* and / or explain that we do not need to add 'es' to *fish*.)

Key: I like dogs: 3; I like hamsters: 4; I like turtles: 1; I like cats: 5; I like rabbits: 2

Look, draw and write. (AB page 60)

- Read the words at the top of the activity.
- Say **Now draw the pet which lives in each home and write the words.** Draw the children's attention to the example.
- The children work individually and draw pictures and write the words.
- Check the answers by asking e.g. **Who lives in number one?** and the children name the pets.

Key: 1 fish 2 mouse 3 bird 4 guinea pig

Ending the lesson

Lesson review

- Briefly ask the children what they can do as a result of the lesson (name pets, sing the song *I like pets!*). Praise the children for their efforts and / or use the finger puppets to do this.

Goodbye and closing routine

- Say **Let's sing the song** *Are you ready to finish?* Play the CD (CD 1, track 12). Hold up the finger puppets on your index fingers and move them rhythmically as the children count, sing and do the actions.

 Are you ready to finish?

Are you ready to finish?   (gesture questioningly)
Count to twenty and say goodbye
         (mime counting fingers)
One, two, three, four, five, six, seven
   (move arms rhythmically as sing each number)
Eight, nine, ten, and now eleven
Twelve, thirteen, fourteen, fifteen, sixteen
Seventeen, eighteen, nineteen, twenty – Hey!
         (make a big circle with arms)
Goodbye! Goodbye!
Goodbye for today!   (wave goodbye)

- Say goodbye to the children yourself and using the finger puppets. Say e.g. **Goodbye everyone. See you on …** Ask a few individual children to say goodbye to the finger puppets in turn.

8 My pets

Lesson 2
Language input and story

Aim:
- To understand and act out episode 8 of the story

Key language:
- *dog, cat, pony, mouse, hamster, rabbit, bird, fish, guinea pig, turtle*
- *pet, goat, troll, bridge, big, small, medium, long, short, fur, eyes, ears, tail, legs, whiskers*
- *It's …*
- *It's got …*
- *Can I …?*
- *alright*

Materials:
- Pupil's Book page 63
- Activity Book page 61
- Finger puppets (Pip and Squeak)
- Flashcards: Alex, Katie, dog, cat, pony, mouse, hamster, rabbit, bird, fish, guinea pig, turtle
- Treasure clue sticker for Unit 8
- CD 1 and CD 3

Starting out

Greetings and opening routine
- Greet the children yourself and using the finger puppets.
- Play the karaoke version of *I like English* (CD 1, track 11 – see Lesson 1). The children sing and do the actions as in Lesson 1.

Revision activity
- Hold up the flashcards in turn and the children say the words.
- Stick the flashcards on the board in the same order as the song *I like pets!* Play the CD (CD 3, track 18 – see Lesson 1). The children sing the song, do the actions and point to the flashcards.
- Repeat with the karaoke version (CD 3, track 19).

Setting objectives
- Say **Today we're going to listen to and act out episode 8 of the story**.

On the learning trail

Listen and act out the story.
Episode 8: The troll (PB page 63)

Before the story (books closed)
- Hold up the finger puppets and stick the flashcards of Alex and Katie on the board. Recap on the last episode of the story using mime and gesture and / or L1 as necessary: **Alex, Katie, Pip and Squeak meet Baby Bear, Daddy Bear and Mummy Bear in the forest. Baby Bear tells them that Goldilocks is his friend. Baby Bear looks for Goldilocks but he can't find her. Baby Bear takes Alex, Katie, Pip and Squeak to his house. Goldilocks is in the house eating Baby Bear's soup. The next treasure clue is in the bowl of soup**.
- Ask **Can you remember the clue from Unit 7?** Hold up page 55 of the Pupil's Book and point to the treasure clue sticker. Read *Follow the footprints! Find three goats!* as a prompt.
- Use L1 to ask the children if they know a story with three goats and listen to their responses. If they are familiar with the story, briefly ask who and what else is in the story. Use their responses to introduce the words *troll* and *bridge*. If they are not familiar with the story, explain these words

to them (a *troll* is an ugly and unpleasant creature which only exists in stories).

- Ask the following questions in turn. Use mime and gesture to clarify meaning, and encourage the children to predict the answers: **1) Who lives under the bridge? 2) Where's the treasure clue? 3) Who gets the treasure clue?**

During the story (books open)

- Say **Now listen to the story and find out.**
- Play the CD (CD 3, track 20) and the children follow in their books.
- Ask the questions in turn again and check the answers, recasting them in English as necessary. *(1 the troll 2 in the troll's pocket 3 the big goat).*
- Elicit or explain the meaning of *dangerous*. Use the pictures to remind the children of the meaning of *ears*, *legs* and *teeth* and to clarify the meaning of *fur*, *tail* and *whiskers*. Clarify the meaning of *alright*.
- Say **Listen again and repeat the story.** Play the CD again. Pause after each sentence and the children repeat the story.
- **Note:** Additional story text is marked with an asterisk* below. The children repeat the whole story, including the language which does not appear in their books.

 Follow the footprints, Episode 8: The troll

Picture 1	
Narrator:	*Alex, Katie, Pip and Squeak follow the footprints to find the three goats.**
Pip:	*I can see a rabbit!*
Squeak:	*And look! A mouse!*
Katie:	*And birds!**
Alex:	*But where are the three goats?*

Picture 2	
Pip:	*Look! Are they the three goats?*
Squeak:	*Ah! A small goat. It's white. It's got small ears.*
Alex:	*A medium goat. It's brown. It's got a short tail.**
Katie:	*And a big goat. It's black. It's got long legs.**
Alex:	*Yes, they're the three goats! Hurray!**

Picture 3	
Alex:	*Look! The rainbow! Let's cross the bridge!**
Big goat:	*Be careful! A hungry troll lives under the bridge.**
Medium goat:	*It's big. It's got brown fur.**
Small goat:	*It's very dangerous.**

Picture 4	
Troll:	*I'm the troll! I'm hungry!*
Pip:	*Can I cross the bridge?*
Troll:	*Oh, alright! You're too small to eat! I'm the troll! I'm hungry!**
Squeak:	*Can I cross the bridge?**
Troll:	*Oh, alright! You're too small to eat!**

Picture 5	
Troll:	*I'm the troll! I'm hungry!*
Katie:	*Can I cross the bridge?*
Troll:	*Oh, alright! You're too small to eat! I'm the troll! I'm hungry!**
Alex:	*Can I cross the bridge?**
Troll:	*Oh, alright! You're too small to eat!**

Picture 6	
Big goat:	*Can I cross the bridge?*
Troll:	*No, I'm hungry and you're big!*
Big goat:	*Yes, I'm big! Off you go!*
Alex, Katie, Squeak, Pip:	*Hurray!**

Picture 7	
Big goat:	*Here's the last treasure clue!*
Pip:	*Oh, great! Follow the footprints! Find the treasure!*
Big goat:	*Goodbye! Good luck!**

After the story

- Ask questions about each picture as follows: **1) What can Pip see?** *(a rabbit)* **What can Squeak see?** *(a mouse)* **What can Katie see?** *(birds)* **2) Are they the three goats?** *(yes)* **A …** *(big)* **goat**, **a …** *(medium)* **goat and a …** *(small)* **goat** (use gesture to convey the differences in size) **3) Alex, Katie, Pip and Squeak need to cross the …** *(bridge)*. **Who lives under the bridge?** *(the troll)* **Is the troll hungry?** *(yes)* **Is it dangerous?** *(yes)* **4 & 5) Can Pip cross the bridge?** *(yes)* **Why? Because he's too …** *(small)* **to eat** (use gesture

and explain in L1, if necessary, that the troll thinks he's too small to be worth eating). Repeat the last two questions for Squeak, Katie and Alex.
6) What's in the troll's pocket? *(the treasure clue)* **Can the big goat cross the bridge?** *(no)* **Why? Because the troll is …** *(hungry)* **and the goat is …** *(big)* **Does the big goat get the treasure clue?** *(yes)* **What does the big goat do? He says 'Off you go!'** *(use gesture to show he pushes the troll off the bridge)* **What do Alex, Katie, Pip and Squeak say?** *(Hurray!)* **7) What does the big goat give them?** *(the treasure clue)*

Put on the treasure clue sticker.

- Say **The treasure clue says** *Follow the footprints! Find the treasure!* Explain that the characters have nearly reached the rainbow and this is the last treasure clue of the story.
- Say **Find the treasure clue sticker for Unit 8 and stick it here.** Demonstrate what you mean.
- The children look for the treasure clue sticker for Unit 8 and stick it in their books.

Act out the story.

- Divide the class into eight groups and assign a role to each group: Alex, Katie, Pip, Squeak, big goat, medium goat, small goat, troll.
- Follow the procedure for *Act out the story* on page 37 of the Teacher's Book.

Option: The children can act out their parts *either* with *or* without their books, depending on how confident and familiar they are with this episode. If you wish to make the activity more challenging, the children can act out the whole story by joining in their character's part as you replay the CD.

Look and match. (AB page 61)

- Hold up your Activity Book. Read the phrases and the children point to the pictures.
- Say **Now match the phrases and pictures.** Draw the children's attention to the example.
- The children work individually.
- Check the answers by asking individual children to read one of the phrases and point to the picture in their book.

Key: 1 big goat – bottom left 2 medium goat – bottom right 3 small goat – top left 4 troll – top right

Read, write and listen. (AB page 61)

- Read Pip's exchange with the troll and the children say the missing words.

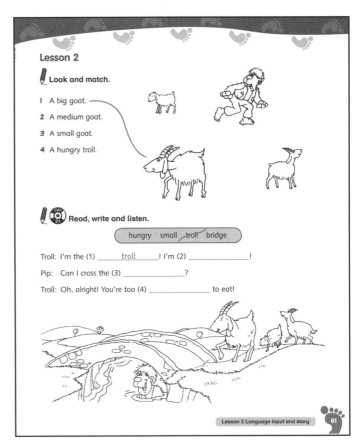

- The children complete the exchange.
- Check the answers on CD (CD 3, track 21).
- Ask individuals to read the exchange to the class.
- The children act out the exchange in pairs. They then change roles and repeat. The children can also pretend to be Squeak, Katie and Alex instead of Pip and act out the exchange several times.

Key: 1 troll 2 hungry 3 bridge 4 small

 Read, write and listen.

Troll: *I'm the <u>troll</u>! I'm <u>hungry</u>!*
Pip: *Can I cross the <u>bridge</u>?*
Troll: *Oh, alright! You're too <u>small</u> to eat!*

Ending the lesson

Lesson review

- Briefly ask the children what they can do as a result of the lesson (understand and act out *The troll*). Praise the children for their efforts and / or use the finger puppets to do this.

Goodbye and closing routine

- Say **Let's sing** *Are you ready to finish?* Play the karaoke version of the song (CD 1, track 13 – see Lesson 1). Hold up the finger puppets and the children sing and do the actions as in Lesson 1.

8 My pets

Lesson 3
Communication and grammar

Aim:
- To practise saying sentences to describe pets

Key language:
- *It's got (a) ...*
- *It's the ...*
- *goat, troll*
- *big, small, medium, long, short*
- *fur, eyes, ears, tail, legs, whiskers, teeth*
- *black, brown, white*
- *dog, cat, pony, mouse, hamster, rabbit, bird, fish, guinea pig, turtle*

Materials:
- Pupil's Book pages 63 and 64
- Activity Book pages 62 and 93
- Finger puppets (Pip and Squeak)
- Flashcards: Alex, Katie, dog, cat, pony, mouse, hamster, rabbit, bird, fish, guinea pig, turtle
- Scissors
- CD 1 and CD 3
- A prepared set of Unit 8 picture cards (AB page 93)

Starting out

Greetings and opening routine

- Greet the children yourself and using the finger puppets.
- *Either* play the karaoke version of *I like English* (CD 1, track 11 – see Lesson 1) and the children sing and do the actions as in Lesson 1 *or* stick the flashcards in the order of the song *I like pets!* on the board and play the karaoke version (CD 3, track 19 – see Lesson 1). The children point to the flashcards, do the actions and sing the song.

Revision activity

- Hold up the finger puppets and stick the character flashcards on the board. Ask **Can you remember who's in the story with Pip, Squeak, Alex and Katie?** *(the troll, the three goats)*

- Ask the children to open their Pupil's Books at page 63. Briefly reconstruct the story, getting the children to supply key words. Say e.g. **Alex, Katie, Pip and Squeak look for the three ...** *goats.* **Pip sees a ...** *rabbit,* **Squeak sees a ...** *mouse,* **Katie sees some ...** *birds.* **Then three goats appear: a ...** *big goat,* **a ...** *medium goat* **and a ...** *small goat.* **Alex sees the ...** *rainbow* **in the distance** (use gesture to convey meaning). **They must cross the ...** *bridge.* **The goats say that a hungry ...** *troll* **lives under the ...** *bridge.* **The troll lets Alex, Katie, Pip and Squeak cross the bridge because they are too ...** *small* **to eat**. **The big goat throws the troll off the bridge** (use gesture to convey meaning) **and gets the ...** *treasure clue.*

- Play the CD (CD 3, track 20 – see Lesson 2). The children listen and follow the story in their books.

Setting objectives

- Say **Today we're going to practise saying sentences to describe pets.**

On the learning trail

Listen, number and say. (PB page 64)

- Hold up your Pupil's Book and ask the children to name who's in each picture, i.e. *small goat, medium goat, big goat, troll*.

- Point to the parts of the body of the goats and say e.g. **Look at the ears / legs / tail.** Point to the parts of the body of the troll and say e.g. **Look at the teeth / fur.**

- Say **Listen and number the pictures in order.** Draw the children's attention to the example.

- Play the CD once (CD 3, track 22). Use the pause button, if necessary, to give the children time to number the pictures.

- Check the answers by asking e.g. **Who's in picture one?** *(the medium goat)*

- Say **Now listen again. Repeat the sentences.** Play the CD again. Use the pause button to give the children time to repeat the sentences.

- Say e.g. **Tell me about the troll** and ask individual children to take turns to say a sentence about one of the pictures.

  Key: 1 medium goat 2 big goat 3 troll 4 small goat

 Listen, number and say.

1 Katie: It's medium. It's brown.
           It's got a short tail.
2 Alex: It's big. It's black.
           It's got long legs.
3 Katie: It's big. It's got brown fur.
4 Alex: It's small. It's white.
           It's got small ears.

Make the picture cards. (PB page 64 and AB page 93)

- Hold up your Pupil's Book and point to the pictures. Say **We're going to make the picture cards and play the game.** You can show the children the set you have already made.

- Say **Find page 93 in your Activity Book. Look at the picture cards for Unit 8.** Point to the picture cards in turn. The children say the words.

- Make sure all the children have scissors.

- Say **Now cut out the cards like this.** Ask the

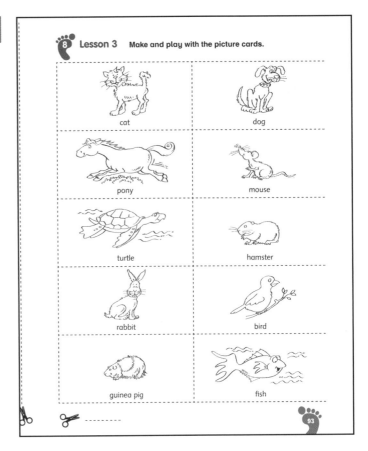

children to write their names or initials on the back of the cards.

- When the children are ready, say e.g. **Hold up the mouse! / Hold up the turtle!** and the children respond by holding up the correct cards.

Play with the picture cards. (PB page 64)

- Hold up one of the flashcards, e.g. cat. Use this to elicit or remind the children of words for parts of the body, e.g. *ears, eyes, fur, tail, legs, whiskers*. Get the children to repeat the words. Draw simple pictures to show each body part on the board as a prompt during the activity if you think the children will need this support.

- Ask the children to lay out the picture cards face up on their desks. Explain that you're going to say a sentence to describe one of the pets and the children can have three attempts to guess which one it is. If they guess correctly, they score a point. If not, you score a point.

- Demonstrate the activity by saying e.g. **It's got big ears.** Ask individual children to guess the pet, e.g.

  P1: *It's the rabbit.*
  T: **No.**
  P2: *It's the pony.*
  T: **No.**

P3: *It's the dog.*

T: **Yes. Very good. One point for you.**

- Play several times with the whole class. Examples of sentences you can use are: **It's got a long tail** *(cat, dog, pony, mouse).* **It's got a short tail** *(rabbit, hamster, guinea pig).* **It's got whiskers** *(rabbit, dog, mouse, cat, guinea pig).* **It's got fur** *(cat, dog, hamster, mouse, guinea pig).* **It's got four legs** *(all except bird and fish).* **It's got two legs** *(bird).* **It's got big eyes** *(cat).*

- Once the children are responding confidently, continue the game by asking individual children to secretly choose an animal and say a sentence, e.g. *It's got small ears* and the rest of the class guess the pet and continue scoring points or not in the same way. At the end, add up the points for you and the class and declare the winners.

- Divide the class into pairs. The children play the game with their partner.

- If there is time, the children can colour the picture cards.

Read, match and colour. (AB page 62)

- Read the sentences and the children identify the correct pictures: small goat, medium goat, big goat, troll.

- Say **Now match the sentences and pictures. Colour the goats and the troll.** Draw the children's attention to the example. Explain that they do not need to colour the small goat, which is white.

- The children work individually and match the sentences and pictures and colour the pictures.

- Check the answers by saying a sentence and asking children to say *It's the ...* and to name the character.

  Key: 1 small goat – bottom right 2 medium goat – bottom left 3 big goat – top left 4 troll – top right

Look, read and write. (AB page 62)

- Read the words at the top of the activity. Ask the children to look at the features of the pets carefully.

- Read the sentences in turn and the children name the pets.

- Say **Now write the words.** Draw the children's attention to the example.

- The children work individually and write the words.

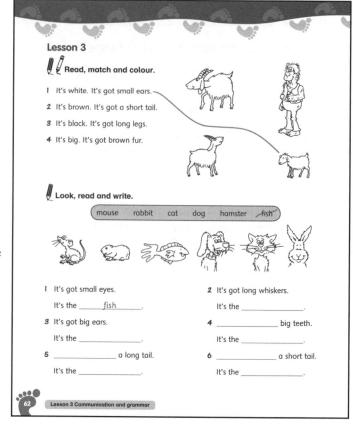

- Check the answers by asking individual children to read one of the sentences.

- The children take turns to read the sentences in pairs.

  Key: 1 fish 2 cat 3 rabbit 4 dog 5 mouse 6 hamster

Ending the lesson

Lesson review

- Briefly ask the children what they can do as a result of the lesson (say sentences to describe pets). Praise the children for their efforts and / or use the finger puppets to do this.

Goodbye and closing routine

- Say goodbye to the children yourself and using the finger puppets. If there is time, you can also play the karaoke version of *Are you ready to finish?* (CD 1, track 13 – see Lesson 1) and the children sing and do the actions as in Lesson 1.

8 My pets

Lesson 4
Communication, grammar and pronunciation

Aims:

- To practise asking and saying the names of pets
- To say a tongue-twister with /h/

Key language:

- *What's its name? Its name is ...*
- *This is ...*
- *What a ...!*
- *lovely, nice, thank you*

Materials:

- Pupil's Book page 65
- Activity Book page 63
- Finger puppets (Pip and Squeak)
- Flashcards: dog, cat, pony, mouse, hamster, rabbit, bird, fish, guinea pig, turtle, Frodo
- Unit 8 picture cards from Lesson 3
- CD 1 and CD 3

Starting out

Greetings and opening routine

- Greet the children yourself and using the finger puppets.
- *Either* play the karaoke version of *I like English* (CD 1, track 11 – see Lesson 1) and the children sing and do the actions as in Lesson 1 *or* stick the flashcards in the order of the song *I like pets!* on the board and play the karaoke version (CD 3, track 19 – see Lesson 1). The children point to the flashcards, do the actions and sing the song.

Revision activity

- Give out or ask the children to get out the picture cards they made in Lesson 3.
- Ask the children to lay out the cards face up on their desks.
- Say e.g. **Show me a pet that's got fur!** As fast as they can, the children choose one picture card of a pet to hold up and show you that fulfils the description.

- Look at all the cards the children are holding up and say e.g. **Yes, very good.** Ask individual children to say what pet they are holding up, e.g. *rabbit / cat / hamster* and e.g. *It's got fur.*
- Repeat several times with different sentences (see *Play with the picture cards* on page 207 of the Teacher's Notes for suggested sentences).

Setting objectives

- Say **Today we're going to practise asking and saying the names of pets. We're also going to practise pronunciation.**

On the learning trail

Listen and say the chant. (PB page 65)

- (Books closed) Explain to the children that they are going to listen to a chant about pets and pets' names.
- Ask **What's the pet? What's its name?** Play the first verse of the chant on the CD (CD3, track 23) and check the answer *(dog, Digger)*.

- Repeat with the remaining three verses *(cat, Cleo; turtle, Terry; bird, Betty)*
- Ask the children to open their Pupil's Books at page 65. The children look at the pictures of the pets and confirm their answers.
- Play the CD again. The children say the chant and point to the pets.
- Divide the children into two groups (to represent the two speakers in each verse of the chant).
- Play the CD again. The children say the chant with their group.
- Get the groups to change roles and repeat.

 This is my dog

This is my dog.	*What a lovely dog!*
Oh, thank you!	*What's its name?*
Its name is Digger.	*Oh, hello Digger.*
Digger's a very nice name.	
This is my cat ...	*(Cleo)*
This is my turtle ...	*(Terry)*
This is my bird ...	*(Betty)*

Ask and say. (PB page 65)

- Ask the children to look at the pictures of pets and to read the name for each one, e.g. *Molly*.
- Get the children to ask in chorus about picture one. They ask *What's its name?* Invite one child to answer, e.g. *Its name is ...*
- Repeat the procedure for the rest of the pictures.
- Divide the class into pairs. The children take turns to ask and say the names of all the pets.

Listen and say: Frodo's word fun. (PB page 65)

- Write the letter '*h*' on the board and make the sound /h/ as in *hamster* and *hungry*.
- Ask the children to put their hands in front of their mouths and to feel the air on their hands as they make the sound /h/ and say the words.
- Read the tongue-twister slowly while the children follow in their books.
- Hold up the flashcard of Frodo. Say **Listen to Frodo and say the tongue-twister.** Play the CD (CD 3, track 25).
- Ask pairs of children to say the tongue-twister in turns.

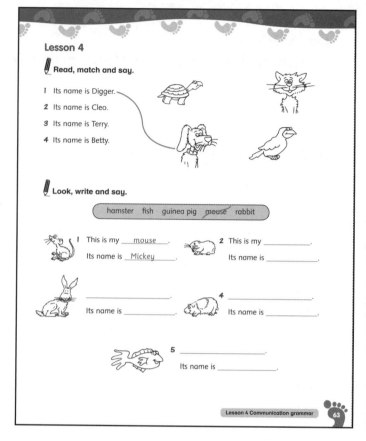

- The children practise saying the tongue-twister with a partner.

 Frodo's word fun. Listen and say.

Harry is a happy, hungry hamster.
Is Harry a happy, hungry hamster? Yes, he is!
Harry is a happy, hungry hamster.
Is Harry a happy, hungry hamster? Yes, he is!
Harry is a happy, hungry hamster.
Is Harry a happy, hungry hamster? Yes, he is!

Read, match and say. (AB page 63)

- Read the sentences and the children point to the pets.
- Say **Now read and match the sentences and pictures.** Draw their attention to the example.
- The children work individually. They match the pictures and sentences.
- Check the answers by pointing to the picture of each pet and asking **What's its name?** and the children say the sentences.

Key: Children match the sentences and pictures.
1 Digger (dog) 2 Cleo (cat) 3 Terry (turtle)
4 Betty (bird)

Look, write and say. (AB page 63)

- Read the example sentence. Explain that you want the children to imagine that these are their pets. They have to complete the sentences and invent a name for each one.
- The children work individually. They complete the sentences by writing the words for the pets and inventing their names.
- When they are ready, ask individual children to take turns to hold up their book, point to one of the pictures and say *This is my ... Its name is ...*

Key: 1 mouse 2 hamster 3 rabbit 4 guinea pig 5 fish

Ending the lesson

Lesson review

- Briefly ask the children what they can do as a result of the lesson (ask and say the names of pets, say a tongue-twister). Praise the children for their efforts and / or use the finger puppets to do this.

Goodbye and closing routine

- Say goodbye to the children yourself and using the finger puppets. If there is time, you can also play the karaoke version of *Are you ready to finish?* (CD 1, track 13 – see Lesson 1) and the children sing and do the actions as in Lesson 1.

8 My pets

Lesson 5
Content input

Aims:
- To read and understand ways to care for a pet
- To recognise that it is important to care for pets

Key language:
- *pet, animal, family, food, water, walks*
- *brush, clean, feed, give, take, play, care for*

Materials:
- Pupil's Book page 66
- Activity Book page 64
- Finger puppets (Pip and Squeak)
- Flashcards: dog, cat, pony, mouse, hamster, rabbit, bird, fish, guinea pig, turtle
- CD 1 and CD 3

Starting out

Greetings and opening routine

- Greet the children yourself and using the finger puppets.
- *Either* play the karaoke version of *I like English* (CD 1, track 11 – see Lesson 1) and the children sing and do the actions as in Lesson 1 *or* divide the class into two groups, play *This is my dog* (CD 3, track 23 – see Lesson 4) and the children say the chant.
- Repeat with the karaoke version of *This is my dog* (CD 3, track 24).

Revision activity

- Hold up one of the flashcards and the children name the pet, e.g. *rabbit*. Elicit sentences to describe the rabbit, e.g. *It's got fur. / It's got small eyes. / It's got big ears. / It's got whiskers.*
- Ask **What's its name?** and invite children to suggest names for the rabbit in the flashcard, e.g. *Its name is Roger.* Listen to several suggestions and get the class to agree on the name they like best.
- Repeat with the flashcards of three or four different pets.

Setting objectives

- Hold up the finger puppets. Say **Let's learn about the world around you! Today we're going to read about pets and ways to care for your pet.** Explain the meaning of *care* by saying e.g. **Your mother and father care for you** and repeat this in L1 if necessary.

On the learning trail

Read, listen and number. (PB page 66)

- (Books closed) Read the questions *What is a pet? How do you care for a pet?*
- Listen to the children's ideas (in L1). Use their suggestions to introduce or remind them of vocabulary, e.g. *play, brush, food, water, clean*.
- Ask the children to open their Pupil's Books at page 66. Read the text at the start of the activity or play part 1 on the CD (CD 3, track 26).
- Ask questions to check comprehension and clarify meaning, e.g. **What is a pet?** *(an animal)* **Do you keep pets at home?** *(yes)* (If appropriate, explain that *home* means the place where you live and may include a garden, garage or, in the case of a pony, even a stable and field as well.) **Is it important to care for your pet?** *(yes)*

- Say **Look at the photos of ways to care for your pet.** Read the sentences while the children follow in their books.
- Say **Now listen and number the photos.** Draw their attention to the example.
- Play the CD (CD 3, track 26). Use the pause button to allow the children time to write the numbers by each photo.
- Check the answers. Say e.g. **Number one is …** (Feed your pet.)
- Play the CD again as a final check.

Key: Give your pet water: 2; Brush your pet: 4; Take your pet for walks: 6; Feed your pet: 1; Play with your pet: 5; Clean your pet: 3;

 Read, listen and number.

Part 1

A pet is an animal you keep at home.
Many people have got pets.
It is important to care for your pet.

Part 2

These are some ways to care for your pet:
Number 1: Feed your pet.
Number 2: Give your pet water.
Number 3: Clean your pet.
Number 4: Brush your pet.
Number 5: Play with your pet.
Number 6: Take your pet for walks.

Play a game. (PB page 66)

- Teach the children a mime for all the ways to care for a pet, e.g. *Feed your pet* – pretend to hold out a bowl of food; *Give your pet water* – pretend to turn on a tap and fill a bowl of water; *Clean your pet* – pretend to wipe the bars of a cage; *Brush your pet* – pretend to brush a pet; *Play with your pet* – pretend to throw a ball; *Take your pet for walks* – pretend to walk an animal on a lead.
- Explain and demonstrate that when you give an instruction that relates to pets, e.g. **Brush your pet!**, the children should mime the action, and when you give a different instruction, e.g. **Close your books!**, the children should stand still, fold their arms and do nothing.

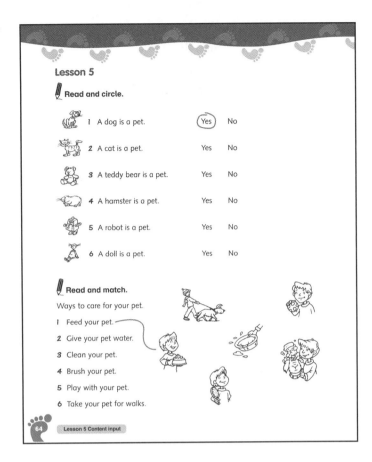

- Play the game by giving different instructions that either relate to pets or don't relate to pets in random order. Examples of instructions you can give which don't relate to pets are: **Sit down! / Jump to the door! / Brush your teeth! / Wash your hands! / Have a shower!** The children respond either by miming the action or by folding their arms and doing nothing. If all the children respond correctly, they win a point. If not, you win a point. Keep a score on the board. Go slowly at first and speed up as the children become familiar with the instructions. Stop the game once the children are winning easily.

Read and circle. (AB page 64)

- Read the sentences and the children say *Yes* or *No* depending on whether they are true or false.
- The children work individually and circle *Yes* or *No*.
- Check the answers by reading the sentences and the children say *Yes* or *No*. If you like, you can also ask them to correct the ones that are wrong, e.g. *A teddy bear is a pet. No, it's a toy.*

Key: 1 Yes 2 Yes 3 No (It's a toy.) 4 Yes
5 No (It's a toy.) 6 No (It's a toy.)

Read and match. (AB page 64)

- Read the ways to care for a pet and the children point to the correct pictures.
- Say **Now match the ways to care for a pet to the pictures**. Draw their attention to the example.
- The children work individually and match the text and pictures.
- The children compare their answers in pairs.
- Check the answers by asking individual children to take turns to read one way to care for a pet and point to the correct picture in their books.

Key: Children match the sentences and pictures.
1 Feed your pet 2 Give your pet water
3 Clean your pet 4 Brush your pet
5 Play with your pet 6 Take your pet for walks

Ending the lesson

Lesson review

- Briefly ask the children what they can do as a result of the lesson (read and understand what a pet is, recognise ways to care for pets). Praise the children for their efforts and / or use the finger puppets to do this.

Goodbye and closing routine

- Say goodbye to the children yourself and using the finger puppets. If there is time, you can also play the karaoke version of *Are you ready to finish?* (CD 1, track 13 – see Lesson 1) and the children sing and do the actions as in Lesson 1.

8 My pets

Lesson 6
Content and personalisation

Aims:
- To identify ways children care for specific pets
- To say what you do to care for a pet

Key language:
- cat, dog, pony, mouse, hamster, rabbit, bird, guinea pig, fish, turtle
- I ... my pet.
- feed, brush, clean, give water to, play with, take for walks
- I've got a ...

Materials:
- Pupil's Book page 67
- Activity Book page 65
- Finger puppets (Pip and Squeak)
- CD 1 and CD 3

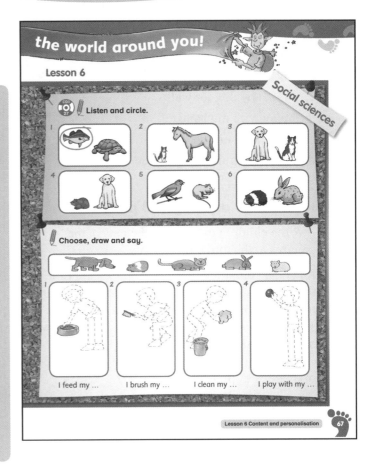

Starting out

Greetings and opening routine

- Greet the children yourself and using the finger puppets.
- *Either* play the karaoke version of *I like English* (CD 1, track 11 – see Lesson 1) and the children sing and do the actions as in Lesson 1 *or* divide the class into two groups, play the karaoke version of *This is my dog* (CD 3, track 24 – see Lesson 4) and the children say the chant.

Revision activity

- Ask the children how many ways they can remember to care for a pet. Listen to their responses. Mime actions as in the game in Lesson 5 (see page 213 of the Teacher's Book) as a prompt if necessary.
- Ask two children to come to the front. Whisper to them one way to care for a pet, e.g. **Brush your pet.** Get the children to mime this to the rest of the class, who guess the action. The child who guesses correctly chooses a partner and has the next turn.
- Repeat several times.

Setting objectives

- Say **In this lesson we're going to identify ways children care for their pets. We're also going to talk about ways you care for a pet.**

On the learning trail

Listen and circle. (PB page 67)

- Say **Look at the pictures.** Ask the children to identify the pets in each one.
- Say e.g. **Listen to the children talking about ways they care for their pet. Circle the correct pet in each picture.** Draw the children's attention to the example.
- Play the CD (CD 3, track 27). Use the pause button, if necessary, to give the children time to circle the correct pictures.
- Check the answers by asking individual children to name the correct pet in each picture.
- Say **Now listen and repeat what the children say.** Play the CD again. The children listen and repeat the sentence for each picture.

Key: 1 fish 2 pony 3 dog 4 hamster 5 mouse 6 guinea pig

Listen and circle.

1 I feed my fish.
2 I brush my pony.
3 I take my dog for walks.
4 I play with my hamster.
5 I clean my mouse.
6 I give my guinea pig water.

Choose, draw and say. (PB page 67)

- Ask the children to name all the pets in the pictures at the top of the activity.

- Read the beginning of each sentence under the four frames. Ask the children to choose one (or more) pet(s) and draw its picture in each frame to show how they care for the pet. They also draw over the dashed outline. Make it clear that the children can draw either pictures of their real pet or pictures of pretend pets.

- When they are ready, ask individual children to take turns to show their pictures and tell the class, e.g. *I feed my rabbit. / I brush my dog.*

  Key: Children's own drawings.

Look, read and write. (AB page 65)

- Say **Look at the pictures.** Read what the children say in the speech bubbles and the children say the missing words.

- Say **Now write the words.** Draw the children's attention to the example.

- The children work individually and write the missing words.

- Check the answers by asking individual children to take turns to read one of the sentences in the speech bubbles.

  Key: 1 rabbit 2 turtle 3 bird 4 cat 5 pony 6 dog

Draw, write and say. (AB page 65)

- Read what Katie and Alex say, while the children follow in their books.

- Ask the children to draw a picture of their pet and to complete the sentences *either* for their real pet *or* for a pretend pet of their choice.

- The children work individually and draw a picture and complete the sentences.

- Ask individual children to take turns to show their picture and tell the class, e.g. *I've got a rabbit. I feed my rabbit.* After each one, ask e.g. **Is the rabbit your real pet? What's its name?** and make positive comments, e.g. **What a lovely rabbit!**

Ending the lesson

Lesson review

- Briefly ask the children what they can do as a result of the lesson (identify ways children care for their pets, say what they do to care for their pet).

- Praise the children for their efforts and / or use the finger puppets to do this.

Goodbye and closing routine

- Say goodbye to the children yourself and using the finger puppets. If there is time, you can also play the karaoke version of *Are you ready to finish?* (CD 1, track 13 – see Lesson 1) and the children sing and do the actions as in Lesson 1.

8 My pets

Lesson 7
Children's culture

Aim:
- To sing a version of a traditional song and play a version of a traditional game

Key language:
- ...'s got ...
- Hurry!
- Here's the ...
- rabbit, cat, mouse, fly
- tail, ears, eyes, nose, leg, whiskers, fur
- long, big, curly, shiny

Materials:
- Pupil's Book page 68
- Activity Book page 66
- Finger puppets (Pip and Squeak)
- Flashcards: Frodo, cat, rabbit
- CD 1 and CD 3

Starting out

Greetings and opening routine

- Greet the children yourself and using the finger puppets.
- *Either* play the karaoke version of *I like English* (CD 1, track 11 – see Lesson 1) and the children sing and do the actions as in Lesson 1 *or* play the karaoke version of *This is my dog* (CD 3, track 24 – see Lesson 4) and the children say the chant.

Revision activity

- Say a sentence, e.g. **I feed my dog**, and do the action (see Lesson 5). Explain and demonstrate that another child should then say a sentence including either the word *feed* or the word *dog* and do the action in the same way. For example, they could say *I feed my turtle* or *I brush my dog*. Ask children to raise their hands if they can contribute the next sentence. Stop the activity after six to ten children have had a turn, depending on the size of the class.

Setting objectives

- Hold up the flashcard of Frodo. Say **In this lesson we're going to learn about children's culture with Frodo. We're going to sing a version of a traditional song and play a version of a traditional game.**

On the learning trail

Listen and sing the song. (PB page 68) (books closed)

- Hold up the flashcard of the rabbit. Say **This is a song about a little rabbit named Peter. Peter's got a fly on his nose.** Move your fingers and make a buzzing noise like a fly to convey the meaning of this.
- Say **Listen to the song and do the actions.** Play the CD (CD 3, track 28) once. The children listen to the song and do the actions with you (see audio script on page 218).
- Play the CD again. The children do the actions again and join in singing the song.
- Ask the children to open their Pupil's Books at page 68. Explain or use the picture to clarify the meaning of *shiny* and *curly*. If you like, you can explain that *flip* means to hit something very

quickly but that *flop* in this context is a nonsense word used because of the similar sound.

- Play the CD again. The children follow in their books and sing the song.

- Sing the song again either using the karaoke version (CD 3, track 29) or without the CD. This time, leave out words or whole phrases progressively and continue to do only the actions, e.g. for the first three lines, sing:
Little Peter Rabbit's got a fly on his …
Little Peter Rabbit's …
Little …

- The children do the actions for each line in the same way as when singing all the words.

 Little Peter Rabbit

Little Peter Rabbit's got a fly on his nose	(waggle hands on head; flap arms; touch nose)
Little Peter Rabbit's got a fly on his nose	(repeat actions as above)
Little Peter Rabbit's got a fly on his nose	(repeat actions as above)
And he flips it and he flops it	(flick nose one way; flick nose the other way)
And it flies away!	(flap arms)
Shiny nose and curly whiskers	(rub nose with circular motion; spiral outwards with both hands, pointing with index fingers)
Shiny nose and curly whiskers	(repeat actions as above)
Shiny nose and curly whiskers	(repeat actions as above)
And he flips it and he flops it	(flick nose one way; flick nose the other way)
And it flies away!	(flap arms)

 Citizenship box: Remember!

Say **Look at the children in the picture. Is it important for them to take care of their pet rabbit?** and listen to the children's responses.

Hold up the flashcard of Frodo, read the *Remember!* note and explain the meaning of *kind*. Ask the children how they can be kind to pets, e.g. not to tease or hurt them, to keep them clean, to feed them, to give them water.

Play *Cat and mouse!* (PB page 68)

- If possible, get the children to stand or sit in a circle, making sure there is plenty of room to walk round behind them (if this isn't possible, see the option below).

- Walk round the circle tapping each child gently on the shoulder and saying **mouse** as you pass. Get the children to join in repeating the word with you.

- After about six children, tap the next child on the shoulder, say **cat** and give them the flashcard of the cat. Demonstrate and explain that the child who you name as 'cat' and give the flashcard to should stand up and walk as fast as possible after you round the circle until you get back to their place, where you sit down.

- As you walk fast round the circle away from the cat say **Hurry! Hurry! Here's the cat!** and repeat this in a rhythmical way, encouraging all the children to join in.

- The child who is the cat then has the next turn, walking round the circle, tapping children on the shoulder and saying *mouse* and *cat* with everyone participating in the same way.

- Repeat the game several times.

Option: If it's not possible for the children to stand or sit in a circle, they can play the game sitting at their desks. In this case, you walk up and down the rows, tapping each child gently and saying **mouse**. When you say **cat** and give the flashcard to a child, they get up and follow you round one row of desks and back to their desk in the same way. For safety reasons, it is important to ensure that the children walk in the game, not run.

Look, read and write. (AB page 66)

- Read the sentences. The children follow in their book, point to where the fly is on Little Peter Rabbit in each picture and say the missing words.

- Say **Now read and write the missing words.** Draw the children's attention to the example.

- Check the answers by asking children to take turns to read a sentence.

Key: 1 nose 2 ear 3 tail 4 leg

Look, write and say. (AB page 66)

- Say **Look at the cat.** Read the words at the top of the activity.
- Say e.g. **Number one. It's got big …** and the children say the words.
- Say **Now write the words** and draw their attention to the example.
- The children work individually and write the words. If you like, they can also colour the cat black.
- Check the answers by asking individual children to take turns to say a sentence about the cat, e.g. *It's got long whiskers*.

Key: 1 ears 2 eyes 3 whiskers 4 fur 5 tail

Ending the lesson

Lesson review

- Briefly ask the children what they can do as a result of the lesson (sing *Little Peter Rabbit*, play *Cat and mouse!*). Praise the children for their efforts and / or use the finger puppets to do this.

Goodbye and closing routine

- Say goodbye to the children yourself and using the finger puppets. If there is time, you can also play the karaoke version of *Are you ready to finish?* (CD 1, track 13 – see Lesson 1) and the children sing and do the actions as in Lesson 1.

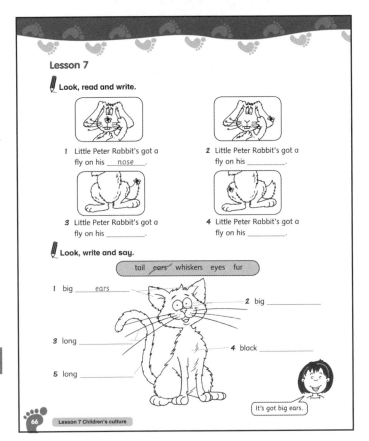

8 My pets

Lesson 8
Unit review / *All About Me* Portfolio Booklet

Aim
- To review learning in Unit 8

Key language:
- *It's got …*
- *What's its name? Its name is …*
- *cat, dog, pony, mouse, hamster, rabbit, bird, guinea pig, fish, turtle*
- *I … my pet.*
- *feed, brush, give water to, play with*
- *This is my …*
- *ears, eyes, tail, whiskers*
- *long, short, big, small*

Materials:
- Pupil's Book page 69
- Activity Book page 67
- *All About Me* Portfolio Booklet pages 20 and 21
- Finger puppets (Pip and Squeak)
- Flashcards: cat, dog, pony, mouse, hamster, rabbit, bird, guinea pig, fish, turtle, Frodo
- Word cards: cat, dog, pony, mouse, hamster, rabbit, bird, guinea pig, fish, turtle
- Stickers for Unit 8
- CD 1 and CD 3

Starting out

Greetings and opening routine

- Greet the children yourself and using the finger puppets.
- *Either* play the karaoke version of *I like English* (CD 1, track 11 – see Lesson 1) and the children sing and do the actions as in Lesson 1 *or* stick the flashcards on the board in the order of the song *I like pets!* and play the karaoke version (CD 3, track 19 – see Lesson 1). The children sing the song and point to the flashcards.

Revision activity

- Ask **Can you remember the song *Little Peter Rabbit*?** Do the actions for each line of the song (see audio script on page 218 of the Teacher's Notes) and encourage the children to reconstruct the words as you do this, with prompting as necessary.
- Play the CD (CD 3, track 28 – see Lesson 7). The children sing the song and do the actions.
- Either play the karaoke version of the song (CD 3, track 29) or sing the song without the CD. Get the children to omit whole phrases of the song but to continue doing the actions (see the final stage of the activity *Listen and sing the song* on page 218 of the Teacher's Book).

Setting objectives

- Say **Today we're going to review what we've learnt in Unit 8.**

On the learning trail

Listen and put on the stickers. Write the words. (PB page 69)

- Make sure the children have the stickers for Unit 8 ready.

- Say **Listen and put on the stickers.** Draw the children's attention to the example.
- Play the CD (CD 3, track 30). Use the pause button to give the children time to put on the stickers.
- Say **Now write the words.** Draw the children's attention to the example.
- Check the answers by saying the numbers and getting the children to say the words.

    Key: 1 cat 2 rabbit 3 hamster 4 dog 5 fish
    6 guinea pig 7 mouse 8 bird 9 rabbit 10 pony

 Listen and put on the stickers.

1 It's got long whiskers. It's a cat.
2 It's got a short tail. It's a rabbit.
3 It's got small ears. It's a hamster.
4 This is my dog. What's its name? Tommy.
5 This is my fish. What's its name? Freda.
6 This is my guinea pig. What's its name? Glenda.
7 I feed my mouse.
8 I give water to my bird.
9 I play with my rabbit.
10 I brush my pony.

Look, write and say. (PB page 69)

- Read the sentences and exchanges and the children say the missing words.
- Draw the children's attention to the example. The children work individually and write the missing words.
- Check the answers by asking individual children to read the exchanges and sentences.

    Key: 1 hamster 2 rabbit 3 dog 4 cat 5 fish
    6 guinea pig

Listen and draw. (AB page 67)

- Say **Listen and draw the missing parts of the body on the pets.** Draw the children's attention to the example.
- Play the CD (CD 3, track 31). Pause, if necessary, to give the children time to complete the pictures.
- Check the answers by getting individual children to say *It's got ...* and name the part of the body they have drawn in one of the pictures.

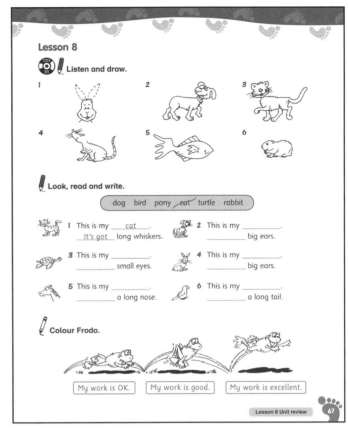

Key: The following body parts should be drawn in:
1 long ears 2 short tail 3 big eyes 4 small ears
5 small eyes 6 long whiskers

 Listen and draw.

1 It's a rabbit. It's got long ears.
2 It's a dog. It's got a short tail.
3 It's a cat. It's got big eyes.
4 It's a mouse. It's got small ears.
5 It's a fish. It's got small eyes.
6 It's a hamster. It's got long whiskers.

Look, read and write. (AB page 67)

- Read the sentences and the children say the missing words.
- Say **Write the words** and draw the children's attention to the example.
- The children work individually and complete the sentences.
- Check the answers by asking individual children to read the sentences.

    Key: 1 cat 2 dog 3 turtle 4 rabbit 5 pony 6 bird

Colour Frodo. (AB page 67)

- Hold up the flashcard of Frodo. Remind the children that in this activity they assess their work in the unit by choosing and colouring the picture of Frodo which corresponds best to how they think they have done.

- Remind the children of the key by pointing to the three pictures of Frodo and saying **Colour this picture if your work is OK but you think you need to try harder or need more practice. Colour this picture of Frodo if you think your work is good. Colour this picture of Frodo with a big smile and jumping very high if you think your work is excellent.** Make sure the children understand that there are no right answers and that it is their own opinion of the work they have done which is important. Be ready to encourage the children to have a positive view if they are too hard on themselves.

Ending the lesson

Lesson review

- Briefly ask the children what they can do as a result of the lesson (use the language and vocabulary they've learnt in Unit 8). Praise the children for their efforts and / or use the finger puppets to do this.

Goodbye and closing routine

- Say goodbye to the children yourself and using the finger puppets. If there is time, you can also play the karaoke version of *Are you ready to finish?* (CD 1, track 13 – see Lesson 1) and the children sing and do the actions as in Lesson 1.

All About Me Portfolio Booklet

The children complete Unit 8 of their personal *All About Me* Portfolio Booklets. They complete their learning journey by colouring the sections on the path to show what they can do. If you like, the children can also sign this page and you can endorse this by adding your own signature and the date.

9 Treasure!

Structures and grammar

- *Where are you?*
- *Let's ... to the ...!*
- *Good idea!*
- *Put it in ...!*
- Recycled: *What's this? It's a ..., Are you ...? Yes, I am. / No, I'm not., Where ...? I'm ..., in / on / under, We ...*

Vocabulary

- Core: *tree, flower, grass, rock, river, hill, bush, path, fence, gate*
- Other: *jump, hop, run, walk, skip*
- Content / culture: *paper, glass, tin cans, bin, know, show, three times*
- Recycled: *put, plastic, clean, blue, yellow, green, red, happy, clap hands,* numbers 1–20

Main receptive language

- *countryside, rubbish, recycle, throw away*

Communicative competence

Understanding

Listening:
- Can recognise words for things in the countryside
- Can understand the episode of the story
- Can understand questions and answers about where you are
- Can understand suggestions
- Can understand what people recycle
- Can identify words which rhyme

Reading:
- Can recognise words for things in the countryside
- Can recognise words to describe where people are
- Can recognise action words
- Can read statements about recycling

Speaking

Spoken interaction:
- Can ask and say where you are
- Can make and respond to suggestions

Spoken production:
- Can sing the song *I like English*
- Can identify things in the countryside
- Can sing the song *Where's the treasure?*
- Can say where you are
- Can say the rhyme *Follow me*
- Can say rhyming words
- Can say what you and your family recycle
- Can sing the song *If you're happy*
- Can sing the song *Are you ready to finish?*

Writing

- Can copy and write words for things in nature
- Can complete sentences about where people are
- Can complete suggestions

Content links

- *Science:* recycling

Learning strategies and thinking skills

- Recognising learning objectives
- Associating vocabulary with pictures
- Using actions to memorise language patterns
- Deducing
- Sorting and counting
- Associating colours and materials
- Reflecting on learning
- Recognising own progress

Children's culture

- Singing a song: *If you're happy*
- Playing a traditional game: *Follow my leader!*

Pronunciation

- Identifying and saying rhyming words

Values and attitudes

- Recognition of the value of recycling
- Sense of achievement in completing *Footprints 1*
- Pleasure in how much English you know

9 Treasure!

Lesson 1
Vocabulary presentation

Aim:
- To name things in the countryside

Key language:
- *tree, flower, grass, rock, river, hill, bush, path, fence, gate, treasure*
- *Where's ...?*
- *What's this? It's a ...*
- *Look at ...*

Materials:
- Pupil's Book page 70
- Activity Book page 68
- Finger puppets (Pip and Squeak)
- Flashcards: Alex, Katie, Frodo, tree, flower, grass, rock, river, hill, bush, path, fence, gate
- Word cards: tree, flower, grass, rock, river, hill, bush, path, fence, gate, Frodo
- CD 1 and CD 3
- Picture of countryside (optional)

Starting out

Greetings and opening routine

- Greet the children yourself and using the finger puppets. Say e.g. **Hello, children. Hello … How are you today?** *Fine, thank you.* Ask a few individual children to greet the puppets in turn.

- Say **Let's sing the song** *I like English*. Play the CD (CD 1, track 10). Hold up the puppets on your index fingers. Stick the character flashcards on the board. Move them as the children sing and do the actions and use them to point to the other characters.

 I like English

I like English.	(thumbs up)
And I like you.	(gesture to a friend)
I like Alex, Katie and Frodo.	(point to the flashcards)
I like Pip and Squeak, too!	(wave to the puppets)

Setting objectives

- Say **Today we're going to learn how to name things in the countryside** (show the children a picture of countryside or draw a simple picture on the board to explain what you mean). **We're also going to sing a song.**

On the learning trail

Vocabulary presentation (books closed)

- Ask the children **What things do you find in the countryside?** and listen to their responses either in English or in L1. As children name items on the flashcards, hold these up and either repeat or recast the words in English.

- Stick the flashcards on the board. Point to them in turn and get the children to repeat the words with you in chorus.

- Divide the class in half. Hold up the Pip finger puppet and say to one half **Say the words with Pip.** Use the puppet to point to the flashcards in turn and the children say the words with you. Make the puppet fly around to praise the children.

- Repeat the procedure with the Squeak puppet and the other half of the class.

Follow the footprints. (PB page 70) (books open)

- Hold up the flashcard of Frodo. Say **Listen and follow the footprints with Frodo the frog. Use your finger** and demonstrate this.

- Play the CD (CD 3, track 32). The children listen and follow the footprints with their fingers. They stop by each picture as they hear the word and repeat the word.

- Say **Now listen and draw a line following the footprints** and demonstrate this. Play the CD again. The children draw a line, stop by each picture and repeat the words as previously.

 Follow the footprints.

tree ... flower ... grass ... rock ... river ... hill ... bush ... path ... fence ... gate

- Stick the word cards on the board in jumbled order (at the children's height and away from the flashcards).

- Point to one word card, e.g. *path* and read the word. Say **Look for the path.** Give the children time to do this.
- Ask a child to come to the front of the class and stick the word card for *path*, by the corresponding flashcard. Ask the rest of the class **Is this right?** and get them to say the word.
- Repeat the procedure with the rest of the word cards.
- Take the flashcards and word cards off the board.

Listen and sing the song. (PB page 70)

- Say **Look at Pip and Squeak. They're looking for the treasure!** Ask **Can they see the treasure?** *(no)* **What can they see?** and the children name the other things in the picture.
- Say **Listen to the song. Point to the pictures** and demonstrate what you mean. Play the CD (CD 3, track 33). The children listen to the song and point to the items in the picture for each verse.
- Elicit or remind the children of the meaning of *Where's ...?* Use gesture to convey or explain the meaning of *Are we too late?*
- Invite four (or eight) children to the front of the class. Give them one (or two) flashcard(s) each and get them to stand facing the class holding up the flashcards in the same order as the song. Explain and demonstrate that the children at the front should hold up their flashcard(s) when they hear the word(s) in the song. The rest of the class should point to the flashcards in turn as they sing and do actions (see audio script below).
- Play the CD again. The children point to the pictures, do the actions and sing the song.
- At the end, ask the children e.g. **Do you think Pip and Squeak will find the treasure? Are they too late?** and listen to their responses.

 Where's the treasure?

Look at the flowers and the grass (mime looking through binoculars)
Look at the bush and the tree
Where's the treasure? (put hands out questioningly)
Oh, please tell me! (point to yourself)

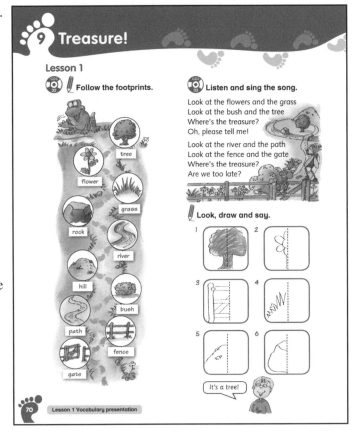

Look at the river and the path (mime as above)
Look at the fence and the gate
Where's the treasure? (put hands out questioningly)
Are we too late? (tap real or imaginary watch)

Look, draw and say. (PB page 70)

- Ask the children to look and name what's in each incomplete picture.
- Say **Now draw and complete the pictures.** Draw the children's attention to the example.
- The children work individually and draw and complete the pictures.
- Check the answers by asking **What's this?** and individual children respond *It's a ...* for each one.

Key: 1 tree 2 flower 3 gate 4 grass 5 hill 6 rock

Read, match and say. (AB page 68)

- Read the sentences and the children point to the pictures.
- Say **Now match the sentences and pictures.** Draw the children's attention to the example.
- The children work individually and match the sentences and pictures.
- Check the answers by asking individual children to hold up their books, point to a picture and say the sentence.

  Key: Children match the sentences and pictures.

1 top left	2 bottom right
3 middle row, right	4 bottom row, middle
5 bottom row, left	6 middle row, left

Look, write and listen. (AB page 68)

- Read the verse of the song *Where's the treasure?* and the children say the missing words.
- Say **Now write the words.** Draw the children's attention to the example.
- The children work individually and write the words.
- Play the song on the CD (CD 3, track 33). The children follow in their books and check their answers.
- If you like, play the karaoke version of the song (CD 3, track 34). The children follow in their books and sing this verse.

  Key: flowers; grass; bush; tree; treasure

Ending the lesson

Lesson review

- Briefly ask the children what they can do as a result of the lesson (name things in the countryside, sing the song *Where's the treasure?*). Praise the children for their efforts and / or use the finger puppets to do this.

Goodbye and closing routine

- Say **Let's sing the song** *Are you ready to finish?* Play the CD (CD 1, track 12). Hold up the finger puppets on your index fingers as the children count, sing and do the actions.

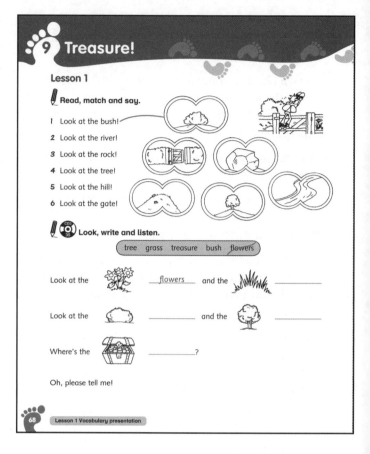

Are you ready to finish?

Are you ready to finish?   (gesture questioningly)
Count to twenty and say goodbye
                    (mime counting fingers)
One, two, three, four, five, six, seven
    (move arms rhythmically as sing each number)
Eight, nine, ten, and now eleven
Twelve, thirteen, fourteen, fifteen, sixteen
Seventeen, eighteen, nineteen, twenty – Hey!
                    (make a big circle with arms)
Goodbye! Goodbye!
Goodbye for today!   (wave goodbye)

- Say goodbye to the children yourself and using the finger puppets. Say e.g. **Goodbye everyone. See you on …** Ask a few individual children to say goodbye to the finger puppets in turn.

9 Treasure!

Lesson 2
Language input and story

Aim:
- To understand and act out episode 9 of the story

Key language:
- *tree, flower, grass, rock, river, hill, bush, path, fence, gate, jump*
- *Where are you? I'm ...*
- *Are you in / on / under ...?*
- *Yes, I am. / No, I'm not.*

Materials:
- Pupil's Book page 71
- Activity Book page 69
- Finger puppets (Pip and Squeak)
- Flashcards: Alex, Katie, Frodo, tree, flower, grass, rock, river, hill, bush, path, fence, gate
- Treasure clue sticker for Unit 9
- CD 1 and CD 3

Starting out

Greetings and opening routine

- Greet the children yourself and using the finger puppets.
- Play the karaoke version of *I like English* (CD 1, track 11 – see Lesson 1). The children sing and do the actions as in Lesson 1.

Revision activity

- Hold up the flashcards in turn and the children say the words.
- Stick the flashcards in pairs on the board in the same order as each verse of the song *Where's the treasure?*
- Play the CD (CD 3, track 33 – see Lesson 1). The children sing the song, do the actions and point to the flashcards.
- Repeat with the karaoke version (CD 3, track 34).

Setting objectives

- Say **Today we're going to listen to and act out episode 9 of the story.**

On the learning trail

Listen and act out the story.
Episode 9: The end of the rainbow
(PB page 71)

Before the story (books closed)

- Hold up the finger puppets and stick the flashcards of Alex and Katie on the board. Recap on the last episode of the story using mime and gesture and / or L1 as necessary: **Alex, Katie, Pip and Squeak find the three goats. They must cross the bridge to get to the rainbow. The goats say that a hungry troll lives under the bridge. The troll lets Alex, Katie, Pip and Squeak cross the bridge because they are too small to eat. The big goat throws the troll off the bridge** (use gesture to convey meaning) **and gets the treasure clue**.

- Ask **Can you remember the clue from Unit 8?** Hold up page 63 of the Pupil's Book and point to the treasure clue sticker. Read *Follow the footprints! Find the treasure!* as a prompt if necessary.

- Ask the following questions in turn. Use mime and gesture to clarify meaning, and encourage the children to predict the answers: **1) Who appears? 2) How do Alex, Katie, Pip and Squeak get to the end of the rainbow? 3) Who is at the end of the rainbow?**

During the story (books open)

- Say **Now listen to the story and find out.** Explain to the children that they will hear a 'beep' noise on the CD to tell them when to move to the next picture in the story.

- Play the CD (CD 3, track 36) and the children follow in their books.

- Ask the questions in turn again and check the answers, recasting them in English as necessary. *(1 Frodo 2 They follow Frodo. 3 Pinocchio, Little Red Riding Hood, Jack, Hansel and Gretel, Aladdin, the three goats, Goldilocks and Baby Bear)*

- Say **Listen again and repeat the story.** Play the CD again. Pause after each sentence and the children repeat the story.

- **Note:** There is more story text on the CD than appears on the Pupil's Book page. This additional text is marked with an asterisk* in the audio script below. The children repeat the whole story, including the language which does not appear in their books.

Follow the footprints, Episode 9: The end of the rainbow

Picture 1

Narrator:	*Alex, Katie, Pip and Squeak follow the footprints to find the treasure.**
Frodo:	*Croak, croak! Hello!**
Squeak:	*Listen! It's Frodo!*
Pip:	*Are you in the river?*
Frodo:	*No, I'm not.**
Alex:	*Are you in the grass?**
Frodo:	*No, I'm not.**
Katie:	*Are you under the bush?**
Frodo:	*No, I'm not.**
Alex:	*Oh, where are you, Frodo?**

Picture 2

Frodo:	*I'm here! I'm on the rock!*

Picture 3

Frodo:	*Follow me! Let's go to the rainbow!*
Pip and Squeak:	*Yes! Let's find the treasure!*
Alex and Katie:	*Yes! Come on!**

Picture 4

Frodo:	*Let's jump ... along the path, past the river, the trees, the flowers, the grass, the rock and the bush to the rainbow!**

Picture 5

Pip:	*Wow! Here's the end of the rainbow!*

Picture 6

Squeak:	*Here's the treasure!*
Katie:	*And here are our friends!*
Alex:	*It's magic!**
Squeak:	*It's amazing!**
Story characters:	*Hurray!**

After the story

- Ask questions about each picture as follows:
  1) Who does Squeak hear? (use gesture to convey meaning) *(Frodo)* **Can they see Frodo?** *(no)* **Where do they look?** (use gesture to convey meaning) *(in the river, in the grass, under the bush)* **2) Where's Frodo?** *(on the rock)* **3) Frodo says *Let's go to the ...*** *(rainbow)*. **Pip and Squeak say *Let's find the ...*** *(treasure)*. **4) Frodo says *Let's ...*** (do the action to convey meaning) *(jump)* **to the rainbow. What do they pass on the way?** *(river, trees, flowers, grass, rock, bush)* **5) What do Pip and Squeak see? The end of the ...** *(rainbow)*. **6) What is at the end of the rainbow?** *(the treasure)* **And who is at the end of the rainbow?** *(Little Red Riding Hood, Jack, Pinocchio, Hansel and Gretel, Aladdin, the three goats, Goldilocks and Baby Bear)*

Put on the treasure clue sticker.

- Read the text on the side of the treasure casket. Say **Find the treasure clue sticker for Unit 9 and stick it here.** Demonstrate what you mean.
- The children look for the treasure clue sticker for Unit 9 and stick it in their books.

Act out the story.

- Divide the class into five groups and assign a role to each group: Alex, Katie, Pip, Squeak or Frodo. Give a finger puppet or character flashcard to one child in each group to hold up during the story.

- Follow the procedure for *Act out the story* on page 37 of the Teacher's Book (five children are needed to act out the story).

> **Option:** The children can act out their parts *either* with *or* without their books, depending on how confident and familiar they are with this episode. If you wish to make the activity more challenging, the children can act out the whole story by joining in their character's part as you replay the CD.

Read and colour. (AB page 69)

- Read the sentences. The children follow in their books and point to the things in the picture. Remind the children of the colours if necessary.

- Say **Now read and colour the pictures.**

- The children work individually and colour the pictures as instructed.

- Check the answers by asking individual children to hold up their books, point to something they've coloured in the picture and say the sentence.

   Key: trees – brown and green; flowers – purple and yellow; grass – green; river – blue; rock – black; bush – red

Read, write and listen. (AB page 69)

- Read the exchanges with Frodo, and the children say the missing words.

- The children work individually and complete the exchanges.

- Check the answers by listening to the CD (CD 3, track 37).

- The children act out the exchanges in pairs.

   Key: 1 river 2 grass 3 bush 4 rock

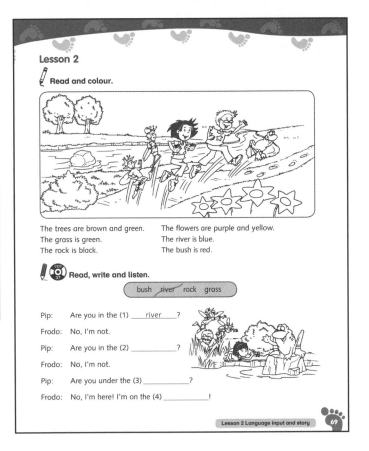

 Read, write and listen.

Pip: *Are you in the river?*
Frodo: *No, I'm not.*
Pip: *Are you in the grass?*
Frodo: *No, I'm not.*
Pip: *Are you under the bush?*
Frodo: *No, I'm here! I'm on the rock!*

Ending the lesson

Lesson review

- Briefly ask the children what they can do as a result of the lesson (understand and act out *The end of the rainbow*). Praise the children for their efforts and / or use the finger puppets to do this.

Goodbye and closing routine

- Say **Let's sing *Are you ready to finish?*** Play the karaoke version of the song (CD 1, track 13 – see Lesson 1). Hold up the finger puppets and the children sing and do the actions as in Lesson 1.

9 Treasure!

Lesson 3
Communication and grammar

Aim:
- To practise asking and saying where you are

Key language:
- *tree, flower, grass, rock, river, hill, bush, path, fence, gate*
- *Where are you? / I'm ...*
- *Are you in / on / under ...?*
- *Yes, I am. / No, I'm not.*

Materials:
- Pupil's Book pages 71 and 72
- Activity Book pages 70 and 95
- Finger puppets (Pip and Squeak)
- Flashcards: Alex, Katie, Frodo, tree, flower, grass, rock, river, hill, bush, path, fence, gate
- Word cards: tree, flower, grass, rock, river, hill, bush, path, fence, gate
- Scissors and stapler
- A prepared little book for Unit 9 (AB page 95)
- CD 1 and CD 3

Starting out

Greetings and opening routine

- Greet the children yourself and using the finger puppets.
- *Either* play the karaoke version of *I like English* (CD 1, track 11 – see Lesson 1) and the children sing and do the actions as in Lesson 1 *or* stick the flashcards on the board in pairs in the order of the song *Where's the treasure?* and play the karaoke version (CD 3, track 34 – see Lesson 1). The children point to the flashcards, sing the song and do the actions.

Revision activity

- Hold up the finger puppets and stick the character flashcards on the board. Ask **Can you remember who's in the story with Pip, Squeak, Alex and Katie?** *(Frodo, Little Red Riding Hood, Pinocchio, Jack, Hansel and Gretel, Aladdin, the three goats, Goldilocks and Baby Bear)*

- Ask the children to open their Pupil's Books at page 71. Briefly reconstruct the story, getting the children to supply key words. Say e.g. **Alex, Katie, Pip and Squeak find ...** *Frodo on a ... rock.* **Frodo says** *Let's go to the ... rainbow.* **Pip and Squeak say** *Let's find the ... treasure.* **Alex, Katie, Pip and Squeak follow Frodo past the ... river, trees, flowers, grass, rock, bush to the end of the ... rainbow. At the end of the rainbow is the ...** *treasure and their friends ... Little Red Riding Hood, Pinocchio, Jack, Hansel and Gretel, Aladdin, the three goats, Goldilocks and Baby Bear.*

- Play the CD (CD 3, track 36 – see Lesson 2). The children listen and follow the story in their books.

Setting objectives

- Say **Today we're going to practise asking and saying where you are.**

On the learning trail

Play a game. (PB page 72)

- Say **Look at the picture**. Ask questions, e.g. **Who's on the gate?** *(Jack and Little Red Riding Hood)* **Who's in the flowers?** *(Gretel and Baby Bear)* **Who's under the tree?** *(Hansel and Squeak)* and the children name the characters. Elicit or remind the children of the difference between *in*, *on* and *under* as you do this.

- Explain that you are going to secretly choose and pretend to be one of the characters. Get the children to ask in chorus *Where are you?* Reply e.g. **I'm under the tree.** Then get the children to ask you in chorus e.g. *Are you Hansel?* **(No, I'm not.)** *Are you Squeak?* **(Yes, I am.)**

- Repeat the game a few times in the same way.

- Once the children are asking and answering the questions confidently, play the game by getting individual children to ask you a question. The child who guesses correctly then has the next turn at secretly choosing and pretending to be one of the characters.

- Play the game several times with the whole class.

- Divide the class into pairs. The children play the game with their partner. They have three turns each.

Make the *My Little Footprints Book*. (PB page 72 and AB page 95)

- Hold up your Pupil's Book and point to the pictures. Say **We're going to make the *My Little Footprints Book* and play the game.**

- Hold up your Activity Book and say **Find page 95 in your Activity Book. Look at the *My Little Footprints Book*.** Say **Let's make the *My Little Footprints Book*** and show the children the book you have prepared (see page 87 of the Teacher's Book for instructions on how to make the little book).

- Say **Cut and fold the pages like this** and demonstrate what you mean. Point out the difference between the dashed lines (cutting lines) and the dotted lines (folding lines).

- Staple the children's books together as soon as they have folded the pages correctly. Then say **Now cut here** and demonstrate cutting along the dotted line at the top to separate the pages.

- Go through the little book page by page. Read the questions and answers and the children say the missing word on each page.

- Explain that the children should draw and colour the picture of themselves on each page and write the missing word. Either stick the word cards on the board for the children to copy or ask them to look at the *Follow the footprints* activity on page 70 of the Pupil's Book to do this.

- The children work individually to draw and colour the pictures of themselves and write the words on each page of their little books.

Play with the *My Little Footprints Book*. (PB page 72)

- Hold up your Pupil's Book and point to the pictures. Ask two pupils to read the first exchange and two other pupils to read the second exchange.

- Explain that you want the children to use their little books to play a guessing game with a partner.

- Demonstrate the game with one child. Get the child to open their little book at any page but not to let you see which one. Ask e.g. **Are you on the gate?** Get the child to respond *Yes, I am* or *No, I'm not* depending on the page they have opened. Demonstrate or explain that you have three chances to guess correctly before changing roles.

- Play the game several times with the whole class. Ask individual children to take turns to come to the front and open a page of their books.

231

Ask other children to ask questions, e.g. *Are you on the rock?*, and to have the next turn if they guess correctly.

- Divide the class into pairs. The children play the game with their partner.

Listen, number and say. (AB page 70)

- Say **Look at the pictures** and ask the children to tell you where the child is in each one, e.g. *under the tree / in the river.*
- Say **Now listen and number the pictures.** Draw the children's attention to the example.
- Play the CD (CD 3, track 38). Use the pause button to give the children time to number the pictures.
- Check the answers by saying the numbers and getting the children to say where the child is in each picture.
- Say **Now listen and repeat.** Play the CD again. The children listen and repeat the question and answer for each picture.

Key: picture 1: 6; picture 2: 2; picture 3: 4; picture 4: 1; picture 5: 3; picture 6: 5

 Listen, number and say.

1 Where are you? I'm on the gate.
2 Where are you? I'm in the river.
3 Where are you? I'm under the bush.
4 Where are you? I'm on the rock.
5 Where are you? I'm in the flowers.
6 Where are you? I'm under the tree.

Look and write. (AB page 70)

- Read the words at the top of the activity while the children follow in their books.
- Say **Look at the pictures.** Read the speech bubbles in turn and the children say the missing words.
- Say **Now write the words.** Draw the children's attention to the example.
- The children work individually and write the words.
- Check the answers by asking individual children to say one of the sentences.

Key: 1 grass 2 flowers 3 bush 4 hill

Ending the lesson

Lesson review

- Briefly ask the children what they can do as a result of the lesson (ask and say where they are). Praise the children for their efforts and / or use the finger puppets to do this.

Goodbye and closing routine

- Say goodbye to the children yourself and using the finger puppets. If there is time, you can also play the karaoke version of *Are you ready to finish?* (CD 1, track 13 – see Lesson 1) and the children sing and do the actions as in Lesson 1.

9 Treasure!

Lesson 4
Communication, grammar and pronunciation

Aims:
- To practise making and responding to suggestions
- To identify and say rhyming words

Key language:
- *Let's ... to the ...*
- *Yes. Good idea. / No.*
- *jump, skip, hop, run, walk*
- *tree, flower, grass, rock, river, hill, bush, path, fence, gate*

Materials:
- Pupil's Book page 73
- Activity Book page 71
- Finger puppets (Pip and Squeak)
- Flashcards: tree, flower, grass, rock, river, hill, bush, path, fence, gate, Frodo
- Unit 9 little books from Lesson 3
- CD 1 and CD 3

Starting out

Greetings and opening routine

- Greet the children yourself and using the finger puppets.
- *Either* play the karaoke version of *I like English* (CD 1, track 11 – see Lesson 1) and the children sing and do the actions as in Lesson 1 *or* stick the flashcards on the board in groups of three in the order of the song *Where's the treasure?* and play the karaoke version (CD 3, track 34 – see Lesson 1). The children point to the flashcards, sing the song and do the actions.

Revision activity

- Give out or ask the children to get out the little books they made in Lesson 3.
- Divide the class into pairs. Explain and demonstrate that the children should take turns to read their little books with their partner. The child looking at their partner's book should read the question *Where are you?* at the top of each page and the child whose book it is should read the answer. They should then change roles.
- The children take turns to read their *My Little Footprints Books* with their partner.

Setting objectives

- Say **Today we're going to practise making and responding to suggestions** (give an example, e.g. Frodo says *Let's go to the rainbow!*, to explain what you mean). **We're also going to practise pronunciation.**

On the learning trail

Listen and say the rhyme. (PB page 73)

- (Books closed) Stick the flashcards of the rock, the flower, the river, the gate and the tree in different places in the classroom. Get the children to name each one as you do this.

- Say **Stand up, please.** Say the action words in the rhyme in turn (*jump, skip, hop, run, walk*). Demonstrate doing the action for each one on the spot.

- Say **Listen to the rhyme. Turn and look at the pictures** (demonstrate turning to face the five flashcards) **and do the actions!** Play the CD (CD 3 track 39). The children listen to the rhyme, turn to face the flashcards, gesture for *Follow me* and do the actions on the spot for each verse.

- Repeat once.

- Ask the children to open their Pupil's Books at page 73. Play the CD again. The children say the rhyme and point to the pictures in their books.

 Follow me

*Follow, follow, follow me
Let's jump to the rock
One, two, three!*

*Let's skip to the flowers …
Let's hop to the river …
Let's run to the gate …
Let's walk to the tree …*

Play a game. (PB page 73)

- Stick the remaining flashcards (i.e. grass, path, hill, fence, bush) in different places in the classroom. Get the children to name each one as you do this.

- Hold up the finger puppets, one on each hand. Explain and demonstrate that if Pip makes a suggestion, e.g. *Let's hop to the tree!*, the children should say *Yes! Good idea!*, repeat the suggestion and start hopping on the spot in the direction of the flashcard of the tree. If Squeak makes a suggestion, e.g. *Let's walk to the path!*, the children should say *No!* One child should then make an alternative suggestion, changing one of the words Squeak says. For example, in this case the child could say *Let's run to the path!* or *Let's walk to the hill!*

- Play the game by holding both finger puppets behind your back. Say e.g. **Let's run to the bush … says Pip!** Hold up the finger puppet suddenly from behind your back as you say the puppet's name and the children respond. Make more suggestions with Pip than with Squeak in the initial stage of the game. Once the children are repeating the suggestions confidently, make more suggestions with Squeak and ask individual children to take turns to make alternative suggestions each time.

Listen and say: Frodo's word fun. (PB page 73)

- Read the words in the speech bubble. Use L1 to explain that *tree, three* and *me* rhyme. In other words, they end in the same sound. If you like, give a few examples of words which rhyme in L1 to illustrate the concept of rhyme.

- Hold up the flashcard of Frodo. Say **Listen to Frodo. Say the words which rhyme.** Play the CD (CD 3, track 41). Use the pause button after each set of words. Ask the children to say the words which rhyme. They then listen and check their answers before continuing.

- Play the CD again. The children listen and repeat the words which rhyme.

 Frodo's word fun. Listen and say.

1 *tree / me / skip / three
   tree / me / three*

2 *gate / grass / eight / late
   gate / eight / late*

3 *run / one / green / fun
   run / one / fun*

4 *mat / hop / cat / hat
   mat / cat / hat*

Read and match. (AB page 71)

- Read the words and the children point to the appropriate pictures.

- Say **Now match the words and pictures.** Draw the children's attention to the example.

- The children work individually. They match the words and pictures.

- Check the answers by getting individual children to say a word, point to the correct picture and demonstrate the action.

Key: Children match the sentences and pictures.
1 skip 2 hop 3 jump 4 run 5 walk

Look, write and say. (AB page 71)

- Read the exchanges and the children say the missing words.
- Say **Now write the words.** Draw their attention to the example.
- The children work individually and complete the exchanges.
- Check the answers by asking individual children to take turns to read one of the exchanges.
- The children practise saying the exchanges in pairs.

Key: 1 tree 2 gate 3 Let's, flowers 4 Let's, fence 5 Let's, river

Ending the lesson

Lesson review

- Briefly ask the children what they can do as a result of the lesson (make and respond to suggestions, recognise and say words which rhyme). Praise the children for their efforts and / or use the finger puppets to do this.

Goodbye and closing routine

- Say goodbye to the children yourself and using the finger puppets. If there is time, you can also play the karaoke version of *Are you ready to finish?* (CD 1, track 13 – see Lesson 1) and the children sing and do the actions as in Lesson 1.

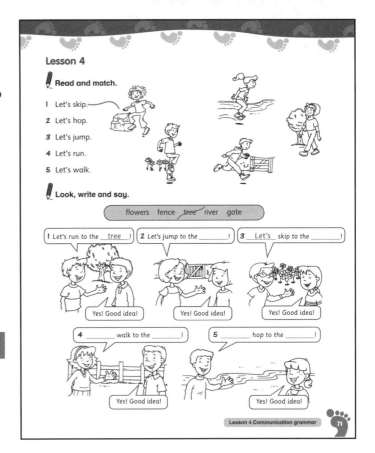

9 Treasure!

Lesson 5
Content input

Aims:
- To read and understand that we recycle some rubbish
- To identify materials that we recycle

Key language:
- *rubbish, paper, plastic, glass, tin can(s)*
- *This is ...*
- *Put it in the ... bin!*
- *blue, yellow, green, red*
- *recycle, throw away*

Materials:
- Pupil's Book page 74
- Activity Book page 72
- Finger puppets (Pip and Squeak)
- Flashcards: tree, flower, grass, rock, river, hill, bush, path, fence, gate
- CD 1 and CD 3
- *Either* examples of paper, glass, tin cans and plastic to recycle *or* old magazine photos of these (optional)

Starting out

Greetings and opening routine

- Greet the children yourself and using the finger puppets.
- *Either* play the karaoke version of *I like English* (CD 1, track 11 – see Lesson 1) and the children sing and do the actions as in Lesson 1 *or* divide the class into two groups, play *Follow me* (CD 3, track 39 – see Lesson 4), hold up the flashcards and the children say alternate verses of the rhyme and do the actions with their group.
- Repeat with the karaoke version of *Follow me* (CD 3, track 40).

Revision activity

- Stick the flashcards in different places in the classroom. Get the children to say the words as you do this.

- Make a suggestion, e.g. **Let's run to the flowers!** Explain and demonstrate that if you have your hand on your chin, the children should agree and say *Yes! Good idea! Let's run to the flowers!* and run on the spot in the direction of the flower flashcard. If you have your arms folded, the children should say *No!* and you then ask a child to make an alternative suggestion, changing one word, e.g. *Let's skip to the flowers!* or *Let's run to the tree!* If you like, introduce a scoring system and turn the activity into a game. If the children respond correctly, they score a point, and if not, you score a point. Add up the points at the end of the game (making sure that the children win!).

Setting objectives

- Hold up the finger puppets. Say **Let's learn about the world around you! Today we're going to read about recycling.** Use English or L1 to explain that *recycling* means using things we throw away (rubbish) to create a new product.

On the learning trail

Read, match and listen. (PB page 74)

- (Books closed) Read the question **What do we recycle?**
- Listen to the children's ideas (in L1). Use their suggestions to introduce or remind them of vocabulary, e.g. *paper, glass, tin cans, plastic, bin, rubbish*. Show the children examples of paper, glass, tin cans and plastic to recycle or old magazine photos if you have these.
- Ask the children to open their Pupil's Books at page 74. Read the text at the start of the activity or play part 1 on the CD (CD 3, track 42).
- Ask a question to check comprehension and clarify meaning, e.g. **What do we throw away?** (use gesture to clarify meaning) *(rubbish)* **Do we use some rubbish again?** *(yes)* **What do we call this?** *(recycling)* **What do we recycle?** *(paper, glass, tin cans, plastic)*
- Read the labels on the four recycling bins. Say **Look at the photos of things to recycle.** Read the sentences and the children identify the correct bin for each one.
- Say **Circle the correct word and match the photos to the correct bins.** Draw the children's attention to the example.

- The children work individually. They circle the words and match the photos and bins.
- Say **Now listen and check your answers.** Play the CD (CD 3, track 42). Use the pause button to allow the children time to check their answers.
- Check the answers by saying e.g. **Number one. This is …** *(paper)*. **Where do we put it? In the …** *(blue bin)*.
- Play the CD again as a final check.

  Key: 1 paper: blue bin 2 plastic: red bin
  3 paper: blue bin 4 glass: green bin
  5 a tin can: yellow bin

 Read, match and listen.

Part 1

We throw away a lot of rubbish.
We recycle some rubbish.
We recycle paper and glass.
We also recycle plastic and tin cans.

Part 2

1 This is paper. Put it in the blue bin!
2 This is plastic. Put it in the red bin!
3 This is paper. Put it in the blue bin!
4 This is glass. Put it in the green bin!
5 This is a tin can. Put it in the yellow bin!

Play a game. (PB page 74)

- Use examples of paper, glass, tin cans and plastic or old magazine photos to play the game, if you have them available. Alternatively, use objects available in the classroom.
- Explain and demonstrate that you are going to show the children objects or photos in turn and say **This is paper / glass / plastic / a tin can.** The children should say *Put it in the … bin!* and name the colour of the bin where it should go to be recycled. Explain that if the children respond correctly, they score a point, and if not, you score a point.

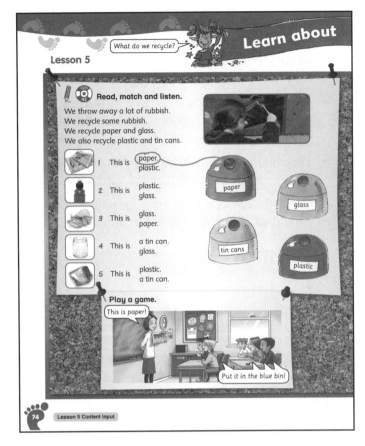

- Start the game and go slowly at first, getting the children to repeat the responses in chorus. Keep a score of the points on the board. Stop the game once the children are responding easily, and add up the scores (making sure that the children win!).

Read, match and say. (AB page 72)

- Read the sentences and the children point to the pictures.
- Say **Now match the sentences and pictures.** Draw the children's attention to the example.
- The children work individually and match the sentences and pictures.
- Check the answers by asking individual children to take turns to read a sentence and point to the appropriate picture.

  Key: Children match the sentences and pictures.
  1 This is paper. 2 This is glass. 3 This is a tin can.
  4 This is paper. 5 This is plastic.

Draw, colour and say. (AB page 72)

- Say **Look at the pictures.** Ask the children to say whether the objects at the top of the activity are *paper*, *glass*, *plastic* or *a tin can*.

- Read the labels on the bins. Say **Now draw the pictures in the correct bins. Colour the bins.** Draw the children's attention to the example.

- The children work individually and draw the pictures in the bins and then colour the bins.

- Check the answers by saying e.g. **paper** and individual children respond *Put it in the blue bin!*

    Key: 1 paper bin (blue): comic and paper
    2 tin can bin (yellow): tuna can
    3 glass bin (green): jar
    4 plastic bin (red): plastic bottle

Ending the lesson

Lesson review

- Briefly ask the children what they can do as a result of the lesson (read and understand that we recycle some rubbish, identify materials that we recycle). Praise the children for their efforts and / or use the finger puppets to do this.

Goodbye and closing routine

- Say goodbye to the children yourself and using the finger puppets. If there is time, you can also play the karaoke version of *Are you ready to finish?* (CD 1, track 13 – see Lesson 1) and the children sing and do the actions as in Lesson 1.

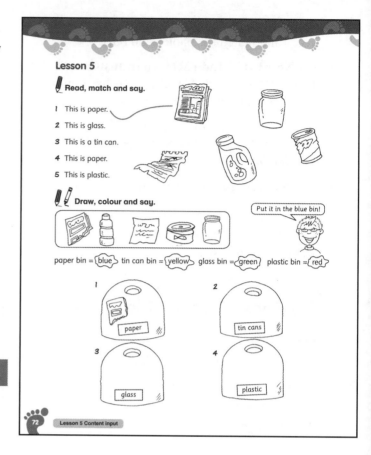

9 Treasure!

Lesson 6
Content and personalisation

Aims:
- To say what you and your family recycle
- To count and sort things to recycle

Key language:
- *We put ... in the ... bin.*
- *paper, glass, plastic, tin cans*
- *blue, yellow, green, red*
- numbers 1–20

Materials:
- Pupil's Book page 75
- Activity Book page 73
- Finger puppets (Pip and Squeak)
- Flashcards: tree, flower, grass, rock, hill, bush, path, fence, gate
- CD 1 and CD 3

Starting out

Greetings and opening routine

- Greet the children yourself and using the finger puppets.
- *Either* play the karaoke version of *I like English* (CD 1, track 11 – see Lesson 1) and the children sing and do the actions as in Lesson 1 *or* divide the class into two groups, play the karaoke version of *Follow me!* (CD 3, track 40 – see Lesson 4), hold up the flashcards and the children say alternate verses of the rhyme and do the actions with their group.

Revision activity

- Recap on Lesson 5 by asking the children **What do we recycle?** *(paper, plastic, glass, tin cans)*
- Say true / false sentences based on the text on page 74 of the Pupil's Book, e.g. **We recycle paper / We don't recycle glass.** The children respond *Yes* or *No* depending on whether the sentences are true or false.

Setting objectives

- Say **In this lesson we're going to talk about what we recycle.** Use L1 to clarify what you mean if necessary.

On the learning trail

Listen and number. (PB page 75)

- Say **Look at the pictures. Listen to Alex saying what he and his family recycle. Listen and number the pictures.** Draw the children's attention to the example.
- Play the CD (CD 3, track 43). Use the pause button, if necessary, to give the children time to number the pictures.
- Check the answers by getting the children to point to the pictures they have numbered in order.
- Say **Now listen and repeat what Alex says.** Play the CD again. The children listen and repeat the sentence for each picture. If you like, remind the children that we use *we* when we're talking about ourselves and other people such as our family.

Key: green bin 2; blue bin 3; yellow bin 4; red bin 1

 Listen and number.

1 We put plastic in the red bin.
2 We put glass in the green bin.

3 We put paper in the blue bin.
4 We put tin cans in the yellow bin.

Draw and say. (PB page 75)

- Say **Look at Katie's picture and read what her mother says**.

- Say **Now draw and colour a picture of what you and your family recycle.** Explain and demonstrate that the children should draw a picture of themselves and what they are putting in the bin. They should then colour the bin the corresponding colour. They can look at the previous activity (*Listen and number*) to check the right colour for the bin.

- When they are ready, ask individual children to take turns to show their picture and tell the class, e.g. *We put glass in the green bin.*

- **Note:** If the colours of recycling bins are different where the children live, then you may like to explain this and get them to use the relevant colours for their local area in this activity.

Colour, count and write. (AB page 73)

- Say **Look at the paper, glass, tin cans and plastic. Let's count the pictures!** Get the children to point first to all the pictures of paper, then glass, tin cans and plastic and to count the objects with you in chorus.

- Read the key at the top of the activity.

- Say **Now colour the pictures. Count how many of each one again to check we are right! Write the number in the box.** Draw the children's attention to the example.

- The children work individually. They colour the pictures and write the numbers in the boxes.

- Check the answers by asking the children to compare and count the items in pairs and then tell the class.

    Key: glass 12; tin cans 9; plastic 10; paper 13

Read, write and tick (✓). (AB page 73)

- Read the words at the top of the activity.

- Read the question and sentences and the children say the missing words.

- Say **Now write the words and tick.** Draw the children's attention to the example.

- The children work individually. They look at the picture and complete the sentences. They tick the ones that are true for them and their families.

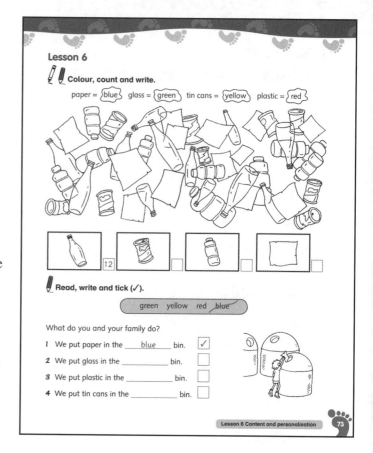

- Ask children to take turns to say a sentence.

    Key: 1 blue 2 green 3 red 4 yellow

Option: If you have previously introduced diferent colours of recycling bins because of where the children live, then the children can complete the sentences with these colours instead of the ones in the book.

Ending the lesson

Lesson review

- Briefly ask the children what they can do as a result of the lesson (count and sort things to recycle, say what they and their family recycle). Praise the children for their efforts and / or use the finger puppets to do this.

Goodbye and closing routine

- Say goodbye to the children yourself and using the finger puppets. If there is time, you can also play the karaoke version of *Are you ready to finish?* (CD 1, track 13 – see Lesson 1) and the children sing and do the actions as in Lesson 1.

9 Treasure!

Lesson 7
Children's culture

Aim:
- To sing a version of a well-known song and play a version of a traditional game

Key language:
- *happy, clap, skip, jump, hop*
- *window, door, board, clock*
- *know, show, three times*
- *Let's ... to the ...!*

Materials:
- Pupil's Book page 76
- Activity Book page 74
- Finger puppets (Pip and Squeak)
- Flashcards: tree, flower, grass, rock, river, hill, bush, path, fence, gate, Frodo
- CD 1 and CD 3
- Leader's cap (can be either real hat or paper hat) (optional)

Starting out

Greetings and opening routine

- Greet the children yourself and using the finger puppets.
- *Either* play the karaoke version of *I like English* (CD 1, track 11 – see Lesson 1) and the children sing and do the actions as in Lesson 1 *or* divide the class into two groups, play the karaoke version of *Follow me!* (CD 3, track 40 – see Lesson 4), hold up flashcards and the children say alternate verses of the rhyme and do the actions with their group.

Revision activity

- Draw four simple pictures of recycling bins on the board. Either label or colour them blue (paper), green (glass), red (plastic) or yellow (tin cans).
- Say true / false sentences in random order, e.g. **I put paper in the blue bin. / I put tin cans in the green bin.** The children repeat the sentences and say e.g. *I put paper in the blue bin, too!* if you name the correct bin or *No! I put tin cans in the yellow bin* if you name the incorrect bin. Each time the children respond correctly, put a tick in the corresponding bin. At the end, count up the number of ticks the children have scored for each bin.

Setting objectives

- Hold up the flashcard of Frodo. Say **In this lesson we're going to learn about children's culture with Frodo. We're going to sing a version of a well-known song and play a version of a traditional game.**

On the learning trail

Listen and sing the song. (PB page 76) (books closed)

- Say **This song is about what you do if you're happy.** Ask the children what actions they do if they're happy and listen to their responses in English or L1.
- Say **Stand up, please. Listen and do the actions in the song.** Play the CD (CD 3, track 44). The children listen to the song and do the actions.
- At the end, ask the children to name the actions in the song (*clap, jump, skip, hop*). Compare these with their responses at the start of the activity.

- Play the CD again. The children do the actions and join in singing the song.
- Ask the children to open their Pupil's Books at page 76. Play the CD (CD 3, track 44) while the children follow in their books, point to the pictures and sing the song.

 If you're happy

If you're happy and you know it, clap three times
If you're happy and you know it, clap three times
If you're happy and you know it, and you really want to show it
If you're happy and you know it, clap three times!

If you're happy and you know it, jump three times
…
If you're happy and you know it, skip three times
…
If you're happy and you know it, hop three times
…

 Citizenship box: Remember!

Smile at the children and say e.g. **I can think of a reason for you to be happy!** and encourage the children to guess what it is.

Hold up the flashcard of Frodo, read the *Remember!* note and clarify the meaning. Point out to the children that they are almost at the end of *Footprints 1* and praise them for how hard they have worked and how much English they now know.

Play *Follow my leader!* (PB page 76)

- *Either* stick the flashcards for Unit 9 on different walls around the classroom *or* play the game using familiar classroom furniture *or* use a mixture of real furniture in the classroom and the flashcards. Review the words for the classroom furniture.
- Put on the leader's cap (either real or paper hat) for the game if you have one. If not, you can simply mime an imaginary hat.
- Ask the children to stand in a line behind you. If you have a large class, you may prefer to ask six to ten children to play the game at a time rather than the whole class together. Explain and demonstrate that the children should have about half a metre between each other in the line and that they mustn't touch anyone else during the game.
- Say e.g. **Let's jump to the window!** Demonstrate this and get the children to jump behind you in a line. Then take the leader's cap off (or mime taking off an imaginary hat) and put it on the child behind you.
- Explain and demonstrate that the child with the cap is now the leader and should suggest an action, e.g. *Let's walk to the door!* After doing the action the child puts the leader's cap on the child next to them (or mimes doing this) and goes to the back of the line. The game continues in the same way until all the children in the line have had a turn being the leader.

Option: If it's not possible for the children to move about the classroom in a line, you can play the game in the following way instead. Put on the leader's cap and ask one child to come and stand with you. Suggest and do an action with the child and then give them the leader's cap. The child puts on the cap and names another child to come and stand with them. They do an action. The game continues in the same way until e.g. six to ten children have had a turn. If you like, you can get the rest of the class to clap and say *Great!* or *Fantastic!* as the children take turns to make suggestions and do the actions correctly.

Read and match. (AB page 74)

- Read the instructions and the children point to the corresponding pictures.
- Say **Now match the sentences and pictures.** Draw the children's attention to the example.
- Check the answers by asking individual children to read a sentence and point to the corresponding picture in their book.

Key: Children match the sentences and pictures.
1 Skip … 2 Jump … 3 Clap … 4 Hop …

Look, write and say. (AB page 74)

- Say **Look at the children playing** *Follow my leader!* Read what the leader says in each picture and the children say the missing words.
- Say **Now write the words** and draw their attention to the example.
- The children work individually and write the words.
- Check the answers by asking individual children to say what the leader says in each speech bubble.
- Divide the class into pairs. The children take turns to be the leader and do the actions with their partner.

Key: 1 window 2 door 3 board 4 clock

Ending the lesson

Lesson review

- Briefly ask the children what they can do as a result of the lesson (sing *If you're happy*, play *Follow my leader!*). Praise the children for their efforts and / or use the finger puppets to do this.

Goodbye and closing routine

- Say goodbye to the children yourself and using the finger puppets. If there is time, you can also play the karaoke version of *Are you ready to finish?* (CD 1, track 13 – see Lesson 1) and the children sing and do the actions as in Lesson 1.

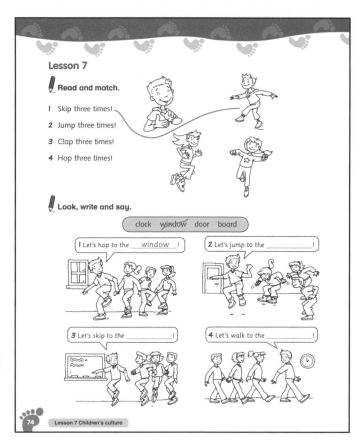

9 Treasure!

Lesson 8
Unit review / All About Me Portfolio Booklet

Aim:
- To review learning in Unit 9

Key language:
- *tree, flower, grass, rock, river, hill, bush, path, fence, gate*
- *Where are you? I'm ...*
- *Are you in / on / under ...?*
- *Yes, I am. / No, I'm not.*
- *Let's ... to the ...!*
- *skip, hop, jump, run, walk*

Materials:
- Pupil's Book page 77
- Activity Book page 75
- *All About Me* Portfolio Booklet pages 22 and 23
- Finger puppets (Pip and Squeak)
- Flashcards: tree, flower, grass, rock, river, hill, bush, path, fence, gate, Frodo
- Word cards: tree, flower, grass, rock, river, hill, bush, path, fence, gate
- Stickers for Unit 8
- CD 1 and CD 3

Starting out

Greetings and opening routine

- Greet the children yourself and using the finger puppets.
- *Either* play the karaoke version of *I like English* (CD 1, track 11 – see Lesson 1) and the children sing and do the actions as in Lesson 1 *or* stick the flashcards on the board in the order of the song *Where's the treasure?* (CD 3, track 33 – see Lesson 1) and the children sing the song, do the actions and point to the flashcards.

Revision activity

- Divide the class into two groups (one for each alternate verse of the song *If you're happy*). Play the CD (CD 3, track 44 – see Lesson 7). The children take turns to stand up and sing their verse and do the actions with their group.
- *Either* change roles and play the CD again *or* play the karaoke version (CD 3, track 45 – see Lesson 7) and the children sing the same verses again.

Setting objectives

- Say **Today we're going to review what we've learnt in Unit 9.**

On the learning trail

Listen and put on the stickers. Write the words. (PB page 77)

- Make sure the children have the stickers for Unit 9 ready.
- Say **Listen and put on the stickers.** Draw the children's attention to the example.
- Play the CD (CD 3, track 46). Use the pause button to give the children time to put on the stickers.

- Say **Now write the words.** Draw the children's attention to the example.
- Check the answers by saying the numbers and getting the children to say the words.

  Key: 1 tree 2 flowers 3 hill 4 river 5 path 6 bush 7 grass 8 fence 9 rock 10 gate

 Listen and put on the stickers.

1 Where are you? I'm under the tree.
2 Where are you? I'm in the flowers.
3 Where are you? I'm on the hill.
4 Are you in the river? Yes, I am.
5 Are you on the path? Yes, I am.
6 Are you under the bush? Yes, I am.
7 Let's walk to the grass! Yes! Good idea!
8 Let's jump to the fence! Yes! Good idea.
9 Let's run to the rock! Yes! Good idea!
10 Let's hop to the gate! Yes! Good idea!

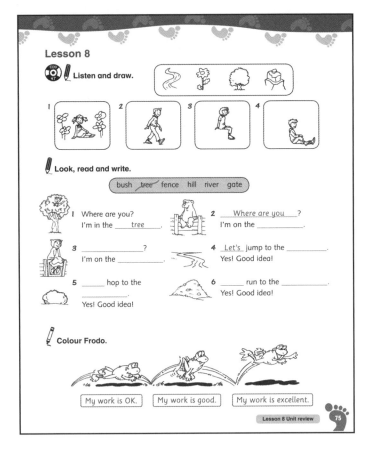

Look, write and say. (PB page 77)

- Read the exchanges and the children say the missing words.
- Say **Now write the words.** Draw the children's attention to the example.
- The children work individually and write the missing words.
- Check the answers by asking individual children to read one of the exchanges.

  Key: 1 grass 2 gate 3 hill 4 rock 5 flowers 6 bush

Listen and draw. (AB page 75)

- Say **Listen and draw where the children are.** Draw the children's attention to the example.
- Play the CD (CD 3, track 47). Pause, if necessary, to give the children time to complete the pictures.
- Check the answers by asking e.g. **What does the child in picture one say?** and the children repeat the replies.

  Key: 1 in the flowers 2 on the path 3 on the rock 4 under the tree

 Listen and draw.

1 Where are you? I'm in the flowers.
2 Where are you? I'm on the path.
3 Where are you? I'm on the rock.
4 Where are you? I'm under the tree.

Look, read and write. (AB page 75)

- Read the exchanges and the children say the missing words.
- Say **Write the words** and draw the children's attention to the example.
- The children work individually and complete the exchanges.
- Check the answers by asking individual children to read one of the exchanges.

  Key: 1 tree 2 fence 3 Where are you?, gate 4 river 5 Let's, bush 6 Let's, hill

Colour Frodo. (AB page 75)

- Hold up the flashcard of Frodo. Remind the children that in this activity they assess their work in the unit by choosing and colouring the picture of Frodo which corresponds best to how they think they have done.

- Remind the children of the key by pointing to the three pictures of Frodo and saying **Colour this picture if your work is OK but you think you need to try harder or need more practice. Colour this picture of Frodo if you think your work is good. Colour this picture of Frodo with a big smile and jumping very high if you think your work is excellent.** Make sure the children understand that there are no right answers and that it is their own opinion of the work they have done which is important. Be ready to encourage the children to have a positive view if they are too hard on themselves.

Ending the lesson

Lesson review

- Briefly ask the children what they can do as a result of the lesson (use the language and vocabulary they've learnt in Unit 9). Praise the children for their efforts and / or use the finger puppets to do this.

- Congratulate the children on finishing Level 1 of *Footprints* and make or add to positive comments you made previously (in Lesson 7) about how hard they have worked and how much they have learnt during the course.

> **Option:** If you like, you can also present the children individually with a personalised, signed and dated copy of the *Footprints 1* Achievement Certificate (see page 265). You can do this *either* as part of the lesson *or* during a special ceremony to which you also invite the children's parents and families.

Goodbye and closing routine

- Say goodbye to the children yourself and using the finger puppets. If there is time, you can also play the karaoke version of *Are you ready to finish?* (CD 1, track 13 – see Lesson 1) and the children sing and do the actions as in Lesson 1.

> ***All About Me*** **Portfolio Booklet**
>
> The children complete Unit 9 of their personal *All About Me* Portfolio Booklets. They complete their learning journey by colouring the sections on the path to show what they can do. If you like, the children can also sign this page and you can endorse this by adding your own signature and the date.

Christmas

Structures and grammar

- ... *has got* ...
- *I like / don't like* ...
- *What* ...!
- *We love you!*
- *Please help me!*
- Recycled: ... *happy / sad*

Vocabulary

- Core: *Christmas, Santa, reindeer, sleigh, short, antlers*
- Recycled: *yellow, happy, sad, present*

Main receptive language

- *Christmas Eve, guide, children*

Communicative competence

Understanding

Listening:
- Can understand a Christmas story

Reading:
- Can read key sentences in the story

Speaking

Spoken interaction
- Can answer questions about the story

Spoken production
- Can act out the story
- Can sing the song *Jingle bells*
- Can sing the *Goodbye song*

Content links

- *Art and craft:* cut-out story book

Learning strategies and thinking skills

- Predicting and hypothesising what happens in a story
- Associating pictures and language patterns
- Using actions to memorise a song

Children's culture

- Listening to a story about a Christmas reindeer
- Singing a version of a well-known Christmas song: *Jingle bells*

Values and attitudes

- Pleasure in celebrating Christmas
- Enjoyment in a Christmas story and song
- Awareness that it's wrong to mock or laugh at others

Christmas

Aims:

- To listen to and act out a Christmas story
- To sing a Christmas song
- To make a Christmas cut-out

Key language:

- *Christmas, Santa, reindeer, sleigh, short, yellow, antlers*
- *… is happy / sad.*
- *I like … / don't like …*
- *… has got …*
- *We love you.*
- *Please help me!*
- *Happy Christmas!*

Materials:

- Pupil's Book page 78
- Finger puppets (Pip and Squeak)
- CD 1 and CD 3
- Flashcards: Santa, sleigh and reindeer
- Photocopies of Christmas cut-out (see page 261), one for each child (optional)
- Coloured card to make book cover, stapler or hole puncher, pieces of wool, glitter, glue, scissors (optional)
- A prepared *Rosa's story* book (optional)

Starting out

Greetings and opening routine

- Greet the children yourself and using the finger puppets. Make the finger puppets dance about and say **Pip and Squeak are very happy. Why are they happy, do you think?** Listen to the children's guesses and then say e.g. **Pip and Squeak are happy because soon it's Christmas!** Check that the children understand the meaning of *Christmas*.

Setting objectives

- Say **Today we're going to do activities to celebrate Christmas in English. We're also going to listen to a Christmas story and we're going to sing a Christmas song. (We're also going to make a Christmas cut-out.)**

Option: If the children don't celebrate Christmas themselves, you may like to say **In many countries, people celebrate a festival called Christmas. We're going to learn about the festival by listening to a Christmas story and singing a Christmas song.**

On the learning trail

Listen and act out the story. 'Rosa's story' (PB page 78)

Before the story (books closed)

- Introduce or revise the vocabulary by holding up the flashcards in turn, pointing to the pictures and asking the children **Who brings presents for children at Christmas?** *(Santa)* **How does he bring them? On a …** *(sleigh)* **Who pulls the sleigh?** *(reindeer)*

- Say **We're going to listen to a story about one of Santa's reindeers called Rosa.**
- Ask the following questions in turn. Use mime to clarify meaning, and encourage the children to predict the answers: **1) Why is Rosa sad? 2) Why is Rosa happy?**

During the story (books open)

- Say **Now listen to the story and find out.** Explain to the children that they will hear a 'beep' noise on the CD to tell them when to move to the next picture in the story.
- Play the CD (CD 3, track 48) and the children follow in their books.
- Ask the questions again and check the answers, recasting them in English and using mime and gesture to clarify meaning as necessary.
(1 Rosa's antlers are short and yellow; the other reindeers don't want to play with her. 2 Rosa helps Santa; her antlers guide the sleigh.)
- Say **Listen again and repeat the story.** Play the CD again. Pause after each sentence and the children repeat the story.
- **Note:** There is more story text on the CD than appears on the PB page. This additional text is marked with an asterisk* in the audio script below. The children repeat the whole story, including the language which does not appear in their books.

 Rosa's story

Picture 1	
Narrator:	*Rosa is a reindeer. Rosa has got short, yellow antlers.**
Rosa:	*Oh, I don't like my short, yellow antlers!**

Picture 2	
Reindeer 1:	*Ha! Ha! What short, yellow antlers!*
Reindeer 2:	*You can't play with us!**
Narrator:	*Rosa is very sad.**

Picture 3	
Narrator:	*It's Christmas Eve and Santa's here.**
Santa:	*Please help me, Rosa! Your antlers can guide my sleigh!**
Rosa:	*Oh, yes!*
Narrator:	*Rosa is very happy.**

Picture 4	
Reindeer 1:	*Hurray!*
Reindeer 2:	*We love you, Rosa!*
Santa:	*Thank you, Rosa! Now the children can get their Christmas presents!**
Rosa:	*Oh, I like my short, yellow antlers now!**

After the story

- Ask questions about each picture as follows:
1) What colour are Rosa's antlers? *(yellow)* **Are they short?** *(yes)* **2) Do the reindeer want to play with Rosa?** *(no)* **Is Rosa happy?** *(No, she's sad.)* **3) Who's here?** *(Santa)* **What does Santa ask Rosa to do? Help guide the ...** *(sleigh)* **with her short, yellow ...** *(antlers).* **Is Rosa sad now?** *(No, she's happy.)* **4) Do the reindeer love Rosa now?** *(yes)* **Does Rosa like her short, yellow antlers now?** *(yes)*

Act out the story.

- Divide the class into five groups and assign a role to each group: Narrator, Rosa, Santa, Reindeer 1, Reindeer 2. Read the story or play the CD again. Point to or stand by each group and join in miming and saying their part with them every time their character speaks.
- Ask five confident children to come to the front of the class (one from each group). The children act out the story to the rest of the class. Either play the CD again or prompt them by reading the story and encouraging them to join in saying their parts with you as they do this. Encourage everyone to clap and say e.g. *Fantastic!* at the end.

Listen, sing and colour. (PB page 78)

- Say **Let's listen to a song about Rosa and Santa's sleigh!** Play the CD (CD 3, track 49) while the children follow in their books. Clarify that Rosa's antlers are so yellow that you can see a light from them in the dark. This is why she can guide Santa's sleigh!
- Say **Stand up please! Let's do actions and sing the song!** Play the CD again. The children join in doing the actions (see audio script below) and singing the song.
- Repeat once or twice. If you like, pause the CD before the last word in each line. The children supply the word and do the action before continuing.

- Say **Now colour the picture of Rosa. What colour is Rosa?** *(brown)* **And what colour are her antlers?** *(yellow)*

- The children work individually and colour the picture of Rosa. If you like, play the karaoke version of the song (CD 3, track 50) and the children sing softly as they do this.

Jingle bells

Jingle bells, jingle bells
                (make fist in front of you like bells)
Jingle all the way
                (make antlers with your hands)
We all love the reindeer
Who pulls Santa's sleigh!

Make the Christmas cut-out (TB page 261) (optional)

- Say **We're going to make a book of Rosa's story** and show the children the cut-out you have prepared.

- Give out copies of the cut-out and say **Cut out the book. Fold the paper in half along the horizontal dotted line. Then fold it in half along the vertical dotted line to make up the book.**

- When the children are ready, say **Now cut out the speech bubbles like this. Stick them on the correct pages in your book** and demonstrate what you mean.

- The children work individually and stick the speech bubbles on the correct pages in their books. If you like, ask the children to look at the story in the Pupil's Book to check that they are doing this correctly.

- Say **Let's listen to the story again. Follow in your books.** Play the CD of the story again.

- If you have coloured card available, give a sheet folded in half to each child.

- Say **Let's make a cover for Rosa's story. Write *Rosa's story by ...* and your name on the front and draw a picture.** Write this on the board for the children to copy.

- The children work individually to prepare their book covers. These can be attached to the folded story pages either by two staples or by punching two holes and threading through and loosely tying a piece of wool. If you like, the book covers can be decorated with glitter and the children can also colour the story pages. They can then take their books home to show and / or give to their parents as a Christmas present.

Ending the lesson

Lesson review

- Briefly ask the children what they can do as a result of the lesson (act out *Rosa's story*, sing the song *Jingle bells*, make a book of the story – optional). Praise the children for their efforts and / or use the finger puppets to do this.

Goodbye and closing routine

- Say **Let's sing the *Goodbye song*.** Play the CD (CD 1, track 4 – see Unit 1, Lesson 1). Hold up the finger puppets on your index fingers as the children sing and do the actions.

- Say **Happy Christmas!** to the children yourself and using the finger puppets and encourage them to say this to you, the puppets and each other. Then say e.g. **Goodbye everyone. See you on ...** as usual.

Easter

Structures and grammar

- *go ...*
- *finds ...*
- Recycled: *It's ...*

Vocabulary

- Core: *Easter, rabbit, egg, little, hunt, eat, run away*
- Recycled: *big, play,* colours, numbers 1–5

Communicative competence

Understanding

Listening:
- Can understand an Easter song
- Can identify numbers and colours

Reading:
- Can read numbers and colour words

Speaking

Spoken interaction:
- Can answer questions about the colour of Easter eggs

Spoken production:
- Can sing the song *Five little rabbits go out to play*
- Can sing the song *Shake your head*

Content links

- *Art and craft:* counting cut-out

Learning strategies and thinking skills

- Identifying key words in a rhyme
- Using rhythm and repetition to memorise language patterns in a rhyme
- Associating counting with manipulating a cut-out

Children's culture

- Singing an Easter song: *Five little rabbits go out to play*
- Identifying coloured eggs in an Easter egg hunt

Values and attitudes

- Pleasure in celebrating Easter
- Enjoyment in a well-known Easter tradition
- Awareness that it's important to share things with others

Easter

Aims:
- To sing an Easter song
- To listen and colour Easter eggs
- To make an Easter cut-out

Key language:
- *Easter, rabbit, egg, little*
- *go, hunt, play, find, run away*
- *Happy Easter!*
- colours
- numbers 1–5

Materials:
- Pupil's Book page 79
- Finger puppets (Pip and Squeak)
- CD 1 and CD 3
- Photocopies of Easter cut-out (see page 262), one for each child (optional)
- Scissors (optional)
- A prepared Easter cut-out (optional)

Starting out

Greetings and opening routine

- Greet the children yourself and using the finger puppets. Make the finger puppets dance about and say **Pip and Squeak are very happy. Why are they happy, do you think?** Listen to the children's guesses and then say **Pip and Squeak are happy because soon it's Easter!** Check that the children understand the meaning of *Easter*.

Setting objectives

- Say **Today we're going to do activities to celebrate Easter in English. We're going to sing an Easter song and do an Easter listening activity. (We're also going to make an Easter cut-out.)**

Option: If the children don't celebrate Easter themselves, you may like to say **In many countries people celebrate a festival called Easter. We're going to learn about an Easter tradition by singing an Easter song and doing a listening activity.**

On the learning trail

Listen and sing the song. (PB page 79)

- (Books closed) Introduce or revise the vocabulary by asking the children **What do you think of at Easter?** *(rabbit, Easter egg, chocolate, etc.)*

- Explain that at Easter it is a tradition in some places to hunt for chocolate eggs.

- Say **We're going to listen to a song about five little rabbits who hunt for eggs on Easter Day. What colour are the eggs, do you think?** Encourage the children to predict the colours of the eggs in the song. Use this as an opportunity to revise colour words if necessary.

- Say **Listen to the song. What colour are the eggs?** Play the CD (CD 3, track 51). Pause after each verse and ask the children to tell you the colour of the egg. At the end, compare the colours of the eggs in the song with the children's predictions.

- Ask the children to open their Pupil's Books at page 79. Say **Look at the picture. Where are the five little rabbits? Let's count them!** The children point to the rabbits in their books and count them with you.

- Say e.g. **Find the red egg! / Find the blue egg!** and the children find and point to the different coloured eggs.

- Say **Let's sing the song. Point to the eggs.** Play the CD. The children point to the appropriate eggs and sing the song.

Five little rabbits go out to play

Five little rabbits go out to play
And hunt for eggs on Easter Day
One little rabbit finds a big, red egg
Eats it all and runs away!

Four little ... yellow
Three little ... blue
Two little ... green
One little ... pink

Listen, colour and say. (PB page 79)

- Say **Look at the rabbits. Listen and colour the eggs they find.** Play the CD (CD 3, track 53). Use the pause button to give the children time to colour the eggs.

- Check the answers by saying the numbers and getting the children to point to the completed pictures in their books and say e.g. **This rabbit finds ... (a red egg).**

    Key: The eggs should be coloured as follows:
    1 red 2 yellow 3 blue 4 green 5 pink

Listen, colour and say.

1 *This rabbit finds a red egg.*
2 *This rabbit finds a yellow egg.*
3 *This rabbit finds a blue egg.*
4 *This rabbit finds a green egg.*
5 *This rabbit finds a pink egg.*

Make the Easter cut-out (TB page 262) (optional)

- Say **Let's make the five little rabbits.** Show the children the cut-out you have prepared.

- Give a photocopy of the cut-out to each child. Make sure that they have scissors available.

- Say **Cut between the rabbits like this. And fold them down like this.** Make sure the rabbits are folded down behind the picture. Demonstrate what you mean.

- When the children are ready, say e.g. **Show me four rabbits! / Show me two rabbits!** The children hold up their cut-outs, showing the number of rabbits you say.

- If you like, do a collaborative colour dictation using the cut-out. Say e.g. **What colour is this rabbit? Brown? Black? OK. How many think it's brown? How many think it's black? OK. This rabbit is black. Colour the rabbit black,** etc.

- Play the karaoke version of the song (CD 3, track 52). The children sing the song and fold down the rabbits in each verse.

Ending the lesson

Lesson review

- Briefly ask the children what they can do as a result of the lesson (sing an Easter song, listen and identify the colours of Easter eggs, make an Easter cut-out – optional). Praise the children for their efforts and / or use the finger puppets to do this.

Goodbye and closing routine

- Say **Let's sing the song *Shake your head*.** Play the CD (CD 1, track 8). Hold up the finger puppets and the children sing and do the actions.

- Say **Happy Easter!** to the children yourself and using the finger puppets and encourage them to say this to you, the puppets and each other. Then say e.g. **Goodbye everyone. See you on ...** as usual.

Father's Day

Structures and grammar

- *I love ...*
- *How about you?*
- *He loves me, too*
- Recycled: *... is ...*

Vocabulary

- Core: *Father, day, Dad, love*
- Recycled: *fantastic, great, brilliant, happy*

Main receptive language

- *shirt, tie*
- *play, read*

Communicative competence

Understanding

Listening:
- Can understand a Father's Day song

Reading:
- Can read a message in a Father's Day card

Speaking

Spoken interaction:
- Can answer questions about what you do with your father

Spoken production:
- Can sing a Father's Day song *I love Dad*
- Can sing the song *Are you ready to finish? / Shake your head*

Writing
- Can complete a Father's Day card

Content links

- *Art and craft:* Father's Day card

Learning strategies and thinking skills

- Using rhythm and repetition to memorise language patterns in a song
- Associating pictures and personal experience
- Personalising a card

Children's culture

- Singing a Father's Day song
- Making a Father's Day card

Values and attitudes

- Pleasure in celebrating Father's Day
- Recognition of the importance of family
- Enjoyment in making a card to give to your father

Father's Day

Aims:
- To sing a song for Father's Day
- To make a card for Father's Day)

Key language:
- *I love ...*
- *How about you?*
- *He loves me, too.*
- *... is ...*
- *Dad, fantastic*
- *Happy Father's Day!*

Materials:
- Pupil's Book page 80
- Finger puppets (Pip and Squeak)
- CD 1 and CD 3
- Photocopies of Father's Day cut-out (see page 263), one for each child (optional)
- Scissors, glue, crayons (optional)
- A prepared Father's Day card (optional)

- **Note:** Before celebrating Father's Day with the children, check the class or school records to find out whether this may be a sensitive area for some children. If so, it may be appropriate for those children to make their cards for someone else in their family, e.g. an uncle or grandfather, or, depending on the circumstances, you may decide it is best not to celebrate this festival.

Starting out

Greetings and opening routine

- Greet the children yourself and using the finger puppets. Make the finger puppets whisper to each other. Say, as if to the puppets, **What is it? Tell us.** Hold the finger puppets to your ear and then say to the children **Ah. It's Father's Day on ... Pip and Squeak want to celebrate Father's Day!** Check that the children understand the meaning of *Father's Day*.

Setting objectives

- Say **Today we're going to sing a song for Father's Day. (And we're going to make a card for Father's Day.)**

On the learning trail

Listen and sing the song. (PB page 80)

- (Books closed) Say e.g. **My Dad is great! And your Dad?** Encourage the children to say sentences about their dads using any language they know, e.g. *My Dad is fantastic. / My Dad is brilliant.*

- Say **Let's listen to a song for Father's Day. What does the song say?** *My Dad is ...?* Play the CD (CD 3, track 54) and the children listen to the song. Check the answer (*fantastic*).

- Ask the children to open their Pupil's Books at page 80. Say **Look at the pictures.** Point to the pictures in turn and ask **Do you read / play with your Dad?** and listen to the children's responses.

- Say **Let's sing the song again.** Play the CD. The children follow in their books and sing the song. At the end, check the children understand *loves* and that *How about you?* means *Do you love your Dad, too?*

- Divide the class into two groups. Explain that group 1 should sing the first sentence each time and group 2 should sing the repetition. Play the CD again. The children sing the song with their groups. They then change roles.

 I love Dad

I love Dad. I love Dad.
How about you? How about you?
My Dad is fantastic.
My Dad is fantastic.
He loves me, too.
He loves me, too!

Make the Father's Day cut-out (TB page 263) (optional)

- Say **Let's make a card with a shirt and a tie for Father's Day.** Show the children the cut-out card you have prepared and point to the shirt and the tie to clarify meaning.

- Give a photocopy of the cut-out to each child. Make sure that they have scissors, glue and crayons available.

- Say **Cut out the card like this. And fold it like this.** The children fold the triangles down to make a shirt collar. Demonstrate what you mean.

- Say **Colour the shirt and the tie** and give the children a few minutes to do this.

- Say **Now cut out the tie and stick it here** and demonstrate what you mean.

- Read the message on the card and say **Write Dad here and write your name here!** and demonstrate what you mean.

- The children work individually and make and complete their cards. If you like, play the karaoke version of the song (CD 3, track 55) and the children can sing softly as they do this. The children then take their cards home to give to their fathers on Father's Day.

Ending the lesson

Lesson review

- Briefly ask the children what they can do as a result of the lesson (sing a song for Father's Day, make a card for Father's Day – optional). Praise the children for their efforts and / or use the finger puppets to do this.

Goodbye and closing routine

- Sing *Are you ready to finish?* or *Shake your head* Play the CD (CD 1, track 12). Hold up the finger puppets and the children sing and do the actions.

- Say **Happy Father's Day!** to the children yourself and using the finger puppets and encourage them to say this to you, the puppets and each other. Then say e.g. **Goodbye, everyone. See you on ...**

Mother's Day

Structures and grammar

- *Make a ...*
- *Give a ...*
- Recycled: *I love ...*

Vocabulary

- Core: *Mother, day, hug, surprise*
- Recycled: *present, card, flowers, Mum*

Main receptive language

- *special, things*

Communicative competence

Understanding

Listening:
- Can understand things to do for Mother's Day

Reading:
- Can read things to do for Mother's Day

Speaking

Spoken interaction:
- Can answer a question about what you'd like to do for Mother's Day

Spoken production:
- Can say things you'd like to do for Mother's Day
- Can sing the song *Shake your head / Are you ready to finish?*

Writing
- Can complete a Mother's Day card

Content links

- *Art and craft:* Mother's Day card

Learning strategies and thinking skills

- Listening and reading in order to make personal choices
- Expressing personal preferences
- Personalising a card

Children's culture

- Reading about ways to celebrate Mother's Day
- Making a Mother's Day card

Values and attitudes

- Pleasure in identifying things to do for Mother's Day
- Recognition of the importance of family
- Enjoyment in making a card to give to your mother

Mother's Day

Aims:
- To read about Mother's Day
- To tick things you'd like to do
- To make a card for Mother's Day

Key language:
- *hug, card, flowers, surprise, present*
- *Make a ... / Give a ...*
- *Happy Mother's Day!*

Materials:
- Pupil's Book page 80
- Finger puppets (Pip and Squeak)
- CD 1 and CD 3
- photocopies of Mother's Day cut-out (see 264), one for each child (optional)
- Scissors, crayons (optional)
- A prepared Mother's Day card (optional)

- **Note:** Before celebrating Mother's Day with the children, check the class or school records to find out whether this may be a sensitive area for some children. If so, it may be appropriate for those children to make their cards for someone else in their family, e.g. an aunt or grandmother, or, depending on the circumstances, you may decide it is best not to celebrate this festival.

Starting out

Greetings and opening routine

- Greet the children yourself and using the finger puppets. Make the finger puppets whisper to each other. Say, as if to the puppets, **What is it? Tell us.** Hold the finger puppets to your ear and then say to the children **Ah. It's Mother's Day on … Pip and Squeak want to celebrate Mother's Day!** Check that the children understand the meaning of *Mother's Day*.

Setting objectives

- Say **Today we're going to read about Mother's Day. (And we're going to make a card for Mother's Day.)**

On the learning trail

Listen, read and tick (✓). (PB page 80)

- (Books closed) Ask the children **What can you do to celebrate Mother's Day?** Listen to their ideas, recasting them in English if necessary. Use this as an opportunity to introduce or remind the children of vocabulary, e.g. *card, present, flowers, surprise.*

- Ask the children to open their Pupil's Books at page 80. Say **Listen and read about things to do to celebrate Mother's Day. How many of the things are the same as your ideas?** Check the children understand the meaning.

- Play the CD (CD 3, track 56). The children listen and read the text. At the end, check how many of the things in the text are the same as or similar to the children's ideas.

- Say **Listen and read the text again. This time, tick the things you'd like to do to celebrate Mother's Day.** Point to the pictures. Explain and demonstrate what you mean. Make it clear that there are no right answers and the children should tick according to their own personal opinions. Play the CD again. Pause after each phrase to give the children time to put ticks.

- At the end ask e.g. **What would you like to do?** and ask individual children to tell the class one idea they have ticked, e.g. *Make a card*. Don't be surprised if children have ticked all six ideas!

 Listen, read and tick.

Mother's Day is a special day for your Mum.
Here are some things to do:
Say 'I love you!'
Give a big hug.
Make a card.
Make a present.
Give flowers.
Give your Mum a surprise!

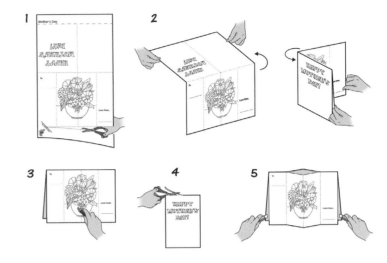

Make the Mother's Day cut-out (TB 264) (optional)

- Ask **Would you like to make a card for your Mum?** *(yes)* **Would you like to give flowers to your Mum?** *(yes)* Say **So let's make a pop-up card with flowers for Mother's Day!** Show the children the cut-out card you have prepared.

- Give a photocopy of the cut-out to each child. Make sure that they have scissors and crayons available.

- Say **Colour the card and the flowers** and give the children a few minutes to do this.

- Say **Now cut out the card like this. Fold the card like this.** Demonstrate how to make the card.

- The children work individually and make their cards. When they are ready, read the message on the front of the card and inside the card. Say **Write *Mum* here and write your name here!** and demonstrate what you mean. The children can then take their cards home to give to their mothers on Mother's Day.

Ending the lesson

Lesson review

- Briefly ask the children what they can do as a result of the lesson (read about Mother's Day, say things they'd like to do for Mother's Day, make a card for Mother's Day – optional). Praise the children for their efforts and / or use the finger puppets to do this.

Goodbye and closing routine

- Sing *Shake your head* or *Are you ready to finish?* Play the (CD 1, track 8 or track 12). Hold up the finger puppets and the children sing and do the actions.

- Say **Happy Mother's Day!** to the children yourself and using the finger puppets and encourage them to say this to you, the puppets and each other. Then say e.g. **Goodbye, everyone. See you on …**

Christmas

Rosa's story

Please help me, Rosa!

Ha! Ha! What short, yellow antlers!

We love you, Rosa!

Easter

Father's Day

To

_____ ,

You're

fantastic!

Love from,

_____

Happy Father's Day!

Mother's Day

HAPPY MOTHER'S DAY!

To

_____,

Love from,

_____

PHOTOCOPIABLE

264

© Macmillan Publishers Limited 2008

This is to certify that

_____

has successfully completed

Footprints 1

Teacher: _____

School: _____

Date: _____

Macmillan Education
4 Crinan Street
London N1 9XW
A division of Macmillan Publishers Limited
Companies and representatives throughout the world

ISBN 978-0-2307-2214-9

Text © Carol Read 2008
Design and illustration © Macmillan Publishers Limited 2008

First published 2008

All rights reserved; no part of this publication may be reproduced, stored in a retrieval system, transmitted in any form, or by any means, electronic, mechanical, photocopying, recording or otherwise, without the permission of the publishers.

Note to Teachers
Permission to copy
The material in this book is copyright. However, the publisher grants permission for copies to be made without fee on those pages marked with the photocopiable symbol. Private purchasers may make copies for their own use or for use by classes of which they are in charge; school purchasers may make copies for use within and by the staff and students of the school only. This permission does not extend to additional branches of an institution, who should purchase a separate master copy of the book for their own use. For copying in any other circumstances, prior permission in writing must be obtained from Macmillan Publishers Limited.

Page make-up by Red Giraffe Limited
Illustrated by Red Giraffe Limited and Paul Gibbs
Cover design by Right On The Line
Cover illustration by Teri Gower

Printed and bound in China

2016 2015 2014
10 9 8 7